World Politics

00/01

Twenty-First Edition

EDITOR

Helen Purkitt
United States Naval Academy

Dr. Helen Purkitt obtained her Ph.D. in international relations from the University of Southern California. She is professor of political science at the U.S. Naval Academy. Her research and teaching interests include political psychology, African politics, international relations theory, and environmental security. She is currently researching South Africa's former biological weapons program and completing an experimental study of framing effects in budget decision-making. Recent publications include "A Problem Centered Approach for Understanding Foreign Policy: Some Examples from U.S. Foreign Policy toward Southern Africa" in S. Nagel (Ed.) *Global international policy: Among and Within Nations. Marcel-Dekker, 2000* (forthcoming); "Predicting Environmental Security Trends and Events in Africa: A Proto-Type Monitoring system of Environmental and Political Problems in Southern Africa," *International Symposium of Forecasting,*" Washington, D.C., U.S. Government, 1999; and "Problem Representations and Political Expertise: Evidence from 'Think Aloud Protocols of South African Elites," in D. Sylvan and J. F. Voss (eds.), *Problem Representation in International Relations* (Cambridge University Press, 1998).

Dushkin/McGraw-Hill
Sluice Dock, Guilford, Connecticut 06437

Visit us on the Internet
http://www.dushkin.com/annualeditions/

World Map

This map has been developed to give you a graphic picture of where the countries of the world are located, the relationship they have with their region and neighbors, and their positions relative to the superpowers and power blocs. We have focused on certain areas to more clearly illustrate these crowded regions.

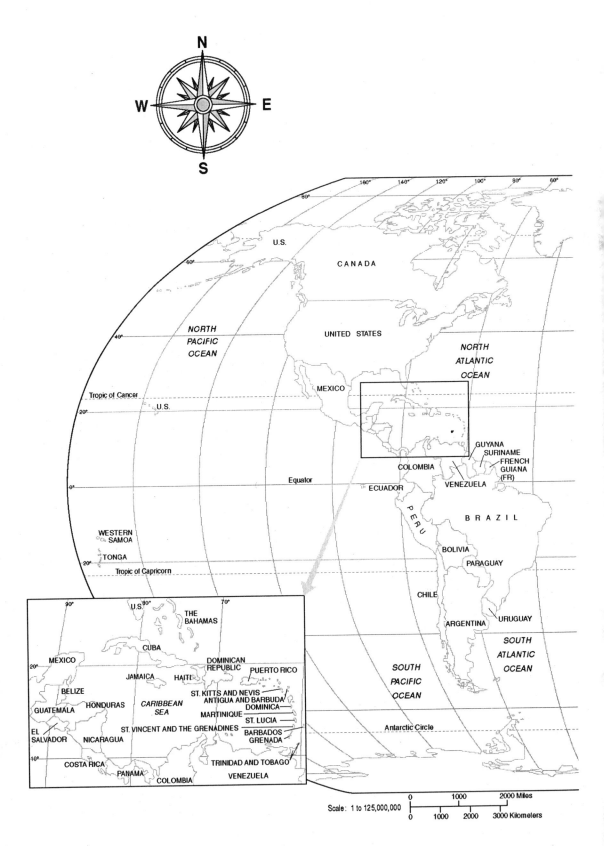

Scale: 1 to 125,000,000

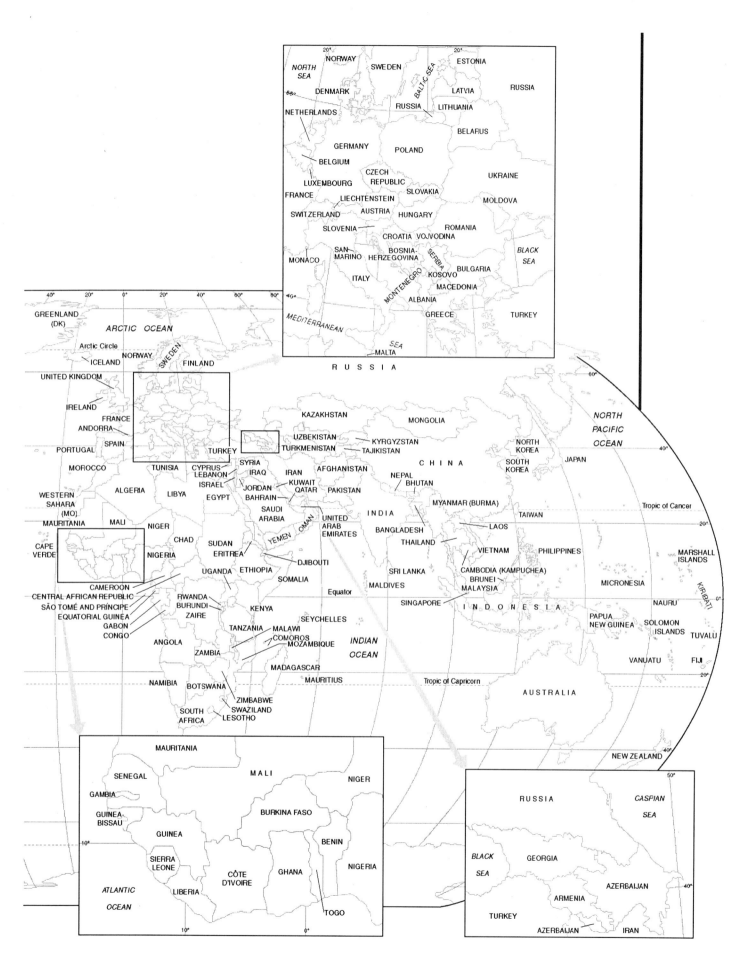

Credits

1. Alternative Visions of World Politics in the Twenty-First Century
Unit photo—United Nations photo by Yutaka Nagata.
2. International Political Economy
Unit photo—Novosti Photo, Moscow, Russia.
3. The Politics of Weapons of Mass Destruction
Unit photo—B-2 Advanced Technology Bomber courtesy of U.S. Air Force.
4. North America
Unit photo—The White House.
5. Latin America
Unit photo—United Nations photo of experimental terracing of yams in Jamaica.
6. Europe
Unit photo—Courtesy of British Information Service.
7. Russia and the Former Soviet States
Unit photo—United Nations photo.
8. The Pacific Basin
Unit photo—United Nations photo by John Isaac.
9. Middle East and Africa
Unit photo—United Nations photo by John Isaac.
10. International Organizations and Global Issues
Unit photo—United Nations photo by John Isaac.

Cataloging in Publication Data
Main entry under title: Annual Editions: World Politics. 2000/2001.
    1. International relations. 2. United States—Foreign relations. I. Purkitt, Helen, *comp.*
II. Title: World politics.
ISBN 0–07–236578–1   327'.05   80–643193   ISSN 0198–0300

Twenty-First Edition

Cover image © 2000 PhotoDisc, Inc.

Printed in the United States of America   1234567890BAHBAH543210   Printed on Recycled Paper

v

In publishing ANNUAL EDITIONS we recognize the enormous role played by the magazines, newspapers, and journals of the public press in providing current, first-rate educational information in a broad spectrum of interest areas. Many of these articles are appropriate for students, researchers, and professionals seeking accurate, current material to help bridge the gap between principles and theories and the real world. These articles, however, become more useful for study when those of lasting value are carefully collected, organized, indexed, and reproduced in a low-cost format, which provides easy and permanent access when the material is needed. That is the role played by ANNUAL EDITIONS.

New to ANNUAL EDITIONS is the inclusion of related World Wide Web sites. These sites have been selected by our editorial staff to represent some of the best resources found on the World Wide Web today. Through our carefully developed topic guide, we have linked these Web resources to the articles covered in this ANNUAL EDITIONS reader. We think that you will find this volume useful, and we hope that you will take a moment to visit us on the Web at **http://www.dushkin.com** to tell us what you think.

Annual Editions: World Politics 00/01 is aimed at filling a void in materials for learning about world politics and foreign policy. The articles are chosen for those who are new to the study of world politics. The objective of this compilation is to stimulate interest in learning more about international issues that often seem remote and irrelevant, but that can have profound consequences for economic well-being, security, and survival.

International relations can be viewed as a complex and dynamic system of actions and reactions by a diverse set of actors that produce new situations that require further actions. The readings in this volume have been chosen to convey the complexities and dynamic interdependence of actors in contemporary international relations.

This interdependence means that events in places as far away as Latin America, Asia, the Middle East, and Africa affect the United States, just as America's actions, and inaction, have significant repercussions for other states. Interdependence also refers to the increased role of nonstate actors such as international corporations, the United Nations, nongovernmental organizations and actors, and the Cable News Network (CNN). These nonstate actors increasingly influence the scope, nature, and pace of change in the international system. International events proceed at such a rapid pace, however, that often what is said about international affairs today may be outdated by tomorrow. It is important, therefore, that readers develop a mental framework or theory of the international system as a complex system of loosely connected and diverse sets of actors who interact around an ever-changing agenda of international issues. This collection of articles about international events provides up-to-date information, commentaries about the current set of issues on the world agenda, and analyses of the significance of these issues and emerging trends for the structure and functioning of the post–cold war international system.

A variety of political perspectives are offered in each unit to make readers more aware of the complex and differing aspects of international relations stressed by different analysts. Usually the underlying ideological assumptions are implicit aspects of the analysis. By becoming more aware of the assumptions underlying contemporary analyses of international relations, one can become a more discriminating consumer of alternative perspectives about the world.

This twenty-first edition of *Annual Editions: World Politics* is divided into 10 units. The end of the cold war means that we can no longer view international relations through the prism of a bipolar system. Instead, national, regional, and subregional issues are increasingly important aspects of international relations in the emerging multipolar and multidimensional world system.

The first three units summarize themes and broad areas of international concerns in a period of high uncertainty about future security threats. Each article in unit 1 offers an alternative view of the important trends emerging in world politics at the start of the twenty-first century.

The continuing global fallout from the Asian financial crisis underscores the importance of understanding the linkages between economic and political trends in an era of increasing globalism. The articles in unit 2 discuss the key actors, issues, and trends relevant to understanding contemporary problems in the international political economic system.

Articles in unit 3 discuss specific issues and emerging trends related to the spread of weapons of mass destruction. As the technology and materials necessary to produce nuclear, chemical, and biological weapons proliferate, the world is faced with new and unprecedented security threats. A number of questions related to how to deter, defend against, and cope with the effects of weapons of mass destruction, which are used against civilians by either hostile nation-states or terrorist groups, must be answered. Authorities must now prepare to defend against these new threats at the local, national, and international levels of world society.

Articles in units 4 through 9 focus on the impact of international and regional trends in six geographical areas or subsystems: North America, Latin America, Europe, Russia and the other independent nation-states of the former Soviet Union, the Pacific Basin, and the Middle East and Africa. A common theme running through these articles is the increased challenges facing local, national, and regional political authorities who must simultaneously cope with the problems generated by economic globalism and subnational political changes.

The final unit of this reader, unit 10, examines unresolved issues and new trends in the post–cold war era related to the role of the United Nations, the IMF and World Bank, and other nonstate actors in coping with international economic and political conflicts. This final section begins with an article that questions the ability of the United Nations' Security Council to be the guardian of international peace and security without more support for major reforms by the United States and other major powers. Subsequent articles focus on the role of new types of international actors and trends, including the role played by modern mercenaries, the increased use of "child soldiers," and the political changes that may occur in our collective security as the populations in developed countries continue to age.

I would like to thank Ian Nielsen and his associates at Dushkin/McGraw-Hill for their help in putting this volume together and previous users of *Annual Editions: World Politics*, who took the time to contribute articles or comments on this collection of readings. Please continue to provide feedback to guide the annual revision of this anthology by filling out the postage-paid *article rating form* on the last page of this book.

Helen Purkitt

Helen E. Purkitt
Editor

Contents

Alternative Visions of World Politics into the Twenty-First Century

Three articles consider some of the challenges facing the world: the impact of local conflicts on foreign policy, major influences on domestic and international security, and the consequences of globalization.

International Political Economy

Five articles examine the global marketplace as politics redefine the rules of the economic game.

UNIT 1

UNIT 2

The concepts in bold italics are developed in the article. For further expansion please refer to the Topic Guide and the Index.

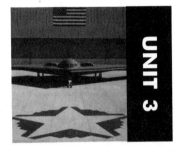

UNIT 3

The Politics of Weapons of Mass Destruction

Four selections discuss nuclear proliferation and the use of toxic weapons.

The concepts in bold italics are developed in the article. For further expansion please refer to the Topic Guide and the Index.

North America

These seven articles discuss
current and future United States
and Canadian roles in world
policy and international trade.

UNIT 5

Latin America

Three selections consider Latin American relations in the Western Hemisphere with regard to politics, economic reform, and trade.

UNIT 6

Europe

Four selections review some of the historic events that will alter Western and Central Europe. Topics include the European Union's search for a foreign policy and Central/Eastern Europe's strivings toward democracy.

The concepts in bold italics are developed in the article. For further expansion please refer to the Topic Guide and the Index.

UNIT 7

Russia and the Former Soviet States

Four articles examine the current state of Russia's economy, politics, military, and foreign policy.

UNIT 8

The Pacific Basin

Five articles examine some of the countries instrumental in the economic evolution of the Pacific Basin.

UNIT 9

Middle East
and Africa

Five articles review the
current state of the Middle East
and Africa with regard to conflict,
extremism, and democratic trends.

The concepts in bold italics are developed in the article. For further expansion please refer to the Topic Guide and the Index.

UNIT 10

International Organizations and Global Issues

Three articles discuss international organizations and world peace, UN reform, and the use of mercenaries and children in the conduct of modern "war."

The concepts in bold italics are developed in the article. For further expansion please refer to the Topic Guide and the Index.   3

This topic guide suggests how the selections and World Wide Web sites found in the next section of this book relate to topics of traditional concern to students and professionals interested in world politics. It is useful for locating interrelated articles and Web sites for reading and research. The guide is arranged alphabetically according to topic.

The relevant Web sites, which are numbered and annotated on pages 6 and 7, are easily identified by the Web icon (◎) under the topic articles. By linking the articles and the Web sites by topic, this ANNUAL EDITIONS reader becomes a powerful learning and research tool.

TOPIC AREA	TREATED IN	TOPIC AREA	TREATED IN
Africa	39. Africa 40. Post-Imperial Africa at War 42. Outsourcing War 43. Children under Arms ◎ **3, 6, 8, 10, 11, 12, 28, 31, 35, 36**		29. Baltics: Between Russia and the West ◎ **3, 6, 14, 20, 21, 22**
Alternative Visions of World Politics	1. Dueling Globalizations 2. Future of Civil Conflict 3. New Interventionism and the Third World ◎ **1, 2, 4, 8, 32, 34, 35, 36**	**Europe (Western)**	24. Enemies and Colleagues ◎ **3, 6, 10, 12, 19, 20, 21, 22**
Arms Control and Arms Trade	9. Against Nuclear Apartheid 10. Russia: The Nuclear Menace Within 11. Troubled Treaties: Is the NPT Tottering? 12. Bombs, Gas and Microbes ◎ **3, 9, 14, 15**	**Foreign Investment**	1. Duelling Globalizations 5. Toward a New International Economic Order 6. Capitalism's Last Chance? 8. Helping the World's Poorest 22. Economic Crisis in Latin America: Global Contagion, Local Pain ◎ **6, 9, 10, 12**
Asia	31. Is the Asian Financial Crisis Over? 32. Tigers Ready to Roar? 33. Does China Matter? 34. Tokyo's Depression Diplomacy 35. Toward a Comprehensive Settlement of the Korean Problem ◎ **3, 4, 6, 11, 12, 25, 26**	**Future Predictions**	1. Dueling Globalization 2. Future of Civil Conflict 6. Capitalism's Last Chance? 20. International Relations 25. Revolutions of 1989 Reconsidered ◎ **32, 35**
Balkans	26. Unlearning the Lessons of Kosovo ◎ **3, 5, 6, 15, 21**	**Globalization**	1. Dueling Globalization 5. Toward a New International Economic Order 6. Capitalism's Last Chance? 8. Helping the World's Poorest 16. Americans and the World 22. Economic Crisis in Latin America: Global Contagion, Local Pain 31. Is the Asian Financial Crisis Over? 32. Tigers Ready to Roar? ◎ **6, 9, 10, 11, 12, 32, 33, 34, 35, 36**
Canada	18. No-First-Use Policy for NATO? 19. Canada's Water—Hands Off ◎ **3, 5, 6, 16, 17, 18**		
Democracy	15. Rethinking United States Policy toward the Muslim World 24. Enemies and Colleagues 25. Revolutions of 1989 Reconsidered ◎ **1, 18, 28**	**Human Rights**	3. New Interventionism and the Third World 43. Children under Arms ◎ **8, 33, 34, 35, 36**
Environment	19. Canada's Water—Hands Off ◎ **7, 17**	**International Organizations and Treaties**	5. Toward a New International Economic Order 7. Trade and the Developing World: A New Agenda 11. Troubled Treaties: Is the NPT Tottering? 37. Iraq and UN's Weapons of Mass Destruction 43. Children under Arms ◎ **8, 10, 12, 14, 17, 32, 34, 36**
Ethnic Conflict	2. Future of Civil Conflict 3. New Interventionism and the Third World 24. Enemies and Colleagues 30. Chaos in the Caucasus 39. Africa 40. Post-Imperial Africa at War ◎ **3, 14, 15, 17, 21, 23, 24, 28**		
Europe (Central)	25. Revolutions of 1989 Reconsidered 26. Unlearning the Lessons of Kosovo 27. Life with Boris	**Latin America and Central America**	20. International Relations 21. Colombia at War 22. Economic Crisis in Latin America: Global Contagion, Local Pain ◎ **17, 18, 35**

AE: World Politics

The following World Wide Web sites have been carefully researched and selected to support the articles found in this reader. If you are interested in learning more about specific topics found in this book, these Web sites are a good place to start. The sites are cross-referenced by number and appear in the topic guide on the previous two pages. Also, you can link to these Web sites through our DUSHKIN ONLINE support site at *http://www.dushkin.com/online/.*

The following sites were available at the time of publication. Visit our Web site—we update DUSHKIN ONLINE regularly to reflect any changes.

General Sources

1. Belfer Center for Science and International Affairs
http://www.ksg.harvard.edu/bcsia/
BCSIA is a center for research, teaching, and training in international affairs.

2. Carnegie Endowment for International Peace
http://www.ceip.org
One of the goals of this organization is to stimulate discussion and learning among experts and the public on a wide range of international issues. The site provides links to the journal *Foreign Policy* and to the Moscow Center.

3. Central Intelligence Agency
http://www.odci.gov
Use this official home page to learn about many facets of the CIA and to get connections to other sites and resources, such as *The CIA Factbook*, which provides extensive statistical information about every country in the world.

4. The Heritage Foundation
http://www.heritage.org
This page offers discussion about and links to many sites of the Heritage Foundation and other organizations having to do with foreign policy and foreign affairs.

5. Political Resources on the Net
http://www.agora.stm.it/politic/
This site contains listing of political sites that are available on the Internet, sorted by country, with links to Parties, Organizations, Governments, Media, and more from all around the world.

6. World Wide Web Virtual Library: International Affairs Resources
http://www.etown.edu/vl/
Surf this site and its links to learn about specific countries and regions, to research think tanks and organizations, and to study such vital topics as international law, development, the international economy, human rights, and peacekeeping.

Alternative Visions of World Politics into the Twenty-First Century

7. Global Trends 2005 Project
http://www.csis.org/gt2005/
The Center for Strategic and International Studies explores the coming global trends and challenges of the new millenium. Read their summary report at this Web site. Also access Enterprises for the Environment, Global Information Infrastructure Commission and Americas at this site.

8. Human Rights Web
http://www.hrweb.org
This useful site offers ideas on how individuals can get involved in helping to protect human rights around the world.

International Political Economy

9. International Political Economy Network
http://csf.colorado.edu/ipe/
This premier site for research and scholarship includes electronic archives.

10. Organization for Economic Cooperation and Development/FDI Statistics
http://www.oecd.org/daf/cmis/fdi/statist.htm
Explore world trade and investment trends and statistics on this site. It provides links to many related topics and addresses global economic issues on a country-by-country basis.

11. Virtual Seminar in Global Political Economy/Global Cities & Social Movements
http://csf.colorado.edu/gpe/gpe95b/resources.html
This site of Internet resources is rich in links to subjects of interest in regional environmental studies, covering topics such as sustainable cities, megacities, and urban planning.

12. World Bank
http://www.worldbank.org
News (e.g., press releases, summaries of new projects, speeches) and coverage of numerous topics regarding development, countries, and regions are provided at this site.

Weapons of Mass Destruction

13. The Bulletin of the Atomic Scientists
http://www.bullatomsci.org
This site allows you to read more about the Doomsday Clock and other issues as well as topics related to nuclear weaponry, arms control, and disarmament.

14. ISN International Relations and Security Network
http://www.isn.ethz.ch
This site, maintained by the Center for Security Studies and Conflict Research, is a clearinghouse for extensive information on international relations and security policy.

15. Terrorism Research Center
http://www.terrorism.com
The Terrorism Research Center features definitions and research on terrorism, counterterrorism documents, a comprehensive list of Web links, and profiles of terrorist and counterterrorist groups.

North America

16. The Henry L. Stimson Center
http://www.stimson.org
Stimson, a nonpartisan organization, focuses on issues where policy, technology, and politics intersect. Use this site to find varying assessments of U.S. foreign policy in the post–cold war world and to research many other topics.

17. The North American Institute
http://www.santafe.edu/~naminet/index.html
NAMI, a trinational public-affairs organization, is concerned with the emerging "regional space" of Canada, the United States, and Mexico and the development of a North American community. It provides links for study of trade, the environment, and institutional developments.

Latin America

18. Inter-American Dialogue
http://www.iadialog.org
This is the Web site for IAD, a premier U.S. center for policy analysis, communication, and exchange in Western Hemisphere affairs. The 100-member organization has helped to shape the agenda of issues and choices in hemispheric relations.

Europe

19. Central Europe Online
http://www.centraleurope.com
This site contains daily updated information under headings such as news on the Web today, economics, trade, and currency.

20. Europa: European Union
http://europa.eu.int
This server site of the European Union will lead you to the history of the EU (and its predecessors), descriptions of EU policies, institutions, and goals, and documentation of treaties and other materials.

21. NATO Integrated Data Service
http://www.nato.int/structur/nids/nids.htm
NIDS was created to bring information on security-related matters to the widest possible audience. Check out this Web site to review North Atlantic Treaty Organization documentation, to read *NATO Review,* and to explore key issues in the field of European security and transatlantic cooperation.

22. Social Science Information Gateway
http://sosig.esrc.bris.ac.uk
A project of the Economic and Social Research Council (ESRC), this is an online catalogue of thousands of Internet resources relevant to political education and research.

Russia and the Former Soviet Union

23. Russia Today
http://www.russiatoday.com
This site includes headline news, resources, government, politics, election results, and pressing issues.

24. Russian and East European Network Information Center, University of Texas at Austin
http://reenic.utexas.edu/reenic.html
This is the Web site for information on Russia and the former Soviet Union.

The Pacific Basin

25. ASEAN Web
http://www.asean.or.id
This site of the Association of South East Asian Nations provides an overview of Asia: Web resources, summits, economic affairs, political foundations, and regional cooperation.

26. Inside China Today
http://www.insidechina.com
Part of the European Internet Network, this site leads you to information on all of China, including recent news, government, and related sites.

27. Japan Ministry of Foreign Affairs
http://www.mofa.go.jp
Visit this official site for Japanese foreign policy statements and press releases, archives, and discussions of regional and global relations.

The Middle East and Africa

28. Africa News Online
http://www.africanews.org
Open this site for up-to-date information on all of Africa, with reports from Africa's leading newspapers, magazines, and news agencies. Coverage is country-by-country and regional. Internet links are among the resource pages.

29. ArabNet
http://www.arab.net
This page of ArabNet, the online resource for the Arab world in the Middle East and North Africa, presents links to 22 Arab countries. Each country page classifies information using a standardized system.

30. Gopher Site: Israel
gopher://israel-info.gov.il
Search the directories in this site for such information as policy speeches, interviews, and briefings; discussion of Israel and the UN; and Web sites of the Israel government.

31. IR-Net
http://www.ir-net.co.za
Examine this site of South Africa's Industrial Relations Network as a sample of how different countries address labor issues. It provides information on mediation and conciliation and notes many library and resource links.

International Organizations and Global Issues

32. Commission on Global Governance
http://www.cgg.ch
This site provides access to *The Report of the Commission on Global Governance,* produced by an international group of leaders who want to find ways in which the global community can better manage its affairs.

33. InterAction
http://www.interaction.org
InterAction encourages grassroots action and engages policymakers on advocacy issues and uses this site to inform people on its initiatives to expand international humanitarian relief and development-assistance programs.

34. Nonprofit Organizations on the Internet
http://www.ui.mil.edu/people/ellens/non.html
This site includes some NGO links and contains a meta-index of nonprofit organizations.

35. The North-South Institute
http://www.nsi-ins.ca/ensi/index.html
Searching this site of the North-South Institute—which works to strengthen international development cooperation and enhance gender and social equity—will help you find information and debates on a variety of global issues.

36. United Nations Home Page
http://www.un.org
Here is the gateway to the United Nations. Also see *http://www.undp.org/missions/usa/usna.htm* for the U.S. Mission at the UN.

We highly recommend that you review our Web site for expanded information and our other product lines. We are continually updating and adding links to our Web site in order to offer you the most usable and useful information that will support and expand the value of your Annual Editions. You can reach us at: *http://www.dushkin.com/annualeditions/.*

www.dushkin.com/online/

Unit Selections

1. **Dueling Globalizations: A Debate between Thomas L. Friedman and Ignacio Ramonet,** Thomas L. Friedman and Ignacio Ramonet
2. **The Future of Civil Conflict,** Shashi Tharoor
3. **The New Interventionism and the Third World,** Richard Falk

Key Points to Consider

❖ What type of conflict do you predict will cause the most serious threats to world peace in the twenty-first century? Explain your reasoning.

❖ What are the most important differences between Thomas L. Friedman's and Ignacio Ramonet's visions of globalization? What are the important points of agreement between these two analysts about the meaning, causes, and consequences of globalization?

❖ Can you describe a recent local conflict with international ramifications whose root causes include some of the factors identified by Shashi Tharoor?

❖ Explain why you agree or disagree with Richard Falk's thesis that the current international legal and current international conflict resolution approaches will not be able to resolve ethnic conflicts. Use one or two current ethnic conflicts to support your answer.

 **Links**   **www.dushkin.com/online/**

7. **Global Trends 2005 Project**
   http://www.csis.org/gt2005/
8. **Human Rights Web**
   http://www.hrweb.org

These sites are annotated on pages 6 and 7.

As we enter the twenty-first century, there is a noticeable increase in efforts to predict important changes and to understand new patterns of relationships that may shape international relations in the future. Anyone can engage in this sport as there is little agreement among "futurists" about what to expect regarding causes of tension, types of conflict, or patterns of interaction that may characterize international relations during the twenty-first century.

With the demise of the cold war, analysts now tend to focus on the political and economic ramifications of the emerging international system. Many analysts now cite "globalization" as the dominant characteristics of this emerging new system. Globalization refers to the increased global interdependence of economic, communication, and transport systems. Globalization also refers to innovations in computer and other high-tech capabilities and the increased use of these innovations by people in all parts of world society.

A number of disintegrative tendencies are frequently associated with "globalization," including the rise of cultural extremism in Islamic, Judaic, and Christian cultures; increased economic inequality between the developed and developing sectors of world society; ethnic strife; and the diffusion of high-technology weaponry. The current uncertainty about the significance and consequences of globalism is reflected in "Dueling Globalizations: A Debate between Thomas L. Friedman and Ignacio Ramonet." These two analysts differ on the meaning, importance, and future significance of emerging global trends.

Since globalization promotes both boundary-broadening and boundary-heightening changes, debates are likely to continue for some time about the consequences of the processes. Many analysts predict that communal conflicts will continue to be the most prevalent type of conflict in future international relations. Many of the deadly local conflicts in remote areas of the developing world are ignored by governments and the media in developed countries. Other communal conflicts receive more world attention and involvement by developed countries because of geographic proximity or strategic value for major powers, or because they raise concerns about the possibility of escalation in a world characterized by the proliferation of weapons of mass destruction. Some complex emergencies in the developing world receive attention because of humanitarian concerns or because more self-interested motives relate to the possibility that conditions in collapsed societies may fuel mass migrations, the spreading of infectious diseases, and other problems. The disintegration of Yugoslavia and the resulting Balkans war, which were largely ignored by most nation-states for nearly 5 years, is frequently cited as the most likely archetypal conflict that may trigger outside involvement in the future. Other communal conflicts, such as the civil war in Angola and the ongoing interstate and civil wars in the Great Lakes region of Africa, are examples of the types of conflicts that are likely to be ignored.

In "The Future of Civil Conflict," Shashi Tharoor, the director of Communications and Special Projects in the Office of the Secretary General of the United Nations, identifies several political factors that are at the root of most contemporary civil conflicts, including invented nationalism, the legacy of colonialism, state fragmentation, failed leadership, expatriate extremism, and the financial incentives that warlords and other actors have in perpetuating violence. Conventional international diplomacy or outside peacekeeping forces are the least suited to manage these types of conflict.

In "The New Interventionism and the Third World," Richard Falk cautions that the legal framework, which emphasizes the right of self-determination and respect for territorial sovereignty of national states, is in disarray, and current international conflict resolution approaches are unable to resolve most ethnic conflicts. Instead, future international peace and stability may depend on how well local, national, or regional actors are able to manage conflict among communal groups.

This debate will occur at the same time that available water, land, and food declines, infant mortality and population growth rates rise, and infectious diseases spread. How a political regime copes with these and related challenges is receiving some attention today because it is now recognized that such factors are root causes or triggers that fuel local conflicts. Conflicts in Somalia and Rwanda were not spontaneous outbreaks of clan warfare or ethnic violence. Rather, the underlying strains of hunger, drought, the longer-term lack of cultivable land, the breakdown of traditional clan structures, and, finally, population increases fueled these recent conflicts as did the residue of past political and economic relationships.

Occasionally, problems caused by environmental factors facilitate peace. A devastating drought in Mozambique, in addition to damage caused by prolonged civil war, led warring factions to agree to a negotiated peace settlement in 1994. In a similar fashion, the worsening problems created by drought throughout the Middle East, along with the desires of aging President Assad of Syria and Prime Minister Barak of Israel, prompted the leaders of the two countries to resume peace talks at the end of 1999. While analysts continue to argue about whether water or oil will be the most important strategic resource in that future, there is an emerging consensus that resource scarcity and environmental degradation will complicate existing relationships among nation-states and other actors in future international relations.

While some analysts focus on the implications of globalization for future conflicts, some Western analysts are more optimistic about future world trends. Many now attribute the spread of democracy in part to the communication revolution and the ability of marginal groups to interact and communicate using new technological tools such as the Internet. The communication revolution and the increased influence of civil society are widely cited as reasons for recent implementations of democratic reforms in many countries. What remains to be seen is whether globalization will promote democracy, establish new international norms of peace and stability or lead to older forms of international conflicts. Optimists and pessimists, holding rival visions of future world politics, will continue to disagree about globalization.

Disagreements will continue because emerging trends call into question long-standing concepts of security based on competition over armaments and national wealth. Instead, future security may be a function of the strength and durability of subnational and transnational as well as interstate relationships. This proposition, if accurate, requires a new vision and model of international relations.

Alternative Visions of World Politics into the Twenty-First Century

Dueling Globalizations:

A DEBATE BETWEEN THOMAS L. FRIEDMAN AND IGNACIO RAMONET

DOSCAPITAL

by Thomas L. Friedman

If there can be a statute of limitations on crimes, then surely there must be a statute of limitations on foreign-policy clichés. With that in mind, I hereby declare the "post–Cold War world" over.

For the last ten years, we have talked about this "post–Cold War world." That is, we have defined the world by what it wasn't because we didn't know what it was. But a new international system has now clearly replaced the Cold War: globalization. That's right, globalization—the integration of markets, finance, and technologies in a way that is shrinking the world from a size medium to a size small and enabling each of us to reach around the world farther, faster, and cheaper than ever before. It's not just an economic trend, and it's not just some fad. Like all previous international systems, it is directly or indirectly shaping the domestic politics, economic policies, and foreign relations of virtually every country.

As an international system, the Cold War had its own structure of power: the balance between the United States and the USSR, including their respective allies. The Cold War

THOMAS L. FRIEDMAN *is a foreign affairs columnist for the* New York Times *and author of* The Lexus and the Olive Tree *(New York: Farrar, Straus, and Giroux, 1999).*

had its own rules: In foreign affairs, neither superpower would encroach on the other's core sphere of influence, while in economics, underdeveloped countries would focus on nurturing their own national industries, developing countries on export-led growth, communist countries on autarky, and Western economies on regulated trade. The Cold War had its own dominant ideas: the clash between communism and capitalism, as well as détente, nonalignment, and perestroika. The Cold War had its own demographic trends: The movement of peoples from East to West was largely frozen by the Iron Curtain; the movement from South to North was a more steady flow. The Cold War had its own defining technologies: Nuclear weapons and the Second Industrial Revolution were dominant, but for many developing countries, the hammer and sickle were still relevant tools. Finally, the Cold War had its own defining anxiety: nuclear annihilation. When taken all together, this Cold War system didn't shape everything, but it shaped many things.

Today's globalization system has some very different attributes, rules, incentives, and characteristics, but it is equally influential. The Cold War system was characterized by one overarching feature: division. The world was chopped up, and both threats and opportunities tended to grow out of whom you were divided from. Appropriately, that Cold War system was symbolized by a single image: the Wall. The globalization system also has one overarching characteristic: integration. Today, both the threats and opportunities facing a country increasingly grow from whom it is connected to. This system is also captured by a single symbol: the World Wide Web. So in the broadest sense, we have gone from a system built around walls to a system increasingly built around networks.

Once a country makes the leap into the system of globalization, its élite begin to internalize this perspective of integration and try to locate themselves within a global context. I was visiting Amman, Jordan, in the summer of 1998 when I met my friend, Rami Khouri, the country's leading political columnist, for coffee at the Hotel Inter-Continental. We sat down, and I asked him what was new. The first thing he said to me was "Jordan was just added to CNN's worldwide weather highlights." What Rami was saying was that it is important for Jordan to know that those institutions that think globally believe it is now worth knowing what the weather is like in Amman. It makes Jordanians feel more important and holds out the hope that they will profit by having more tourists or global investors visiting. The day after seeing Rami I happened to interview Jacob Frenkel, governor of the Bank of Israel and a University of Chicago-trained economist. He remarked to me: "Before, when we talked about macroeconomics, we started by looking at the local markets, local financial system, and the inter-relationship between them, and then, as an afterthought, we looked at the international economy. There was a feeling that what we do is primarily our own business and then there are some outlets where we will sell abroad. Now, we reverse the perspective. Let's not ask what markets we should export to after having decided what to produce; rather, let's first study the global framework within which we operate and then decide what to produce. It changes your whole perspective."

Integration has been driven in large part by globalization's defining technologies: computerization, miniaturization, digitization, satellite communications, fiber optics, and the Internet. And that integration, in turn, has led to many other differences between the Cold War and globalization systems.

Unlike the Cold War system, globalization has its own dominant culture, which is why integration tends to be homogenizing. In pre-vious eras, cultural homogenization happened on a regional scale—the Romanization of Western Europe and the Mediterranean world, the Islamization of Central Asia, the Middle East, North Africa, and Spain by the Arabs, or the Russification of Eastern and Central Europe, and parts of Eurasia, under the Soviets. Culturally speaking, globalization is largely the spread (for better and for worse) of Americanization—from Big Macs and iMacs to Mickey Mouse.

Whereas the defining measurement of the Cold War was weight, particularly the throw-weight of missiles, the defining measurement of the globalization system is speed—the speed of commerce, travel, communication, and innovation. The Cold War was about Einstein's mass-energy equation, $e=mc^2$. Globalization is about Moore's Law, which states that the performance power of microprocessors will double every 18 months. The defining document of the Cold War system was "the treaty." The defining document of the globalization system is "the deal." If the defining anxiety of the Cold War was fear of annihilation from an enemy you knew all too well in a world struggle that was fixed and stable, the defining anxiety in globalization is fear of rapid change from an enemy you cannot see, touch, or feel—a sense that your job, community, or workplace can be changed at any moment by anonymous economic and technological forces that are anything but stable.

If the defining economists of the Cold War system were Karl Marx and John Maynard Keynes, each of whom wanted to tame capitalism, the defining economists of the globalization system are Joseph Schumpeter and Intel chairman Andy Grove, who prefer to unleash capitalism. Schumpeter, a former Austrian minister of finance and Harvard University professor, expressed the view in his classic work *Capitalism, Socialism, and Democracy* (1942) that the essence of capitalism is the process of "creative destruction"—the perpetual cycle of destroying old and less efficient products or services and replacing them with new, more efficient ones. Grove took Schumpeter's insight that only the paranoid survive for the title of his book about life in Silicon Valley and made it in many ways the business model of globalization capitalism. Grove helped popularize the view that dramatic, industry-transforming innovations are taking place today faster and faster. Thanks to these technological breakthroughs, the speed at which your latest invention can

A Tale of Two Systems	Cold War	Globalization
"The Cold War had its own dominant ideas: the clash between communism and capitalism. . . . The driving idea behind globalization is free-market capatalism."	In 1961, dressed in military fatigues, Cuban president Fidel Castro made his famous declaration: "I shall be a Marxist-Leninist for the rest of my life." In February 1972, President Richard Nixon traveled to China to discuss a strategic alliance between the two countries against the USSR.	This January, Castro donned a business suit for a conference on globalization in Havana. Financier George Soros and conservative economist Milton Friedman were invited. In April 1999, Chinese premier Zhu Rongji came to Washington to discuss China's admission to the World Trade Organization.
"These countries that are most willing to let capitalism quickly destroy inefficient companies, so that money can be freed up and directed to more innovative ones, will thrive in the era of globalization. Those which rely on governments to protect them from such creative destruction will fall behind."	Many countries raised trade barriers and tried import substitution industrialization, nationalization, price controls, and interventionist policies. The International Monetary Fund (IMF) and the World Bank were always present but rarely heeded. **Result:** Hyperinflation, overwhelming external debt, corruption, and inefficient industries ruled the day. Only 8 percent of countries had liberal capital regimes in 1975 and foreign direct investment was at a low of $23 billion.	Economic development relies on private-sector ownership, transparency and accountability, as well as investments in human capital and social infrastructure. The IMF plays a critical role, but must be enmeshed in a web of other organizations that support social welfare and the environment while promoting economic growth. **Result:** Foreign direct investment increased five fold between 1990 and 1997, jumping into $644 billion, and the number of countries with liberal regimes tripled to 28 percent.
The balance between individuals and nation-states [has changed]. . . . So you have today not only a superpower, not only Supermarkets, but . . . Super-empowered individuals."	In 1956, there were 973 international nongovernmental organizations (NGOs) in the world. In 1972, the total volume of world trade was only a fraction larger than the gross national product of the USSR. In 1970, there were only 7,000 transnational corporations (TNCs) in the world.	In 1996, there were 5,472 international NGOs in the world. The estimated annual revenue of transnational organized crime as of 1997, $750 billion, is larger than the gross domestic product of Russia. By 1994 the number of TNCs grew to 37,000 parent companies with 200,000 affiliates worldwide— controlling 33 percent of the world's productive assets.

SOURCE: Quotes taken from *The Lexus and the Olive Tree,* by Thomas Friedman (New York: Farrar, Straus, and Giroux, 1999).

be made obsolete or turned into a commodity is now lightening quick. Therefore, only the paranoid will survive—only those who constantly look over their shoulders to see who is creating something new that could destroy them and then do what they must to stay one step ahead. There will be fewer and fewer walls to protect us.

If the Cold War were a sport, it would be sumo wrestling, says Johns Hopkins University professor Michael Mandelbaum. "It would be two big fat guys in a ring, with all sorts of posturing and rituals and stomping of feet, but actually very little contact until the end of the match, when there is a brief moment of shoving and the loser gets pushed out of the ring, but nobody gets killed." By contrast, if globalization were a sport, it would be the 100-meter dash, over and over and over. No matter how many times you win, you have to race again the next day. And if you lose by just one-hundredth of a second, it can be as if you lost by an hour.

Last, and most important, globalization has its own defining structure of power, which is much more complex than the Cold War structure. The Cold War system was built exclusively around nation-states, and it was balanced at the center by two superpowers. The globalization system, by contrast, is built around three balances, which overlap and affect one another.

The first is the traditional balance between nation-states. In the globalization system, this balance still matters. It can still explain a lot of the news you read on the front page of the paper, be it the containment of Iraq in the Middle East or the expansion of NATO against Russia in Central Europe.

The second critical balance is between nation-states and global markets. These global markets are made up of millions of investors moving money around the world with the click of a mouse. I call them the "Electronic herd." They gather in key global financial centers, such as Frankfurt, Hong Kong, London, and New York—the "supermarkets." The United States can destroy you by dropping bombs and the supermarkets can destroy you by downgrading your bonds. Who ousted President Suharto in Indonesia? It was not another superpower, it was the supermarkets.

The third balance in the globalization system—the one that is really the newest of all—is the balance between individuals and nation-states. Because globalization has brought down many of the walls that limited the movement and reach of people, and because it has simultaneously wired the world into networks, it gives more direct power to individuals than at any time in history. So we have today not only a superpower, not only supermarkets, but also super-empowered individuals. Some of these super-empowered individuals are quite angry, some of them quite constructive—but all are now able to act directly on the world stage without the traditional mediation of governments or even corporations.

Jody Williams won the Nobel Peace Prize in 1997 for her contribution to the International Campaign to Ban Landmines. She managed to build an international coalition in favor of a landmine ban without much government help and in the face of opposition from the major powers. What did she say was her secret weapon for organizing 1,000 different human rights and arms control groups on six continents? "E-mail."

By contrast, Ramzi Ahmed Yousef, the mastermind of the February 26, 1993, World Trade Center bombing in New York, is the quintessential "super-empowered angry man." Think about him for a minute. What was his program? What was his ideology? After all, he tried to blow up two of the tallest buildings in America. Did he want an Islamic state in Brooklyn? Did he want a Palestinian state in New Jersey? No. He just wanted to blow up two of the tallest buildings in America. He told the Federal District Court in Manhattan that his goal was to set off an explosion that would cause one World Trade Center tower to fall onto the other and kill 250,000 civilians. Yousef's message was that he had no message, other than to rip up the message coming from the all-powerful America to his society. Globalization (and Americanization) had gotten in his face and, at the same time, had empowered him as an individual to do something about it. A big part of the U.S. government's conspiracy case against Yousef (besides trying to blow up the World Trade Center in 1993, he planned to blow up a dozen American airliners in Asia in January 1995) relied on files found in the off-white Toshiba laptop computer that Philippine police say Yousef abandoned as he fled his Manila apartment in January 1995, shortly before his arrest. When investigators got hold of Yousef's laptop and broke into its files, they found flight schedules, projected detonation times, and sample identification documents bearing photographs of some of his co-conspirators. I loved that—Ramzi Yousef kept all his plots on the C drive of his Toshiba laptop! One should have no illusions, though. The super-empowered angry men are out there, and they present the most immediate threat today to the United States and the stability of the new globalization system. It's not because Ramzi Yousef can ever be a superpower. It's because in today's world, so many people can be Ramzi Yousef.

So, we are no longer in some messy, incoherent "post–Cold War world." We are in a new international system, defined by globalization, with its own moving parts and characteristics. We are still a long way from fully understanding how this system is going to work. Indeed, if this were the Cold War, the year would be about 1946. That is, we understand as much about how this new system is going to work as we understood about how the Cold War would work in the year Churchill gave his "Iron Curtain" speech.

Nevertheless, it's time we recognize that there is a new system emerging, start trying to analyze events within it, and give it its own name. I will start the bidding. I propose that we call it "DOScapital."

A NEW TOTALITARIANISM

by Ignacio Ramonet

We have known for at least ten years that globalization is the dominant phenomenon of this century. No one has been waiting around for Thomas Friedman to discover this fact. Since the end of the 1980s, dozens of authors have identified, described, and analyzed globalization inside and out. What is new in Friedman's work—and debatable—is the dichotomy he establishes between globalization and the Cold War: He presents them as opposing, interchangeable "systems." His constant repetition of this gross oversimplification reaches the height of annoyance.

Just because the Cold War and globalization are dominant phenomena in their times does not mean that they are both systems. A system is a set of practices and institutions that provides the world with a practical and theoretical framework. By this fight, the Cold War never constituted a system—Friedman makes a gross error by suggesting otherwise. The term "Cold War," coined by the media, is shorthand for a period of contemporary history (1946—89) characterized by the predominance of geopolitical and geostrategic concerns. However, it does not explain a vast number of unrelated events that also shaped that era: the expansion of multinational corporations, the development of air transportation, the worldwide extension of the United Nations, the decolonization of Africa, apartheid in South Africa, the advancement of environmentalism, or the development of computers and high-tech industries such as genetic engineering. And the list goes on.

Furthermore, tension between the West and the Soviet Union, contrary to Friedman's ideas, dates from before the Cold War. In fact, that very tension was formative in shaping the way democratic states understood Italian fascism in the 1920s, Japanese militarism in the 1930s, German rearmament after the rise of Adolf Hitler in 1933, and the Spanish Civil War between 1936 and 1939.

Friedman is right, however, to argue that globalization has a systemic bent. Step by step, this two-headed monster of technology and finance throws everything into confusion. Friedman, by contrast, tells a tale of globalization fit for Walt Disney. But the chaos that seems to delight our author so much is hardly good for the whole of humanity.

Friedman notes, and rightly so, that everything is now interdependent and that, at the same time, everything is in conflict. He also observes that globalization embodies (or infects) every trend and phenomenon at work in the world today—whether political, economic, social, cultural, or ecological. But he forgets to remark that there are groups from every nationality, religion, and ethnicity that vigorously oppose the idea of global unification and homogenization.

Furthermore, our author appears incapable of observing that globalization imposes the force of two powerful and contradictory dynamics on the world: fusion and fission. On the one hand, many states seek out alliances. They pursue fusion with others to build institutions, especially economic ones, that provide strength—or safety—in numbers. Like the European Union, groups of countries in Asia, Eastern Europe, North Africa, North America, and South America are signing free-trade agreements and reducing tariff barriers to stimulate commerce, as well as reinforcing political and security alliances.

But set against the backdrop of this integration, several multinational communities are falling victim to fission, cracking or imploding into fragments before the astounded eyes of their neighbors. When the three federal states of the Eastern bloc—Czechoslovakia, the USSR, and Yugoslavia—broke apart, they gave birth to some 22 independent states! A veritable sixth continent!

The political consequences have been ghastly. Almost everywhere, the fractures provoked by globalization have reopened old wounds. Borders are increasingly contested, and pockets of minorities give rise to dreams of annexation, secession, and ethnic cleansing. In the Balkans and the Caucasus, these tensions unleashed wars (in Abkhazia, Bosnia, Croatia, Kosovo, Moldova, Nagorno-Karabakh, Slovenia, and South Ossetia).

The social consequences have been no kinder. In the 1980s, accelerating globalization went hand in hand with the relentless ultraliberalism of British prime minister Margaret

Thatcher and U.S. president Ronald Reagan. Quickly, globalization became associated with increased inequality, hikes in unemployment, deindustrialization, and deteriorated public services and goods.

Now, accidents, uncertainty, and chaos have become the parameters by which we measure the intensity of globalization. If we sized up our globalizing world today, what would we find? Poverty, illiteracy, violence, and illness are on the rise. The richest fifth of the world's population owns 80 percent of the world's resources, while the poorest fifth owns barely .5 percent. Out of a global population of 5.9 billion, barely 500 million people live comfortably, while 4.5 billion remain in need. Even in the European Union, there are 16 million people unemployed and 50 million living in poverty. And the combined fortune of the 358 richest people in the world (billionaires, in dollars) equals more than the annual revenue of 45 percent of the poorest in the world, or 2.6 billion people. That, it seems, is the brave new world of globalization.

Beware of Dogma

Globalization has little to do with people or progress and everything to do with money. Dazzled by the glimmer of fast profits, the champions of globalization are incapable of taking stock of the future, anticipating the needs of humanity and the environment, planning for the expansion of cities, or slowly reducing inequalities and healing social fractures.

According to Friedman, all of these problems will be resolved by the "invisible hand of the market" and by macroeconomic growth—so goes the strange and insidious logic of what we in France call the *pensée unique*. The *pensée unique*, or "single thought," represents the interests of a group of economic forces—in particular, free-flowing international capital. The arrogance of the *pensée unique* has reached such an extreme that one can, without exaggerating, call it modern dogmatism. Like a cancer, this vicious doctrine imperceptibly surrounds any rebellious logic, then inhibits it, disturbs it, paralyzes it, and finally kills it. This doctrine, this *pensée unique*, is the only ideology authorized by the invisible and omnipresent opinion police.

The *pensée unique* was born in 1944, at the time of the Bretton Woods Agreement. The doctrine sprang from the world's large economic and monetary institutions—the Banque de France, Bundesbank, European Commission, International Monetary Fund, Organisation for Economic Cooperation and Development, World Bank, and World Trade Organization—which tap their deep coffers to enlist research centers, universities, and foundations around the planet to spread the good word.

Dazzled by the glimmer of fast profits, the champions of globalization are incapable of taking stock of the future.

Almost everywhere, university economics departments, journalists (such as Friedman), writers, and political leaders take up the principal commandments of these new tablets of law and, through the mass media, repeat them until they are blue in the face. Their dogma is echoed dutifully by the mouthpieces of economic information and notably by the "bibles" of investors and stockbrokers—the *Economist*, *Far Eastern Economic Review*, Reuters, and *Wall Street Journal*, for starters—which are often owned by large industrial or financial groups. And of course, in our media-mad society, repetition is as good as proof.

So what are we told to believe? The most basic principle is so strong that even a Marxist, caught offguard, would agree: The economic prevails over the political. Or as the writer Alain Minc put it, "Capitalism cannot collapse, it is the natural state of society. Democracy is not the natural state of society. The market, yes." Only an economy disencumbered of social speed bumps and other "inefficiencies" can steer clear of regression and crisis.

The remaining key commandments of the *pensée unique* build upon the first. For instance, the market's "invisible hand corrects the unevenness and malfunctions of capitalism" and, in particular, financial markets, whose "signals orient and determine the general movement of the economy." Competition and competitiveness "stimulate and develop businesses, bringing them permanent and beneficial modernization." Free trade without barriers is "a factor of the uninterrupted development of commerce and therefore of societies." Globalization of manufactured production and especially financial flows should be encouraged at all costs. The international division of labor "moderates labor demands and lowers labor costs." A strong currency is a must, as is deregulation and privatization at every turn. There is always "less of the state" and a constant bias toward the interests of capital to the detriment of the interests of labor, not to mention a callous indifference to ecological costs. The constant repetition of this catechism in the media by almost all political decision makers, Right and Left alike (think of British and German prime ministers Tony Blair and Gerhard Schroder's "Third Way" and "New Middle"), gives it such an intimidating power that it snuffs out every tentative free thought.

Magnates and Misfits

Globalization rests upon two pillars, or paradigms, which influence the way globalizers such as Friedman think. The first pillar is communication. It has tended to replace, little by little, a major driver of the last two centuries: progress. From schools to businesses, from families and law to government, there is now one command: Communicate.

The second pillar is the market. It replaces social cohesion, the idea that a democratic society must function like a clock. In a clock, no piece is unnecessary and all pieces are unified. From this eighteenth-century mechanical metaphor, we can derive a modern economic and financial version. From now on, everything must operate according to the criteria of the "master market." Which of our new values are most fundamental? Windfall profits, efficiency, and competitiveness.

In this market-driven, interconnected world, only the strongest survive. Life is a fight, a jungle. Economic and social Darwinism, with its constant calls for competition, natural selection, and adaptation, forces itself on everyone and everything. In this new social order, individuals are divided into "solvent" or "nonsolvent"—i.e., apt to integrate into the market or not. The market offers protection to the solvents only. In this new order, where human solidarity is no longer an imperative, the rest are misfits and outcasts.

Thanks to globalization, only activities possessing four principal attributes thrive—those that are planetary, permanent, immediate, and immaterial in nature. These four characteristics recall the four principal attributes of God Himself. And in truth, globalization is set up to be a kind of modern divine critic, requiring submission, faith, worship, and new rites. The market dictates the Truth, the Beautiful, the Good, and the Just. The "laws" of the market have become a new stone tablet to revere.

Friedman warns us that straying from these laws will bring us to ruin and decay. Thus, like other propagandists of the New Faith, Friedman attempts to convince us that there is one way, and one way alone—the ultraliberal way—to manage economic affairs and, as a consequence, political affairs. For Friedman, the political is in effect the economic, the economic is finance, and finances are markets. The Bolsheviks said, "All power to the Soviets!" Supporters of globalization, such as Friedman, demand, "All power to the market!" The assertion is so peremptory that globalization has become, with its dogma and high priests, a kind of new totalitarianism.

DOSCAPITAL 2.0

by Thomas L. Friedman

Ignacio Ramonet makes several points in his provocative and impassioned anti-globalization screed. Let me try to respond to what I see as the main ones.

Ramonet argues that the Cold War was not an international system. I simply disagree. To say that the Cold War was not an international system because it could not explain everything that happened during the years 1946 to 1989—such as aerial transport or apartheid—is simply wrong. An international system doesn't explain everything that happens in a particular era. It is, though, a dominant set of ideas, power structures, economic patterns,

Diplomacy then: Soviet premier Nikita Khruschev and U.S. vice president Richard Nixon argue over the merits of capitalism in 1959's "Kitchen Debate" . . .

and rules that shape the domestic politics and international relations of more countries in more places than anything else.

Not only was the Cold War such an international system, but France had a very comfortable, unique, and, at times, constructive niche in that system, bridging the two superpower camps. Now that this old order is gone, it is obvious France is looking for a new, singular, and equally comfortable niche in today's system of globalization. Just as in the Cold War, France, like every other country, will have to define itself in relation to this new system. The obsession with globalization in the pages of *Le Monde diplomatique* is eloquent testimony to the fact that this search is alive and well in France.

Ramonet says that I "forget to remark that there are groups from every nationality, religion, ethnicity, etc., who vigorously oppose . . . globalization." In my book *The Lexus and the Olive Tree*, however, I have five separate chapters dealing with different aspects of that backlash. The penultimate chapter, in fact, lays out why I believe that globalization is not irreversible and identifies the five major threats to it: Globalization may be "just too hard" for too many people; it may be "just too connected" so that small numbers of people can disrupt the whole wired world today; it may be "just too intrusive" into people's lives; it may be 'just too unfair to too many people"; and lastly, it may be "just too dehumanizing." My approach could hardly be

called the Walt Disney version of globalization.

Frankly, I can and do make a much stronger case for the downsides of globalization than Ramonet does. I know that globalization is hardly all good, but unlike Ramonet I am not utterly blind to the new opportunities it creates for people—and I am not just talking about the wealthy few. Ask the high-tech workers in Bangalore, India, or Taiwan, or the Bordeaux region of France, or Finland, or coastal China, or Idaho what they think of the opportunities created by globalization. They are huge beneficiaries of the very market forces that Ramonet decries. Don't they count? What about all the human rights and environmental nongovernmental organizations that have been empowered by the Internet and globalization? Don't they count? Or do only French truck drivers count?

Ramonet says I am "incapable of observing that globalization imposes the force of two powerful contradictory dynamics on the world: fusion and fission." Say what? Why does he think I called my book *The Lexus and the Olive Tree*? It is all about the interaction between what is old and inbred—the quest for community, nation, family, tribe, identity, and one's own olive tree—and the economic pressures of globalization that these aspirations must interact with today, represented by the Lexus. These age-old passions are bumping up against, being squashed by, ripping through, or simply learning to live in balance with globalization.

What Ramonet can accuse me of is a belief that for the moment, the globalization system has been dominating the olive-tree impulses in most places. Many critics have pointed out that my observation that no two countries have ever fought a war against each other while they both had a McDonald's was totally disproved by the war in Kosovo. This is utter nonsense. Kosovo was only a temporary exception that in the end proved my rule. Why did airpower work to bring the Balkan war to a close after only 78 days? Because NATO bombed the Serbian tanks and troops out of Kosovo? No way. Airpower alone worked because NATO bombed the electricity stations, water system, bridges, and economic infrastructure in Belgrade—a modern European city, a majority of whose citizens wanted to be integrated with Europe and the globalization system. The war was won on the power grids of Belgrade, not in the trenches of Kosovo. One of the first things to be reopened in Belgrade was the McDonald's. It turns out in the end the Serbs wanted to wait in line for burgers, not for Kosovo.

Ramonet falls into a trap that often ensnares French intellectuals, and others, who rail against globalization. They assume that the rest of the world hates it as much as they do, and so they are always surprised in the end when the so-called little people are ready to stick with it. My dear Mr. Ramonet, with all due respect to you and Franz Fanon, the fact is the wretched of the earth want to go to Disneyworld, not to the barricades. They want the Magic Kingdom, not *Les Misérables* Just ask them.

Finally, Ramonet says that I believe all the problems of globalization will be solved by the "invisible hand of the market." I have no idea where these quotation marks came from, let alone the thought. It certainly is not from anything I have written. The whole last chapter of my book lays out in broad strokes what I believe governments—the American government in particular—must do to "democratize" globalization, both economically and politically. Do I believe that market forces and the Electronic Herd are very powerful today and can, at times, rival governments? Absolutely. But do I believe that market forces will solve everything? Absolutely not. Ramonet, who clearly doesn't know a hedge fund from a hedge hog, demonizes markets to an absurd degree. He may think governments are powerless against such monsters, but I do not.

I appreciate the passion of Ramonet's argument, but he confuses my analysis for advocacy. My book is not a tract for or against globalization, and any careful reader will see that. It is a book of reporting about the world we now live in and the dominant international system that is shaping it—a system driven largely by forces of technology that I did not start and cannot stop. Ramonet treats globalization as a choice, and he implicitly wants us to choose something different. That is his politics. I view globalization as a reality, and I want us first to understand that reality

... and now: Microsoft boss Bill Gates gives Russia's former first deputy premier Anatoly Chubais a crash course on the new economy in Moscow, 1997.

and then, by understanding it, figure out how we can get the best out of it and cushion the worst. That is my politics.

Let me share a secret with Ramonet. I am actually rooting for France. I hope that it can preserve all that is good and unique in its culture and way of life from the brutalizing, ho-

---

The wretched of the earth want to go Disneyworld, not to the barricades. They want the Magic Kingdom, not Les Misérables. Just ask them.

---

mogenizing forces of globalization. There is certainly room for a different path between the United States and North Korea, and good luck to France in finding it. But the readers of *Le Monde diplomatique* will get a lot better idea of how to find that middle path by reading my book than by reading Ramonet's critique.

Unfortunately, his readers will have to read *The Lexus and the Olive Tree* in a language other than French. The book is coming out in Arabic, Chinese, German, Japanese, and Spanish. There is only one major country where my American publisher could not find a local publisher to print it: France.

LET THEM EAT BIG MACS

by Ignacio Ramonet

It is truly touching when Thomas Friedman says, "The wretched of the earth want to go to Disneyworld, not to the barricades." Such a sentence deserves a place in posterity alongside Queen Marie-Antoinette's declaration in 1789, when she learned that the people of Paris were revolting and demanding bread: "Let them eat cake!"

My dear Mr. Friedman, do reread the 1999 *Human Development Report* from the United Nations Development Programme. It confirms that 1.3 billion people (or one-quarter of humanity) live on less than one dollar a day. Going to Disneyworld would probably not displease them, but I suspect they would prefer, first off, to eat well, to have a decent home and decent clothes, to be better educated, and to have a job. To obtain these basic needs, millions of people around the world (their numbers grow more numerous each day) are without a doubt ready to erect barricades and resort to violence.

I deplore this kind of solution as much as Friedman does. But if we are wise, it should never come to that. Rather, why not allocate a miniscule part of the world's wealth to the "wretched of the earth"? If we assigned just 1 percent of this wealth for 20 years to the development of the most unhappy of our human brothers, extreme misery might disappear, and with it, risks of endemic violence.

But globalization is deaf and blind to such considerations—and Friedman knows it. On the contrary, it worsens differences and divides and polarizes societies. In 1960, before globalization, the most fortunate 20 percent of the planet's population were 30 times richer than the poorest 20 percent. In 1997, at the height of globalization, the most fortunate were 74 times richer than the world's poorest! And this gap grows each day. Today, if you add up the gross national products of all the world's underdeveloped countries (with their 600 million inhabitants) they still will not equal the total wealth of the three richest people in the world. I am sure, my dear Mr. Friedman, that those 600 million people have only one thing on their minds: Disneyworld!

It is true that there is more to globalization than just the downsides, but how can we overlook the fact that during the last 15 years of globalization, per capita income has decreased in more than 80 countries, or in almost half the states of the world? Or that since the fall of communism, when the West supposedly arranged an economic miracle cure for the former Soviet Union—more or less, as Friedman would put it, new McDonald's restaurants—more than 150 million ex-Soviets (out of a population of approximately 290 million) have fallen into poverty?

If you would agree to come down out of the clouds, my dear Mr. Friedman, you could perhaps understand that globalization is a symptom of the end of a cycle. It is not only the end of the industrial era (with today's new technology), not only the end of the first capitalist revolution (with the financial revolution), but also the end of an intellectual cycle—the one driven by reason, as the philosophers of the eighteenth century defined it. Reason gave birth to modern politics and sparked the American and French Revolutions. But almost all that modern reason constructed—the state, society, industry, nationalism, socialism—has been profoundly changed. In terms of political philosophy, this transformation captures the enormous significance of globalization. Since ancient times, humanity has known two great organizing principles: the gods, and then reason. From here on out, the market succeeds them both.

Now the triumph of the market and the irresistible expansion of globalization cause me to fear an inevitable showdown between capitalism and democracy. Capitalism inexorably leads to the concentration of wealth and economic power in the hands of a small group. And this in turn leads to a fundamental question: How much redistribution will it take to make the domination of the rich minority acceptable to the majority of the world's population? The problem, my dear Mr. Friedman, is that the market is incapable of responding. All over the world, globalization is destroying the welfare state.

What can we do? How do we keep half of humanity from revolting and choosing violence? I know your response, dear Mr. Friedman: Give them all Big Macs and send them to Disneyworld!

WANT TO KNOW MORE?

An insightful overview of the social transformations that globalization has ushered in can be found in Malcolm Waters' *Globalization* (New York: Routledge, 1995). In *Capitalism, Socialism, and Democracy* (London: Harper, 1942), Joseph Schumpeter argues that only innovation can compensate for the destructive forces of the market. Benjamin Barber looks at culture clash in his book *Jihad versus McWorld* (New York: Times Books, 1995). William Greider argues for more managed globalization in *One World Ready or Not: The Manic Logic of Global Capitalism* (New York: Simon & Schuster, 1997). In his book, *The Post-Corporate World: Life after Capitalism* (San Francisco: Berrett-Koehler, 1999), David Korten stipulates that corporate capitalism could unravel the cohesion of society. Robert Reich considers how international labor markets will react to a shrinking world in *The Work of Nations: Preparing Ourselves for the 21st Century* (New York: Alfred A. Knopf, 1991). For a view on how information technology has changed the world economy, see Frances Cairncross' *The Death of Distance* (Cambridge: Harvard Business School Press, 1997). For a provocative advocate of Americanization, see David Rothkopf's **"In Praise of Cultural Imperialism"** (FOREIGN POLICY, Summer 1997). Refraining from taking sides, Dani Rodrik reexamines some of the faulty assumptions made on both sides of the globalization debate in *"Sense and Nonsense in the Globalization Debate"* (FOREIGN POLICY, Summer 1997). Ignacio Ramonet's wide-ranging commentary can be found in back issues of *Le Monde diplomatique*, archived online. Rigorous critiques of Thomas Friedman's new book, *The Lexus and the Olive Tree* (New York: Farrar Straus and Giroux, 1999) can be found in the *New Yorker* (May 10, 1999), *Nation* (June 14, 1999), *Financial Times* (May 15, 1999) and *New Statesman* (July 5,1999).

For links to relevant Web sites, as well as a comprehensive index of related FOREIGN POLICY articles, access **www.foreignpolicy.com**.

The Future of Civil Conflict

Shashi Tharoor

"The defining mode of conflict in the era ahead," Sen. Daniel Patrick Moynihan declared in 1993, "is ethnic conflict. It promises to be savage. Get ready for 50 new countries in the world in the next 50 years. Most of them will be born in bloodshed."

Moynihan's apocalyptic vision is not untypical of the prevailing wisdom. History, it seems to many, has exacted its own revenge on what Francis Fukuyama so rashly suggested was the posthistorical world, in the form of conflicts sparked and sustained by ancient and incomprehensible hatreds and bloodlusts. To many analysts, class conflict is passé; the "proxy wars" of the Cold War era can, by definition, no longer occur; and even realpolitik, with rational states pursuing their clearly defined interests, seems dated. Ethnicity, it seems, is the new, dominant causality.

Of course, one of the problems of looking at the future is that the future is never quite what it used to be. There is no doubt that in some parts of the world contemporary civil conflict has an ethnic cast to it. The question is how pervasive that cast is, and whether it is possible to both recognize and look beyond ethnicity to other forms of violent confrontation in our world.

Postmodern Tribalism

Although actual figures may vary marginally from year to year, it is clear that most violent conflicts today occur within states rather than between them. It is also true that the overwhelming majority of the world's wars are taking place in what used to be called the Third World. Despite the global media's preoccupation with the tragic events in the Balkans, more ordnance is being expended, and more lives lost, in civil conflict on any typical day in Asia and Africa than in the more mediagenic "North." Finally, studies looking at the incidence of conflict show that, if one

were to list all the wars that have occurred since 1945, fully a quarter are still active. In other words, ours is an age of blazing civil conflict, and there is no reason to suppose that the foreseeable future will be any different.

The ethnic dimension to many of these conflicts is striking. Ethnic conflict may best be understood as conflict between aggregations or groups that share a collective view of themselves as being distinctly different from other aggregations or groups because of their shared inherent characteristics—essentially characteristics related to identity from birth, such as race, religion, language, cultural heritage, clan or tribal affiliation. How else to explain why Armenian victims of the 1988 earthquake refused blood donated by their Azerbaijani neighbors? Or why Latvian lawmakers in 1993 wanted to cleanse their military cemeteries of Russian corpses? Or why Hutus and Tutsis, Turks and Kurds, or Serbs and Croats, have so tragically reveled in what Freud called "the narcissism of minor differences"?

At times, it can appear that we are indeed living in a world of postmodern tribalism. Certainly, ethnicity enjoys a role in the formation of identity quite different from the one it occupied in the era when nationality was preeminent. Its claims find support from ideas both on the left and on the right. Even the contemporary acknowledgement of ethnicity in "politically correct" policies of multiculturalism and affirmative action has contributed to legitimizing it. More crucial, the language of human rights is increasingly being used to advance a particularist-ethnic agenda of separatism in many parts of the world, from Abkhazia and Chechnya to Sri Lanka and Bougainville. And ethnic identity is frequently promoted as a vehicle for the socioeconomic advancement of the particular ethnic group, with separatism seen as the only way to gain power and control over material resources.

But do these tendencies really support the contemporary commonplace that ours is an age of ethnic conflict? Certainly, the conflicts in the former Yugoslavia and Rwanda occurred along ethnic lines. But there is contradictory evidence as well. The recent conflicts in Cambodia and Guatemala, to cite two of the most horrifying examples of civil conflict of the past 30 years, did not. And while some scholars have suggested that

Shashi Tharoor is director of Communications and Special Projects in the Office of the Secretary General of the United Nations. The views expressed here are the author's own and do not necessarily reflect the positions of the United Nations.

ethnically homogeneous states are less vulnerable to civil war, the examples of Somalia, Cambodia, and Nicaragua—all essentially uni-ethnic states that have been riven in recent years by fratricidal conflict—should give us pause.

Even when ethnicity is overtly the fault line in a civil conflict, as in a war where the sides identify themselves by ethnic labels, it is rarely, if ever, a sufficient explanation for conflict. There are always the more prosaic political ambitions of ethnic leaders to be considered, not to mention straightforward economic motivations. Indeed, it would be safer to proceed from the assumption that politics is at the root of most contemporary civil conflict than to take at face value the ethnic explanation that is so much in vogue today—particularly in the media.

Invented Nationalisms
It should be remembered that while ethnicity is often adduced as the root cause of civil conflict, those who emphasize its centrality most stridently and implacably are often the same opportunistic local political leaders who find in it the ideal vehicle to preserve or enhance their power, or to distract their citizens from other domestic failures, often when ethnic division is nowhere as profound as is being claimed. Yugoslavia after 1989 is often cited as a classic example of this phenomenon, though the practice is common enough. This is not to deny the potency or appeal of ethnic images, emblems, and folklore, particularly in periods of social and political flux when the "traditional" appears to offer the only anchor for people for whom every other certainty has failed. Sometimes this is dressed up as an ethnic form of irredentism: not so much the notion that a country should recapture all its lost territories but rather that it should reclaim all its "lost" peoples by annexing the foreign territories on which they live. This phenomenon is one more confirmation of the postmodern notion that all nationalisms are essentially invented (or reinvented) in modern times, through a combination of imagining ethnic, linguistic, or historical communities that have no greater basis than communal indoctrination.

But although ethnic symbols can, and sometimes do, serve to mobilize beleaguered communities even when the original reasons for their problems are not rooted in ethnicity, it should be remembered that not every ethnic group feels the need to assert itself through conflict; still less should one extrapolate that ethnic aspirations will inevitably result in wars in quest of new nationhoods. Not every distinct ethnic minority seeks secession; it is safe to assume that the Turks in Germany will not seek a new state, nor Asians in Britain or Hispanics in the United States. Other minorities, in societies with seemingly intractable problems, will accept their status as minorities, if their legitimate aspirations are fulfilled within their

states. India, which in essence is a national aggregation of minorities, is a striking example of this rule (and also of exceptions that prove it). Democracies that offer minorities the opportunities to find their place in the sun and to determine their own political future within a national framework usually do not need to fear ethnic rebellion.

Exceptions exist, of course. The Tamils in Sri Lanka might conceivably be seen as one, though it could also be argued that the ongoing guerrilla struggle there has more to do with the obduracy of a single-minded secessionist leader and his fanatically loyal core of supporters than with any unalterably fervent secessionist feeling among the Tamil masses as a whole, especially in light of the political concessions made by the current Sri Lankan government.

Of course, this does not mean that societies that are relatively resistant to the risk of secession are immune from ethnic conflict that falls short of becoming a full-fledged civil war. One has only to think of the effects of racism in this regard. Where, for example, certain groups are perceived as inassimilable and are discriminated against systematically, violence is always a possible outcome—as recent events in Kosovo have demonstrated. But again, there is nothing inevitable about such an outcome. Anti-Tutsi feeling in the Democratic Republic of Congo led to bloodshed, but while violence seemed possible between ethnic Russians and their neighbors in Latvia, bloodshed has so far been averted.

In a world where, increasingly, one man's fundamentalist is another's true believer, religious sectarianism and chauvinism can play at least as dangerous a role. Religious chauvinism can manifest itself as intolerance on either side of the divide between the state and the rebel. The persecution of minority faiths or heretical sects of the dominant faith often leaves their practitioners with nothing to lose if they were to riot or even take up arms against their tormentors. Nondiscriminatory policies on the part of enlightened governments would prevent this, but all too often discrimination is built into the constitution or the state structure in countries where the state identifies itself with an established faith or religious identity. The mirror image of this phenomenon is when a secular government confronts a religiously fanatical rebel group, such as the Armed Islamic Group in Algeria or the Sikh fundamentalist warriors of Sant Jarnail Singh Bhindranwale in Indian Punjab, or (at least initially) the "Lord's Resistance Army" in Uganda.

Triggers of Conflict
In assessing the likely causes of future civil conflict, the evidence of the recent past makes a useful guide. The process of decolonization, which was for so long a significant generator of conflicts, is no longer the factor it was. But residual problems from the end of the

2. Future of Civil Conflict

era of colonization, whether the consequence of badly managed departures by the colonial power or simply the result of the fact that boundaries drawn in colonial times create enormous problems of national unity, still remain dangerously alive, as is evidenced by the continuing crises in Kashmir, East Timor, and Western Sahara, not to mention the old standbys of Cyprus and Israel-Palestine. Any one of them could erupt at any time, as they have done, much to everyone's surprise, in the dispute between Eritrea and Ethiopia over old colonial boundaries.

The tensions that have sometimes erupted into violence in the postcolonial period stemming from conflicts between groups that were materially favored by the colonial power and those that were disadvantaged are all too well known, whether one is talking about the Ibos in Nigeria trying to secede in 1967 or the Sinhalese resentment of the privileges Tamils enjoyed when Britain ruled Sri Lanka. But the intellectual legacy of the colonial period also continues to exact its toll—from careless anthropology to politically motivated sociology. It was the partly spurious and certainly oversimplified and careless division of the peoples of the Great Lakes region of Africa into two rigidly differentiated tribes—Hutus and Tutsis—that lies at the root of the slaughter going on today. And the theoretical underpinnings of British colonialism in India, from the invention of "martial races" to the policy of "divide and rule" on religious lines, led to the savage partition of the subcontinent and episodes of communal bloodletting since.

A "mixed" colonial history within a modern state can also be a source of danger. When a state has had more than one colonial past, its coherence is often imperiled. After all, secession can be prompted by historical, geographical, and cultural factors as easily as by ethnic ones. Ethnicity and language hardly seem to have been factors in the secessions (one recognized, the other not) of Eritrea from Ethiopia and the Republic of Somaliland from Somalia. Rather, it was different colonial experiences (Italian rule in Eritrea and British rule in Somaliland) that set the secessionists apart—at least in their own self-perceptions—from the rest of their ethnic compatriots. A similar case can be made about the former Yugoslavia, where areas that had been under Hapsburg rule for 800 years were joined to parts that had been under Ottoman suzerainty for more than 500 years.

The Shape of Things to Come?

Overall, however, the colonial legacy is less relevant to contemporary civil conflict than state fragmentation and re-formation. There is nothing new about this, of course. In the aftermath of the First World War, the Ottoman and Austro-Hungarian empires dissolved and a number of new nation-states emerged. The end of the Second World War gave rise not only to the dismantling of the Third Reich and the redrawing of a number of borders but also to the consolidation of the Soviet bloc and the beginning of the era of decolonization. As with the period immediately after the two world wars, the end of the Cold War also brought about the breakdown of structures and barriers that had been maintained by (and for) the purposes of the belligerents. What is less clear is whether crises and wars in such places as Kosovo, the Former Yugoslav Republic of Macedonia, Georgia, and Nagorno-Karabakh are the shape of things to come or whether the wars of communist succession, as they are sometimes called, are coming to an end now that the Soviet Union and the former Yugoslavia have disintegrated.

What is unarguably a continuing source of danger are the many instances in the world of failed states. Somalia is the best-known example of this; Liberia after the end of the hegemony of the True Whig Party is another. The fact that there is a crisis in governance in many other African countries as well makes the possibility of other Somalias and Liberias alarmingly real, as has been shown by recent events in Sierra Leone, Congo-Brazzaville, and the Democratic Republic of Congo.

And, though the point is not always emphasized strongly enough, at the root of these state failures is the enduring problem of underdevelopment, which is itself frequently a cause of civil conflict. The uneven distribution of infrastructure in a poor country, for instance, can lead to resources being distributed unequally, which in turn leads to increasing fissures in a society between those from "neglected regions" and those better served by roads, railways, power stations, telecommunications, bridges, and canals.

The transformation of many formerly statist economies to capitalism—a feature of our age, in which, apparently, liberal capitalism's triumph is almost complete—has accentuated this problem. It is ironic but true that paternalistic economies do not generate as much conflict over economic spoils as do economies in the process of conversion to capitalism, where resource distribution follows the law of the market rather than the political imperatives of the state.

Advancing underdevelopment in many countries of the South, which are faring poorly in their desperate struggle to remain players in the game of global capitalism, has created conditions of desperate poverty, ecological collapse, and rootless, unemployed populations beyond the control of atrophying state systems. And of course, resource competition and environmental degradation can themselves be a source of conflict, as groups battle for control of ever diminishing natural resources in a deteriorating environment.

Intriguingly, however, the idea that wealth-producing regions might increasingly pursue greater prosperity by breaking away from larger nations that are acting as a drag on their economic advancement—a situation in which, as the French political scientist Pascal Boniface has suggested, "a secessionist movement is just a press release away"—has little evidence to back it. Despite the press releases of the Lombard League in northern Italy, there are no examples of successful secessions of the rich regions of the world, however much the wealthy Northern Mexicans might complain about their poverty-stricken southern compatriots, or the Catalans might grumble about the rest of Spain.

Leadership, Ideology, and Circumstance

If there are times when civil conflict is the result of circumstances that individuals have little power to influence, there are other instances of conflict that are the result of the failure of political leadership. By this I do not mean only the willingness of political leaders to manipulate their followers into acts of criminality and destruction, but also the abject failure of many leaders to rule effectively or imaginatively, to inspire their citizens and contain the destructive forces that were simmering under the surface of their societies. The examples of President Gamsakhurdia in Georgia, elected in a landslide but unable to rule, or President Mobutu in Zaire, come readily to mind.

We know that political leadership plays a role in either accentuating or mitigating differences within a state. But what tends to get lost when the causes of conflict are anatomized are the circumstantial factors. The mere proliferation of weapons, for instance, can serve as a cause of conflict, rather than just an intensifier of it: many of the clashes that occurred within the larger conflict in Afghanistan, such as between different factions of the so-called Northern Alliance, reflected this "Have Gun, Will Unravel" tendency. The role of external incitements is one to which successive would-be peacemakers in that conflict have repeatedly drawn attention: foreign arms flows and external support for rival factions in Afghanistan contributed in key ways to the nature, duration, and intensity of the civil war there throughout the 1990s. The current conflict in the Democratic Republic of Congo features, even more starkly, the determining role of external powers on both sides.

It is too often forgotten, however, that not all external actors are foreigners. Ethnic diasporas are often a potent source of both the intellectual and financial underpinnings of civil conflict. There seems to be something about expatriation that breeds extremism. The American ethnic mosaic is full of imported bigotry, from the Muslim fundamentalists who have been trying with commendable ineptitude to blow up New York, to Miami's fanatical Cuban exiles.

The Expatriate Extremist

Exile, it is clear, nurtures political extremists: one has only to look at the Brooklyn-born settlers in the West Bank to confirm the point. Many nations around the world have had to face the reality of zeal abroad for radicalism at home. Examples abound: expatriate Sikhs pouring money, weapons, and organizational skills into the cause of a separate "Khalistan," while some expatriate Hindus finance Hindu chauvinism in India; Irish Americans supporting, willfully or otherwise, IRA terrorism; Jaffna Tamils in England financing the murderous drive for "Eeelam" in Sri Lanka; and American Jewish groups lobbying for positions on Palestinian issues that are far less accommodating than those of a number of Israeli leaders, including Shimon Peres and the late Yitzhak Rabin.

The roots of this political extremism from afar may lie in the very nature of expatriation. Most of the contemporary world's emigrants are people who left their homelands in quest of material improvement, looking for financial security and professional opportunities that, for one reason or another, they could not attain in their own countries. Most of them left intending to return: a few years abroad, a few more dollars in the bank, they told themselves, and they would come back to their own hearths, triumphant over the adversity that had led them to leave. But the years kept stretching on, and the dollars were never quite enough, or their needs mounted with their acquisitions, or they developed new ties (career, spouse, children, schooling) to their new land, and then gradually the realization seeps in that they would never go back. And with this realization, often only half acknowledged, came a welter of emotions: guilt, at the abandoning of the motherland, mixed with rage that the motherland had somehow—through its own failings, political, economic, social—forced them into this abandonment. The attitude of this kind of expatriate to his homeland is that of the faithless lover who blames the woman he has spurned for not having sufficiently merited his fidelity.

Of course, all generalizations are dangerous, and the vast majority of expatriates adjust to this dilemma and assimilate into new lands. But for a small but influential minority, the psychology I have described makes the support of extremism at home doubly gratifying: it appeases the expatriate's sense of guilt at not being involved in his homeland, and it vindicates his decision to abandon it. (If the homeland he has left did not have the faults he detests, he tells himself, he would not have had to leave it.)

But that is not all. The troubled expatriate desperately needs to define himself in his new society. He is reminded by his mirror, if not by the nationals of his new land, that he is not entirely like them. In the midst of racism and alienation, second-class citizenship and self-hatred, he needs an identity to assert—a label of which he can be proud, yet which does not undermine his choice of expatriation. He has rejected the reality of his country but not, he declares fervently, the essential values he had derived from his roots. As his children grow up "American" or "British" or "Canadian," as they slough off the assumptions, prejudices, and fears of his own childhood, he becomes even more assertive about them. But his nostalgia is based on the selectiveness of memory; it is a simplified, idealized recollection of his roots, often reduced to their most elemental—family, caste, clan, sect, region, religion. In exile among foreigners, he clings to a vision of what he really is that admits no foreignness.

The tragedy is that the culture he remembers, with both nostalgia and rejection, has itself evolved—in interaction with others—on its national soil. His perspective distorted by exile, the expatriate knows nothing of this. His view of what used to be home is divorced from the experience of home. This kind of expatriate is no longer an organic part of the culture, but a severed digit that, in its yearning for the hand, can only twist itself into a clenched fist.

The New Zeitgeist

If I have gone into this phenomenon at some length, it is because ours is a world increasingly defined by displacement: the movement of populations across frontiers everywhere means that expatriation is a central feature of the Zeitgeist. There is some fascinating recent work on the role of expatriate intellectuals in creating, practically out of whole cloth, an Oromo national self-consciousness where none had existed, and in financing a "liberation army" to win a state in the Horn of Africa for a nation that had never existed before in the minds of most of its putative citizenry. Perhaps 5 percent of the earth's people today live in countries other than those in which they were born. The consequences for future civil conflicts should not be underestimated.

Civil conflicts, of course, have many roots at home. One aspect that bears close examination is their political economy. It is a commonplace among humanitarian aid workers, who are all too familiar in any case with relief becoming part of the calculations of the belligerents, that a major motivation of the warring parties in a civil conflict is to promote, or resist, a change in the structures and processes through which resources are distributed within a given society. It is hardly a new maxim that profits flow in the midst of conflict, but the point is that conflict itself may be kept alive by the opportunities for profit, and the issue of who actually profits becomes key. Political leaders, businessmen, smugglers, sanctions evaders, drug traffickers, may all find material benefits in the continuation of a war that is decimating their own people. (Lebanon was probably a good example of this.)

The Economics of Ethnic Conflict

The running of a war economy requires both power and skills, and often international connections: there is no point controlling diamond mines if you cannot sell the diamonds to people who are willing to pay you in dollars, as was demonstrated during the civil war in Sierra Leone, where diamonds are a churl's best friend. In Cambodia, the thriving cross-border trade between Khmer Rouge-controlled parts of the country and Thailand became a factor in the progress of that country's civil war. Thus, the economics of warfare can thwart political and diplomatic attempts at resolution, whether directly or indirectly.

There is also the factor of the complicity of warring elites in each other's exactions. As the British scholar David Keen has observed, some civil wars become very civil indeed. It was said of the Khmer Rouge and the army generals of the official state of Cambodia that they fought each other during the day and drank together at night. I remember being told by a journalist of an episode during the three-cornered Bosnian war in 1993 when a Serb gunnery captain in the hills above the city of Mostar accepted $10,000 from a Muslim unit to shell the Croats. "Fine, we'll start shelling them promptly at 6:00 P.M.," the Serb allegedly informed the Muslim. Why not sooner, the Muslim asked. "Because from 10:00 to 6:00, we've been paid $10,000 by the Croats to shell you," came the reply. The story may well be apocryphal, but to those who heard many such stories throughout the war in the former Yugoslavia, it has an undeniable ring of plausibility. Joseph Heller's Milo Minderbinder is alive and well and flourishing in the Balkans.

So war can be lucrative for the warriors. Precious commodities and natural resources have played a decisive role in a number of recent civil conflicts: diamonds in Sierra Leone, Liberia, and Angola; drugs in Colombia, Afghanistan, and Myanmar; oil in the Democratic Republic of Congo. The political economy of civil wars is not only about the most direct and crude material advantage, of course. There are sometimes fundamental economic issues at stake as well. Land distribution, for instance, was a central part of the conflict in El Salvador. But it would be difficult to make the case that all, or even the majority, of civil conflicts are driven principally by economic interests, even if they are largely sustained by them.

The conventional wisdom about economic globalization has been that it would contribute to curbing war, which would be seen as no longer profitable. It has not turned out that way. Indeed, some of the poster children for globalization proved that they were more, not less, vulnerable to civil strife as a result. The riots, looting, and rapes that occurred in Indonesia in May-June 1998 provided a stark example of civil conflict—albeit fortunately not civil war—sparked by an economy's inability to cope with the demands as well as the opportunities of globalization. As the American political scientist David Turton has put it, in many countries globalization has made the state "both too small and too big at the same time . . . too small to act as an autonomous and independent political and economic entity and too big to satisfy the aspirations and claims of its ethnic and other minorities."[1]

This seems to bring us back to ethnicity again: the principal targets of the Indonesian violence were the ethnically distinct Chinese minority. After all, however counterintuitive it may seem, ethnic identities are intimately bound up with globalization. As Turton has argued, "One cannot think locally unless one already has an idea of a global context in which localities can coexist. One cannot assert a right to local identity and self-determination except by appealing to some general principles. To make such a claim, then, is also to assert global identity."

Ethnicity, in short, is a "relational concept: it refers to the way cultural differences are communicated and is therefore created and maintained by contact, not by isolation." In the politicization of identities, ethnicity can distort elements that might otherwise have been considered positive. Indeed, it has been argued that the factors that scholars normally point to as promoting good and friendly relations between states—such as liberalization and democracy—are not necessarily assets in promoting positive relations within a state. Freedom, after all, too often includes the freedom to incite hatred.

It seems reasonable to suggest that the sources of civil conflict I have identified will remain valid in the foreseeable future. And while no single one of them is adequate in itself to serve as a predictor of future civil conflict, the interaction of two or more of these elements—economics overlaid on ethnicity, for instance—could go a long way toward explaining the nature and intensity of violent attempts to overturn internal national political arrangements.

Era of the Warlord
It is a truism that civil conflict is not always driven by rational and objective factors: the irrational and the subjective are equally vital, as is the role of collective historical memory. The corollary to this is that such conflicts are all the more difficult to resolve.

There is usually a multiplicity of actors and factors. The fighters are often a divided and disorganized lot, poorly disciplined, with little by way of a coherent chain of command or supply. They may owe allegiance to an immediate leader rather than to the larger cause on whose side they profess to be fighting, with the result that alliances may change and commitments may be broken with bewildering ease. This is the era of the warlord, accountable to no one, who thinks with his stomach and speaks with a Kalashnikov. Negotiating cease-fires or agreements with the

likes of such leaders is never simple, and they are rarely durable. It should come as no surprise that civil wars last longer than wars between states. In the twentieth century, 20 months has been the average duration of interstate wars, in contrast to 120 months for civil wars.

The ferocious destructive capacity of civil conflict has become evident in recent and ongoing conflicts, in which the scale of destruction also reflects the fact that in such wars damage to civilians is often the intention, rather than the by-product, of military action. Often, brutality is an end in itself, meant to terrorize and intimidate; sometimes it is a means to an end, as when "ethnic cleansing" is conducted to drive "alien" populations away from territory that is sought in the name of a single ethnic group.

Matters are further complicated by the all-consuming nature of civil conflicts, whose participants often seem prepared to endure human and material costs out of all proportion to the likely benefits because they are often fighting for values that they consider priceless—identity, nation, *volk*. Soldiers in such conflicts often abandon all hopes of another way of life, and when the wars in which they are engaged do end they may find the transition to peacetime activities all but impossible. For such soldiers, it is easier to heed the exhortation to carry on fighting than to reconcile themselves to a peace in which they might become both irrelevant and unemployed.

In addition, the political economy of civil conflict often makes warfare a rational rather than an irrational choice for many of the participants. Sometimes it is a "win-win" proposition for fighters who can divide the spoils with fighters from the enemy side. In short, there are a variety of incentives to continue a civil conflict, and a number of disincentives to compromise, both emerging from the conflict itself.

The situation is made worse by the availability of cheap and easily acquired weaponry. The fact that obtaining landmines and AK-47s is far simpler than acquiring more sophisticated inventories is enough, in and of itself, to make civil conflicts easier to sustain. The international arms trade, sadly, also reflects the bizarre and tragic phenomenon of the poor of the South killing each other with weaponry sold to them by the rich of the North (including, too often, by the five permanent members of the United Nations Security Council).

And although high technology has not yet become a decisive factor in civil conflicts, three other trends of the 1990s have acquired greater importance than before. The first is the role of television, powerfully enhanced by advances in satellite technology, which bring shattering images from the battlefield into people's homes almost as they occur. The visual media has always been the most emotive source of nationalist demagoguery; the role of television in whipping up passions and hatreds (and not much more benignly, overweening nationalist pride) in assorted civil conflicts in Europe can scarcely be overstated. (I will always remember with sick horror how, in the early days of the Yugoslav war, both Serbs and Croats displayed the same pictures of the same massacred babies, demanding mutual retribution.)

A second contemporary trend appears to be that civil wars are not particularly amenable to negotiated solutions, and on the relatively few occasions that a peace has been successfully negotiated, the settlements reached have too often been unstable. This of course does not mean that all peacemaking is futile, but it points to the severity of the challenge confronting diplomats attempting to put an end to such civil conflagrations.

The third contemporary trend is the involvement of professional combatants in civil conflicts—with "private armies" and "military companies" providing expert military services to their combatant clients. Despite recent episodes in places as far apart as Sierra Leone and Papua New Guinea, it is too early to estimate the impact such firms may have on the future of civil wars.

Much has been made of the role of "national character" in determining the severity and duration of a particular conflict. This is controversial. But there is one structural aspect to national character that is undeniably crucial—the construction of state systems that can prevent, or easily succumb to, civil conflict.

In many states, divisive constitutional and political structures, state repression, mobilization along ethnic or regional lines, unequal economic distribution patterns, the weakness of the middle class and its inability to compete in a globalizing world market, and widespread poverty and environmental degradation combine to create a propitious ground for violence between groups who feel they have little to lose and everything to gain by taking up arms. This aspect is crucial in any attempt to cope with civil conflict.

Coping with the Future

A comprehensive discussion of strategies for coping with future civil conflict is beyond the scope of this article, but a few basic thoughts come to mind. In our increasingly multiethnic, interdependent, globalizing world, how can issues of identity and ethnicity be dealt with so that they do not manifest themselves in violent conflict? What structures might prevent the processes of division within states and the demonization of "others" within communities? Clearly, Senator Moynihan's apocalyptic vision, with which I began, is not an appealing prospect; a proliferation of secessions can never answer the real challenges of managing diversity within states. Instead, solutions short of secession have to be found, preferably before civil conflict erupts into full-scale civil war.

Much has already been written on the challenges and possibilities of international responses to civil conflicts, and on the extent to which the international system can prevent or resolve them. It is worth bearing in mind the subjective considerations that affect preventive action by the U.N. Security Council—the judgment of the political leaders of the five permanent members, their willingness to act on early warnings, their perceptions of how the civil conflict in question affects their own direct strategic interests, and indeed their policy preferences (the U.S. administration's understanding of the likelihood of East Pakistan's secession in 1971, for instance, did not preclude Washington's "tilt" toward the military junta in Islamabad, a useful ally in the then-secret opening to China). The attitude of the parties to potential civil conflict is also crucial: some are more amenable to international influence than others.

My principal concern here is with domestic arrangements that prevent civil conflict; there is no better place to stop a conflict before it starts than within the country itself. I would submit that there is nothing inherently wrong with identity-consciousness, even if this is based on ethnicity, provided it does not manifest itself in hatred for, and resultant mobilization against, other identities. Theoreticians have proposed a variety of models to achieve this—"consociationism" (governing through alliances with groups of different identities), "federalism" (governing through decentralization of power to different geographical regions), and "ethnic syncretism" (governing by according ethnic identities full cultural expression, but not political articulation). I am no theoretical scholar and would prefer to focus on an empirical example that appears to cut across all three categories. India, the country I know best, offers an instructive paradigm.

One Land Embracing Many

Few Indians today would advance their country as a paragon, but it is truly remarkable that for 51 years after its savage and sad "freedom at midnight," marred by the carnage of a traumatic partition with Pakistan, India has avoided both the large-scale civil conflict and the political disintegration that was widely predicted for it in the 1950s and 1960s. No other country in the world, after all, embraces the extraordinary mixture of ethnic groups, the profusion of mutually incomprehensible languages, the varieties of topography and climate, the diversity of religions and cultural practices, and the range of levels of economic development that India does. Yet Indian democracy, rooted in the constitutional rule of law and free elections, has managed the processes of political change and economic transformation necessary to develop the country and forestall political and economic disaster.

India is united not by a common ethnicity, language, or religion, but by the experience of a common history within a shared geographical space, reified in a liberal constitution and the repeated exercise of democratic self-governance in a pluralist polity. India's founding fathers wrote a constitution for a dream; we in India have given passports to their ideals. Instead of the "narcissism of minor differences," in India we celebrate the commonality of major differences. To stand Michael Ignatieff's famous phrase on its head, India is a land of belonging rather than of blood.

So the idea of India is of one land embracing many. It is the idea that a nation may endure differences of caste, creed, color, culture, conviction, cuisine, costume, and custom, and still rally around a democratic consensus. That consensus is about the simple principle that in a democracy you do not really need to agree—except on the ground rules of how you will disagree. The reason India has survived all the stresses and strains that have beset it for 50 years is that it maintained consensus on how to manage without consensus. Indians are comfortable with the idea of multiple identities and multiple loyalties, all coming together in allegiance to a larger idea of India.

Yet this has occurred while politicians have opportunistically made Indians more conscious than ever of what divides us—religion, region, caste, language, ethnicity—by seeking to mobilize support on ever narrower lines of identity. But it is electoral, not military, support they have sought to mobilize; and the electoral system is focused on a common national structure of governance. Politicians understand that no one identity can ever triumph in India: both the country's chronic pluralism and the logic of the electoral marketplace make this impossible. In a pluralist state, it is essential that each citizen feels secure in his or her identity. But Indians have come to understand that while they may be proud of being Muslims or Marwaris or Mallahs, they will be secure in these religious, regional, or caste identities only because they are also Indians.

India is perhaps too singular a case to serve as a model, but it embodies many of the strategies that could help multiethnic states ward off the perils of civil conflict in the future. It is not that India is free of civil conflict—though the Punjab troubles are over, for all practical purposes—but rather that when such a conflict has occurred, it has usually been because of India's failure, in those specific circumstances, to follow the very prescriptions it has applied with such success to the country as a whole.

And even if there are unique aspects to the Indian case, it is no accident that pluralist democracies have dealt better with civil conflict than other types of societies. The proposition that pluralist democracy is therefore the best antidote to the risk of infection of civil conflict seems to me an unexceptional one. This does not mean democracy will satisfy every extremist minority group—as some Basques have proven in Spain and some Tamils in Sri Lanka. But democracy, both as precept and practice, has never sought or assumed the mantle of perfection.

Instead of looking at postconflict military interventions for which the mandate or the resources required may not be available, should the world not be devoting more attention to the promotion of democracy and pluralism across the globe? There are obvious political dangers in such a course, and there is no doubt that democracy, like love, must come from within; it cannot be instilled from the outside. But encouraging democracy for all the peoples of the world would be an eminently worthwhile objective for policymakers. This century has, despite all its setbacks, given us a world safe for democracy; let us work, in the next century, to establish a world safe for diversity.

Notes

The author wishes to acknowledge the valuable comments and insights provided by Edward Mortimer, Ian Johnstone, Andrew Mack, Nader Mousavizadeh, and Paul Lewis.

1. For this and subsequent quotes, see David Turton, "Introduction: War and Ethnicity," in *War and Ethnicity: Global Connections and Local Violence*, ed. David Turton (Univ. of Rochester Press, 1997).

The New Interventionism and the Third World

> **"The legal framework defining the right of self-determination and respect for territorial sovereignty is in disarray. Deference to the state has weakened in recent years by changes in geopolitics, greater support for human rights, the impact of globalization, and the countervailing emergence of a variety of micronationalisms and ethnic causes."**

RICHARD FALK

The most vexing problems in the 1990s have arisen from human catastrophes in economically and politically disadvantaged countries. Somalia, Bosnia, Rwanda, Chechnya, Kosovo, Sierra Leone, Liberia, and Sudan are some of the most prominent instances. These countries are either in the geographical South or in two dismantled states, the Soviet Union and Yugoslavia. Their plight is linked to a circumstance of "new world disorder" that emerged after the end of the cold war and continued through the 1990s.

Because they are no longer of strategic interest to the world power structure or from the perspectives of globalization, leading states have had no incentive to invest heavily in rescue operations. At the same time, however, the global media have highlighted with vivid images the suffering associated with these crises of governance.

Furthermore, there has been a strong buildup of support for international human rights in recent decades, the result of concerted activity by nongovernmental organizations around the world, as well as the success of the anti-apartheid campaign directed at South Africa and the struggle for civil and political rights in Eastern Europe. This recent emphasis on human rights has added poignancy to the tragedy of societies seemingly caught in a deadly downward spiral of events with no serious prospects of a reversal through self-help.

SUMMONING THE UN . . .

Pressure to do something about humanitarian catastrophes has mounted, but what to do, and by whom, has proved controversial, with undertakings in response often leading to despair and disappointment. The most obvious approach was to turn for urgent help to the United Nations. After all, cooperation within the Security Council seemed much more feasible than it had during the gridlock of the cold war era. The UN had made major contributions even before the collapse of the Soviet Union, playing useful peacekeeping roles in ending regional conflicts in a series of countries, including Afghanistan, El Salvador, Angola, Mozambique, and Namibia. Such optimism about an expanding UN role reached its climax with the 1991 Persian Gulf War, when the Security Council joined together in support of action to restore Kuwaiti sovereignty after Iraq's invasion the previous year.

RICHARD FALK *is Albert G. Milbank Professor of International Law and Practice at Princeton University. His books include* Law in an Emerging Global Village: A Post-Westphalian Perspective *(Ardsley, N.Y.: Transnational Publishers, 1998), and* Predatory Globalization: A Critique *(Cambridge: Polity Press, 1999).*

1 ❖ ALTERNATIVE VISIONS OF WORLD POLITICS IN THE TWENTY-FIRST CENTURY

But relying on the UN to address humanitarian crises was not a problem-free solution. First, constitutional problems arose associated with the limitation of UN authority. Article 2(7) of the UN Charter declared that internal matters were beyond the reach of the organization. This principle had been designed to reassure member states that their sovereign rights would be respected, and that they would not become targets of collective intervention in the future. Beyond this, it was not clear that the UN could mobilize the political will or the capabilities to address internal problems in weak states whose destiny seemed unrelated to the strategic interests of those that are rich and powerful. Concerns were also voiced that the UN mandate was being appropriated by the United States to disguise the unilateral character of an essentially military undertaking. During the Gulf War, the Security Council did not appear to play a significant role after its initial act of authorization was given, and all decisions about the scope, the tactics, and even the goals of the war were reached in Washington after only limited consultation with coalition partners.

Yet the non-Western world itself is divided as to what is the appropriate UN role. It is split between those who advocate a stronger United Nations able and willing to mount effective humanitarian interventions as needed, and those who fear that such action serves as a cover for geopolitics and offers a pretext for new forms of postcolonial intervention by the North in the South. In the background is the tension between protecting the sovereign rights of weaker states, an essential value for recently independent countries, and providing the international capabilities needed to rescue people from extreme ethnic violence and other conditions of life-threatening chaos.

This background had drawn into question two overlapping arenas of action and influence. The first is the United Nations, especially the Security Council. The last three secretaries-general of the UN have each called for an expanded peace and security mandate that limits the sovereignty of states by reference to norms of international human rights. Given the experience of the last decade, it is extremely doubtful whether the UN can act effectively, independently, and consistently in response to these essentially internal challenges.

The Gulf War is misleading as a model. The main theater of conflict was international, with several major powers acting in collective self-defense on behalf of Kuwait. Furthermore, the preconditions for successful UN action were satisfied because the geopolitical interests at stake coincided with the basic UN mission to restore Kuwaiti sovereignty. In all subsequent undertakings, the UN has been given an uncertain mandate and insufficient capabilities by the UN Security Council, reflecting the ambivalence and divisions among the five permanent members of the Security Council. The ideological fervor of the cold war has happily vanished from UN undertakings, but funda-

The spread of consumerism has threatened traditional identities in many societies, producing a backlash against threats of Westernization, or even "McDonaldization."

mental differences on global policy continue to put Russia and China on one side and the three Western states of France, the United Kingdom, and the United States on the other side of many issues. At bottom, the opposition arises from Russian and Chinese fears of what they regard as a Euro-American effort to exert control over the UN and world politics more generally.

The other related arena of potential action is that of the United States government, as the "sole surviving superpower" and the state that provides diplomatic leadership for global peace and security. Its own shifting assessments of the importance and method of responding to internal political turbulence have often undermined the UN's role and created confusion as to the character of its foreign policy.

In the early 1990s, Washington was an enthusiastic advocate of humanitarian activism within a UN framework, but it seriously underestimated the potential costs and nature of such rescue operations in the setting of what was then referred to as "failed states." This American ebullience received a rude shock in 1993 when an incident during a peacekeeping operation in Somalia resulted in the death of 18 American soldiers. A sharp political backlash produced an abrupt shift in approach by the Clinton administration that saw the United States use its leadership role in 1994 to minimize the UN response to genocide in Rwanda, and generally to favor extremely limited responses to humanitarian catastrophes elsewhere, thereby degrading UN credibility.

The failure of the UN mission to protect the victims of Serbian ethnic cleansing in Bosnia gave rise to considerable criticism directed at the ineffectuality of the United Nations and contributed to a rethinking of how to address future humanitarian catastrophes, especially if they occurred in Europe. The ordeal of the Bosnian war was finally brought to an end by a combination of NATO bombing missions and a forceful diplomatic initiative spearheaded by the United States that produced the Dayton Accords at the end of 1995. Although the wisdom, justice, and durability of these arrangements are still being debated, they did represent a clear shift away from reliance on the United Nations.

. . . ONLY TO ABANDON IT

Then came the challenge of ethnic cleansing in Kosovo during the late 1990s. The crimes against humanity attributed to Yuglosav President Slobodan Milosevic's government directly challenged Europe and the United States to protect these new victims of ethnic cleansing before it was too late. Remembering the failures to stop genocidal outbreaks in Rwanda, and especially the mass killings in Bosnia, Western states favored a strong response for Kosovo. Partly for domestic political reasons in the United States, and partly because of the difficulty of gaining the support of Russia and China in the Security Council, a regional approach was adopted. It led to a diplomatic effort to induce Belgrade to accept a NATO peacekeeping force for Kosovo, and when that failed, to launch a 78-day air campaign under NATO auspices. Finally, in mid-1999 Yugoslavia relented, and an occupying international force under a NATO commander, but within a UN framework, was agreed upon.

Contrary to stated NATO objectives, Kosovo was then moved closer to a condition of independence under the authority of its Albanian population, a group that previously had been the victim of Serbian oppression but was now apparently engaged in ethnic cleansing of its own. The result seems to be an ethnic Albanian ministate rather than the sort of multiethnic entity being destroyed by Milosevic. It is also noteworthy that NATO and the United States felt obliged to rely on Russian diplomacy to negotiate an end to military operations that lasted much longer than hoped, straining public support and alliance unity. The ironic result of the essentially one-sided war was to allow the Milosevic regime a face-saving way out of Kosovo, almost the very one that had been refused before the war commenced.

Although effective as a show of force and political will, the alliance's approach to Kosovo was exceedingly controversial and unsatisfactory in several respects, producing anxieties in third world settings and a debate virtually everywhere. The legal authority of the UN with respect to the use of force was bypassed, and the explicit UN Charter prohibition on unauthorized regional enforcement action was ignored. A threatening precedent under the rubric of humanitarian intervention was established.

The form of intervention was also troublesome. The stark unevenness of the war-fighting capabilities, with no NATO casualties despite thousands of bombing sorties, suggested that an intimidating military predominance was now lodged in the West, specifically under the control of the United States with its mastery of the application of information technology to warfare. The threatening character of this military predominance as abetted by the unilateral use of force by Washington in recent years in response to allegations of complicity with international terrorism or in its struggle against so-called rogue states. Sudan and Afghanistan, for example, were bombed in 1998 without any authorization from the UN. Yet these bombings were only speculatively and rather remotely connected with the terrorist incidents against American embassies in Kenya and Tanzania that allegedly justified such recourse to force outside the area of self-defense, the sole legal grounds for the use of force by a state under contemporary international law.

Then came East Timor, outside the European sphere and in the immediate aftermath of doubts about the Kosovo approach. Again the UN seemed indispensable. The Indonesian military had encouraged a brutal response to a UN-sponsored referendum in which 78.5 percent of those voting indicated support for an independent East Timor. In response to Indonesian state-sponsored terror, a combination of geopolitical pressure from the United States on the government in Jakarta, regional responsibility by Australia to supply most of the personnel for a peacekeeping mission, and a formal UN mandate have seemed to provide some relief for the East Timorese. However, the future of this long-suffering people remains in doubt.

What emerges from this chronology of events is a wavering sequence of international responses in which several elements are moved back and forth on a case-by-case basis that reflects shifting political moods, foreign policy calculations, and a variety of distinct patterns of humanitarian catastrophe. Of greatest importance seems to be the attitude taken by the United States with regard to the degree of response and under whose auspices.

Three main ideas are woven together in different patterns in each specific instance: unilateral action by the United States; a UN undertaking; and reliance on the primacy of regional responsibility. It needs to be realized that often the main priority of potential intervenors is to minimize responses to humanitarian catastrophes so as to avoid being drawn into costly undertakings of uncertain outcome and little strategic value. The common element in these crises is to raise crucial policy choices between preserving the territorial unity of existing sovereign states and upholding the rights of self-determination for oppressed peoples.

UNITY VERSUS SELF-DETERMINATION

A special section of the July 31 *Economist* was devoted to "The Road to 2050," involving what the editors called "the new geopolitics." It contained an inquiry into whether state-shattering turbulence would reshape the world map of the future, either moving in the direction of adding many new states to the current 193, or cutting back to a small number of regional giants. The humanitarian catastrophe in East Timor, coming so quickly after the Kosovo campaign, provides a vivid reminder of the centrality of political turbulence within states to the quality of world order as we edge closer to the twenty-first century.

What makes these challenges so bewildering is that they often appear to arise at the intersection of two conflicting fundamental principles: that of respect for the state's territorial sovereignty and that of the right of self-determination enjoyed by "the peoples" of the world. Throughout the cold war a modus vivendi between these two principles generally prevailed. It consisted of limiting self-determination claims for political independence to those situations that did not involve the dismemberment of any existing state. The main context of self-determination was associated with the dynamics of decolonization, and both East and West, along with the leadership of the third world, accepted the idea that colonial borders would be respected during the transition to independence. Challenges along the way have involved Tibet and China, the Ibos and Nigeria, and Kashmir and India, but in each instance the territorial sovereign has successfully resisted secessionist moves. Only Bangladesh, with India's help, was able to shatter the unity of Pakistan after a bloody genocidal ordeal in 1971 that sent as many as 10 million refugees temporarily into India.

This pattern of limiting self-determination was accepted as operative international law, and was endorsed unanimously by the UN General Assembly's 1970 Declaration of Principles of International Law Concerning Friendly Relations among States. A kind of Faustian bargain, it meant consigning restive minority peoples, in effect, "captive nations," to oppressive regimes that persistently abused their rights in exchange for an agreed principle of order that recognized the primacy of the sovereign state within its own territory. Occasionally, as in South Africa in the apartheid period or in Kosovo, the oppressed group was actually the large majority of the affected population. Such bargains always seem like moral backsliding when one recalls the tragic inaction of the international community toward the plight of the Jews during the Nazi period before and during World War II, persecution ignored because it was occurring within German territory.

Several developments eroded, if not altogether destroyed, the bargain between advocates of self-determination and defenders of sovereignty. The first and foremost was the political current unleashed by the ending of the cold war. By moving quickly to recognize the recovery of statehood by the Baltic countries, and then the other republics that had composed the Soviet Union, a major precedent seemed to be set: self-determination could be realized under certain conditions in a manner that disrupted the former unity of a state. In the Soviet instance, the process seemed spontaneous, and appeared to be a largely voluntary adjustment to the collapse of the Soviet Union and its internal empire. Subsequent developments in the former Yugoslavia were less reconcilable with the older bias against state-shattering involuntary claims of secession. European diplomacy, led by Germany, quickly moved to recognize Slovenia and Croatia as states, and appeared to deny Belgrade the right to maintain the unity of Yugoslavia.

As had been understood from the moment it was given currency in the days after World War I, the idea of self-determination is a highly combustible concept that can be used in many contradictory ways. Even at its inception, President Woodrow Wilson regarded self-determination as pertaining mainly to the peoples emerging out of the collapsing Austro-Hungarian and Ottoman Empires, while Lenin regarded it as primarily applicable to the overseas colonies of the European powers. More recently, self-determination has been used to assert the claims of indigenous peoples to safeguard their traditional homelands and way of life and by minorities that are targets of ethnic hatred. As international law vests this right in "peoples" rather than either "nations" or "states," there is considerable room for interpretation.

But it is not plausible to explain the turbulence of this period merely by reference to the ambiguities of practice and concept associated with self-determination. Another powerful effect of the ending of the cold war has been a weakening of what might be called "geopolitical discipline." The Soviet state successfully suppressed ethnic nationalisms within its sphere of influence, but with its collapse, these sentiments erupted in many parts of the former empire. A wide array of Euro-Asian nationalisms smoldered during the ordeal of Soviet rule, but were never extinguished. After the Soviet collapse, these ethnic nationalisms resurfaced as passionate movements for independent statehood.

The West also relaxed its geopolitical grip with the ending of the cold war. It no longer was as fearful of realignment emerging out of internal political turbulence, or the risks of competitive interventions that had occurred during the cold war in many countries of the South, especially Vietnam and Afghanistan. It stopped subsidizing friendly artificial or weak states, thereby allowing the strains within civil society to exert themselves more potently. This could be seen in Yugoslavia, where the West had invested heavily in the country's stability during the cold war years when the anti-Soviet Yugoslav army was seen as important to the defense of Europe. After 1989 such considerations no longer applied, and a sharp reduction in external financial support contributed to the rise of various expressions of anti-Serb nationalism.

> *It is late in the day to get the genie of self-determination back into the bottle of state sovereignty.*

This loss of strategic value dramatically affected the stability of sub-Saharan Africa. Whereas both Moscow and Washington had once worked hard to keep particular governments in firm control, the incentives to do so in the post-cold war years evaporated. These countries were no longer strategic battlegrounds. Additionally, human rights considerations often reinforced this impulse, especially in instances where authoritarian and corrupt regimes had been long kept in power solely because they were geopolitically reliable.

A further set of factors associated with economic globalization has intensified these state-shattering challenges. The worldwide spread of consumerism has threatened traditional identities in many societies, producing a chauvinistic backlash against alleged threats of Westernization, or even "McDonaldization." The state often appears to be weak and ineffectual, while many extremist movements are seen to be gaining strength by appealing to particular ethnic or religious identities. The rise of market forces, including the pressures exerted on states by the IMF and World Bank, have further seemed to erode the capacity of the state, shifting loyalty to ethnic and civilizational identities, and often provoking severe conflict.

PUTTING CONFLICTS INTO CONTEXT

In contrast, East Timor can be viewed as unfinished business from the colonial era. Shortly after Portugal granted independence to East Timor, Indonesia moved in 1975 to annex by brute force the new state in an aggression that more than anything else resembled Iraq's attack on Kuwait. The revealing difference involves the geopolitical climate, which encouraged winking at Indonesia's aggression while mounting a full-scale counterattack in support of Kuwait. Now with moves toward independence for East Timor provoking a bloody repression of horrifying magnitude, the geopolitical climate is different. Indonesia is no longer, as in 1975, seen as a vital cold war ally. Human rights and self-determination have grown far more important in recent years. The East Timorese have made their case effectively in the global court of public opinion, making it difficult for the world to turn away from their torment, especially since the chaos was created by their reliance on democratic means in the form of a UN-monitored referendum on the future of East Timor.

Where does this pattern of ethnic conflict and humanitarian catastrophe lead? Where should it lead? Because each situation presents such a unique set of relevant factors, it is impossible to offer convincing generalizations. The legal framework defining the right of self-determination and respect for territorial sovereignty is in disarray. Deference to the state has weakened in recent years by changes in geopolitics, greater support for human rights, the impact of globalization, and the countervailing emergence of a variety of micro-nationalisms and ethnic causes. Furthermore, the United Nations has been viewed as incapable of addressing these challenges in a consistent or principled manner. It is either unable to produce a consensus among its members or tries to act on the basis of a vague mandate without having access to sufficient financial and military capabilities.

Both Kosovo and East Timor illustrate experiments in forging cooperation between regional actors of the UN, with a strong orchestrating role being played by the United States. And always, there is need to take account of the strategic calculus and the relation of a given country to the world economy. Thus, it is impossible to do much about Tibet or Chechnya because the political costs of intervention seem too high or to address the plight of ethnic strife and genocidal politics in sub-Saharan Africa because the public concern and geo-economic stakes seems so small.

So where does this leave us? I would anticipate an ongoing debate in the United States and elsewhere on the broad theme of humanitarian intervention and self-determination that will not be resolved in the next decade. Unfortunately, the best guess is that a series of humanitarian catastrophes will invite response, but that neither Washington nor the UN often will be successful.

On the level of international law, it is late in the day to get the genie of self-determination back into the bottle of state sovereignty. The best we can now hope for is compromise. Both Kosovo and East Timor suggest the form it might take: no support for claims of self-determination that would shatter an existing state unless a "people" was being victimized either by genocidal behavior or through repeated crimes against humanity, and in exceptional cases, as a result of severe abuses of basic human rights targeted at a given ethnic community and sustained over a period of years.

A longer-term view would be to rethink the role of the United Nations. It could become a more responsible vehicle for response if it were allowed to form a voluntary professional military and police force on a secure financial basis that ensured much higher degrees of political independence than currently exists. Many cases would still require the collaboration of the United States and regional actors, as can be seen with Australia's leading role in the UN operation in East Timor, but the UN could bear the burden of political responsibility, and there would not be raised so directly the issue of whether a country should risk the lives of its young citizens in the pursuit of humanitarian goals.

Still, the trend toward further breakdowns in state-society relations seems likely to continue unabated. Perhaps, as seems the case for micro-nationalisms in Western Europe, the formation of strong regional communities will lessen the insistence on separate statehood. Another promising line of response is to establish various arrangements that maintain the unity of the state but grant substantial rights of autonomy and self-administration, an approach that might finally address the Kurdish challenge afflicting several Middle East countries. Also helpful would be placing greater reliance on preventive diplomacy, heeding early warning signals, as were abundantly present in the settings of both Kosovo and East Timor. The successful deployment of a small deterrent peace force has seemed helpful in preventing the spread of ethnic violence to Macedonia, until it was recently terminated for extraneous reasons because of a Chinese veto at the UN.

No challenge is more likely to test the maturity and morality of American global leadership in the years ahead than its ability to address these various instances of humanitarian catastrophe that threaten the unity and even survival of the afflicted state.

Unit 2

Key Points to Consider

❖ What are the most important aspects of the international economy that cannot be explained by contemporary economic theories? Identify important political factors that played a role in each of these events or trends.

❖ Explain why you believe the financial crisis in East Asia in 1997 and spreading effects worldwide indicate the need for either a tune-up or major overhaul of the international financial system.

❖ Explain why you agree or disagree with billionaire investor George Soros's assessment that the world is in the midst of an acute financial and political crisis that may lead to the disintegration of the global capitalist system.

❖ Which countries in the world may be able to greatly expand their market share of service exports in the future? Will this growth translate into increased international political influence or power? How important are the principles of fairness and comprehensiveness for the continued trend towards trade liberalization worldwide?

❖ Do you agree or disagree with Jeffrey Sachs's analysis that rich countries need to mobilize global science and technology in order to address specific problems in the poorest countries? Defend your answer.

 **Links**   # www.dushkin.com/online/

These sites are annotated on pages 6 and 7.

Today, economic problems, like the Asian financial crisis, the rapid flow of global capital, and the possibility of world recession, are important features of international relations. Stories about the linkages between expanded free trade zones and national trade deficits or worker dislocations are often featured in the media. Governments increasingly focus on issues related to how to promote market shares for national industries in world markets as competition becomes more intense. As the global economy becomes integrated, national governments must scramble to ensure that deep-seated political disagreements do not interfere with the pursuit of commercial gain by industry.

Recently the United States repealed several laws requiring the imposition of mandatory sanctions as a tool of persuasion while retaining sanctions against a few longstanding enemies—Cuba, Iraq, and Libya. During 1999, the United States lobbied hard to gain China's admission into the World Trade Organization (WTO) and avoided criticizing other important trading partners for human rights violations. The pattern illustrates how a powerful nation-state increasingly shifts national priorities to promote economic prosperity.

As the effects of the Asian financial crisis illustrate, it is important to understand how political factors contribute to major economic problems. Helen Milner summarizes what is known about important economic and political linkages in "International Political Economy: Beyond Hegemonic Stability." The article explains how and why the distribution of power among countries allows hegemonic powers to play key roles in international economics. Milner also discusses how the activities of key international institutions, widely held ideas and beliefs, and domestic politics affect problems and trends in the international economic system.

Even though the economies of most Asian nation-states continue to show signs of recovery, concern lingers about the rapidity with which the economic downturn in Asia spread to Russia and Latin American nation-states. Thomas Palley in "Toward a New International Economic Order," explains that different interpretations of the financial crisis in Asia highlight more fundamental disagreements about whether the international financial system needs a tune-up or a major overhaul.

The disagreements are more than academic debates as economic policies affect the economic well-being of citizens in both the developed and developing world. Recognition is growing that the International Monetary Fund's (IMF) prescriptions for coping with financial crisis aggravated economic and political problems in several "bail-out countries." The rapid withdrawal of investment flows from countries that experienced short-term liquidity problems also fueled debate about how and how much to reform international institutions and practices that regulate capital flows. The debates reflect more basic disagreements about whether the recent international economic slowdown is a sign of temporary or fundamental problems associated with the modern world capital system. In "Capitalism's Last Chance?" billionaire investor George Soros argues that the world is in the midst of an acute financial and political crisis. According to this contrarian capitalist, it is not too late to fix the system. However, Soros warns that if this crisis is left unchecked, it will lead to the disintegration of the global capitalist system.

As competition increases among nation-states, multinational corporations and units of transnational companies located in different states become involved in deciding how to regulate international trade effectively. The decisions are central in determining which corporations and nations will win or lose in terms of market shares, profits, and national and international political influences. The trend underscores the growing importance of the World Trade Organization (WTO). With 120 member-nations, WTO, established in 1995, acts as a global referee of international trade issues, including national "competition polices," international investment, internationally recognized labor rights, and global trade liberalization. The World Trade Organization is moving toward tackling a host of thorny issues related to domestic antitrust practices, labor standards, and the environment that heretofore were the exclusive province of national governments.

Trans-Atlantic trade disputes between the United States and the European Union over bananas and the use of genetically altered substances in agriculture continue to divide the United States and European countries and to fuel conflicts among nation-states within the European Union. The violent protests at the WTO talks in Seattle, Washington, in 1999 underscored the increased role that trade policies are likely to play in domestic politics. The protests reflect the reality that service sector businesses with leading-edge knowledge, skills, or processes in any country are now exportable across national borders. America benefits from this trend in many sectors.

The organized labor and environmental protesters who demanded tighter labor and environmental standards at the World Trade Organization meeting in Seattle, Washington, reflected a number of organized interests in the developed world. However, vocal and highly visible protesters did not reflect the concerns of most people in developing countries. In most developing countries, trade issues link to larger problems related to poverty. As the number of poor and unemployed people in developing countries increases, developing nation-states increasingly complain that three-fourths of humanity is not benefiting from recent trade agreements. In "Trade and the Developing World: A New Agenda," Joseph Stiglitz warns that if the current round of trade talks is seen as unbalanced, support for trade liberalization in the developing world will falter. Since inequalities and conflicts between rich and poor countries are likely to increase, Stiglitz stresses that the Millennium Round of world trade talks should empha- size the principles of fairness and comprehensiveness.

Unfortunately, too many developing countries find it difficult to compete and prosper in the emerging global economy, since many of these countries have to pay 40 to 80 percent of their GNP to service past international debts. Jeffrey Sachs, a well-known economist, in "Helping the World's Poorest," argues that recent efforts to provide partial debt relief to Highly Indebted Poor Countries (HIPCs) is only one step in the direction needed to close the gap between the richest and poorest countries in the world. Since conditions for most people in many HIPCs are worsening dramatically, Sachs emphasizes the need for rich countries to mobilize global science and technology in order to address specific problems that help to keep poor countries poor.

International Political Economy: Beyond Hegemonic Stability

by Helen V. Milner

International political economy is a growth industry. Beginning its boom after the oil crises in the 1970s shook both world markets and states, the field now encompasses not only a great deal of political economy but of comparative and international politics as well. The end of the Cold War also helped shift attention to the field's main focus: how markets and states affect one another.

Scholars in the field have tried to explain at least four aspects of the international political economy. First, many of its pioneers thought that economics was too narrow to explain central aspects of the international economy. Consider one of the more visible theoretical gaps: Although economic theory showed that free trade was optimal, in reality, protectionism characterized most states' trade policies for years. Seeking to explain such paradoxes created by economic theory, scholars have proposed explanations that are more political. In particular, they have emphasized how politics determines the stability and openness of the international economy, a focus inspired by the trauma of the Great Depression in the 1930s and the desire to avoid repeating any such experience.

Second, scholars have focused on explaining states' foreign economic policy choices. In part, many believe that these choices are the most important factor shaping the nature of the international economy. For example, explaining why states choose to protect their economies, or how they set their exchange rates, or why they give foreign aid have been

central preoccupations for the field. These explanations, however, have sought to interpret such choices by adducing domestic and international factors as well as economic and political ones.

Third, the field has paid attention to why certain states grow rapidly and develop over time, while others fail to do so or decline. This interest in the changing positions of states in the world economy has also been approached eclectically. Economic causes for such changes are usually supplemented by political ones, while domestic causes of the rise and decline of states are paired with international factors.

Finally, scholars have been interested in the impact of the international economy on domestic politics, an issue often explored under the rubric of the globalization of national economies.

Researchers in this field have generally sought answers to these kinds of questions by looking into four categories of explanatory factors: 1) the distribution of world power, especially the role of a hegemonic state; 2) the structure, function, and consequences of international institutions; 3) the impact of nonmaterialist factors such as ideas and beliefs; and 4) the effect of domestic politics.

DOES HEGEMONY BREED STABILITY?

Robert Gilpin, Stephen Krasner, and other scholars from the realist tradition have identified the distribution of power among states as a central factor in explaining the openness and stability of the international economy. "Hegemonic stability theory," first espoused by Charles Kindleberger in the 1970s, focuses on the role of leading states—for example,

HELEN V. MILNER *is professor of political science at Columbia University.*

Reprinted by permission of *Foreign Policy*, Spring 1998, pp. 82-96. © 1998 by the Carnegie Endowment of International Peace.

Great Britain in the nineteenth and the United States in the twentieth centuries—and on how changes in the distribution of capabilities affect the world economy. This theory argued that the overwhelming dominance of one country was necessary for the existence of an open and stable world economy. Such a hegemon served to coordinate and discipline other countries so that each could feel secure enough to open its markets and avoid beggar-thy-neighbor policies. Conversely, the theory asserted that the decline of a hegemon tends to be associated with economic closure, instability, and the creation of competing regional blocs.

During the nineteenth century, Britain exercised a form of economic hegemony over much of the world. Britain's leadership was associated with the globalization of markets, the openness of international trade and capital movements, the rise of multinational corporations, and the general economic and political stability that characterized at least Europe. World War I brought an abrupt end to both British hegemony and the conditions that it had promoted. Increasing protectionism, the formation of regional blocs, and the decline in capital mobility in the 1920s and early 1930s ate away at the foundations of the global economy, contributing to growing economic instability and the depression.

The cause of this tragic chain of events has often been laid at America's doorstep. The United States was, at the end of World War I, the world's strongest economic power. But it steadfastly refused to take on the leadership role that Britain could no longer play. This "irresponsibility" was most vividly exemplified in the minds of many people by the infamous Smoot-Hawley Tariff (1930), which raised the average tax on imports to the United States by about 40 percent. At the beginning of the depression, the United States shut its markets to foreign goods and thus helped propel the world economy into its worst swoon ever. The unwillingness of the United States to coordinate its monetary and currency policies with other countries merely exacerbated the situation. This isolationist posture on the part of the world's economic hegemon had negative consequences for most other countries and the United States itself.

The perils of isolationism seemed to have been well learned by American policymakers after the end of World War II. Then, the United States quickly assumed a leadership role and steadily moved forward to create an open international trade system based on the General Agreement on Tariffs and Trade (GATT) and a stable monetary system founded on the Bretton Woods system. The Marshall Plan was perhaps the direct antithesis of the Smoot-Hawley tariff. It symbolized recognition of America's special role and responsibility for peace and prosperity beyond its borders—indeed, globally. U.S. leadership, it is asserted, helped create the conditions necessary for the steady economic growth experienced by the industrial countries up to the 1970s and the rapid development of countries such as Japan and South Korea.

Concerns about U.S. power arose again in the late 1960s and early 1970s. America's economic advantages over the rest of the world seemed to be rapidly dissipating, while other countries were catching up. In response, protectionist sentiment within the United States grew, leading to many domestic challenges to the traditional policy of freer trade. The stability of international currency markets was also disrupted by American behavior. The simultaneous pursuit of the Vietnam War and the Great Society program helped fuel inflation in the United States, which was exported abroad because of the dollar's role in international exchange. America's allies, especially France and Germany, became very concerned over the impact of this erosion in the dollar's value as the world's reserve currency. Ultimately, these problems led to the U.S. abandonment of the Bretton Woods fixed exchange rate system and to the emergence of a more volatile era of floating exchange rates. Hence, although American policy may have laid the groundwork for the growing globalization of markets, the decline of American leadership prompted many, especially in the United States, to worry about the future stability and direction of the world economy. Critics of U.S. power, however, especially Susan Strange, have either denied any decline in U.S. capabilities or lauded the effects of the decline of "irresponsible" U.S. power.

WHY POWER ISN'T EVERYTHING

Nowadays, such concerns about American power have receded. By the mid-1990s, the decline of U.S. hegemony no longer seemed so assured. Claims about the decrease in U.S. power appeared exaggerated given the demise of the Soviet Union, persistent recession in Japan, high unemployment and slow growth in Europe combined with the challenge of integrating Eastern Europe into the European Union, and American industry's return to competitiveness. Moreover, the relationship between hegemony and an open, stable world economy has been cast into doubt by a number of scholars, such as Robert Keohane and David Lake. As U.S. behavior during the interwar period illustrates, the possession of superior resources by a nation does not translate automatically into great influence or beneficial outcomes for the world.

Institutions to Govern the World Economy

One reason why the distribution of power among countries is not seen as the exclusive factor shaping the workings of the international economy is the important role played by international institutions. Keohane has made the most ambitious claims about the role of these institutions. He argues that although hegemony might be necessary for creating such institutions, once begun, they take on a life of their own, and states come to see them as worth preserving. Multilateral institutions such as the United Nations, International Monetary Fund (IMF), World Bank, World Trade Organization (WTO), and EU provide information to states about each others' behavior, reduce the cost of negotiating agreements, and can expose, and sometimes even punish, violations of agreements by states. The claim is that without these institutions the international economy—and international politics—would be much more unstable, less open, and more conflictual. In the case of the EU, for example, many see peace in Western Europe over the past 40 years as partially a product of this institution; and scholars and politicians often cite the maintenance of peace in Europe as a primary motivation for monetary union.

The impact and role of international institutions are controversial. Realists, with their emphasis on power, denigrate the role of such institutions, often seeing them as having little independent impact, and argue that their influence is derived from the actions of the states within them. In the EU example, they might cite the hegemonic role of Germany as the key to monetary union. Others, especially European scholars, believe that many international institutions are controlled by the United States, and thus reflect its interests. In particular, the United States is seen as using the IMF and World Bank as subtle mechanisms to exert its influence on countries. As realists, these scholars emphasize the impact of state power over the character of the institutions themselves.

The Power of Values

The emphasis on power and international institutions misses a central element necessary to explain political behavior: the purposes or goals that states and their leaders choose to pursue with their resources. Nonmaterialist explanations of the international political economy attach key interest to how states' purposes or goals are defined. Two central approaches have taken on the task of explaining this. The "ideas approach," exemplified by the work of Keohane and Judith Goldstein, proposes that the ideas that policymakers carry in their heads are very important in explaining their policy choices. Ideas, whether about the proper role of the state in the economy or the means-ends relationship between economic policy instruments and outcomes, shape how policymakers act.

Dominant ideas—ones that capture the attention of large segments of the policy-making community—define states' actions and coordinate their behaviors in critical ways. Scholars have identified both the rise of the belief in Keynesian macroeconomics after World War II and the later dominance of monetarist beliefs as central explanations for the creation of various international institutions and the coordination of states' policies within them. Some attribute the movement toward European monetary union to the spread of monetarist ideas among European policymakers. In another area, Anne Krueger has shown how changes in the prevailing ideas on how to induce economic development led, in the 1950s, to the use of import substitution policies and, more recently, to their abandonment.

Like scholars who emphasize ideas, the so-called constructivists focus on how policymakers' and states' purposes are defined. This approach goes beyond the adoption of ideas to the definition of social identity. A core proposition of this approach is that the social construction—hence, the term "constructivism"—of states' identities constrains the choices that states can make and propels them toward certain behaviors. For instance, Peter Katzenstein has argued that the Japanese embrace of pacifism since the end of World War II has affected Japan's behavior and its policy choices in the security area. Others have suggested that the construction of a European social identity has helped promote European integration. And certainly the growing concern with nationalism and national identity as sources of conflict or cooperation in international politics has been part of the constructivists' agenda, as evidenced in the work of Ronald Jepperson and Alexander Wendt. These nonmaterialist explanations of the international political economy emphasize states' purposes and choice of goals, which their proponents see as fundamental to states' behavior.

The Impact of Domestic Politics

Domestic political explanations of the international political economy also focus on the definition of states' purposes, but they tend to emphasize political processes and examine the way that national interests are defined through a struggle among domestic actors. Scholars in this area usually focus on two sets of factors: In the first case, they see social groups such as labor organizations, capitalists, multinational corporations, import-competing firms, and ethnic groups as having identifiable preferences about international economic policy that often translate into national policy. Those domestic groups who benefit from international economic exposure or have strong international ties already will favor greater international openness and stability and press their governments to enact policies that promote such market characteristics. The more such groups exist domestically, the greater will be the pressure on policymakers to orient their policies in this direction. For example, Jeffrey Frieden has argued that European monetary union has become more tenable because of the growing external orientation of European firms and banks and their concomitant interest in European economic openness and currency stability.

In the second case, some scholars point to a greater role for the state and policymakers in both the definition and execution of international economic policy. For them, the character of the state is what matters. The institutional structure of the state and its imperviousness to societal pressures shape the policy preferences of political actors and their capacity to implement these preferences. For example, Katzenstein and others identified France and Japan as states with institutional structures that allow technocratically inclined policymakers to play a leading role in defining foreign economic policy and pursuing interventionist policies.

The impact of a state's institutional structures on its development prospects has also been a topic of interest. Why is it that in some countries (mostly in East Asia) the state has played a central role in fostering economic development, while in others (mostly in Africa and Latin America) state action seems to have impaired economic progress? Some scholars such as Chalmers Johnson and Stephan Haggard have concluded that certain institutional characteristics are more conducive than others to making the state an effective promoter of economic development. These institutional traits often enable the state to mediate between the international and domestic economies. More recently, concerns have grown about the extent of democracy within states. Some scholars such as Donald Wittman and Gerald Scully have argued that economic growth and international openness depend greatly on whether a state's institutions are democratic or not.

In more recent work, scholars such as Judith Goldstein, Beth Simmons, and I have tried to focus on both societal actors and state institutions, realizing that each plays a role in shaping foreign economic policy. Moreover, scholars have tried to connect international and domestic factors. Thus, two-level games, which link both the international and domestic environments and societal and state actors, have become more prominent. Robert Putnam's early version of this approach has been refined by others seeking to derive more specific propositions about how all of these factors interact. For example, a number of scholars have shown how divided government affects trade policy choices. These two-level models promise a better understanding of the interaction of the complex factors that create the international political economy.

THE PRESSURES OF GLOBALIZATION

Globalization refers to the increasing integration of national economies into a global one. As mentioned before, globalization peaked in the late nineteenth century, reached its nadir in the early 1940s, and has since rebounded to levels comparable to the earlier highs. Globalization has thus increased, as most agree, but it is far from being complete. For many economists, globalization is a beneficial process since it produces net gains for most countries. More concern has been raised by political scientists over its political effects, especially domestic ones.

In the 1970s, the buzzword for globalization was interdependence. It was argued that rising interdependence was not only changing international politics but also rendering the nation-state obsolete. The expectation was that it would severely limit the range of action that states could take. The state would gradually become less and less important to its citizens as interdependence rose. This debate aroused much controversy and inspired a strong defense of the continuing relevance of the state in international and domestic politics.

In the 1990s, this debate has revived as globalization reaches new heights. Three issues are central to it: First, globalization has been seen as exerting pressure on all states to change their policies and institutions in certain ways. Globalization, scholars have argued, is forcing convergence in policies among countries most exposed to it. Liberalizing trade policy, removing capital controls, opening financial markets to foreign investors, and downsizing the role of the state in the economy are the generic policy prescriptions for effective participation in a global economy. Pressure for the reduction—or even abandonment—of the welfare state in developed countries, and for the liberalization of the economy in developing ones, has been seen as a byproduct of globalization.

Second, globalization has been seen as giving increased power to the holders of capital—investors, multinational firms, and global financial institutions. These actors now can demand that states make changes in their economic policies and can punish them if they do not comply by exiting the country or, better yet, speculating against the country in world currency markets. In contrast, labor has been weakened. Having less freedom to move from country to country, workers find their power to bargain with firms impaired. Membership in unions worldwide has declined, and unions have faced challenges to their acquired power in many states. Globalization moves jobs around the world and imposes constraints on wage increases as never before.

Finally, globalization, it is sometimes claimed, is irreversible. That is, no actor can resist its advance. This again calls into question the role of the nation-state. Can any state resist, or even reshape, the pressures generated by global markets? Or must a state submit to the ineluctable pressures of globalization and lose the capacity to direct its national economy?

On none of these issues is there much consensus. Although many events seem to support the above views—the rush to free trade and capital market liberalization, the reforms of many welfare states, and the creation of independent central banks globally—some critics have seen the other side of the coin. They note that the percentage of government spending in the economy has declined only slightly or not at all (even in Margaret Thatcher's England), countries have maintained extensive and distinct welfare systems, national ways of doing business have persisted, and unions have actually made a resurgence lately in some nations, including in the United States and France. These events suggest that globalization is neither producing convergence nor undermining labor, and may not be irreversible. States in fact are ever more important, for they are the means for countries to resist and reshape the pressures generated by globalization. In this view, strengthening the institutions of the state may be the most effective way for countries to reap the maximum benefits from a world of global markets. These contradictory perspectives on globalization are likely to persist until we have more evidence about its effects.

The relationship between American power and globalization is also a topic of much interest. It is undeniable that U.S. policies have helped create the current international economy. But some claim that globalization is not only a creation of the United States but also a creature controlled by it. Countries such as France and Malaysia have vehemently expressed the view that globalization is basically the extension of American economic practices and ideals to the world, and a tool for the exertion of American power. They see resistance to global market pressures as defiance of the United States. Or, as some South Koreans have claimed during the recent financial crisis there, the IMF is just doing America's bidding. That may be leadership, but it is not the type of leadership these countries would like to see.

Ironically, many Americans see globalization as beyond their country's control. Indeed, in their eyes, the United States is ever more constrained by global forces, just like everyone else: All states must heed the dictates of international bond traders and investors or face the consequences. The United States let globalization out of the bottle and now cannot contain it. This loss of national control is bemoaned by some and applauded by others, but none doubt its reality. What is striking in this debate is the difference in perception between Americans and the rest of the world about the relationship between globalization and American influence.

The impact of globalization remains an area of intense research. The recent economic travails in Asia have underlined how even well-developed states can be affected by international investors and the vast capital flows they now control. How this crisis is resolved will have important consequences for many countries and for the future of the global economy. Will the pressures exerted by international financial actors fundamentally change the relationship between Asian governments and their economies? Will the crisis lead to greater convergence between the economic practices of Asian institutions and those common in the West? Will the famed "industrial policy" practiced by many Asian governments disappear? This issue is especially important for China and other developing countries seeking models of how best to foster economic development.

Such questions beg a look at the role of the state in economic policy, both foreign and domestic. In the aftermath of the two world wars, government intervention in the economy became accepted practice at both the micro and macro levels for eliminating boom and bust cycles in the economy. Indeed, the twentieth century has witnessed the greatest growth in government intervention in the economy ever seen. Globalization and the spread of more "orthodox" economic ideas, however, have undermined confidence in such intervention in many areas. As states' roles in their economies are reduced, what will happen to both the economy and the states? Or is the withdrawal of the state from the economy a passing trend? Will new ideas arise that sanction a greater role for the state in the economy?

Finally, the impact of power and international policies on the global economy is of great interest. After all, political conflict and war after 1914 destroyed the global economy created in the late nineteenth century. What effects will the post-Cold War international system have on the world economy? Will major international conflicts reappear, thus fracturing it into blocs? Will institutions that have helped to keep the peace such as the EU, NATO, and UN disappear, while new political alliances form, reshaping economic flows? Critically, what impact will such changes in the distribution of power and the organization of international politics have on the global economy? These issues will form some of the general research agendas for scholars in international political economy.

WANT TO KNOW MORE?

While students of international political economy hold contradictory perspectives on the causes and effects of globalization, they admire the work of several scholars who have illuminated the pillars of the world economy. A respected primer is Robert Gilpin's *The Political Economy of International Relations* (Princeton, NJ: Princeton University Press, 1987). The father of hegemonic stability theory is Charles Kindleberger; see his seminal work, *The World in Depression, 1929–39* (Berkeley, CA: University of California Press, 1973). David Lake presents an updated case for the theory in **"Leadership, Hegemony, and the International Economy"** (*International Studies Quarterly*, Winter 1993–94).

The spirited debate over the role of ideas is presented in *Ideas and Foreign Policy* (Ithaca, NY: Cornell University Press, 1993), edited by Judith Goldstein and Robert Keohane. Those wanting to learn how societal actors shape foreign economic policy can turn to Ronald Rogowski's *Commerce and Coalitions* (Princeton, NJ: Princeton University Press, 1990). Beth Simmons' *Who Adjusts? Domestic Sources of Foreign Economic Policy During the Interwar Years* (Princeton, NJ: Princeton University Press, 1994) provides an in-depth exploration of how domestic politics can affect a state's approach to the world economy. Helen Milner's *Interests, Institutions and Information* (Princeton, NJ: Princeton University Press, 1997) develops two-level games. Keohane makes ambitious claims about the role of international institutions in *International Institutions and State Power* (Boulder, CO: Westview Press, 1989). The national security aspect of this field is outlined in Joanne Gowa's *Allies, Adversaries, and International Trade* (Princeton, NJ: Princeton University Press, 1993). Chalmers Johnson considers the effects of a state's institutional structures in his book *MITI and the Japanese Miracle* (Stanford, CA: Stanford University Press, 1982). FOREIGN POLICY has published several articles on globalization, including Dani Rodrik's **"Sense and Nonsense in the Globalization Debate"** (Summer 1997).

For links to relevant Web sites, as well as a comprehensive index of related articles, access **www.foreignpolicy.com**.

Toward a New International Economic Order

Washington Consensus, Main Street Alternative

Thomas I. Palley

THE FINANCIAL crisis that erupted in east Asia in mid-1997 has thrust millions of workers back into dire poverty and shattered an entire decade of economic development in the region. The crisis has also flared and spread within the global economy. Russia has undergone a financial collapse. South Africa, which is Africa's largest economy, has had to raise interest rates to defend its currency and faces a significant economic slow down. Now, the process of financial contagion has added Brazil to the ranks of crisis countries, and most economists are predicting a severe Latin American economic downturn in 1999. In light of Brazil's troubles, Newsweek recently went so far as to compare the winter recovery in world financial markets as akin to the "phony war" of 1940, a period when people falsely reassured themselves that calamity would be avoided.

Under such circumstances it is hard to be optimistic. Yet, it is possible that there may be a silver lining to the crisis in that it has forced an opening of debate at the highest levels about the future course of globalization. This opening provides an opportunity to remake the process of globalization in a manner that shifts it away from its current path of unstable and inequitable development, on to a path of stable and equitable growth. If policy makers in the industrialized countries also take steps to ward off a recession, the suffering caused by the crisis will not have been all in vain.

The crisis and its subsequent spread have raised two distinct sets of issues. One set has concerned how to react immediately to the crisis and prevent it from deepening. Here,

the focus has been on the appropriateness of the International Monetary Fund's (IMF's) policy recommendations for east Asia and the need for global reflation. The IMF initially recommended a dose of fiscal and monetary austerity in the afflicted economies (Thailand, South Korea, and Indonesia), while the U.S. Federal Reserve viewed the crisis as exclusively regional in impact. The IMF's policies threatened to worsen east Asia's deflation; it has now been grudgingly compelled to allow east Asian governments to run deficits, and east Asian interest rates have also been lowered somewhat. Meanwhile, the Federal Reserve Board has reluctantly come to recognize the U.S. economy's own exposure to east Asia's misfortune, and last October it cut interest rates. However, there is a real danger of Federal Reserve policy turning out to be "too little, too late." In particular, the Fed continues to claim that rate cuts were only needed to calm financial markets, which indicates that it may not yet have recognized the magnitude of weakening of global demand. Moreover, though the Fed has cut interest rates by three-quarters of a percent, this reduction does not match the fall in inflation over the last eighteen months. This means that real interest rates have actually risen.

A second set of issues concerns the structure of the international economic order. Here, the question is to what extent are fundamental flaws in the structure responsible for the crisis, and to what extent are these flaws responsible for the trend of slowing economic development and worsening of global income distribution. This second set of issues is at the

 Originally appeared in *Dissent* magazine, Spring 1999, pp. 48-52.

heart of the debate over the international financial architecture. How this debate is resolved will critically determine the path of future prosperity.

Though IMF policy in east Asia and Federal Reserve interest-rate policy have both shifted in a more expansionary direction, this shift risks being short lived unless accompanied by recognition of the fundamentally flawed character of the existing global economic order. This is because the thinking that gave rise to the IMF's initial mistaken prescription for east Asia is the same thinking that underlies the structure of the existing order. Absent a rejection of this thinking, the world economy will remain brutally exposed to the unstable deflationary forces inherent in today's global economic order, while policy makers will ineluctably be drawn back toward policies of contraction.

THE DIFFERENCES in thinking regarding the validity of the existing global economic order are reflected in disagreements over the interpretation of the current crisis. On one hand, there is the IMF-Treasury view, which interprets it as a narrow crisis of international financial markets. Hence, Treasury Secretary Robert Rubin's call to "modernize the architecture of the international financial markets." On the other hand there is a view that reads the situation as a full-fledged crisis of globalization that has revealed deep flaws in the design of the existing global economic order.

The narrow financial-markets crisis view is promoted by supporters of the "Washington consensus" that has dominated economic policy making for the last twenty years. It maintains that global economic growth is best furthered by more open trade, export-led growth, greater deregulation, and more liberalized financial markets. It is epitomized by the IMF, which has sought to characterize the crisis as resulting from inadequate financial transparency, and in the aftermath of the crisis the IMF has actually called for greater liberalization of international financial capital flows. All that is required is a minor tune-up of the international financial system, combined with some learning from experience. Thus, "sequencing of reforms" has become a hot new issue, the argument being that countries like South Korea engaged in wrong sequencing whereby they mistakenly liberalized short-term capital flows before long-term flows. Learning means that policy makers will

not make this mistake next time, and meanwhile the underlying recommendations of the Washington consensus remain correct.

The Treasury view is broadly similar to that of the IMF. Both the Treasury and the IMF were slow to recognize that east Asia's troubles were triggered by a bank run that had foreign investors rushing to repatriate funds. They therefore both initially supported mistaken policies of economic austerity predicated upon high interest rates, government spending cuts, and higher taxes. Since then, both have reversed these policy prescriptions to a significant degree. However, they continue to see the long-run solution in terms of limited financial market reforms. Thus, we have Secretary Rubin's claim that "these reform programs have at their core strengthening financial systems, improving transparency and supervision, eliminating the inter-relationships between banks, the government, and commercial entities, opening capital markets, and appropriate monetary and fiscal policies."

Whereas proponents of the Washington consensus think that the existing model of globalization merely needs a tune-up, there is a "Main Street alternative" that thinks the model is fundamentally bankrupt. The issue is not one of recalibrating the model, but rather one of designing a new model that is stable, equitable, and pro-growth. For the last twenty years, the Washington consensus has dominated policy making, yet global economic growth has been slower and inequality has risen. In industrialized countries, wages have stagnated, workers are working longer hours, and there has been an increase in job insecurity. Rather than being an isolated event, east Asia's financial crisis represents one more in a succession of crises. As World Bank chief economist Joseph Stiglitz puts it, the world economy has been having "a boom in busts."

At the most abstract level, the Main Street alternative begins by challenging the fatalistic notion that markets and the process of globalization are natural phenomena. All markets and all economies operate on rules, and this applies as much to the markets that have been fashioned by the Washington consensus as it did to markets fashioned under Franklin Roosevelt's New Deal. If there is any doubt about this, consider the North American Free Trade Agreement (NAFTA), which is widely represented as a model free trade agreement. In fact, the actual treaty consists of one thousand pages of rules governing trade. Viewed from this perspective, the debate is not one of regulation versus deregulation. Instead, it is about what type of market rules we will have, and whose economic interests they will serve.

The Main Street alternative seeks to modernize the financial architecture, as does the IMF-Treasury view. However, it maintains that the measures to improve financial transparency and accounting standards are nowhere near enough. Instead, a more fundamental reconfiguration of the international economic order is needed. The conversation cannot be restricted to discussion of financial markets. Trade, finance, economic growth, and income distribution are all intimately connected, and this means much more must be on the table. Financial market governance, labor market governance, and the international trading system interact. Producing stable equitable growth requires that all elements of the international economic order be designed in a mutually consistent and reinforcing manner.

When it comes to the financial architecture discussion of specifics quickly reveals fundamental differences between the Main Street alternative and the Washington consensus. The latter seeks more international openness of domestic financial markets, better accounting standards, more financial transparency, and disclosure, and more IMF market surveillance. The claim is that more daylight and more market openness will enhance market discipline, thereby producing efficiency and stability. The Main Street alternative also maintains that improved accounting standards and financial transparency and disclosure are needed, but there is also a need to reduce speculation and make investors invest with an eye to the long term and proper regard to risk. This requires taxes on the buying and selling of currencies to reduce speculative trading, as well as requirements that oblige investors to commit for a minimum time period. To the Washington consensus, these are interventions that distort the market's natural rhythms; to the Main Street alternative, they are rules that diminish speculation and encourage productive long-term investment.

There is also nominal agreement on the need to strengthen demand conditions to foster growth, but once again there is fundamental disagreement on the specifics. Thus, whereas the Washington consensus sees export-led growth as a solution to each country's demand problem, the Main Street alternative sees it as a source of competitive devaluation and de-

flation. In an attempt to gain a competitive advantage on international markets, countries are led to try to lower the value of their currencies relative to those of their rivals. This in turn risks producing a vicious circle of currency crises, as market speculators quickly realize that one country's devaluation renders rival-country currencies over-valued. Indeed, some economists identify the Chinese devaluation of 1994 as the trigger behind east Asia's financial crisis.

EVEN MORE problematic is the tendency of export-led growth strategies to promote global deflation. One country's exports are another country's imports, and this means that all cannot rely on export-led growth. Attempts to do so result in a beggar-thy-neighbor dynamic in which countries seek to export by relying on demand in other countries, thereby generating a global shortage of demand that risks plunging the global economy into a deflationary spiral.

Export-led growth must therefore be replaced with domestic demand-led growth. This is a strategy that lifts all boats, because demand growth in one country pulls in exports from others, so that all grow together.

Achieving domestic demand-led growth in turn requires strengthening domestic demand, and this brings to the fore even deeper divisions between the Washington consensus and the Main Street alternative. Growing domestic demand calls for rising wages to support domestic consumption, and achieving this requires evening the balance of power between capital and labor. For this reason, core labor standards that give workers rights of free association allowing them to form unions and bargain collectively are essential. Absent the protections granted by core labor standards, individual workers will face a ceaseless uphill struggle for higher wages, thereby confounding the possibility of shifting to a path of domestic demand-led growth. Whereas the Washington consensus views independent trade unions as a market distortion, the Main Street alternative sees them as the private-sector solution to the imbalance of power created by capital's ability to roam the globe in search of the cheapest, most exploitable workers.

The intelligence and humanity that mark Treasury Secretary Rubin have placed him on record as supporting core labor standards and human rights for ethical reasons, but the problem is that this issue remains peripheral in the

Treasury's economic construction of the current crisis. The reality is that it is central. Escaping the trap of export-led growth and making globalization work for all can happen only if the playing field between workers and capital is leveled. This will ensure that the benefits of economic development are shared and that domestic consumption demand can absorb the growth of output.

There is another reason why human rights, labor standards, and strong independent trade unions are vital. The IMF has emphasized the problem of political corruption and economic cronyism that has given rise to misallocation of borrowed resources. It has proposed solving this problem through increased market discipline imposed by increased financial transparency and increased international openness of domestic financial markets. The argument is that market competition will drive out cronyism. This belief is mistaken. The reality is that these behaviors are politically sponsored, and changing them requires political reform. This in turn requires putting in place countervailing forces that can block such behavior. Human and labor rights that give workers the right of free association and confer the ability to organize independent trade unions are the foundation of such reforms. Strong well-functioning democracy is needed to prevent economic cronyism, and unions are an essential ingredient for such an outcome.

Debt relief for developing countries is another measure that can help shift the world economy toward a path of domestic demand-led growth. Debt-service burdens now hinder much of the developing world from following an equitable pro-growth agenda. They also force the third world to focus on export-led growth, which has contributed to deteriorating terms of trade, as well as causing job loss in developed countries. Debt relief is a means out of this box.

WHAT IS true for workers also holds for governments. Just as footloose capital is able to threaten workers, so too it is able to threaten governments. As a result of their increased mobility, corporations are increasingly able to win tax exemptions by threatening to move jobs overseas. This has contributed to shifting the tax burden on to working households. The same process threatens to undermine environmental and workplace safety standards. Thus, with business

perceiving these measures as a cost, the threat of relocation will be used to get such standards repealed. This is the hallmark of the race to the bottom that has been unleashed by globalization Washington consensus style. For these reasons, the Main Street alternative advocates that international trading agreements incorporate rules that disallow the environment and workplace safety as dimensions of business competition. Also needed are measures that prevent tax competition, whereby governments compete against one another by lowering business tax rates to attract investment.

Finally, it is worth pointing out a third view associated with Jeffrey Sachs, which straddles the debate. Sachs was one of the early architects of Washington consensus "shock" therapy in Eastern Europe, the premise of which was that the old command style economies had to be opened to the bracing wind of the market by rapid privatization and deregulation. However, he has broken with the Washington consensus over east Asia's crisis, and was one of the first to point out that austerity was the wrong response to a bank run.

A key difference between the IMF-Treasury view and Sachs concerns the relationship between stabilization and growth. All are for growth. However, the IMF-Treasury view maintains that stabilization must come first, and only then will growth be possible; hence, the inclination to high interest rates and fiscal austerity to placate financial markets. Sachs implicitly argues that stabilization is not possible without growth. Policy makers must therefore focus on jump-starting the world economy through a variety of initiatives, from coordinated interest rate cuts to debt relief and development assistance.

This growth versus stabilization difference is important, but we should not be misled about its ultimate significance. In all other regards Sachs shares the Washington consensus. In particular, he is committed to "fast-track" style free trade, which fosters an international race to the bottom. International wage competition and shifting of jobs in response to cross-country differences in workplace and environmental standards are legitimate dimensions of free trade. At the macroeconomic level, export-led growth, which has countries relying on foreign demand to ensure full employment, is also legitimate. This is so even if exports are achieved through reliance on depreciated currencies. In sum, Sachs may have broken with the Washington consensus over east Asia, but he has not broken with the global economic architecture that the Washington consensus has fostered in the last twenty years.

East Asia's collapse has revealed a clear need to refashion globalization so as to render it stable and share its benefits. The recent spreading of the crisis to Brazil provides further evidence that the existing system is unstable. Brazil's currency devaluation now risks spreading financial contagion to other Latin American countries and China, while its attempt to export its way out of trouble will aggravate the problem of global deflation.

The policies of the Washington consensus have failed. There is now a historic opportunity to break with the Washington consensus and replace it with the new internationalism of the Main Street alternative. Both common sense and economic logic tell us that globalization can work only if there is a level playing field between business and labor, and if economic growth is predicated on expanding domestic markets. This is the only way to ensure equitable growth with full employment. For these reasons it is time to say "Goodbye Washington consensus, hello Main Street alternative."

THOMAS I. PALLEY is assistant director of public policy for the AFL-CIO. He is the author of *Plenty of Nothing: The Downsizing of the American Dream and the Case for Structural Keynesianism* (Princeton University Press).

Capitalism's Last Chance?

by George Soros

The world is in the grip of an acute financial and political crisis. This crisis, if left unchecked, will lead to the disintegration of the global capitalist system. It is a crisis that will permanently transform the world's attitude toward capitalism and free markets. It has already overturned some of the world's longest established, and seemingly immovable, political regimes. Its effects on the relationships between advanced and developing nations are likely to be permanent and profound.

This situation came about unexpectedly, almost out of a clear blue sky. Even the people who expected an Asian crisis—and my firm, Soros Fund Management, was the first to anticipate the inevitability of the 1997 devaluation of the Thai baht that started the global chain reaction—had no idea of its extent or its destructive power.

What makes this crisis so politically unsettling and so dangerous for the global capitalist system is that the system itself is its main cause. More precisely, the origin of this crisis is to be found in the mechanism that defines the essence of a globalized capitalist system: the free, competitive capital markets that keep private capital moving unceasingly around the globe in a search for the highest profits and, supposedly, the most efficient allocation of the world's investment and savings.

The Asian crisis was originally attributed to various contingent weaknesses in specific countries and markets. Most economists focused initially on policy misjudgments that re-

sulted in overvalued currencies and excessive reliance on foreign-currency borrowing. As the crisis spread, it became clear that such economic misjudgments were symptomatic of deeper sociopolitical problems. Political commentators have put the blame on the nexus of sociopolitical arrangements now described pejoratively as "crony capitalism" but previously extolled as "Confucian capitalism" or "the Asian model." There is some truth to these claims. Most Asian governments did make serious policy misjudgments, in some cases encouraged by international investors and the International Monetary Fund (IMF). They allowed investment and property booms to go unchecked and kept their currencies tied to the dollar for too long. In general, the Asian model was a highly distorted and immature form of the capitalist regime.

However, as the crisis has continued to develop, it has become apparent that its spread cannot be attributed simply to macroeconomic errors or specifically Asian characteristics. Why, after all, is the contagion now striking Eastern Europe, Latin America, and Russia, and even beginning to affect the advanced economies and efficient financial markets of Europe and the United States?

FINANCIAL PENDULUM OR WRECKING BALL?

The inescapable conclusion is that the crisis is a symptom of pathologies inherent in the global system. International financial markets have served as more than just a passive transmission mechanism for the global contagion; they have themselves been the main cause of the economic epidemic.

If it is true that the operation of free financial markets was in and of itself the funda-

GEORGE SOROS is *chairman of Soros Fund Management and author of* The Crisis of Global Capitalism *(New York: PublicAffairs, 1998).*

Reprinted with permission from *Foreign Policy,* Winter 1998-99, pp. 55-66. © 1999 by the Carnegie Endowment of International Peace.

mental cause of the present crisis, then a radical reconsideration of the dominant role that deregulated financial markets play in the world is inevitable. In the absence of urgent reforms, this rethinking could produce a powerful backlash against the global capitalist system, particularly in the developing countries on its periphery.

The essential point is that the global capitalist system is characterized not just by global free trade but more specifically by the free movement of capital. The system can be envisaged as a gigantic circulatory system, sucking capital into the financial markets and institutions at the center and then pumping it out to the periphery, either directly in the form of credits and portfolio investments or indirectly through multinational corporations.

Until the Thai crisis, the center was vigorously sucking in and pumping out money, financial markets were growing in size and importance, and countries on the periphery were obtaining an ample supply of capital from the center by opening up their capital markets. There was a global boom in which the emerging markets fared especially well. At one point in 1994, more than half the total inflow of capital to U.S. mutual funds went into emerging-market funds. The Asian crisis reversed the direction of the flow. Capital started fleeing emerging markets such as Korea and Russia. At first, the reversal benefited the financial markets at the center. But since the Russian meltdown in August 1998, the banking and financial systems at the center have also been adversely affected. As a result, the entire world economy is now under threat.

With the growing realization that the underlying cause of this threat is the inherent instability of deregulated financial markets, the ideology of world capitalism faces a historic challenge. The financial markets are playing a role very different from the one assigned to them by economic theory and the prevailing doctrine of free market capitalism. According to the ideology of free market fundamentalism, which has swept the world since it was pioneered in the early 1980s by Ronald Reagan and Margaret Thatcher, competitive markets are always right—or at least they produce results that cannot be improved on through the intervention of nonmarket institutions and politicians. The financial markets, in particular, are supposed to bring prosperity and stability—the more so, if they are completely free from government interference in their operations and unrestricted in their global reach.

> *Today's crisis cannot be attributed simply to macroeconomic errors or specifically Asian characteristics.*

The current crisis has shown this market fundamentalist ideology to be irredeemably flawed. Free market ideology asserts that fluctuations in stock markets and credit flows are transient aberrations that can have no permanent impact on economic fundamentals. If left to their own devices, financial markets are supposed to act in the long run like a pendulum, always swinging back toward equilibrium. Yet it can be demonstrated that the very notion of equilibrium is false. Financial markets are inherently unstable and always will be. They are given to excesses, and when a boom/bust sequence progresses beyond a certain point, it inevitably transforms the economic fundamentals, which in turn can never revert to where they began. Instead of acting like a pendulum, financial markets can act like a wrecking ball, swinging from country to country and destroying everything that stands in their way.

The current crisis presents policymakers with what may be a final opportunity to recognize that financial markets are inherently unstable before the wrecking ball takes aim at the foundations of the global capitalist system itself. What, then, needs to be done?

SAVING CAPITALISM FROM ITSELF

Many of the widely discussed solutions to today's crisis are designed to improve the efficiency of financial markets and impose more market discipline through such means as deregulation, privatization, transparency, and so on. But imposing market discipline means imposing instability. Financial markets are discounting a future that is contingent on the bias that prevails in markets, and the reflexive interplay between expectations and outcomes yields unstable results. Market discipline is desirable, but it needs to be supplemented by another kind of discipline: Public-policy measures are needed to stabilize the flows of international finance required by the global capitalist system and to keep the inherent instability of financial markets under control.

Within the main capitalist countries, strong frameworks of state intervention already exist to protect against financial instability. The United States has the Federal Reserve Board and other financial authorities whose mandates are to prevent a breakdown in its domestic financial markets and, if necessary, act as lenders of last resort. They have been quite successful. I am confident that they are capable of fulfilling their responsibilities. Indeed, now, in the second phase of the current crisis, as the problems of the periphery have begun to spill over into the center and threaten serious financial instability in U.S. markets, stabilizing mechanisms have been brought powerfully into play. The Federal Reserve has urgently eased monetary policy and made clear that it will continue to print money if that is what financial stability requires. More controversially, the Fed has pressured the private sector into organizing a lifeboat for Long Term Capital Management, a hedge fund that the Fed itself declared to be too big to fail.

The trouble is that international mechanisms for crisis management are grossly inadequate. Most policymakers in Europe and the United States worry today whether their countries can be protected from the global financial contagion. But the issue at the global level is much broader and more historically important. Even if the Western economies and banking systems do survive the present crisis without too much harm, those on the periphery have been significantly damaged.

The choice confronting the world today is whether to regulate global financial markets internationally to ensure that they carry out their function as a global circulatory system or leave it to each individual state to protect its own interests. The latter course will surely lead to the eventual breakdown of global capitalism. Sovereign states act as valves within the system. They may not resist the in-

Stop us before we kill again.

flow of capital, but they will surely resist the outflow, once they consider it permanent. Malaysia has shown the way. A rapid spread of foreign-exchange controls will inevitably be accompanied by the drying up of international investment and a return to inward-looking economic strategies on the periphery. Economic withdrawal from world markets is likely to be accompanied by political disengagement and domestic repression. (Again, Malaysia stands out as an example.) In short, the global capitalist system will disintegrate.

What can be done to stop this process of disintegration? It is necessary to look beyond transparency, regulation, and other mechanisms that simply improve the efficiency of free markets. The flow of capital—and most importantly of private capital—from the center to the periphery must be revived and stabilized.

In seeking solutions to today's crisis, two common fallacies must be avoided. The first is the mistake of shutting the stable door after the horse has bolted. Reforms designed to improve the global financial architecture in the long term may be desirable, but they will do nothing to help the afflicted economies of today. In fact, the opposite may be true: Greater transparency and tougher prudential requirements are likely to discourage capital flows in the short term, just as the austere financial policies imposed by the IMF to restore the long-term soundness of stricken economies tend to make matters worse in the short term. The second fallacy is to embrace the delusion of market fundamentalism: that if markets can be made more transparent, more competitive, and generally more "perfect," their problems will be automatically solved. Today's crisis cannot be solved by market forces alone.

Emergency efforts to stabilize the world economy must focus on two goals: arresting the reverse flow of capital from the periphery of the global capitalist system to the center and ensuring the political allegiance of the peripheral countries to that system.

President Bill Clinton and Treasury Secretary Robert Rubin spoke in September 1998 about the need to establish a fund that would enable peripheral countries following sound economic policies to regain access to international capital markets. Although the two men did not say so publicly, I believe that they had in mind financing it with a new issue of Special Drawing Rights (SDRS), an international reserve asset created by the IMF to supplement members' existing assets.

Although their proposal did not receive much support at the annual meeting of the IMF in October 1998, I believe that it is exactly what is needed. Loans could be made available to countries such as Brazil, Korea, and Thailand that would have an immediate calming effect on international financial markets. Furthermore, such a mechanism would send a powerful signal because it would reward countries doing their utmost to play by the rules of the global capitalist system rather than succumbing, like Malaysia, to the temptation to cut themselves off. The IMF programs in countries such as Korea and Thailand have failed to produce the desired results because they do not include any scheme for reviving the flow of private capital to these countries or reducing their foreign debt. A debt reduction scheme could clear the decks and allow their domestic economies to recover, but it would force international creditors to accept and write off losses. The problem is that creditors would be unwilling and unable to make new loans, making it impossible to finance recovery in these countries without finding an alternate source of international credit. That is where an international credit guarantee scheme would come into play. It would significantly reduce the cost of borrowing and enable the countries concerned to finance a higher level of domestic activity. By doing so, such a mechanism would help revive not only the countries concerned but also the world economy. It would reward countries for playing by the rules of the global capitalist system

and discourage defections along Malaysian lines.

At present, the Clinton proposal is not being seriously pursued because European central banks are adamantly opposed to the issue of SDRS. Their opposition stems from doctrinaire considerations: Any kind of money creation is supposed to fuel inflation. But in using SDRS as guarantees, there would be no new money created; the guarantees would kick in only in case of default.

Reforms designed to improve the global financial architecture in the long term will do nothing to help today's affected economies.

After the German elections, left-of-center governments are now in power in most of Europe. These governments are likely to prove more amenable to a loan guarantee scheme than their central banks, especially when the recovery of important export markets hinges on it. Japan too is likely to support such a scheme as long as it covers Asia as well as Latin America.

NEEDED: INTERNATIONAL CREDIT INSURANCE

Although I strongly endorse the Clinton proposal, I would go even further. Earlier in 1998, I proposed establishing an International Credit Insurance Corporation. My proposal, however, was premature, as the reverse flow of capital had not yet become a firmly established trend. Moreover, the Korean liquidity crisis in late 1997 was followed by a temporary market recovery that lasted until April 1998. My proposal fell flat then, but its time has now come.

A credit insurance mechanism managed by the IMF could provide the cornerstone for the "new architecture" that policymakers and pundits are talking about these days. The new institution, which could become a permanent part of the IMF, would explicitly guarantee, up to defined limits, the loans that private lenders make to countries. If a country defaults,

The Big Fix

The global financial crisis has spawned countless proposals on what to do with the International Monetary Fund (IMF). Herewith some examples:

Tear it down: "Let the IMF be abolished," says economics giant **Milton Friedman** in a November 1998 interview with *Forbes.* "Distribute the assets to each country and let the markets take care of the fallout." His fellow Hoover Institution scholar and former secretary of state **George Shultz** agrees. Instead of throwing money at the IMF, remarks Schultz, Congress should boost the global economy by cutting U.S. taxes by 10 percent across the board.

Clip its wings: The IMF can play a constructive role in crisis management if it avoids finger wagging and excessive interference in a nation's fiscal and monetary policies, says Harvard economics professor and former chairman of the President's Council of Economic Advisers **Martin Feldstein.** He urges the fund to focus on coordinating the rescheduling of international obligations for creditors and debtors and to create a collateralized credit facility to lend to governments that are illiquid but able to repay foreign debts through future export surpluses. The Columbia Business School's **Charles Calomiris** says that instead of doling out cash, the IMF should simply offer advice and encouragement and closely monitor government attempts at macroeconomic reform.

Make it bigger and better: Fleshing out proposals made by President Bill Clinton and British prime minister Tony Blair, the **Group of Seven** (G-7) announced in October 1998 a plan for the fund to extend short-term credit lines to any government that implements IMF—approved reforms, drawing from the recently approved $90 billion increase in the IMF's lendable resources. The G-7 ministers also called for increased collaboration between private-sector creditors and national authorities and the adoption by IMF member nations of a code of financial transparency enforced by annual IMF audits.

Create a new institution: Forget the IMF and World Bank, says **Jeffrey Garten,** dean of the Yale School of Management. Instead, create a global central bank that could provide liquidity to ailing nations by purchasing bonds from national central banks; encourage spending and investment by acquiring national debts at discounted prices; and set uniform standards for lending and provide markets with detailed, credible information on the world's banks.—FP

the IMF would pay the international creditors and then work out a repayment process with the debtor country. The borrowing countries would be obliged to provide data on all borrowings, public or private, insured or not. This information would enable the authority to set a ceiling on the amounts it would be willing to insure. Up to those amounts, the countries concerned would be able to access international capital markets at prime rates plus a modest fee. Beyond these limits, the creditors would be at risk. Ceilings would be set taking into account the macroeconomic policies pursued by individual countries, as well as other overall economic conditions in each country and throughout the world. The new institution would function, in effect, as a kind of international central bank. It would seek to avoid excesses in either direction, and it would have a powerful tool in hand.

The thorniest problem raised by this proposal is how the credit guarantees allocated to an individual country would be distributed among that country's borrowers. To allow the state to make this decision would be an invitation for abuse. Guarantees ought to be channeled through authorized banks that would compete with each other. The banks would have to be closely supervised and prohibited from engaging in other lines of business that could give rise to unsound credits and conflicts of interest. In short, international banks would have to be as closely regulated as U.S. banks were after the breakdown of the American banking system in 1933. It would take time to reorganize the global banking system and introduce the appropriate regulations, but the mere announcement of such a scheme would calm financial markets and allow time for a more thorough elaboration of the details.

The credit insurance plan would obviously help the peripheral countries and the Western banking system to weather the immediate crisis. By providing some inducements for lenders scarred by recent and impending losses, it would help restart the flow of funds from the financial markets toward the peripheral countries. But credit insurance would also strengthen the entire global financial architecture and improve financial stability in the long term. At present, the IMF does not have much influence in the internal affairs of its member countries except in times of crisis when a member country turns to the IMF for assistance. The fund may send its staff to visit and consult with country leaders, but it has neither the mandate nor the tools to shape economic policy in normal times. Its mission is crisis management, not prevention. By giving the new agency a permanent role in the surveillance of participating countries, the credit insurance scheme would help avoid both feast and famine in international capital flows.

Credit insurance would also help counteract the IMF's perverse role in the unsound expansion of international credit. IMF programs have served to bail out lenders, which encourages them to act irresponsibly, thereby creating a major source of instability in the international financial system. This defect of the current architecture is often described as "moral hazard." Moral hazard is caused by the asymmetry in the way that the IMF treats lenders and borrowers. It imposes conditions on borrowers (countries) but not on lenders (financial institutions); the money it lends enables debtor countries to meet their obligations, indirectly assisting the banks to recover their unsound loans. This asymmetry developed during the international crisis of the 1980s and became blatant in the Mexican crisis of 1995. In that case, foreign lenders to Mexico came out whole, even though the interest rates that the Mexican government paid them before the crisis clearly implied a high degree of risk. When Mexico could not pay, the U.S. Treasury and the IMF stepped in and took investors off the hook. The asymmetry and the moral hazard in IMF operations could be corrected by loan guarantees. Instead of bailing out foreign lenders to Mexico in 1995, the IMF would have guaranteed investors up to insured levels and then allowed uninsured debt to be converted into long-term bonds and written off. Had this happened, lenders and investors (myself included) would have been much more cautious about investing in Russia or Ukraine.

THE WILL TO STABILITY?

Some will wonder whether it would be possible for the IMF, let alone any new institution, to carry out the complex tasks I propose. Would it establish the right limits on sound international borrowing and be able to supervise the global circulatory system? A new institution would be bound to make mistakes, but the markets would provide valuable feed-

back and the mistakes could be corrected. After all, that is how all central banks operate and on the whole they do a pretty good job. It is much more questionable whether such a scheme is politically feasible. There is already a lot of opposition to the IMF from market fundamentalists who are against any kind of market intervention, especially by an international organization. If the banks and financial-market participants that currently benefit from moral hazard and asymmetry cease to support the IMF, it is unlikely to survive even in its present inadequate form.

Constructive reform will require governments, parliaments, and market participants to recognize that they have a stake in the survival of the system—and that this stake is far more valuable than any short-term gains that they may make from exploiting the flaws in the existing deregulated system. The question is whether this change of mentality will occur before or after the global capitalist system has fallen apart.

WANT TO KNOW MORE?

The flaws of the global financial system have been the focus of much analysis and debate. Karl Polanyi, in *The Great Transformation* (New York: Rinehart & Co., 1944), argues that capitalism is an anomaly since it embodies a system wherein social relations are defined by economic relations. In previous economic systems, he observes, economic interactions followed from social relations. Robert Kuttner's *Everything for Sale: The Virtues and Limits of Markets* (New York: Alfred A. Knopf, 1997) makes a case for the market's insufficiency in many fields and argues for intelligent intervention to produce better outcomes. In *Has Globalization Gone too Far?* (Washington: Institute for International Economics, 1997), Dani Rodrik posits that the world's leaders must ensure that international economic integration does not further domestic social disintegration.

For more analysis of the link between social relations and economic arrangements, see George Soros' **"The Capitalist Threat"** (*Atlantic Monthly*, February 1997), which argues that the free market undermines efforts to achieve open and democratic societies. Other works by Soros include: **"Toward Open Societies"** (FOREIGN POLICY, Spring 1995) in which he proposes that the creation of open societies should be a primary foreign-policy objective;

"**After Black Monday**" (FOREIGN POLICY, Spring 1988), which advocates a reform of the international currency system; and *The Alchemy of Finance* (New York: John Wiley & Sons, 1987), which describes the "theory of reflexivity" that guides his investment strategies.

Other excellent recent articles include "**The Crisis of Global Capitalism**" (*The Economist*, September 12–18, 1998) in which Jeffrey Sachs argues that world leaders should focus on a "development agenda" and suggests a Group of Sixteen summit—the Group of Eight countries plus eight developing nations—to tackle international financial reform, specifically, the international assistance process. Ricardo Hausmann's article, "**Will Volatility Kill Market Democracy?**" (FOREIGN POLICY, Fall 1997) describes alternatives to the common solutions for stabilizing the intense boom-and-bust cycles that characterize today's markets.

Speeches by Treasury Secretary Robert Rubin over the last six months track the evolution of the official U.S. position on reforming the global financial system. Especially useful are his "**Statement at the Special Meeting of Finance Ministers and Central Bank Governors**" on April 16, 1998, the transcript of the "**Post-Group of Seven Press Conference**" on April 15, 1998, the "**Statement at the 58th Annual Development Committee of the World Bank and the International Monetary Fund**" of October 5, 1998, and the "**Statement to the IMF Interim Committee**" on October 4, 1998.

For links to the texts of these speeches and relevant Web sites, as well as a comprehensive index of related FOREIGN POLICY articles, access **www.foreignpolicy.com**.

Trade and the Developing World: A New Agenda

"If the new round of trade talks is seen as unbalanced and support for liberalization in the developing world falters, then we are likely to see the emergence of even greater inequalities between rich and poor countries, and even more people in poverty.... The implications for global economic and political security of an increasing gap between the haves and the have-nots should be obvious."

JOSEPH F. STIGLITZ

The gap between the developed and the less developed countries is widening, a gap the international community is doing too little to narrow. Even as the ability of developing countries to use aid effectively has increased, the level of development assistance has diminished, with aid per capita to the developing world falling by nearly a third in the 1990s.[1] Cuts in aid budgets have been accompanied by the slogan of "Trade, not aid," together with exhortations for the developing world to participate fully in the global marketplace. At the same time, developing countries have been lectured about how government subsidies and protectionism distort prices and impede growth.

Yet all too often these exhortations ring hollow. As developing countries take steps to open their economies and expand their exports, they find themselves confronting significant trade barriers—leaving them, in effect, with neither aid nor trade. They quickly run up against dumping duties (when no economist would say they are really engaged in dumping), or they face protected or restricted markets in their areas of natural comparative advantage, such as agriculture or textiles.

In these circumstances, it is not surprising that critics of liberalization within the developing world quickly raise cries of hypocrisy. Developing countries often face great pressure to liberalize quickly. When they raise concerns about job loss, they receive the doctrinaire reply that markets create jobs, and that the resources released from the protected sector can be redeployed productively elsewhere. Often, however, the jobs do not appear quickly enough for those who have been displaced; and all too often the displaced workers have no resources to buffer themselves, nor is there a public safety net to catch them as they fall. These are genuine concerns. What are developing countries to make of rhetoric in favor of rapid liberalization, when rich countries—countries with full employment and strong safety nets—argue that they must impose protective measures to help those adversely affected by trade? Or when rich countries play down the political pressures within developing countries—insisting that their polities "face up to the hard choices"—but at the same time excuse their own trade barriers and agricultural subsidies by citing "political pressures"?

I do not doubt that trade liberalization will be of benefit to the developing countries, and to the world more generally. But trade liberalization must be balanced in its agenda, process, and outcomes, and it must reflect the concerns of the developing world. It must take in not only those sectors in which developed countries have a comparative advantage, like finan-

---

JOSEPH F. STIGLITZ *is senior vice president and chief economist at the World Bank.*

[1] Aid per developing country resident in 1990 was $32.27; in 1997 it was only $22.41.

cial services, but also those in which developing countries have a special interest, like agriculture and construction services. It must not only include intellectual property protections of interest to the developed countries, but also address issues of current or potential concern for developing countries, such as property rights for knowledge embedded in traditional medicines, or the pricing of pharmaceuticals in developing country markets.[2]

Success in trade liberalization requires understanding the sources of opposition, and assessing the legitimacy of that opposition and whether and how these concerns can be addressed. Standard economic analysis argues that trade liberalization—even unilateral opening of markets—benefits a country. In this view, job loss in one sector will be offset by job creation in another, and the new jobs will generate higher productivity than the old. This movement from low- to high-productivity jobs represents the gain from the national perspective, and explains why, in principle, everyone can become better off as a result of liberalization. This economic logic requires markets to be working well, however, and in many countries, underdevelopment is an inherent reflection of poorly functioning markets. Thus new jobs are not created, or not created automatically (moving workers from a low-productivity sector to unemployment does not increase output). A variety of factors contribute to the failure of jobs to be created, from government regulations, to rigidities in labor markets, to lack of access to capital. But whatever the causes, they must be addressed simultaneously with trade liberalization if a convincing case is to be made for that liberalization.

The case for trade liberalization is undermined both when developed countries act hypocritically and when market imperfections that are not dealt with result in trade liberalization policy to lower output and wages and increase unemployment. There are some sectors where these markets are particularly important, where the standard competitive paradigm does not work well even in developed countries, let alone developing countries. A stark lesson of the recent East Asia crisis is that weak financial institutions can wreak havoc on an economy, and that strong financial institutions require strong government regulation. But the increased frequency and depth of financial crises in recent years—with close to 100 countries suffering through such crises over the past quarter-century—have shown how hard it is establish strong financial institutions, even in developed countries. It also has shown that liberalization—both capital market and financial sector liberalization—without the requisite accompanying improvements in regulation and

Special interests, regrettably, often masquerade as general interests, using concerns for the poor to justify sustaining their ill-gotten gains.

supervision can contribute to financial-sector instability. That instability in turn has exacted great costs in terms of growth, deepening poverty in the crisis countries.

Finally, we must recognize that while enormous progress has been made in trade liberalization over the past 50 years under the General Agreement on Tariffs and Trade (GATT) and the World Trade Organization (WTO), today real threats exist to that progress. It is not just that future progress may be slow, but there may be, in effect, backsliding, as nontariff barriers replace tariff barriers, with the former far less transparent than the latter. Perhaps the most egregious of these barriers are antidumping and countervailing duties. While there are few topics on which economists agree, one with almost universal consensus is that, as implemented, antidumping and countervailing duties make little economic sense; instead, they are thinly disguised protectionist measures. But, sadly, developing countries do learn from their developed counterparts. They now know how to use these protectionist measures, both against each other and against the more developed countries. Indeed, last year, two of the top four users of antidumping measures were developing countries. (Not surprisingly, the United States and the European Union head the list of developed country users.)

WHY TRADE LIBERALIZATION MATTERS

For both the developed and developing worlds, the stakes are high. First, the developing countries represent a substantial share of international trade—nearly a third of exports of goods, and nearly a quarter of exports of services. It therefore should be obvious that any meaningful world trading system must take into full account the interests and concerns of these countries. Second, as was mentioned earlier, unless we continue to move forward, there is a real danger of backsliding, as nontariff barriers replace tariff barriers as impediments to the free movement of goods and services across national boundaries. Third, even to stay still we must move forward: the changing composition of national output, and in particular the increasing role of services, mean that we must broaden the scope of international trade agreements. Fourth, for developing countries, more is at stake than just the efficiency gains from exploitation of comparative advantage; there are also long-term dynamic gains to openness. Trade liberalization, thus, is an essential element of an effective development strategy. But if developing countries believe that the playing field of international trade is not level but sloped against them, their resulting suspicion and lack of commitment to liberalization will set back not only the trade liberalization agenda, but also the broader reform agenda. Fifth, for the developed countries more is at risk than just a sense of fair play and a humanitarian concern for the nearly 1.5 billion individuals who live in absolute poverty. An

---

[2]The marked disadvantage that developing countries have in participating meaningfully in negotiations should be noted. For example, as the new *World Development Report* points out, 19 of the 42 African World Trade Organization members do not have a trade representative at WTO headquarters in Geneva. In contrast, the average number of trade officials from OECD countries is just under seven.

open and vibrant international trade and investment regime benefits the entire world.

I have argued that trade liberalization is essential for successful development, and that progress in that area depends on a new round of truly balanced and inclusive trade talks. The inverse is also true: if the new round of trade talks is seen as unbalanced and support for liberalization in the developing world falters, then we are likely to see the emergence of even greater inequalities between rich and poor countries, and even more people in poverty. The end of the cold war and the seeming passing of the threat of Communism should not lull us into a sense of contentment. The implications for global economic and political security of an increasing gap between the haves and the have-nots should be obvious. Terrorism and political chaos take their toll no less than does the clash of competing superpowers.

THE POLITICS OF LIBERALIZATION

While the costs associated with liberalization animate much of the support for restrictive trade practices, the benefits of trade liberalization far outweigh these costs. But this does not grant us license to ignore them. Developed countries have recognized the costs, including the political costs, within their own borders and have introduced provisions in trade agreements to begin to address them. But there has yet to develop a widespread understanding of: (1) the real costs of these protective measures; (2) the even greater political and economic costs facing developing countries; or (3) the need to develop a framework that responds effectively to the differentiated needs of developed and developing countries.

Indeed, the perceived costs of liberalizing may well be higher in developing than in more developed countries. But the costs of *not* liberalizing loom even larger: poor countries simply cannot afford either the costs associated with inefficient resource allocation that result from protection or the costs that protection incurs when it results in reduced outside flows of investment and ideas.

Let me elaborate this point briefly. I have argued elsewhere that true development entails a transformation of society.[3] For poorer countries especially, excessive protection shields local residents from a key transformative mechanism. Trade and investment can bring knowledge. Openness to trade not only makes it possible for consumers to consume at lower cost, as suggested by standard models of trade, it also forces firms to innovate, and it offers firms new inputs and intermediate goods, many of which embody new knowledge. Foreign direct investment can bring with it investment capital and scarce human capital, new ways of organizing production, and access to international marketing channels and knowledge networks.

In this view then, the costs of protectionism are potentially very high for poorer countries. Yet in democratic developing countries, governments must persuade their citizens of the vir-

tues of liberalization, and demagogues always are ready to exploit worries about liberalization—just as in more developed countries. As I have noted, when unemployment rates are high and job opportunities are limited, as is so often the case in developing countries, worries about job losses will be far greater. And more developed countries—through both their rhetoric and their actions—too often have failed to be helpful to those genuinely committed to the cause of liberalization in developing countries.

First, we must provide some context for current efforts to increase market access in developing countries. Today those appeals are based on sound economic arguments, but it was not so long ago that gunboat diplomacy—or worse, as in the case of the Opium Wars—was used to persuade recalcitrant countries to open their markets. No pretense at reciprocity was made: it was a sheer show of power. The trade treaties imposed from outside were far from evenhanded.

I raise this not to reopen sore wounds of the colonial era, but to point out that these experiences remain part of the consciousness in developing countries. What has caused these historical wounds to fester is the seeming hypocrisy exercised by those in the developed countries: although they preach the virtues of openness, too often we see that in areas where they lack comparative advantage—areas such as agriculture, textiles, and steel—the developed countries engage in strong protectionist measures.

Thus, to many in the developing world, trade policy in the more developed countries seems more a matter of self-interest than of general principle. When good economic analysis works in favor of self-interest, it is invoked, but when it does not, so much the worse for economic principles. "Yes," the advanced countries seem to be telling the economies in transition (and the emerging economies), "produce what you can—but if you gain a competitive advantage over our firms, beware!" Too often, a not-so-subtle subtext can be read: "Clearly, if there were a level playing field, we could outperform you. Since you seem to be underselling us, it could only be because you are engaging in unfair trade practices."

Several recent events have reinforced this impression. Consider the crisis in East Asia. The conditions imposed through the rescue packages include trade liberalization measures unrelated to the crisis. To many, it seemed simply that those who wanted to force market-opening measures had seized on an opportune time to make use of their temporary power. Subsequent events strengthened the view that market-opening measures were not always advocated with the crisis countries' best interests at heart. As the crisis economies weakened further and excess capacity proliferated, natural market adjustments led to a decline in the pries of a number of commodities, including oil and steel. In capital-intensive industries, where short-run marginal costs lies far below long-run marginal costs, this drop in prices can be quite large. This is part of the market-equilibrating forces; it is not dumping, and should not be interpreted as such.

In sum, although real gains are to be had—both for developed and developing countries—from trade liberalization, there are also losers. The political process is one in which

[3]Joseph Stiglitz, "Towards a New Paradigm for Development: Strategies, Policies, and Processes." Delivered as the 1998 Prebisch Lecture at UNCTAD, Geneva, October 19, 1998.

special interests often triumph over general interests. In a democratic society, the majority must be convinced that they will benefit from—or at least do not face significant risks of being hurt by—liberalization. The special interests, regrettably, often masquerade as general interests, using concerns for the poor to justify sustaining their ill-gotten gains. All too often, more developed countries, both through their actions and their rhetoric, worsen the plight of the honest politician in a developing country who is trying to persuade his or her electorate to support liberalization.

TWO PRINCIPLES

Two basic principles should govern the next set of trade negotiations: fairness, especially fairness to the developing countries, and comprehensiveness. By comprehensiveness I refer to the need to include in the round not only issues of central importance to the developed countries, such as financial market liberalization and information technology, but also those, such as construction and maritime services, that are important to developing countries. One might ask how can either principle be opposed? Yet closer examination raises doubts about the extent to which previous rounds have embodied these principles.

For example, the Uruguay Round and previous GATT trade rounds focused heavily on liberalizing tariffs on manufacturing. They did little to reduce protection in agriculture, a sector in which many developing countries have a comparative advantage. The agricultural liberalization that occurred was driven largely by the interests of developed exporters such as the United States and Australia, and developing country exporters in the Cairns group.[4] Exporters of tropical products did not play an active role in the design of the agricultural liberalization agenda.

Moving ahead on the agricultural issue in this round would have big payoffs. Abolition of agricultural export subsidies and achievement of sharp cuts in import tariffs would benefit many developing countries. Recent research suggests that a 40 percent reduction in agricultural support policies globally would contribute almost exactly the same amount to global welfare as a 40 percent cut in manufacturing tariffs, despite the fact that manufacturing value added is 2.5 times that of agriculture globally. This reflects the huge size of distortions in agriculture relative to manufacturing.

Comprehensiveness is necessary for an equitable agreement, but there are other elements of perceived fairness. Over the years, many developing countries have unilaterally (though often under strong pressure) engaged in a wide variety of trade

Trade liberalization is not sufficient for developing countries to reap the full benefits from integration with the world economy.

liberalization measures. As we approach a new round of trade talks, those countries must be given credit for their concessions, in return for making them binding.

Another aspect of fairness entails sensitivity to the special needs of developing countries. This sensitivity has at least three dimensions. First, developed countries should recognize the higher costs of liberalization in developing countries. Allowing longer transition times for liberalization measures, as was done during the Uruguay Round, lowers the cost of adjustment. In addition to this concession, the more developed countries should consider establishing a formal program of trade adjustment assistance. And we should be clear: the costs of implementation can be high (It has been argued that implementation of just a few of the Uruguay Round agreements can swallow up a year's worth of development assistance for a country). The World Bank has played an important role in the provision of such support for implementation, and will continue to do so in the future. Nevertheless, more assistance is clearly needed.

The second point concerns the special problems posed by human needs, such as health. It has been alleged that some developed country drug companies, for example, sell their drugs to some developing countries at prices that exceed those in some developed country markets. That they might be able to do so is not surprising: intellectual property rights give drug firms scope for price discrimination; in particular, the larger developed countries with national health systems can win more favorable pricing from pharmaceutical firms. Yet as reasonable and rational as price discrimination might seem for profit-maximizing enterprises, to those in less developed countries it appears exploitative. Within the United States and other countries, such exercises of monopoly power—that is, price discrimination not justified by differences in costs of serving different customers—is illegal. It might be appropriate to consider a similar provision in the next round of trade negotiations. We must explore various ways to achieve the goal of ensuring that developing countries achieve "most favored pricing" status.

Third, the negotiations should pay special attention to the long-term growth aspirations of the less developed countries. This has several dimensions. Poorly designed financial services liberalization, for example, can lead to greater instability and perhaps even starve small and medium-sized enterprises of needed capital. Similarly, definitions of intellectual property rights must take into account the interests of users of knowledge as well as producers of knowledge. Within the developed countries, political debates have striven to achieve a balance, with both users' and producers' voices being heard. At the international level, a similar balance is necessary.

More problematic in this vein are issues related to promotion of infant industries, which has justified so much protectionism in the past. Certain types of technology subsidies were

---

[4]The Cairns Group was formed by Australia in 1986 and consists of 15 "fair trading" agricultural producing countries: Argentina, Australia, Brazil, Canada, Chile, Colombia, Fiji, Hungary, Indonesia, Malaysia, New Zealand, Paraguay, Philippines, Thailand, and Uruguay. These countries account for about 20 percent of world agricultural exports.

LIBERALIZING FINANCIAL MARKETS

Modern financial markets are clearly important for economic efficiency, and international financial institutions play an important role in promoting global economic integration, including trade expansion. But financial markets are different from ordinary markets, in that our standard theorems about the gains from trade liberalization in the presence of competitive markets may not apply. The central functions of financial markets are related to the provision of information, and markets for information function differently from markets for ordinary goods and services.

This fundamental difference explains why countries accept a need for financial regulation that all agree would be totally inappropriate for the typical manufacturing sector. Indeed, the recent and ongoing global financial crisis should have sensitized us to the downside risks of rapid liberalization of financial markets in countries that lack the appropriate regulatory structure. If domestic banks in the liberalizing country are weak, then providing an easy avenue for depositors to switch funds to a safer, foreign-owned bank could spark a run on the domestic banking system. Even short of that, the additional competition may erode the franchise value of the bank, and that itself may led to more risk taking, or more broadly imprudent behavior on the part of domestic banks. Thus, even countries with reasonably good systems of bank regulation will need to tighten and improve their financial sector regulations even as they liberalize the market more broadly.

But countries liberalizing their financial systems have not taken these precautions. Typically, these countries not only have failed to recognize the need to do so, but instead have moved in the opposite direction, loosening their regulatory frameworks in the euphoria of liberalization. In retrospect, it should be clear that in many countries the objective should not have been deregulation, but the establishment of a suitable regulatory framework. Even with the appropriate objectives, however, policymakers and regulators would have found the going tough. In country after country, the new foreign entrants into the financial system have recruited away the best and most talented individuals from the government regulating agencies. Unable to compete on salaries, regulatory agencies have found themselves much weaker just at the time that they need to be strengthened.

Nor should we ignore the longer-run development problems that can arise when foreign banks displace domestic banks: these foreign banks may focus their lending efforts on providing finance to multinationals or large national firms, but may show little interest in small and medium-sized enterprises, which are often the engines of growth.

To be sure, if countries manage to strengthen their financial sector regulation as they liberalize, and if they manage to ensure that funds reach small and medium-sized enterprises and other underserved groups, then financial sector liberalization has the potential for improving the performance of this vital part of the economy. The induced competition can be an important spur to efficiency of the sector. But there are clear examples (Kenya, for one) where foreign entry, even in the presence of financial sector liberalization, has failed not only in that objective, but also in the broader goal of reducing interest-rate spreads and bringing down the rates at which funds are available to borrowers. Thus, the liberalization of financial services in developing countries should be approached with some caution.

J.F.S.

---

given the green light under the Uruguay Round, but clearly developed countries use a variety of other, hidden subsidies under the rubric of "defense." This point was illustrated by the recent debates about dual-use technologies and subsidies to aircraft manufacturers. The technology issues facing developing countries are different, but no less important. These countries must absorb new technologies; to do so, they must have the space to engage in a process of learning-by-doing, during which costs fall. With imperfect capital markets, firms cannot simply borrow against future profits, and governments may need to intervene. We must find some way of accommodating these very real concerns of developing countries.[5]

THE BROADER AGENDA

Trade liberalization, while necessary, is not sufficient for developing countries to reap the full benefits from integration with the world economy. Much of the trade agenda now penetrates into areas such as domestic regulation, intellectual property rights, the efficiency of customs administration, and conformity with standards. Further, the ability of a country, and particularly of the more isolated communities within a country, to participate in trade depends upon the quality of the transport and communications infrastructure that allows them to access the world trading system.

The new, broader agenda for international trade involves many issues much more difficult to implement than trade liberalization, which, after all, can be implemented at the stroke of a pen once the necessary agreement has been obtained. Efficient infrastructure requires years of investment both in the regulatory framework under which it is supplied, and in the infrastructure itself. Similarly, improving the efficiency of customs is likely to require strengthening of the customs administration in many countries. Establishing a strong financial regulatory structure—so that opening up markets for financial services strengthens economic performance rather than contributing to economic instability—is no easy task, even for more developed countries.

The broader agenda raises the prospect that trade liberalization may yield even more benefits than it has in the past. But I should quickly add that from the perspective of the de-

---

[5] Article XVIII, Section A of the GATT does provide an explicit mechanism for infant industry protection, but that provision has been little used, presumably because of the requirement for compensation of trading partners, as well as the backlash in recent years against abuse of infant-industry arguments. But going forward, it will be important to ensure that the legitimate development concerns of poorer countries are reflected in the international trade rules—even while guarding against the development-impeding types of protectionism that have so often been justified using infant-industry arguments. Part of the task will be to preserve and raise awareness of provisions already available within the trade rules that may serve some development needs. One example is the Article XIX safeguard provisions, which permit transparent protection of limited duration without requiring compensation.

veloping country, access to markets abroad, especially in the developed countries, is crucial for growth. The East Asia miracle was based on export-oriented policies that took advantage of increasing access. Such policies play a critical role in raising quality within the developing countries, in promoting the transfer of technology, and in enforcing the discipline of competition. I have previously described the development process as a transformation of society, and have argued that openness to the outside in general, and trade in particular, can play a central role in that transformation. In short, for developing countries more is at stake than simply the exploitation of the gains from comparative advantages, as important as those gains are for static economic efficiency. Trade is vital to the dynamics of successful development.

FAIRNESS, COMPREHENSIVENESS, AND THE MILLENNIUM ROUND

The two principles of fairness and comprehensiveness are strongly linked. A comprehensive approach to trade will not only be more effective in attaining the objectives of trade liberalization, but it will also be perceived as fairer. This perception will not only enhance the chances of trade liberalization within developing countries, but also increase their enthusiasm for a broader range of market reforms. A comprehensive round of trade talks that adequately represents the interests of developing countries will deflate the sentiment that market economics is a theory invoked only in the pursuit of developed country interests, and it will increase awareness that vigorous market competition benefits any economy.

Both the political and economic stakes are high. If we fail—if the developed countries allow their special interests to prevail over their national interests, both in terms of their offers of market access and their demands on the developing world for market access—then our failure will undermine confidence in democratic processes everywhere. Clearly, the developed countries have much to gain from a more integrated global economy, and they have much to gain from reducing their distortionary policies. But they can afford the luxury of the inefficiencies of the existing distortions, and they have demonstrated an impressive capacity to dismiss or overlook the intellectual inconsistencies—to use a mild term—in some of their positions.

The developing countries cannot afford such economic distortions; the evidence of the last three decades strongly supports the conclusion that market-oriented policies, including outward-oriented policies, provide their best hope for sustained growth. Such growth is absolutely necessary if poverty within these countries is to be eradicated.

The Millennium Round of trade talks that begins November 30 in Seattle provides a great opportunity. It can reinforce the movement toward true market economies, enhancing competition and promoting economic and societal transformation. At the same time, by reducing trade barriers, and thereby eliminating some of the major sources of corruption and lack of transparency, the round can strengthen democratic processes.

But the round also poses great risks. If negotiations follow historical patterns—hard bargaining motivated by special interests within developed countries, with too little attention paid to the interests of the developing countries—the Millennium Round could strengthen the hand of those in the developing world who resist market reforms and an outward orientation. It could give confirmation and ammunition to those who see relations between the third world and the developed countries through the prism of conflict and exploitation, rather than recognizing the potential for cooperation and mutual gain. Outward-oriented policies will succeed only to the extent that there are markets in which developing countries can sell their products, as well as international rules that allow developing countries to make good use of their current areas of comparative advantage and to develop new areas of economic strength.

Helping the world's poorest

Jeffrey Sachs, a top academic economist, argues that rich countries must mobilise global science and technology to address the specific problems which help to keep poor countries poor

IN OUR Gilded Age, the poorest of the poor are nearly invisible. Seven hundred million people live in the 42 so-called Highly Indebted Poor Countries (HIPCS), where a combination of extreme poverty and financial insolvency marks them for a special kind of despair and economic isolation. They escape our notice almost entirely, unless war or an exotic disease breaks out, or yet another programme with the International Monetary Fund (IMF) is signed. The Cologne Summit of the G8 in June was a welcome exception to this neglect. The summiteers acknowledged the plight of these countries, offered further debt relief and stressed the need for a greater emphasis by the international community on social programmes to help alleviate human suffering.

The G8 proposals should be seen as a beginning: inadequate to the problem, but at least a good-faith prod to something more useful. We urgently need new creativity and a new partnership between rich and poor if these 700m people (projected to rise to 1.5 billion by 2030), as well as the extremely poor in other parts of the world (especially South Asia), are to enjoy a chance for human betterment. Even outright debt forgiveness, far beyond the G8's stingy offer, is only a step in the right direction. Even the call to the IMF and World Bank to be more sensitive to social conditions is merely an indicative nod.

A much more important challenge, as yet mainly unrecognised, is that of mobilising global science and technology to address the crises of public health, agricultural productivity, environmental degradation and demographic stress confronting these countries. In part this will require that the wealthy governments enable the grossly under-financed and underempowered United Nations institutions to become vibrant and active partners of human development. The failure of the United States to pay its UN dues is surely the world's most significant default on international obligations, far more egregious than any defaults by impoverished HIPCS. The broader American neglect of the UN agencies that assist impoverished countries in public health, science, agriculture and the environment must surely rank as another amazingly misguided aspect of current American development policies.

The conditions in many HIPCS are worsening dramatically, even as global science and technology create new surges of wealth and well-being in the richer countries. The problem is that, for myriad reasons, the technological gains in wealthy countries do not readily diffuse to the poorest ones. Some barriers are political and economic. New technologies will not take hold in poor societies if investors fear for their property rights, or even for their lives, in corrupt or conflict-ridden societies. *The Economist's* response to the Cologne Summit ("Helping the Third World", June 26th) is right to stress that aid without policy reform is easily wasted. But the barriers to development are often more subtle than the current emphasis on "good governance" in debtor countries suggests.

Research and development of new technologies are overwhelmingly directed at rich-country problems. To the extent that the poor face distinctive challenges, science and technology must be directed purposefully towards them. In today's global set-up, that rarely happens. Advances in science and technology not only lie at the core of long-term economic growth, but flourish on an intricate mix of social institutions—public and private, national and international.

Currently, the international system fails to meet the scientific and technological needs of the world's poorest. Even when the right institutions exist—say, the World Health Organisation to deal with pressing public health disasters facing the poorest countries—they are generally starved for funds, authority and even access to the key negotiations between poor-country governments and the Fund at which important development strategies get hammered out.

Jeffrey Sachs is director of the Centre for International Development and professor of international trade at Harvard University. A prolific writer, he has also advised the governments of many developing and East European countries.

The ecology of underdevelopment

If it were true that the poor were just like the rich but with less money, the global situation would be vastly easier than it is. As it happens, the poor live in different ecological zones, face different health conditions and must overcome agronomic limitations that are very different from those of rich countries. Those differences, indeed, are often a fundamental cause of persisting poverty.

Let us compare the 30 highest-income countries in the world with the 42 HIPCS (see table below). The rich countries overwhelmingly lie in the world's temperate zones. Not every country in those bands is rich, but a good rule of thumb is that temperate-zone economies are either rich, formerly socialist (and hence currently poor), or geographically isolated (such as Afghanistan and Mongolia). Around 93% of the combined population of the 30 highest-income countries lives in temperate and snow zones. The HIPCS by contrast, include 39 tropical or desert societies. There are only three in a substantially temperate climate, and those three are landlocked and therefore geographically isolated (Laos, Malawi and Zambia).

Not only life but also death differs between temperate and tropical zones. Individuals in temperate zones almost everywhere enjoy a life expectancy of 70 years or more. In the tropics, however, life expectancy is generally much shorter. One big reason is that populations are burdened by diseases such as malaria, hookworm, sleeping sickness and schistosomiasis, whose transmission generally depends on a warm climate. (Winter may be the greatest public-health intervention in the world.) Life expectancy in the HIPCS averages just 51 years, reflecting the interacting effects of tropical disease and poverty. The economic evidence strongly suggests that short life expectancy is not just a result of poverty, but is also a powerful cause of impoverishment.

All the rich-country research on rich-country ailments, such as cardiovascular diseases and cancer, will not solve the problems of malaria. Nor will the biotechnology advances for temperate-zone crops easily transfer to the conditions of tropical agriculture. To address the special conditions of the HIPCS, we must first understand their unique problems, and then use our ingenuity and co-operative spirit to create new methods of overcoming them.

Modern society and prosperity rest on the foundation of modern science. Global capitalism is, of course, a set of social institutions—of property rights, legal and political systems, international agreements, transnational corporations, educational establishments, and public and private research institutions—but the prosperity that results from these institutions has its roots in the development and applications of new science-based technologies. In the past 50 years, these have included technologies built on solid-state physics, which gave rise to the information-technology revolution, and on genetics, which have fostered breakthroughs in health and agricultural productivity.

Science at the ecological divide

In this context, it is worth noting that the inequalities of income across the globe are actually exceeded by the inequalities of scientific output and technological innovation. The chart below shows the remarkable dominance of rich countries in scientific publications and, even more notably, in patents filed in Europe and the United States.

The role of the developing world in one sense is much greater than the chart indicates. Many of the scientific and technological breakthroughs are made by poor-country scientists working in rich-country laboratories. Indian and Chinese engineers account for a significant proportion of Silicon Valley's workforce, for example. The basic point, then, holds even more strongly: global science is directed by the rich countries and for the rich-country markets, even to the extent of mobilising much of the scientific potential of the poorer countries.

The imbalance of global science reflects several forces. First, of course, science follows the market. This is especially true in an age when technological leaps require expensive scientific equipment and well-provisioned research laboratories. Second, scientific advance tends to have in-

creasing returns to scale: adding more scientists to a community does not diminish individual marginal productivity but tends to increase it. Therein lies the origin of university science departments, regional agglomerations such as Silicon Valley and Route 128, and mega-laboratories at leading high-technology firms including Merck, Microsoft and Monsanto. And third, science requires a partnership between the public and private sectors. Free-market ideologues notwithstanding, there is scarcely one technology of significance that was not nurtured through public as well as private care.

If technologies easily crossed the ecological divide, the implications would be less dramatic than they are. Some technologies, certainly those involving the computer and other ways of managing information, do indeed cross over, and give great hopes of spurring technological capacity in the poorest countries. Others—especially in the life sciences but also in the use of energy, building techniques, new materials and the like—are prone to "ecological specificity". The result is a profound imbalance in the global production of knowledge: probably the most powerful engine of divergence in global well-being between the rich and the poor.

Consider malaria. The disease kills more than 1m people a year, and perhaps as many as 2.5m. The disease is so heavily concentrated in the poorest tropical countries, and overwhelmingly in sub-Saharan Africa, that nobody even bothers to keep an accurate count of clinical cases or deaths. Those who remember that richer places such as Spain, Italy, Greece and the southern United States once harboured the disease may be misled into thinking that the problem is one of social institutions to control its transmission. In fact, the sporadic transmission of malaria in the sub-tropical regions of the rich countries was vastly easier to control than is its chronic transmission in the heart of the tropics. Tropical countries are plagued by ecological conditions that produce hundreds of infective bites per year per person.

Different ecologies
1995

	HIPCs* (42)	Rich countries (30)
GDP per person, PPP$†	1,187	18,818
Life expectancy at birth, years†	51.5	76.9
Population by ecozones, % in:		
tropical	55.6	0.7
dry	17.6	3.7
temperate and snow	12.5	92.6
highland	14.0	2.5

Source: J. Sachs *Highly indebted poor countries †Unweighted averages

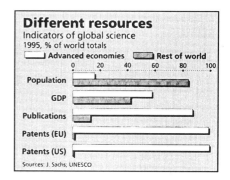

Different resources
Indicators of global science
1995, % of world totals

Mosquito control does not work well, if at all, in such circumstances. It is in any event expensive.

Recent advances in biotechnology, including mapping the genome of the malaria parasite, point to a possible malaria vaccine. One would think that this would be high on the agendas of both the international community and private pharmaceutical firms. It is not. A Wellcome Trust study a few years ago found that only around $80m a year was spent on malaria research, and only a small fraction of that on vaccines.

The big vaccine producers, such as Merck, Rhône-Poulenc's Pasteur-Mérieux-Connaught and SmithKline Beecham, have much of the in-house science but not the bottom-line motivation. They strongly believe that there is no market in malaria. Even if they spend the hundreds of millions, or perhaps billions, of dollars to do the R&D and come up with an effective vaccine, they believe, with reason, that their product would just be grabbed by international agencies or private-sector copycats. The hijackers will argue, plausibly, that the poor deserve to have the vaccine at low prices—enough to cover production costs but not the preceding R&D expenditures.

The malaria problem reflects, in microcosm, a vast range of problems facing the HIPCS in health, agriculture and environmental management. They are profound, accessible to science and utterly neglected. A hundred IMF missions or World Bank health-sector loans cannot produce a malaria vaccine. No individual country borrowing from the Fund or the World Bank will ever have the means or incentive to produce the global public good of a malaria vaccine. The root of the problem is a much more complex market failure: private investors and scientists doubt that malaria research will be rewarded financially. Creativity is needed to bridge the huge gulfs between human needs, scientific effort and market returns.

Promise a market

The following approach might work. Rich countries would make a firm pledge to purchase an effective malaria vaccine for Africa's 25m newborn children each year if such a vaccine is developed. They would even state, based on appropriate and clear scientific standards, that they would guarantee a minimum purchase price—say, $10 per dose—for a vaccine that meets minimum conditions of efficacy, and

perhaps raise the price for a better one. The recipient countries might also be asked to pledge a part of the cost, depending on their incomes. But nothing need be spent by any government until the vaccine actually exists.

Even without a vast public-sector effort, such a pledge could galvanise the world of private-sector pharmaceutical and biotechnology firms. Malaria vaccine research would suddenly become hot. Within a few years, a breakthrough of profound benefit to the poorest countries would be likely. The costs in foreign aid would be small: a few hundred million dollars a year to tame a killer of millions of children. Such a vaccine would rank among the most effective public-health interventions conceivable. And, if science did not deliver, rich countries would end up paying nothing at all.

Malaria imposes a fearsome burden on poor countries, the AIDS epidemic an even weightier load. Two-thirds of the world's 33m individuals infected with the HIV virus are sub-Saharan Africans, according to a UN estimate in 1998, and the figure is rising. About 95% of worldwide HIV cases are in the developing world. Once again, science is stopping at the ecological divide.

Rich countries are controlling the epidemic through novel drug treatments that are too expensive, by orders of magnitude, for the poorest countries. Vaccine research, which could provide a cost-effective method of prevention, is dramatically underfunded. The vaccine research that is being done focuses on the specific viral strains prevalent in the United States and Europe, not on those which bedevil Africa and Asia. As in the case of malaria, the potential developers of vaccines consider the poor-country market to be no market at all. The same, one should note, is true for a third worldwide killer. Tuberculosis is still taking the lives of more than 2m poor people a year and, like malaria and AIDS, would probably be susceptible to a vaccine, if anyone cared to invest in the effort.

The poorer countries are not necessarily sitting still as their citizenry dies of AIDS. South Africa is on the verge of authorising the manufacture of AIDS medicines by South African pharmaceutical companies, despite patents held by American and European firms. The South African government says that, if rich-country firms will not supply the drugs to the South African market at affordable prices (ones that are high enough to meet marginal production costs but do not include the patent-generated monop-

oly profits that the drug companies claim as their return for R&D), then it will simply allow its own firms to manufacture the drugs, patent or no. In a world in which science is a rich-country prerogative while the poor continue to die, the niceties of intellectual property rights are likely to prove less compelling than social realities.

There is no shortage of complexities ahead. The world needs to reconsider the question of property rights before patent rights allow rich-country multinationals in effect to own the genetic codes of the very foodstuffs on which the world depends, and even the human genome itself. The world also needs to reconsider the role of institutions such as the World Health Organisation and the Food and Agriculture Organisation. These UN bodies should play a vital role in identifying global priorities in health and agriculture, and also in mobilising private-sector R&D towards globally desired goals. There is no escape from such public-private collaboration. It is notable, for example, that Monsanto, a life-sciences multinational based in St Louis, Missouri, has a research and development budget that is more than twice the R&D budget of the entire worldwide network of public-sector tropical research institutes. Monsanto's research, of course, is overwhelmingly directed towards temperate-zone agriculture.

People, food and the environment

Public health is one of the two distinctive crises of the tropics. The other is the production of food. Poor tropical countries are already incapable of securing an adequate level of nutrition, or paying for necessary food imports out of their own export earnings. The HIPC population is expected to more than double by 2030. Around one-third of all children under the age of five in these countries are malnourished and physically stunted, with profound consequences throughout their lives.

As with malaria, poor food productivity in the tropics is not merely a problem of poor social organisation (for example, exploiting farmers through controls on food prices). Using current technologies and seed types, the tropics are inherently less productive in annual food crops such as wheat (essentially a temperate-zone crop), rice and maize. Most agriculture in the equatorial tropics is of very low productivity, reflecting the fragility of most tropical soils at high temperatures combined with heavy rainfall.

High productivity in the rainforest ecozone is possible only in small parts of the tropics, generally on volcanic soils (on the island of Java, in Indonesia, for example). In the wet-dry tropics, such as the vast savannahs of Africa, agriculture is hindered by the terrible burdens of unpredictable and highly variable water supplies. Drought and resulting famine have killed millions of peasant families in the past generation alone.

Scientific advances again offer great hope. Biotechnology could mobilise genetic engineering to breed hardier plants that are more resistant to drought and less sensitive to pests. Such genetic engineering is stymied at every point, however. It is met with doubts in the rich countries (where people do not have to worry about their next meal); it requires a new scientific and policy framework in the poor countries; and it must somehow generate market incentives for the big life-sciences firms to turn their research towards tropical foodstuffs, in co-operation with tropical research centres. Calestous Juma, one of the world's authorities on biotechnology in Africa, stresses that there are dozens, or perhaps hundreds, of underused foodstuffs that are well adapted to the tropics and could be improved through directed biotechnology research. Such R&D is now all but lacking in the poorest countries.

The situation of much of the tropical world is, in fact, deteriorating, not only because of increased population but also because of long-term trends in climate. As the rich countries fill the atmosphere with increasing concentrations of carbon, it looks ever more likely that the poor tropical countries will bear much of the resulting burden.

Anthropogenic global warming, caused by the growth in atmospheric carbon, may actually benefit agriculture in high-latitude zones, such as Canada, Russia and the northern United States, by extending the growing season and improving photosynthesis through a process known as carbon fertilisation. It is likely to lower tropical food productivity, however, both because of increased heat stress on plants and because the carbon fertilisation effect appears to be smaller in tropical ecozones. Global warming is also contributing to the increased severity of tropical climatic disturbances, such as the "one-in-a-century" El Niño that hit the tropical world in 1997–98, and the "one-in-a-century" Hurricane Mitch that devastated Honduras and Nicaragua a year ago. Once-in-a-century weather events seem to be arriving with disturbing frequency.

The United States feels aggrieved that poor countries are not signing the convention on climatic change. The truth is that these poor tropical countries should be calling for outright compensation from America and other rich countries for the climatic damages that are being imposed on them. The global climate-change debate will be stalled until it is acknowledged in United States and Europe that the temperate-zone economies are likely to impose heavy burdens on the already impoverished tropics.

New hope in a new millennium

The situation of the HIPCS has become intolerable, especially at a time when the rich countries are bursting with new wealth and scientific prowess. The time has arrived for a fundamental rethinking of the strategy for co-operation between rich and poor, with the avowed aim of helping the poorest of the poor back on to their own feet to join the race for human betterment. Four steps could change the shape of our global community.

First, rich and poor need to learn to talk together. As a start, the world's democracies, rich and poor, should join in a quest for common action. Once again the rich G8 met in 1999 without the presence of the developing world. This rich-country summit should be the last of its kind. A G16 for the new millennium should include old and new democracies such as Brazil, India, South Korea, Nigeria, Poland and South Africa.

Second, rich and poor countries should direct their urgent attention to the mobilisation of science and technology for poor-country problems. The rich countries should understand that the IMF and World Bank are by themselves not equipped for that challenge. The specialised UN agencies have a great role to play, especially if they also act as a bridge between the activities of advanced-country and developing-country scientific centres. They will be able to play that role, however, only after the United States pays its debts to the UN and ends its unthinking hostility to the UN system.

We will also need new and creative institutional alliances. A Millennium Vaccine Fund, which guaranteed future markets for malaria, tuberculosis and AIDS vaccines, would be the right place to start. The vaccine-fund approach is administratively straightforward, desperately needed and within our technological reach. Similar efforts to merge public and private science activities will be needed in agricultural biotechnology.

Third, just as knowledge is becoming the undisputed centrepiece of global prosperity (and lack of it, the core of human impoverishment), the global regime on intellectual property rights requires a new look. The United States prevailed upon the world to toughen patent codes and cut down on intellectual piracy. But now transnational corporations and rich-country institutions are patenting everything from the human genome to rainforest biodiversity. The poor will be ripped off unless some sense and equity are introduced into this runaway process.

Moreover, the system of intellectual property rights must balance the need to provide incentives for innovation against the need of poor countries to get the results of innovation. The current struggle over AIDS medicines in South Africa is but an early warning shot in a much larger struggle over access to the fruits of human knowledge. The issue of setting global rules for the uses and development of new technologies—especially the controversial biotechnologies—will again require global co-operation, not the strong-arming of the few rich countries.

Fourth, and perhaps toughest of all, we need a serious discussion about long-term finance for the international public goods necessary for HIPC countries to break through to prosperity. The rich countries are willing to talk about every aspect except money: money to develop new malaria, tuberculosis and AIDS vaccines; money to spur biotechnology research in food-scarce regions; money to help tropical countries adjust to climate changes imposed on them by the richer countries. The World Bank makes mostly loans, and loans to individual countries at that. It does not finance global public goods. America has systematically squeezed the budgets of UN agencies, including such vital ones as the World Health Organisation.

We will need, in the end, to put real resources in support of our hopes. A global tax on carbon-emitting fossil fuels might be the way to begin. Even a very small tax, less than that which is needed to correct humanity's climate-deforming overuse of fossil fuels, would finance a greatly enhanced supply of global public goods. No better time to start than as the new millennium begins.

Unit Selections

Key Points to Consider

❖ Why did India and Pakistan test nuclear weapons?

❖ Do you agree with experts who predict that future Russian leaders will be more likely now than during the cold war to use nuclear weapons in the event of an international crisis? Support your answer.

❖ What measures could be implemented to increase support for the Nuclear Nonproliferation Treaty and the Comprehensive Nuclear Test Ban Treaty in the United States and worldwide?

❖ Should local, national, or international authorities be doing more to prepare civilians to cope with the effects of chemical, biological, or nuclear attacks?

 **Links**   **www.dushkin.com/online/**

These sites are annotated on pages 6 and 7.

Proliferating weapons of mass destruction—chemical, biological, and nuclear (CBN)—are an important feature of contemporary international relations. Today scholars and politicians debate theoretical issues related to the magnitude of the threat, how to deter or counter weapons of mass destruction, and whether the spread of CBN weapons encourages or acts as a disincentive to interstate war. Meanwhile, proliferation continues unabated.

At least 25 countries either have, or are in the process of developing, weapons of mass destruction. Two dozen are researching, developing, or stockpiling chemical weapons. It is difficult to see how the genie of nuclear weapons technology will be kept in the bottle. India and Pakistan's nuclear tests in May 1998, despite the threat of U.S. sanctions, reawakened the world to the dangers of nuclear weapons and underscored how difficult it is to achieve nuclear disarmament while also slowing down the use of chemical and biological weapons.

In "Against Nuclear Apartheid," Jaswant Singh outlines how India's decision to test nuclear weapons was linked to the lack of concern by declared nuclear powers for India's security problems. Singh predicts that India will remain a declared nuclear power unless there is meaningful progress towards total nuclear disarm-ament. Faced with U.S. economic sanctions and international diplomatic pressure, Pakistan, which was on the verge of defaulting on outstanding international loans even before the nuclear tests, agreed to sign a treaty banning further nuclear tests. A regime change in Pakistan in 1999 as a military coup replaced an elected government did not change Pakistan's nuclear policy. India has also agreed in principle to such a treaty. Neither country, however, has yet indicated a willingness to dismantle their nuclear bomb program. The continuing commitment to retain nuclear weapons supports the proposition that more countries now believe that it is important for a country to obtain at least one or a few nuclear bombs.

Many security analysts remain focused on potential threats created by the seepage of weapons, materials, and expertise from the former Soviet Union and by "rogue" states who are developing nuclear capabilities. Concerns about the spread of nuclear expertise and capabilities from the former Soviet Union stimulated cooperation between the United States, Russia, and a number of former Soviet states. Since 1991, the United States and Russia have dismantled parts of the old nuclear structure in certain former Soviet republics. In 1992 the ex-Soviet republics of Kazakhstan and Belarus agreed to eliminate nuclear weapons from their territory, and Ukraine eliminated much of its nuclear stockpile by the mid-1990s.

The momentum of diplomatic initiatives slowed in recent years as the economic and political environment changed in the former Soviet Union and in the United States. Several programs designed to improve the security of Russia's deteriorating stockpile of weapons of mass destruction are no longer funded by the United States at their original levels. The funds were cut at the same time that growing economic problems in Russia posed additional threats to the security of Russia's stockpiles of nuclear, chemical, and biological weapons, materials, and human expertise. The ease with which these resources can disappear is a source of increasing worry among Western security analysts.

As the economy, conventional armed forces, and equipment deteriorate and Russia is relying more on nuclear weapons for national defense. The scenario of a future Russian government feeling forced to use nuclear weapons is more credible today than during the cold war. As the preparedness and morale of the troops guarding Russia's weapons of mass destruction decline, weapons stocks deteriorate, the reliability of the country's network of early-warning satellites and computer-based launch facilities degrade, and the risk of an accidental use of nuclear weapons increases.

The current slowdown in nuclear arms cooperation between the United States and Russia is likely to continue in the future. Ronald Powaski explains in "Russia: The Nuclear Menace Within," that the main sticking point in further progress between the United States and Russia on securing nuclear materials in Russia and reducing nuclear arms is the Clinton administration's desire to build a national ballistic missile defense system.

The failure of the Clinton administration to win support from the U.S. Senate, during the fall of 1999, for the Comprehensive Test Ban Treaty that would impose a worldwide ban on underground testing triggered wide and highly vocal protests from America's friends and foes around the world. Rebecca Johnson in "Troubled Treaties: Is the NPT Tottering?" describes how the enhanced review process of the NPT is exposing serious problems and disagreements.

The weakness of current international enforcement mechanisms is disturbing because everyone is now a potential victim of a future nuclear, biological, or chemical attack. The realization that weapons of mass destruction are being dispersed throughout the world prompted the United States to ratify the Chemical Weapons Convention (CWC). The United States became one of 100 countries to ratify the CWC in 1997 after a contentious debate in the U.S. Senate.

In 1998 the U.S. government also proposed new measures to bolster the 1972 Biological and Toxic Weapons Convention by adding an international inspection system. The new unified American position means that U.S. negotiators are taking a more active role in international talks. Despite the increase in recent incidents involving alleged biological and chemical weapons, a recent federal study concluded that authorities in the United States at the federal, state, and local level are not prepared to launch coordinated emergency response measures in the event of a chemical or biological attack on civilians. The high visibility of threatened attacks by international and domestic terrorists and malcontents in the United States fuels concerns among Americans about the possibility of a terrorist attack within the United States.

Threats from proliferating weapons of mass destruction have changed in complex ways. As writers for *The Economist* note in "Bombs, Gas and Microbes: The Desperate Efforts to Block the Road to Doomsday," chemical and biological weapons may be just as hard to control as nuclear weapons. Even if a verification protocol is eventually added to the existing biological weapons convention, the spread of weapons technologies seems inexorable.

The Politics of Weapons of Mass Destruction

Against Nuclear Apartheid

Jaswant Singh

THE CASE FOR INDIA'S TESTS

WHILE THE end of the Cold War transformed the political landscape of Europe, it did little to ameliorate India's security concerns. The rise of China and continued strains with Pakistan made the 1980s and 1990s a greatly troubling period for India. At the global level, the nuclear weapons states showed no signs of moving decisively toward a world free of atomic danger. Instead, the nuclear nonproliferation treaty (NPT) was extended indefinitely and unconditionally in 1995, perpetuating the existence of nuclear weapons in the hands of five countries busily modernizing their nuclear arsenals. In 1996, after they had conducted over 2,000 tests, a Comprehensive Test Ban Treaty (CTBT) was opened for signature, following two and a half years of negotiations in which India participated actively. This treaty, alas, was neither comprehensive nor related to disarmament but rather devoted to ratifying the nuclear status quo. India's options had narrowed critically.

India had to ensure that its nuclear option, developed and safeguarded over decades, was not eroded by self-imposed restraint. Such a loss would place the country at risk. Faced with a difficult decision, New Delhi realized that its lone touchstone remained national security. The nuclear tests it conducted on May 11 and 13 were by then not only inevitable but a continuation of policies from almost the earliest years of independence. India's nuclear policy remains firmly committed to a basic tenet: that the country's national security in a world of nuclear proliferation lies either in global disarmament or in exercise of the principle of equal and legitimate security for all.

THE TESTS OF MAY

IN 1947, when a free India took its rightful place in the world, both the nuclear age and the Cold War had already dawned. Instead of aligning with either bloc, India rejected the Cold War paradigm and chose the more difficult path of nonalignment. From the very beginning, India's foreign policy was based on its desire to attain an alternative global balance of power that, crucially, was structured around universal, nondiscriminatory disarmament.

Nuclear technology had already transformed global security. Nuclear weapons, theorists reasoned, are not actually weapons of war but, in effect, military deterrents and tools of possible diplomatic coercion. The basis of Indian nuclear policy, therefore, remains that a world free of nuclear weapons would enhance not only India's security but the security of all nations. In the absence of universal disarmament, India could scarcely accept a regime that arbitrarily divided nuclear haves and have-nots. India has always insisted that all nations' security interests are equal and legitimate. From the start, therefore, its principles instilled a distaste for the self-identified and closed club of the five permanent members of the U.N. Security Council.

During the 1950s, nuclear weapons were routinely tested above ground, making the mushroom cloud the age's symbol. Even then, when the world had witnessed only a few dozen tests, India took the lead in calling for an end to all nuclear weapons testing, but the calls of India's first prime minister, Jawaharlal Nehru, went unheeded.

In the 1960s, India's security concerns deepened. In 1962, China attacked India on its Himalayan border. The nuclear age entered India's neighborhood when China became a nuclear power in October 1964. From then on, no responsible Indian leader could rule out the option of following suit.

JASWANT SINGH is Senior Adviser on Defense and Foreign Affairs to Indian Prime Minister Atal Bihari Vajpayee and a Member of Parliament for the Bharatiya Janata Party.

With no international guarantees of Indian security forthcoming, nuclear abstinence by India alone seemed increasingly worrisome. With the 1962 war with China very much on his mind, Indian Prime Minister Lal Bahadur Shastri began tentatively investigating a subterranean nuclear explosion project. A series of Indian nonproliferation initiatives had scant impact. In 1965, to make matters worse, the second war between India and Pakistan broke out. Shastri died in 1966 and was succeeded by Indira Gandhi, who continued the fruitless search for international guarantees. In 1968, India reaffirmed its commitment to disarmament but decided not to sign the NPT. In 1974, it conducted its first nuclear test, Pokharan I.

The first 50 years of Indian independence reveal that the country's moralistic nuclear policy and restraint paid no measurable dividends, except resentment that India was being discriminated against. Disarmament seemed increasingly unrealistic politics. If the permanent five's possession of nuclear weapons increases security, why would India's possession of nuclear weapons be dangerous? If the permanent five continue to employ nuclear weapons as an international currency of force and power, why should India voluntarily devalue its own state power and national security? Why admonish India after the fact for not falling in line behind a new international agenda of discriminatory nonproliferation pursued largely due to the internal agendas or political debates of the nuclear club? If deterrence works in the West—as it so obviously appears to, since Western nations insist on continuing to possess nuclear weapons—by what reasoning will it not work in India? Nuclear weapons powers continue to have, but preach to the have-nots to have even less. India counters by suggesting either universal, nondiscriminatory disarmament or equal security for the entire world.

India is alone in the world in having debated the available nuclear options for almost the last 35 years. No other country has deliberated so carefully and, at times, torturously over the dichotomy between its sovereign security needs and global disarmament instincts, between a moralistic approach and a realistic one, and between a covert nuclear policy and an overt one. May 11, 1998, changed all that. India successfully carried out three underground nuclear tests, followed on May 13 by two more underground, sub-kiloton tests. These five tests, ranging from the sub-kiloton and fission variety to a thermonuclear device, amply demonstrated India's scientific, technical, and organizational abilities, which until then had only been vaguely suspected. A fortnight later, on May 28 and 30, neighboring Pakistan predictably carried out its own tests in the bleak vastness of the Chagai Hills in Baluchistan, near the Afghan border. Suddenly the strategic equipoise of the post–Cold War world was rattled. The entire nonproliferation regime and the future of disarmament were at the forefront of international agendas.

THE FAILURE OF THE OLD REGIME

SINCE INDEPENDENCE, India has consistently advocated global nuclear disarmament, convinced that a world without nuclear weapons will enhance both global and Indian security. India was the first to call for a ban on nuclear testing in 1954, for a nondiscriminatory treaty on nonproliferation in 1965, for a treaty on nonuse of nuclear weapons in 1978, for a nuclear freeze in 1982, and for a phased program for complete elimination of nuclear weapons in 1988. Unfortunately, most of these initiatives were rejected by the nuclear weapons states, who still consider these weapons essential for their own security. What emerged, in consequence, has been a discriminatory and flawed nonproliferation regime that damages India's security. For years India conveyed its apprehensions to other countries, but this did not improve its security environment. This disharmony and disjunction between global thought and trends in Indian thought about nuclear weapons is, unfortunately, the objective reality of the world. Nuclear weapons remain a key indicator of state power. Since this currency is operational in large parts of the globe, India was left with no choice but to update and validate the capability that had been demonstrated 24 years ago in the nuclear test of 1974.

India's May 1998 tests violated no international treaty obligations. The CTBT, to which India does not subscribe, permits parties to withdraw if they believe their supreme national interests to be jeopardized. Moreover, the forcing of an unconditional and indefinite extension of the NPT on the international community made 1995 a watershed in the evolution of the South Asian situation. India was left with no option but to go in for overt nuclear weaponization. The Sino-Pakistani nuclear weapons collaboration—a flagrant violation of the NPT—made it obvious that the NPT regime had collapsed in India's neighborhood. Since it is now argued that the NPT is unamendable, the legitimization of nuclear weapons implicit in the unconditional and indefinite extension of the NPT is also irreversible. India could have lived with a nuclear option but without overt weaponization in a world where nuclear weapons had not been formally legitimized. That course was no longer viable in the post–1995 world of legitimized nuclear weapons. Unfortunately, the full implications of the 1995 NPT extension were debated neither in India nor abroad. This fatal setback to nuclear disarmament and to progress toward delegitimization of nuclear weapons was thoughtlessly hailed by most peace movements abroad as a great victory.

Nor was the CTBT helpful. In negotiations on the CTBT in 1996, India for the first time stated that the nuclear issue is a national security concern for India and advanced that as one reason why India was unable to accede to the CTBT. Presumably this persuaded the nuclear hegemons to introduce a clause at the last minute pressing India, along with 43 other nations, to sign the treaty to bring it into force. This coercive clause violates the Vienna Convention on Treaties, which stipulates that a nation not willing to be a party to a treaty cannot have obligations arising out of that treaty imposed on it. Even more galling, this clause was introduced at the insistence of China—the provider of nuclear technology to Pakistan. When the international community approved the coercive CTBT, India's security environment deteriorated significantly.

India's plight worsened as the decade wore on. In 1997 more evidence surfaced on the proliferation between China and Pakistan and about U.S. permissiveness on this issue. During Chinese President Jiang Zemin's recent visit to Washington, the United States insisted on a separate agreement with China on Chinese proliferation to Iran and Pakistan, which the Chinese signed instead of professing their innocence. Both the U.S. unease and the Chinese signature attest to Chinese proliferation as a threat to India's security. After all these assurances, China continued to pass missile technology and components to Pakistan. Despite this, the Clinton administration was still willing to certify that China was not proliferating or—even worse for India—that the United States was either unable or unwilling to restrain China. As the range of options for India narrowed, so, too, did the difficulties of taking corrective action.

A FINE BALANCE

TODAY INDIA is a nuclear weapons state. This adds to its sense of responsibility as a nation committed to the principles of the U.N. Charter and to promoting regional peace and stability. During the past 50 years, India made its nuclear decisions guided only by its national interest, always supported by a national consensus. The May 1998 tests resulted from earlier decisions and were possible only because those decisions had been taken correctly.

The earliest Indian forays into the question of nuclear disarmament were admittedly more moralistic than realistic. The current disharmony, therefore, between India and the rest of the globe is that India has moved from being totally moralistic to being a little more realistic, while the rest of the nuclear world has arrived at all its nuclear conclusions entirely realistically. With surplus of nuclear weapons and the technology for fourth-generation weapons, the other nuclear powers are now beginning to move toward a moralistic position. Here is the cradle of lack of understanding about the Indian stand.

The first and perhaps principal obstacle in understanding India's position lies in the failure to recognize the country's security needs; of the need in this nuclearized world for a balance between the rights and obligations of all nations; of restraint in acquisition of nuclear weaponry; of ending today's unequal division between nuclear haves and have-nots. No other country in the world has demonstrated the restraint that India has for the nearly quarter-century after the first Pokharan test in 1974.

Now, as the century turns, India faces critical choices. India had witnessed decades of international unconcern and incomprehension as its security environment, both globally and in Asia, deteriorated. The end of the Cold War created the appearance of American unipolarity but also led to the rise of additional power centers. The fulcrum of the international balance of power shifted from Europe to Asia. Asian nations began their

process of economic resurgence. The Asia-Pacific as a trade and security bloc became a geopolitical reality. But the rise of China led to new security strains that were not addressed by the existing nonproliferation regime. The 1995 indefinite extension of the NPT—essentially a Cold War arms control treaty with a heretofore fixed duration of 25 years—legitimized in perpetuity the existing nuclear arsenals and, in effect, an unequal nuclear regime. Even as the nations of the world acceded to the treaty, the five acknowledged nuclear weapons powers—Britain, China, France, Russia, and the United States—stood apart; the three undeclared nuclear weapons states—India, Israel, and Pakistan—were also unable to subscribe. Neither the world nor the nuclear powers succeeded in halting the transfer of nuclear weapons technology from declared nuclear weapons powers to their preferred clients. The NPT notwithstanding, proliferation in India's back yard spread.

Since nuclear powers that assist or condone proliferation are subject to no penalty,

the entire nonproliferation regime became flawed. Nuclear technologies became, at worst, commodities of international commerce and, at best, lubricants of diplomatic fidelity. Chinese and Pakistani proliferation was no secret. Not only did the Central Intelligence Agency refer to it but, indeed, from the early 1990s on the required U.S. presidential certification of nonproliferation could not even be provided. India is the only country in the world sandwiched between two nuclear weapons powers.

Today most nations are also the beneficiaries of a nuclear security paradigm. From Vancouver to Vladivostok stretches a club: a security framework in which four nuclear weapons powers, as partners in peace, provide extended deterrent protection. The Americas are under the U.S. nuclear deterrent as members of the Organization of American States. South Korea, Japan, and Australasia are also under the U.S. umbrella. China is, of course, a major nuclear power. Only Africa and southern Asia remain outside this new international nuclear paradigm where nuclear weapons and their role in international conduct are paradoxically legitimized. These differentiated standards of national security—a sort of international nuclear apartheid—are not simply a challenge to India but demonstrate the inequality of the entire nonproliferation regime.

In the aftermath of the Cold War, an Asian balance of power is emerging with new alignments and new vacuums. India, in exercise of its supreme national interests, has acted in a timely fashion to correct an imbalance and fill a potentially dangerous vacuum. It endeavors to contribute to a stable balance of power in Asia, which it holds will further the advance of democracy. A more powerful India will help balance and connect the oil-rich Gulf region and the rapidly industrializing countries of Southeast Asia.

To India's north is the Commonwealth of Independent States, a reservoir that has yet to be fully developed. The Soviet Union's successor, Russia, has considerably less international prestige. Inevitably, the previously existing alliance between India and the former U.S.S.R. has eroded.

On India's western flank lies the Gulf region, a critical source of the world's energy. India has ancient links to the area, as it does to the former Soviet lands. It also has extensive energy import requirements. The Gulf employs Indian labor and talent. However, this region and its neighbors have been targets of missile and nuclear proliferation. Long-range missiles entered this area in the mid-1980s. Since 1987, nuclear proliferation in the Gulf, with extraregional assistance, has continued unchecked.

Faced as India was with a legitimization of nuclear weapons by the haves, a global nuclear security paradigm from which it was excluded, trends toward disequilibrium in the Asian balance of power, and a neighbor-

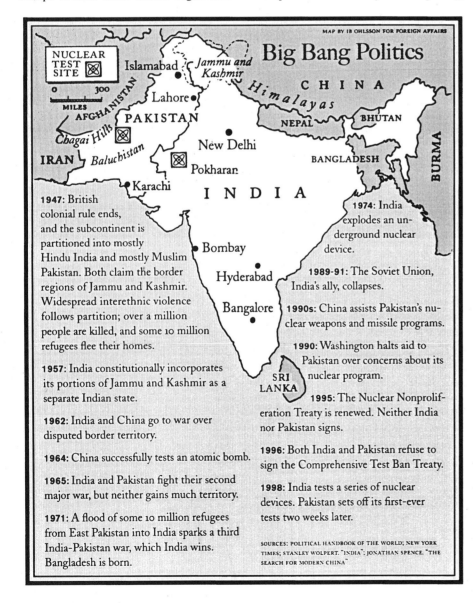

MAP BY IB OHLSSON FOR FOREIGN AFFAIRS

Big Bang Politics

NUCLEAR TEST SITE ⊠

0 — 300 MILES

1947: British colonial rule ends, and the subcontinent is partitioned into mostly Hindu India and mostly Muslim Pakistan. Both claim the border regions of Jammu and Kashmir. Widespread interethnic violence follows partition; over a million people are killed, and some 10 million refugees flee their homes.

1957: India constitutionally incorporates its portions of Jammu and Kashmir as a separate Indian state.

1962: India and China go to war over disputed border territory.

1964: China successfully tests an atomic bomb.

1965: India and Pakistan fight their second major war, but neither gains much territory.

1971: A flood of some 10 million refugees from East Pakistan into India sparks a third India-Pakistan war, which India wins. Bangladesh is born.

1974: India explodes an underground nuclear device.

1989-91: The Soviet Union, India's ally, collapses.

1990s: China assists Pakistan's nuclear weapons and missile programs.

1990: Washington halts aid to Pakistan over concerns about its nuclear program.

1995: The Nuclear Nonproliferation Treaty is renewed. Neither India nor Pakistan signs.

1996: Both India and Pakistan refuse to sign the Comprehensive Test Ban Treaty.

1998: India tests a series of nuclear devices. Pakistan sets off its first-ever tests two weeks later.

SOURCES: POLITICAL HANDBOOK OF THE WORLD; NEW YORK TIMES; STANLEY WOLPERT, "INDIA"; JONATHAN SPENCE "THE SEARCH FOR MODERN CHINA"

hood in which two nuclear weapons countries act in concert, India had to protect its future by exercising its nuclear option. By so doing, India has brought into the open the nuclear reality that had remained clandestine for at least the past 11 years. India could not accept a flawed nonproliferation regime as the international norm when all realities conclusively demanded the contrary.

India's policies toward its neighbors and others have not changed. The country remains fully committed to the promotion of peace, stability, and resolution of all outstanding issues through bilateral dialogue and negotiations. The tests of May 11 and 13 were not directed against any country. They were intended to reassure the people of India about their own security. Confidence-building is a continuous process to which India remains committed.

India's motive remains security, not, as some have speciously charged, domestic politics. Had the tests been motivated simply by electoral exigencies, there would have been no need to test the range of technologies and yields demonstrated in May. In the marketplace of Indian public life, a simple low-yield device would have sufficed. Since that marketplace did not govern the decision to experiment, the tests encompassed the range of technologies necessary to make a credible nuclear deterrent.

JOIN THE CLUB

INDIA IS now a nuclear weapons state, as is Pakistan. That reality can neither be denied nor wished away. This category of "nuclear weapons state" is not, in actuality, a conferment. Nor is it a status for others to grant. It is, rather, an objective reality. India's strengthened nuclear capability adds to its sense of responsibility—the obligation of power. India, mindful of its international duties, is committed to not using these weapons to commit aggression or to mount threats against any country. These are weapons of self-defense, to ensure that India, too, is not subjected to nuclear coercion.

India has reiterated its desire to enter into a no-first-use agreement with any country, either negotiated bilaterally or in a collective forum. India shall not engage in an arms race, nor, of course, shall it subscribe to or reinvent the sterile doctrines of the Cold War. India remains committed to the basic tenet of its foreign policy—a conviction that global elimination of nuclear weapons will enhance its security as well as that of the rest of the world. It will continue to urge countries, particularly other nuclear weapons states, to adopt measures that would contribute meaningfully to such an objective. This is the defining difference. It is also the cornerstone of India's nuclear doctrine.

That is why India will continue to support initiatives, taken individually or col-

lectively, by the Non-Aligned Movement, which has continued to attach the highest priority to nuclear disarmament. This was reaffirmed most recently at the NAM ministerial meeting held soon after India had conducted its recent series of underground tests. The NAM ministers reiterated their call at the Conference on Disarmament to establish, as the highest priority, an ad hoc committee to start negotiations in 1998 on a phased program for the complete elimination of nuclear weapons within a specified time, including a nuclear weapons convention. The collective voice of 113 NAM countries echoes an approach to global nuclear disarmament to which India has remained committed.

One NAM initiative, to which great importance is attached, resulted in the International Court of Justice's unanimous July 1996 declaration that there is an international obligation to pursue in good faith and bring to a conclusion negotiations leading to comprehensive nuclear disarmament under strict and effective international control. India was one of the countries that appealed to the ICJ on this issue. No other nuclear weapons state has supported this judgment; in fact, they all have decried it. India has been and will continue to be in the forefront of the calls for opening negotiations for a nuclear weapons convention. This challenge should be confronted with the same vigor that has dealt with the scourges of biological and chemical weapons. In keeping with its commitment to comprehensive, universal, and nondiscriminatory approaches to disarmament, India is an original party to the conventions against both. In recent years, in keeping with these new challenges, India has actively promoted regional cooperation—in the South Asian Association for Regional Cooperation, in the Indian Ocean Rim Association for Regional Cooperation, and as a member of the Association of Southeast Asian Nations Regional Forum. This engagement will continue. The policies of economic liberalization introduced in recent years have increased India's regional and global linkages, and India shall deepen and strengthen these ties.

India's nuclear policy has been marked by restraint and openness. It has not violated any international agreements, either in 1974 or 1998. This restraint is a unique example. Restraint, however, has to arise from strength. It cannot be based upon indecision or hesitancy. Restraint is valid only when it removes doubts, which is precisely what India's tests did. The action involved was balanced—the minimum necessary to maintain an irreducible component of the country's national security calculus.

Even before 1990, when Congress passed the Pressler amendment cutting off economic and military aid to Pakistan to protest its development of a nuclear program, the genie of nuclear proliferation on the Indian subcontinent was out of the bottle. The

much-quoted 1987 interview in which Abdul Qadeer Khan, the chief Pakistani nuclear scientist, verified the existence of Islamabad's bomb simply confirmed what New Delhi had long suspected. The United States, then still engaged in Afghanistan, continued to deny that Pakistan had crossed the nuclear threshold. The explosions at the Chagai Hills on May 28 and 30 testify to the rightness of India's suspicions.

After the tests, India stated that it will henceforth observe a voluntary moratorium and refrain from conducting underground nuclear test explosions. It has also indicated a willingness to move toward a de jure formalization of this declaration. The basic obligation of the CTBT is thus met: to undertake no more nuclear tests. Since India already subscribes to the substance of the test ban treaty, all that remains is its actual signature.

India has also expressed readiness to participate in negotiations in the Conference on Disarmament in Geneva on a fissile material cut-off treaty. The basic objective of this pact is to prohibit future production of fissile materials for use in nuclear weapons. India's approach in these negotiations will be to ensure that this treaty is universal, nondiscriminatory, and backed by an effective verification mechanism. That same constructive approach will underlie India's dialogue with countries that need to be persuaded of India's serious intent. The challenge to Indian statecraft remains to reconcile India's security imperatives with valid international concerns regarding nuclear weapons.

Let the world move toward finding more realistic solutions and evolving a universal security paradigm for the entire globe. Since nuclear weapons are not really usable, the dilemma lies, paradoxically, in their continuing deterrent value. This paradox further deepens the concern of statesmen. How are they to employ state power in the service of national security and simultaneously address international concerns? How can they help the world create an order that ensures a peaceful present and an orderly future? How are they to reconcile the fact that nuclear weapons have a deterrent value with the objective global reality that some countries have this value and others do not? How can a lasting balance be founded? While humanity is indivisible, national security interests, as expressions of sovereignty, are not. What India did in May was to assert that it is impossible to have two standards for national security—one based on nuclear deterrence and the other outside of it.

The end of the Cold War did not result in the end of history. The great thaw that began in the late 1980s only melted down the ancient animosities of Europe. We have not entered a unipolar order. India still lives in a rough neighborhood. It would be a great error to assume that simply advocating the new mantras of globalization and the market makes national security subservient to global trade. The 21st century will not be the century of trade. The world still has to address the unfinished agenda of the centuries.

Russia: The Nuclear Menace Within

"The United States and Russia have made some progress on securing nuclear materials [in Russia], but they have been unable to move forward on the more traditional issue of strategic arms control. . . . The main sticking point has been the Clinton administration's apparent desire to build a national ballistic missile defense system."

RONALD E. POWASKI

This decade began with considerable reason to be optimistic that the nuclear arms race might be winding down. The cold war was over. Only a few years earlier, in 1987, President Ronald Reagan had concluded, with Soviet President Mikhail Gorbachev, the Intermediate-Range Nuclear Forces Treaty, which eliminated for the first time an entire class of nuclear weapons. By 1993 Reagan's successor, George Bush, had completed the negotiation of two Strategic Arms Reduction Treaties (START I and START II), which together would bring about massive reductions in the strategic nuclear arsenals of the two former adversaries. Bush's successor, Bill Clinton, gained Senate ratification of START I by persuading Belarus, Kazakhstan, and Ukraine to surrender to Russia the nuclear weapons they had inherited from the Soviet Union and to join the nuclear Non-Proliferation Treaty (NPT) as nonweapon states, all of which were prerequisites to Russian ratification of START I. Clinton has not been successful in implementing START II, however. Although the treaty was ratified by the Senate in January 1996 by an overwhelming 87 to 4 vote, it has yet to be approved by the Russian Duma.

As an incentive for the Duma to ratify START II, in 1997 Clinton and Russian President Boris Yeltsin signed START III, which would leave each side with between 2,000 and 2,500 strategic nuclear warheads by 2008. But START III's reductions will not be implemented, the Clinton administration insists, until START II is ratified.

Thus, the optimism about nuclear weapons with which the decade began has been tempered considerably. Whether humanity can avert nuclear catastrophe in the new millennium remains an open question.

RUSSIA'S DETERIORATING DETERRENT

The Duma has delayed ratifying START II partly because of concerns that the reductions mandated by the treaty would disadvantage Russia. The treaty requires Russia to give up its great advantage in heavy intercontinental ballistic missiles (ICBMS) armed with multiple warheads, while allowing the United States to retain its advantage in bombers and submarine-launched ballistic missiles (SLBMS). Eliminating Russia's land-based multiple-warhead ICBMS yet maintaining the maximum 3,500 deployed warheads permitted by START II would require the Russians to build hundreds of new single-warhead missiles, which they obviously cannot afford.

Perhaps more disconcerting to the Russians is the aging of their entire strategic nuclear force, creating the possibility that, solely through attrition, the force will degrade to 2,000 to 2,500 warheads within 10 years—with or without START II or START III. Indeed, the number may fall even lower. Russian Defense Minister Igor Sergeyev has stated publicly that, for economic reasons, Russia may have no more than 500 deployed strategic warheads by 2012. (In 1990 the Soviet Union had 10,779 strategic nuclear warheads, compared with fewer than 6,000 now.)

Not only does Russia have fewer nuclear warheads, it also has fewer reliable missiles on which to launch them. Russian military officials have admitted that 58 percent of Russia's ballistic missiles are well past their operational life span, which averages 10 years of service. Today, 20-year-old ICBMS sit in hundreds of silos across Russia.

The precipitous decline in the size and quality of the Russian strategic nuclear arsenal stems from Russia's financial in-

---

RONALD E. POWASKI *is an instructor in history at Cleveland State University. His most recent book,* Return to Armageddon: The United States and the Nuclear Arms Race, 1981–1999, *was published by Oxford University Press in February 2000.*

ability to replace the nuclear-armed submarines, long-range bombers, and ICBMs built by the Soviet Union during the cold war. Russian opponents of START II have argued that the reductions required by the treaty, when placed alongside the perceived conventional threat posed to Russia by NATO, would threaten Russia's security.

The Russian military leadership, which had initially supported START II—in part because it mistakenly expected it would free funds for conventional forces—is also increasingly concerned that lower defense budgets have reduced the capabilities of Russia's conventional and strategic nuclear forces to an unsafe level. (The Russian military budget is now $65 billion per year, compared with $260 billion for the United States.) This helps explain why Russia, on December 17, 1997, formally abandoned the Soviet pledge never to be the first power to use nuclear weapons.

Unfortunately, Russia's adoption of a nuclear first-use strategy, and its related launch-on-warning strategy (which theoretically will enable Russia to launch its missiles before they can be destroyed by incoming United States missiles), places more emphasis on Russia's increasingly questionable ability to differentiate between real and false attacks. But Russia's early warning system, like its aging strategic missile force, is also deteriorating. Russian officials have publicly acknowledged that 70 percent of Russia's early warning satellites either are past their designed operational life or are in serious disrepair.

The potential for a nuclear catastrophe was demonstrated in January 1995, when Russian radar operators misinterpreted a scientific rocket launched by Norway as an attack. For the first time, Yeltsin's nuclear briefcase, containing Russian missile launch codes, was activated before the true nature of the Norwegian missile was determined.

The shakiness of the Russian alert system has been aggravated by the Y2K problem, which creates the possibility that computer software that uses only two digits to designate a year will on January 1, 2000, misread the year 2000 for 1900 and produce erroneous information. In August 1998 the Russian government admitted that half the 50 operating systems and 100 software programs it uses will have serious Y2K problems. With 2,440 American and 2,000 Russian nuclear warheads still on 15- to 30-minute alert status, erroneous computer information could cause another false alarm similar to the 1995 missile launch off Norway.

One month after the government's admission, Clinton and Yeltsin agreed to establish a system for exchanging information on missile launches and early warning systems. The United States has also provided funds and expertise to Russia to help it counter potential Y2K problems; however, a joint United States–Russian early warning center, planned for Moscow, may not be ready until after January 1, 2000.

NUCLEAR LEAKAGE

The general deterioration in nuclear capabilities has been matched by a breakdown in controls on nuclear materials. This

has increased the possibility that nuclear weapons or materials will be smuggled out of Russia and into the hands of terrorists.

Today, the former Soviet Union holds vast amounts of bomb-making materials—plutonium and highly enriched uranium (HEU). Estimates of the Russian stockpile of weapons-grade materials exceed 1,200 tons of uranium and 150 tons of plutonium. Ukraine recently possessed about 100 kilograms of HEU but no plutonium, and Kazakhstan approximately 300 kilograms of HEU and perhaps 100 kilograms of plutonium. Because primitive nuclear weapons require relatively small amounts of plutonium or HEU—as little as 3 kilograms of enriched uranium or between 1 and 8 kilograms of plutonium—the diversion of only a small fraction of the fissile material from Russia could have dangerous consequences.

An indication of Russia's declining ability to monitor and safeguard these materials came to light in September 1998, when a team of American experts visiting Moscow observed a building containing 100 kilograms of HEU—enough for several nuclear bombs—that was unguarded because the facility could not afford the $200-a-month salary for a security guard. Some nuclear facilities have been forced to shut down their security systems after their electrical service was terminated for nonpayment of bills. And the potential for smuggling nuclear materials out of Russia was illustrated in December 1998, when the chief of the Russian Federal Security Service in the Chelyabinsk region reported that his agents had prevented the theft of 18.5 kilograms of nuclear materials suitable for use in nuclear weapons.

It is also possible that Russian nuclear expertise will become available for purchase by would-be terrorists or countries. The Russian economy's continuing downward spiral has deprived nuclear programs of the funds needed for operations and salaries. In September 1998 some 47,000 unpaid Russian nuclear workers protested nationwide over $400 million in back wages owed them.

In an attempt to reduce the chance that these conditions might tempt unpaid Russian nuclear workers to divert nuclear material for financial gain, the United States promised in September 1998 to provide Russia with $20 million toward retraining 30,000 to 50,000 Russian nuclear scientists for civilian work. The money is also to be used to convert nuclear weapons and missile manufacturing plants to commercial operations.

Since 1991 the Nunn-Lugar program also has been expanded to include assistance to reduce the threat of illicit transfers of nuclear materials.[1] This assistance has included funds to construct and purchase operating equipment for a fissile-material storage facility, and to help establish national and fa-

---

[1]To help Russia defray the cost of eliminating strategic nuclear weapons, as called for in the strategic reduction treaties, in 1991 Congress funded the Comprehensive Threat Reduction Program, more commonly called the Nunn-Lugar program after its cosponsors, Senator Sam Nunn (D-GA) and Senator Richard Lugar (R-IN). Since, $2.7 billion has been spent under the program in helping Russia, Kazakhstan, Ukraine, Belarus, Uzbekistan, and other former Soviet republics reduce, control, and eliminate nuclear, chemical, and biological weapons. According to the Defense Department, the program has helped Russia deactivate 1,538 nuclear warheads; destroy 254 intercontinental ballistic missiles, 30 submarine-launched ballistic missiles and 40 heavy bombers; and eliminate 50 silos for long-range missiles and 148 launchers for submarine-launched missiles.

A START Chronology

1991

July 31—Presidents George Bush and Mikhail Gorbachev sign the Treaty on the Reduction and Limitation of Strategic Offensive Arms (START I), which calls for the United States and the Soviet Union to reduce their strategic nuclear forces over seven years to 1,600 deployed land- and sea-based ballistic missiles and heavy bombers for each side and 6,000 "accountable" warheads, of which no more than 4,900 may be on ballistic missiles. Ballistic missile throw-weight (lifting power) is to be limited to 3,600 metric tons on each side.

November 27—The US Congress passes the Cooperative Nuclear Threat Reduction Program (the Nunn-Lugar program) to help the Soviet Union destroy nuclear, chemical, and other weapons; transport, store, disable, and safeguard weapons in connection with their destruction; and establish safeguards against the proliferation of such weapons.

December 25—The Soviet Union dissolves and is replaced by 12 independent states, including four with nuclear weapons on their territory.

1992

May 23—The United States, Belarus, Kazakhstan, Russia, and Ukraine sign the START protocol at a ceremony in Lisbon, Portugal. Under the Lisbon Protocol, all five countries become parties to START, and the three non-Russian former Soviet republics agree to join the nuclear Non-Proliferation Treaty (NPT) as non-nuclear-weapon states.

July 2—The Kazakhstan parliament ratifies START I.

October 1—The US Senate ratifies START I.

November 4—The Russian Duma ratifies START I. Russia says it will not exchange the instruments of ratification until Belarus, Kazakhstan, and Ukraine reach agreement on the dismantlement of their nuclear forces and join the NPT.

1993

January 3—Presidents George Bush and Boris Yeltsin sign the Treaty on Further Reduction and Limitation of Strategic Offensive Arms (START II). The treaty calls for a reduction in US and Russian strategic warheads to no more than 3,000 to 3,500 each on land- and sea-based ballistic missiles and heavy bombers. The treaty also bans multiple warheads on land-based ballistic missiles and requires Russia to destroy all SS-18 "heavy" Russian missiles. The reductions are to be completed in two phases by the year 2003—or by the end of 2000 if the United States helps finance the destruction and dismantling of weapons in Russia.

February 4—Belarus ratifies START I, the NPT, and the Lisbon Protocol.

1994

January 14—The United States, Russia, and Ukraine sign a statement in which Ukraine agrees to transfer strategic nuclear warheads on Ukrainian territory to Russia in exchange for compensation in the form of fuel assemblies for nuclear power stations and security assurances once Ukraine becomes a non-nuclear-weapon state party to the NPT.

February 3—The Ukrainian parliament accepts the statement and orders the exchange of the instruments of ratification of START I.

February 14—Kazakhstan accedes to the NPT.

May 30—The United States and Russia complete the detargeting of their strategic nuclear missiles. Britain also detargets its missiles under a separate agreement with Russia.

November 16—The Ukrainian parliament approves Ukraine's accession to the NPT as a non-nuclear-weapon state.

December 5—The five parties to the START I Treaty—the United States, Belarus, Kazakhstan, Russia, and Ukraine—exchange instruments of ratification for START I.

1995

April 25—Kazakhstan announces that it has completed the transfer of 104 SS-18s and that it is now nuclear-free.

June 20—President Yeltsin submits START II to the Russian Duma for ratification.

1996

January 26—The US Senate ratifies START II.

June 1—President Leonid Kuchma announces that Ukraine has transferred the last strategic nuclear warhead on its territory to Russia.

November 23—Belarus transfers its last 16 former Soviet SS-25 ICBMs and associated nuclear warheads to Russia and becomes a nonnuclear state.

1997

March 21—At the Helsinki Summit, Presidents Bill Clinton and Boris Yeltsin issue a Joint Statement on Parameters on Future Reductions in Nuclear Forces (START II extension protocol) that calls for the United States and Russia to immediately begin negotiations on a START III agreement once START II enters into force, to extend the elimination deadline for strategic nuclear delivery vehicles under START II from 2003 to December 31, 2007, and to initiate separate talks concerning "possible measures relating to nuclear long-range sea-launched cruise missiles and tactical nuclear systems." The agreed-on framework for START III includes reductions to 2,000 to 2,500 deployed strategic nuclear warheads by December 31, 2007 (coterminus with the extended START II deadline); measures to establish transparency in warhead inventories and their destruction; and the goal of making the START treaties permanent.

April 9—The Russian Duma votes to indefinitely postpone debate over START II ratification.

September 26—Russia and the United States sign the START II extension protocol.

1998

April 13—President Yeltsin submits the START II extension protocol to the Duma.

December 17—In response to US-British military action against Iraq, the Russian Duma postpones an expected vote on START II.

1999

April 9—In response to the start of NATO's bombing campaign against Yugoslavia on March 24, the Duma announces it will indefinitely postpone a vote to ratify START II.

June 16—The United States and Russia agree to extend the Nunn-Lugar program for another seven years. The Clinton administration will ask for $2.8 billion in total funding through 2006 for the program; $2.7 billion was provided between 1992 and 1999; $1.7 billion of that total was allocated for projects in Russia.

June 21—Duma speaker Gennady Seleznyov says that START II ratification will be on the Duma's fall agenda.

Sources:
Federation of American Scientists, *Arms Control Today,* and Rodney W. Jones, et al., *Tracking Nuclear Proliferation,* (Washington, D.C.: Carnegie Endowment, 1998).

cility-level systems for material control and accountability and for physical protection of civil nuclear material.

In addition, the Clinton administration has attempted to eliminate Russian plutonium stockpiles. In a program that began in 1993, the United States has purchased highly enriched uranium and plutonium from Russia to dispose of weapons-grade material that could be smuggled out of the country. As part of this agreement, in 1993 Russia was awarded an advance payment of $100 million against future deliveries of HEU. In September 1998 Russia and the United States signed an agreement that would require each country to remove 50 tons of plutonium from its military stockpile and use it as fuel in nuclear reactors or mix it with nuclear waste. While the 50 tons of Russian plutonium to be reallocated represents only a quarter of Russia's estimated supply, American officials called the accord an important precedent, since it made clear that plutonium is not a resource to be husbanded, as the Russian nuclear establishment often claimed.

Still, there are dozens of research reactors in the former Soviet Union that use weapons-grade fuel. To deal with the problem, the United States Department of Energy is conducting a program to develop low-enriched uranium (LEU) fuels for these reactors. However, because the conversion of HEU to LEU fuel is costly, ending the reliance of these reactors on HEU will come slowly.

OFFENSIVE DEFENSE

The United States and Russia have made some progress on securing nuclear materials, but they have been unable to move forward on the more traditional issue of strategic arms control. Although movement on START I, II, and III has been stalled by nonnuclear . . . matters—especially NATO's expansion and the NATO air campaign against Yugoslavia—the main sticking point has been the Clinton administration's apparent desire to build a national ballistic missile defense system (NMD). Clinton has been under considerable pressure from congressional Republicans to revive the Reagan-Bush "Star Wars" antiballistic missile (ABM) system and, partly for this reason, stated on January 20, 1999, that the administration would announce next year whether the United States would build a limited NMD, with ABMS deployed at two sites, the first probably in Alaska or North Dakota, and eventually another on the East Coast. Such a system, its proponents argue, will protect the United States against a nuclear missile accidentally launched from Russia or China as well as an intentional attack from a "rogue state" such as North Korea.

Not surprisingly, the Russians—who cannot afford to compete in a NMD race—initially refused to amend the 1972 ABM Treaty (which allows for the deployment of 100 ABM interceptors, but only at one site) to permit the expanded ABM deployment envisioned in the Clinton NMD. Russia has also threatened to scrap the still-unratified START II if the United States withdraws from the ABM Treaty to go ahead with NMD.

United States withdrawal from the ABM Treaty would have dire consequences. Not only would the START process die, but the Russians—despite the cost it would entail—would most

likely respond by adding more nuclear warheads to their arsenal to overcome American ABM interceptors, thereby preserving their ability to respond to a United States first strike.

However, at the annual summit of the Group of 8 this June, Yeltsin said Russia would be willing to discuss possible amendments to the ABM Treaty that could enable the United States to deploy a limited NMD. Yeltsin obviously realizes that Clinton may no longer be able to resist the pressure to deploy NMD, and that it is better to get something rather than nothing in return for amending the treaty to permit a limited NMD. But Yeltsin also realizes that survival of the ABM Treaty is in the interest of Russia. Without it, START will surely expire and a new nuclear arms race, in both defensive as well as offensive nuclear weapons, one that Russia can neither win nor afford, is likely to ensue.

Indeed, under Yeltsin Russia agreed in 1997 to modify the ABM Treaty to permit the deployment of so-called theater nuclear defenses (TMD), such as the army's Theater High Altitude Area Defense (THAAD) system, intended to protect United States forces deployed overseas from the threat posed by theater-range ballistic missiles.

In an attempt to develop TMD systems without vitiating the ABM Treaty, the Clinton administration initiated talks with the Russians in November 1993 to establish a "demarcation line" between permitted TMD and restricted ABM systems. On August 21, 1997, the two governments—along with Ukraine, Belarus, and Kazakhstan, which were declared the other successor parties to the Soviet Union to the ABM Treaty—agreed to a statement that defined permitted TMD systems as those whose interceptors possessed velocities below 5 kilometers per second or ranges less than 3,500 kilometers. The agreement also banned the development, testing, or deployment of space-based TMD interceptor missiles, and required an annual data exchange of TMD plans and programs. Before the proposed ABM Treaty amendments contained in the pact can be implemented, however, they must be ratified by the five involved parties.

The Clinton administration has dragged its feet on submitting the amendments to the Senate, missing a June 1, 1999, deadline because it fears that the two-thirds vote required for ratification would not be achieved. The submission deadline had been imposed by Senator Jesse Helms (R-NC), chair of the Senate Foreign Relations Committee, which must approve the amendments before they are considered by the entire Senate.

Like most of his Republican colleagues, Helms opposes any limitations on TMD programs, and therefore would like the opportunity to vote down the proposed amendments as soon as possible, a move he believes will abrogate the unamended ABM Treaty as well. Indeed, Helms has called "the Clinton administration's stubborn adherence to the antiquated and defunct ABM treaty" the greatest obstacle to development of a national missile defense system.

Clinton may be able to overcome Helms's opposition to the ABM Treaty amendments with Yeltsin's decision to consider modifying the treaty to permit deployment of limited NMDs. If the additional modifications proposed by the United States are accepted by the Russians, the administration has announced that it will submit all the amendments to the Senate by next

June. The submission will likely coincide with the administration's decision to deploy a limited NMD, which will no doubt be contingent on the Senate's approval of the ABM Treaty amendments.

BREAKING THE LOGJAM

On February 25, 1999, the Committee on Nuclear Policy released a report that recommended a number of steps to end the current strategic nuclear arms control logjam.[2] The committee called on the Clinton administration to initiate a proposal for deep, mutual strategic force reductions without waiting for START II's ratification by the Russian Duma. Specifically, the committee recommended the reduction of strategic nuclear arsenals to 1,000 deployed warheads on each side within a decade (with a later goal of 1,000 total nuclear warheads on each side).

The committee also called on both sides to eliminate launch-on-warning and massive attack options from their nuclear war strategies. It proposed that all nuclear forces should be immediately taken off hair-trigger alert status to ensure that the Y2K problem does not cause a nuclear-weapon accident or unintended nuclear war. In addition, the committee has recommended continued and enhanced efforts to safeguard fissile materials and control warheads to reduce costs and risks and set the stage for a larger, more cooperative multilateral security framework for the twenty-first century.

---

[2]The Committee on Nuclear Policy was formed in 1997 by project directors of several independent nongovernmental organizations dealing with nuclear weapon policy issues. Its members include scholars, scientists, and researchers, as well as retired military leaders and national lawmakers. A summary of its report, "Jump-START: Retaking the Initiative to Reduce Post–Cold War Nuclear Dangers," appears in *Arms Control Today,* January–February 1999, pp. 15–19.

The Committee on Nuclear Policy believes that greater transparency is also required. It can be enhanced through detailed exchanges of data on stockpiles of warheads and fissile materials and reciprocal monitoring of sites where warheads are stored pending dismantlement. The relaxation of nuclear secrecy that would result from greater transparency would require a major change in the psychology of both sides. Indeed, it would require a degree of trust that has not been achieved so far in the post–cold war era.

As for the ABM Treaty, its maintenance is essential; if it were to expire, the entire arms control regime could unravel. Although the prospects for building an effective NMD remain poor, a system will probably be put into place in the next decade. It is difficult to resist the argument that the United States must have some protection—even if less than foolproof—against a nuclear-armed ballistic missile fired from a country such as North Korea.

To save the ABM Treaty, the United States should make NMD development an international effort, which would include cooperation with Russia and China as well as American allies. In the same spirit in which Ronald Reagan offered to share Star Wars technology with the Soviet Union, the United States should allow all the nuclear-weapon states to share ABM technology. Clearly, the United States will not be secure unless these nations feel secure as well. Reciprocally, they will not feel secure unless they have ABM protection.

If the Russians feel secure from a first-strike attack from the United States, or any other quarter, they will be more likely to continue the START process and with it the effort of further reducing the number of nuclear warheads aimed at the United States. The alternative—allowing their retaliatory capability to be degraded by an American NMD—would require a buildup of offensive missiles designed to overcome it. The result would be another dangerous, costly, and unnecessary nuclear arms race.

Troubled Treaties: Is the NPT tottering?

By Rebecca Johnson

After a failed PrepCom, it's clear that the treaty's indefinite extension has exposed more problems than it cured.

THE NUCLEAR NONPROLIFERATION regime is in deep trouble—but not only because of last year's nuclear tests by India and Pakistan, the threat of "loose nukes" from Russia's disintegrating facilities, and the actions of Saddam Hussein and other nuclear-weapon wannabes. It is also under threat from its own internal contradictions and stresses.

The Nuclear Non-Proliferation Treaty's (NPT) enhanced review process, set up when the treaty was indefinitely extended in 1995, was intended to strengthen the regime; instead it has exposed serious problems.

The new process includes at least three preparatory committee meetings (PrepComs) during the five-year period between review conferences. The second preparatory meeting, held in May 1998, was a mess. Delegates could not agree on anything except when and how to hold the next meeting, which will take place in New York in April.

Last year's meeting deadlocked over two important issues: the Middle East—specifically Israel's nuclear weapons—and nuclear disarmament. All eyes are now on the third PrepCom, with frantic preparations among key players deter-mined to avoid another impasse, which they fear could weaken the credibility of the treaty in the run-up to 2000.

The "Western group" of more than 40 countries, which includes the United States, Europe, Japan, and Australasia, is likely to focus on reinforcing the regime by inducing India and Pakistan to join the Comprehensive Test Ban Treaty (CTBT) and concluding a fissile material cut-off treaty, now being negotiated in Geneva. They will also stand for a strong export control regime and for beefing up the inspection powers of the International Atomic Energy Agency (IAEA).

The non-aligned, for their part, will focus on nuclear disarmament and call for a nuclear-weapon-free zone in the Middle East and security assurances in the form of legally binding pledges from the nuclear weapon powers not to use or threaten to use nuclear weapons against countries without nuclear arms. They will also seek to widen the fissile materials treaty to include current stockpiles.

Most important, however, will be proposals on nuclear disarmament—and the nuclear weapon states' responses to them. The more realistic the proposals are, the greater the pressure on the nuclear weapon states, which have long been let off the hook by the presumed exigencies of the Cold War and the "all or nothing" rhetoric of much of the nuclear disarmament crowd. But now, Ireland, Sweden, and New Zealand are members of the "New Agenda Coalition," which has formed a like-minded group with non-aligned Brazil, Mexico, Egypt, and South Africa. In June 1998, the group called for more action on nuclear disarmament.

When a resolution based on the New Agenda's call was put to the vote in the U.N. General Assembly in December, it garnered 114 votes. And despite heavy arm-twisting by Britain, the United States, and France, Japan and 12 of the 16 NATO countries abstained, refusing to oppose the resolution outright. The only votes against the resolution came from four nuclear weapon states (the NATO three plus Russia), the three de facto weapon states (India, Israel, and Pakistan), Turkey, and a tranche of NATO/European Union applicant states from the former Soviet bloc.

Among other things, the New Agenda resolution called for the full

Reprinted by permission of *The Bulletin of the Atomic Scientists*, March/April 1999, pp. 16-17. © 1999 by the Educational Foundation for Nuclear Science, 6042 South Kimbark, Chicago, Illinois 60637, USA. A one year subscription is $28.

implementation of the decisions adopted by the NPT parties in 1995. And it provoked a fierce debate about NATO's continuing dependence on the potential first use of nuclear weapons. With Canada prepared to vote in favor of the resolution if another NATO country pledged to do likewise, Germany, the Netherlands, Norway, Belgium, and Japan came under heavy domestic pressure.

NATO'S NUCLEAR POLICY HAS BEEN CHAL-lenged by NPT member states as well. In 1995, Mexico questioned NATO's arrangement for U.S. nuclear weapons to be stationed in Europe under NATO command, with provisions for control to be transferred to a non-nuclear weapon state in time of war. At the 1997 NPT meeting, South Africa raised concerns about the "non-proliferation implications" of NATO's planned expansion. Britain objected vehemently, saying that NATO arrangements were irrelevant to the treaty and denying the implication that the transfer of nuclear weapons among NATO members might violate the NPT's Articles I and II.

By 1998, however, the collective statement from the Non-Aligned Movement, which includes more than 100 developing countries, addressed the issue head on. The group opposed "nuclear sharing for military purposes under any kind of security arrangements." Egypt, especially concerned about alleged transfers of nuclear know-how to Israel, also criticized those who argued that the NPT would apply only in times of peace. Egypt proposed that the Review Conference in 2000 should unambiguously state that Articles I and II allow for no exceptions and that the NPT is binding on its signatories at all times.

NATO is undergoing a review of its strategic concept, last updated in 1991. The New Agenda resolution and high-level appeals from former military and diplomatic luminaries such as Gen. Lee Butler and Amb. Thomas Graham have stimulated arguments in several European coun-tries about NATO's nuclear-sharing and first-use policies. These debates are likely to come to a head when heads of state adopt a new posture at the alliance's fiftieth anniversary summit in Washington in April.

The Non-Aligned Movement and some members of the New Agenda Coalition will no doubt question NATO's nuclear sharing and first-use policy at the NPT's preparatory committee meeting, although the NATO states may be able to steer clear of a debate in that forum. But if NATO confirms its reliance on nuclear deterrence, nuclear sharing, and ambiguity regarding first use, it could lead to a major confrontation at the 2000 Review Conference.

THE ISSUE LIKELY TO BE HARDEST FOUGHT in the Review Conference is nuclear disarmament. Plainly put, a growing number of non-nuclear countries want more action and more participation in achieving the NPT's stated goal of eliminating nuclear weapons. Of course they welcome any and all reductions undertaken unilaterally or through the start process, but as long as the United States or other nuclear powers continue to issue statements emphasizing the fundamental importance to their security of nuclear deterrence and nuclear weapons, they reinforce the perception that they are engaged in post-Cold War nuclear rationalization, not disarmament.

Resistance to rethinking a nuclear NATO—and a weakened Russia's growing attachment to its nuclear weapons—are destroying the view that nuclear weapons were primarily a product of the Cold War. Instead, they signal an assumption that the desire for nuclear superiority will remain preeminent for the foreseeable future. But that is not what the non-nuclear countries had in mind when they signed the NPT, nor is it what they agreed to when they made it permanent.

India's explosive demand for rights similar to those of the first five nuclear weapon states has com-pounded the non-nuclear countries' worries. They now fear that the nuclear weapon states intend to hang on to their weapons and retool their nuclear doctrines to counter biological and chemical weapons—and nonproliferation will be doomed. As a result, many NPT parties have intensified their demands for systematic steps leading to the abolition of nuclear weapons.

The non-aligned continue to press their long-standing demand for a time-bound framework for nuclear disarmament. But the nuclear weapon states were more troubled in 1998 by the practical proposals being put forward by moderate countries, such as South Africa, and allies such as Canada. These two played a pivotal role in achieving the indefinite extension of the NPT, and they want the treaty to work. They and many others regard the intransigence of the United States and other members of the nuclear club, as displayed in 1998, as threatening the stability and fabric of the nonproliferation regime. The nuclear weapon states pay lip service to Article VI, but they have not yet grasped that nuclear disarmament is a fundamental tenet of the consensus for nonproliferation.

South Africa's proposal for addressing nuclear disarmament stood out in 1998 because it was practical and geared to the realities of the NPT process. The decisions taken in 1995 included a program of action on nuclear disarmament consisting of three commitments: to the CTBT, to a ban on the production of fissile materials, and to making "systematic and progressive efforts" to reduce nuclear arsenals.

The first two parts of the program were under way in 1998, if not fully in the bag. South Africa therefore focused on the third part, and argued for "a structured opportunity to deliberate on the practical steps" of disarmament. The depth of the nuclear weapon states' refusal to accept the logic of their NPT obligations was clear from the outrage and closed ranks they exhibited when faced with modest proposals for focusing on the implementation of the nuclear disarmament provisions of the treaty.

Canada's proposal that PrepCom reports should reflect important contemporary issues, such as the CTBT's entry into force, was similarly stonewalled.

Both proposals, which were popular, may well be reintroduced in 1999, perhaps with modifications. The nuclear weapon states seem to want the enhanced review to become a four-year text-drafting process, but that will not do. If they do not respond more positively to practical proposals for addressing nuclear disarmament, the third PrepCom will fail, with potentially disastrous consequences.

At this year's preparatory conference, the Non-Aligned Movement will again back Egypt and the Arab League in calling for Israel to accede to the treaty and for full implementation of the 1995 Resolution on the Middle East, which advocated regional negotiations on a zone free of nuclear and other weapons of mass destruction. However, there are hopeful signs that Egypt and the United States are discussing in advance of the PrepCom how the Middle East question can be addressed in the NPT context without either ignoring Israel's nuclear capabilities or overloading the treaty with regional agendas. If the talks are successful, the Middle East issue will not be a major obstacle, although of course it will be raised and discussed.

But the hidden conflict underlying all the debates concerns the purpose and role of the enhanced review process itself. Some regarded it merely as a gambit—a device used to achieve the treaty's permanence in 1995. Unless the nuclear and nonnuclear weapon states agree on their treaty obligations, all debate about the review process will continue to be conducted in conflicting language, without coherence or honest intention. In that context, no amount of earnest statements on the CTBT, fissile materials, security assurances, or even export controls will take the nonproliferation regime onto more secure ground.

The nuclear weapon states may complacently believe that the nonnuclear countries will not rock the boat, no matter how frustrated they become, because they do not want to see India and Pakistan, let alone Iraq or North Korea, lead the way to unbridled nuclear proliferation.

But such complacency is misplaced. Those pushing hardest for a genuine process to oversee nuclear nonproliferation and disarmament are the regime's staunchest advocates. Their desperation stems from a growing fear that the short-sighted policies and complacency of the nuclear weapon states themselves are undermining the basis of the NPT consensus. They fear that 2000 will be a more serious watershed than 1995.

Rebecca Johnson, the executive director of the Acronym Institute in London, is the author of numerous reports on the CTBT, NPT, and multilateral treaty negotiations.

BOMBS, GAS AND MICROBES

The desperate efforts to block the road to doomsday

India and Pakistan have reawakened the world to the dangers of nuclear weapons. Chemical and biological ones may be just as hard to control

IT DID not need the nuclear tests conducted last month by India and Pakistan to show that the nuclear age, which has dominated the second half of this century, is destined for a longer half-life than many had begun to hope. Indeed, almost a decade since the cold war ended and the threat of nuclear Armageddon that had hung over the world for more than 40 years was supposedly lifted, fears about the spread of weapons of mass destruction—nuclear, chemical and biological weapons and the missiles to deliver them—have, if anything, intensified.

Such fears are not irrational. The collapse of the otherwise unlamented Soviet Union brought with it the danger that ex-Soviet weapons scientists might start to hawk their skills abroad—as some have. In any event, the secrets of building nuclear and chemical weapons are now decades old

and increasingly hard to keep. Moreover, regional rivalries that used to be bottled up by America and the Soviet Union lest they led to a superpower confrontation are bottled up no longer. The rivalry between India and Pakistan had long driven a slow-motion arms race, in both missile and nuclear technology, before last month's tit-for-tat testing of bombs. Other potential flashpoints include the Korean peninsula and the Middle East, where tensions between Israel and its Arab neighbours are rising as hopes for peace collapse.

As India and Pakistan have proved, such regional pressures to proliferate should not be underestimated. Yet so far only a few countries have actually crossed the threshold to build weapons of mass destruction. One reason is general abhorrence of their use. The destruction visited on Hiroshima and

Nagasaki in 1945 ensured that nuclear weapons were from then on held in reserve as a deterrent, rather than used as weapons for waging war. Similarly, most countries have ruled out the use of chemical weapons as too nasty for the battlefield (though Iraq has already proved one exception, both in its war with Iran and in its determination to suppress its own Kurdish population). Biological weapons—less useful in the heat of the battle, as their awful effects may take several days to appear—have likewise been stigmatised.

Restraint, however, has not rested entirely on moral injunctions. As important in halting the spread of the horrible new weapons have been arms-control regimes. These work by raising the technical barriers and the costs to would-be proliferators. The question raised by the decisions of India and Pakistan to step across the nuclear

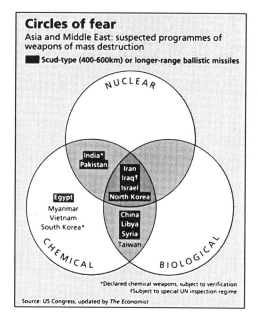

Circles of fear

Asia and Middle East: suspected programmes of weapons of mass destruction

■ Scud-type (400-600km) or longer-range ballistic missiles

NUCLEAR

India*
Pakistan

Iran
Iraq†
Israel
North Korea

Egypt
Myanmar
Vietnam
South Korea*

China
Libya
Syria
Taiwan

CHEMICAL

BIOLOGICAL

*Declared chemical weapons, subject to verification
†Subject to special UN inspection regime

Source: US Congress, updated by The Economist

threshold, however, is whether such regimes can really work.

The most intensive efforts have gone into controlling nuclear weapons. The Nuclear Non-Proliferation Treaty (NPT), which came into force in 1970 and was extended indefinitely in 1995, divides the world into two groups: the five nuclear haves (America, Russia, China, Britain and France, which had tested a nuclear weapon before January 1st 1967) and the rest. The haves promise to work towards nuclear disarmament, as part of an effort towards general and complete disarmament, and the have-nots promise not to acquire nuclear weapons of their own, in return for help with their civilian nuclear industry.

Is it a fair bargain? It is certainly one freely entered into by the 186 states that have signed the treaty: only India, Pakistan, Israel, Brazil and Cuba still sit outside.

In its near-universality, the NPT is one of the most successful arms-control regimes on record. Its system of obligations and checks has persuaded many countries that could have built nuclear weapons not to do so. In the 1980s Argentina and Brazil used the monitoring help and methods of the International Atomic Energy Agency (IAEA), the NPT's watchdog, when they decided to roll back their competing nuclear-weapons programmes. In 1993 South Africa announced that it had built, then dismantled, six nuclear devices before it joined the NPT in 1991—and then invited the IAEA in to check its nuclear records.

Yet the NPT regime at one point nearly collapsed under the burden of its own complacency. After the Gulf

war ended in 1991, it emerged that Iraq, which had signed the treaty, had secretly come within a year or two of building itself a bomb, despite regular IAEA inspections. Since the hardest part of building a bomb is getting hold of the highly enriched uranium or plutonium for its explosive core, the inspectors had been spending most of their time—at the behest of member governments—simply accounting for the nuclear material that was known to exist (because countries had declared they had made it). After Iraq had shown up the flaws in that cosy system of checking, and IAEA inspectors had caught North Korea telling lies about exactly how much plutonium it had produced, the agency was asked to devise a new, far more intrusive inspection system that would do more to deter cheats.

Under the new rules, inspectors have to be given much more information about nuclear activities and facilities in a country—and not just those where nuclear fuel is present; countries are also required to pass on more information about their trade in sensitive nuclear materials; and inspectors can use much more sophisticated equipment and sampling, including environmental monitoring, to ensure that no secret nuclear activity is taking place. The new protocol to the NPT incorporating the extra powers required came into force in 1997. It is not binding on a country unless that country has explicitly accepted it, and so far only a handful have.

Alongside the NPT and the work of the IAEA, there are two groups that seek to prohibit or control trade in sensitive nuclear technologies. The Zangger Committee is made up of 33 nuclear-exporting countries and provides a list to the IAEA of items which, if exported to an NPT member, should trigger the application of IAEA safeguards; the group also exchanges confidential information on exports to countries that are outside the treaty. The Nuclear Suppliers' Group has a slightly larger membership and operates a code that goes beyond strict NPT obligations, laying down rules about trade in nuclear exports, including any that could be used for either civilian or military purposes.

However, most recent efforts to control nuclear proliferation have concentrated on bringing into force the Comprehensive Test-Ban Treaty that was opened for signature in 1996, and on negotiating a new treaty to cut off the production of fissile material for bomb making. Both treaties are seen

as crucial if support for the NPT among the non-nuclear states is not to waver. Yet neither will be easy to achieve.

Although 149 countries have put their signatures to a ban on tests, only 13 have fully ratified the treaty. Yet, to ensure that a test ban is truly comprehensive, the treaty cannot come fully into force until ratified at least by all 44 countries that have nuclear reactors on their territory. These include both India and Pakistan, neither of which has signed the test ban, but also other countries, such as Israel (which has signed but not ratified it) and North Korea (which shows no sign of doing either). Assuming the treaty is still in limbo, its members will meet next year to decide how to proceed. One possibility would be to try to bring the proposed monitoring and information-gathering system into effect, as a confidence-building step, before the treaty itself comes legally into force.

Neither a test ban nor a fissile-materials cut-off treaty (which has a lot of support but has been caught up in bickering at the United Nations Conference on Disarmament in Geneva) would actually oblige countries that have nuclear weapons to abandon them. However, each in its own way would help to cap the ability of those with nuclear weapons to keep building more such weapons and testing ever more sophisticated designs.

Confounded chemicals

The guardians of the Chemical Weapons Convention (CWC), which came into force just over a year ago, have in many ways an even harder task. Whereas it takes a lot of deliberate and nowadays increasingly noticeable effort to build up a nuclear-weapons capability, many countries have sizeable chemicals industries. Moreover, many chemicals with humdrum civilian uses can be combined to make deadly weapons.

For many years, it was against international law to use chemical weapons, but not to manufacture or stockpile them. The CWC, by contrast, outlaws all chemical weapons and requires the destruction of all stockpiles. It also bans trade in some chemicals and restricts it in others (non-signatories will find it increasingly difficult to buy chemicals from CWC members). Within 30 days of signing the convention, governments must give an account of the chemicals industry on their territory, with declarations subject to inspection, including short-notice "anywhere, anytime" checks. And, unlike the NPT's rules, the CWC's apply equally to all.

Already the convention has had its successes. Among the handful of countries that declared a chemical-weapons stockpile, which must now be destroyed under the supervision of the Organisation for the Prohibition of Chemical Weapons (OPCW), were India and South Korea, neither of which had previously admitted to having a chemical-weapons programme. France and China, which had both previously had chemical-weapons programmes, said they destroyed their weapons shortly before signing the convention (those claims are subject to verification by OPCW inspectors). America and Russia, with the world's biggest stockpiles of chemical weapons (33,000 tonnes and 40,000 tonnes of them respectively), are destroying theirs, although Russia, which has only just started, is desperately short of funds for the job.

In their first year the OPCW's inspectors set a furious pace, with over 200 inspections in 25 countries, checking both on the destruction of weapons stocks and on the accuracy of industrial declarations. The danger, to some of the convention's critics, is that all this could prove ineffectively costly—with inspectors spending too much time on official declarations and too little ferreting out illicit activity.

The convention's chief deterrent power against cheats is the right to carry out short-notice challenge inspections, but none has yet been tried. That is in part because many countries are still in "technical non-compliance", taking an age to pass the national legislation and work through the bureaucratic procedures necessary to collect the industrial information that the convention demands. Governments with these problems are reluctant to challenge information supplied by others, however dubious it looks (Pakistan, Iran and some countries in the Balkans were thought to have chemical-weapons programmes but have not declared any), until they have their own house in order. But challenge inspections have to be shown to be possible if they are to have their intended deterrent effect. The real strength of the convention has therefore yet to be shown.

Other problems loom: barely noticed in the recent furore over the Indian and Pakistani nuclear testing, the American Senate last month attached amendments to enabling legislation that, if allowed to stand, would give the president the right to refuse challenge inspections. Many countries are uneasy about such inspections, which

they fear might enable others to walk off with their commercial secrets. But for America to give itself the right to block them, contrary to the convention it has already ratified, sets a bad precedent that others might seek to exploit for sinister purposes.

Another big problem is the number of hold-outs. So far a gratifying 168 countries have signed and 110 have ratified the convention. But the CWC's most obvious bald spot, the Middle East, is also a region of serious concern about proliferation: though Israel and Jordan have signed the convention, they are still to ratify it, and so are not yet bound by the reporting and inspection regime. Meanwhile, most other Arab states, led by Egypt, have refused to sign, citing Israel's refusal to sign the NPT.

Devilish brew

If searching out hidden chemical weapons is like looking for a needle in a haystack, trying to track a hidden biological-weapons programme is like looking for the eye of a needle in a haystack. In theory it takes only a tiny amount of a biological agent, such as botulinum, anthrax or plague, to spread destruction on a vast scale (making biological weapons closer to nuclear weapons in their potential effects). Luckily, turning biological agents into usable weapons is not always easy.

So far more than 130 countries have ratified the 1972 Biological and Toxins Weapons Convention (BWC), which prohibits development and production of such weapons (their use has been outlawed since 1925). But as yet the convention has no built-in checks. Groups of experts have been trying for several years to devise a new verification protocol, but it is difficult to strike a balance between useful checks and the need for bio-tech companies to preserve their legitimate commercial secrets. Even more so than chemical inspections, biological ones would need to rely heavily on the right to carry out sudden searches to investigate suspicious activity or unusual outbreaks of disease.

But if the biological-weapons convention has survived this long without such weapons being used, why worry? One reason is that, like any other arms-control regime, unless it is seen to be enforced it will fall into disrepute. What is more, as other proliferation loopholes are plugged, biological weapons, which are easier to make than nuclear weapons and more destructive than chemical ones, may be-

come the weapon of choice for rogue governments or terrorist groups.

In 1992 Russia, one of the sponsoring governments for the convention, admitted that in the past it had illegally built biological weapons. Although it now claims to have abandoned the programme, not everyone is convinced. Aum Shinrikyo, the Japanese sect that released a nerve gas, sarin, on the Tokyo metro in 1995, killing a dozen people, is now known to have experimented with biological agents too, which it attempted to spray from rooftops and trucks both in central Tokyo and near American military bases in Japan. None of the experiments appears to have worked.

But it was Iraq's industrial-sized biological-weapons programme, uncovered by UN inspectors after the Gulf war, that injected the new urgency into efforts to bolster the BWC. After repeated denials, Iraq eventually confessed to producing biological weapons. Some biological agents had even been loaded into missile warheads and artillery shells ready for use against American and allied troops. Although inspectors have since uncovered many of the details of the programme, Iraq has still failed to account for several tonnes of the medium used for growing microbes and other specialised materials. The fear is that Iraq could restart production of anthrax and other substances within weeks unless the inspectors are allowed to complete their job.

Iraq and other countries suspected of trying to develop biological weapons often got their start in the business by ordering toxic microbes from western germ banks, ostensibly for the development of vaccines and suchlike. This has added to calls for much tighter controls. At the moment trade in such substances is monitored only by the Australia Group, an informal body of more than 20 supplier countries formed in 1985 to harmonise export controls on chemicals that could be used to produce either chemical or biological weapons.

Range of possibilities

But even if a verification protocol is eventually bolted on to the BWC, some governments are getting nervous about the threat from biological weapons, which can be distributed by anything from crop-spraying aircraft to aerosol canister. America is considering the stockpiling of vaccines for use in the event of a biological threat against civilians (vaccines are already available for American troops).

Usually, however, the quickest way to deliver a bomb, and the one that is hardest to defend against, is by missile. The Missile Technology Control Regime (MTCR) was set up in 1987 in an attempt to restrict the sales of equipment and technology for missiles with a range (300 kilometres, or 190 miles) and payload (500kg, or 1,100lb) that would enable them to carry nuclear warheads. Export guidelines were later extended to cover missiles capable of carrying any type of weapon of mass destruction. The MTCR now has some 30 members.

But the controls are far from perfect. Russia is a member of the MTCR, but Russian companies have long been accused of supplying technology and know-how to anyone who will pay for it, most recently Iran, which is thought to be trying to build a new

missile with a range of up to 1,300km, capable of striking Israel, Saudi Arabia and Turkey. China, a major exporter of missile technology in the past, has said it will keep to the basic guidelines of the MTCR, but refuses to join it. It has been repeatedly criticised by America for providing missiles and know-how to others, including Pakistan. Other hard cases include Iraq (which is banned by UN rules from building missiles of more than 150km range but has been caught trying to circumvent the restrictions), Libya, Syria and North Korea. Both Iran and Pakistan are thought to have benefited from North Korea's missile programme to develop longer-range missiles.

The spread of weapons technologies seems inexorable. The best protection is to persuade countries to forgo particularly dangerous technologies in their own interests. Both India and

Pakistan may find that, once the euphoria over their demonstrated nuclear prowess has faded, their security is not improved, indeed may even be worsened, by having—and facing—powerful new weapons loaded on missiles that bring a hair-trigger instability to any future crisis.

In the end, getting at the roots of regional disputes is the only sure way to reduce the danger of a hideously lethal exchange. Arms-control regimes can help by building confidence that obligations not to build or to deploy certain deadly weapons are being kept. Yet such regimes are only as strong as the will of those whose task it is to enforce them. It is the hard cases that will test the world's resolve to prevent the further spread of nuclear, chemical or biological weapons. India and Pakistan are the latest of these. They will not be the last.

Unit 4

Key Points to Consider

❖ What are the most important national security threats facing the United States today?

❖ Should the United States continue to supply military forces to NATO operations in Europe?

❖ What are the pluses and minuses of expanding U.S. cooperative military assistance and training programs to countries bordering Russia? Should NATO membership be extended to these countries?

❖ What policies towards Russia should the United States pursue in the future?

❖ What policies could the United States take to promote freedom, democracy, and human rights in Muslim states?

❖ What type of event or trend would cause Americans to pay more attention to foreign affairs?

❖ Explain why you agree or disagree with the proposition that American will support the loss of American lives in a military operation overseas if the operation promises to be a success.

❖ Is Canada likely to pursue its high profile niche diplomacy and provide troops for UN peacekeeping operations in the future?

❖ How likely is it that conflicts over water will increase tensions between the United States and Canada?

 **Links**

www.dushkin.com/online/

16. **The Henry L. Stimson Center**
   http://www.stimson.org

17. **The North American Institute**
   http://www.santafe.edu/~naminet/index.html

These sites are annotated on pages 6 and 7.

As President Clinton completed his second term in office, it became clear that his administration would not accomplish many of its foreign policy goals. Madeleine Albright, the first female to be appointed Secretary of State, failed to convince most Americans that the United States is the world's one "indispensable power" in the world. Instead, a majority of Americans continued to show a lack of interest in foreign affairs. Despite the success of NATO's military campaign in Kosovo—to accomplish its mission without the loss of American active duty military personnel—many Americans continue to display an unwillingness to support new U.S. commitments abroad. Meanwhile, international trends suggest that political and economic power will continue to diffuse in an international system that is in transition towards a multipower system.

Charles Kupchan, in "Life after Pax Americana," describes how decisions taken by the first American administration of the twenty-first century will play a critical role in determining whether multipolarity reemerges peacefully or brings with it great-power wars. According to Kupchan, the most dangerous consequence of a return to multiparity will be the reemergence of national rivalries and competitive balancing within Europe and East Asia.

The end of the twentieth-century was marked by the expansion of NATO and a continued U.S. military presence in Europe. After the successful air campaign against Serbia, the United States remained the unrivaled military superpower. However, the dynamics of relations among NATO members are becoming more complex as alliance members work to prevent growing economic competition between the United States and members of the European Union from interfering with continued cooperation among members of an expanded NATO alliance. Despite the growth of noninterventionist sentiments among some U.S. politicians and members of the public, the United States continues its commitment of European integration and increased national military capabilities of member-states in an expanded NATO. These goals are being pursued at the same time that the United States continues to encourage Russia's integration with Europe.

One mechanism for strengthening the military capabilities of potential U.S. allies is a growing number of military exercises, training missions, and exchange programs that the U.S. military conducts with the military in 110 countries worldwide. The scope and stakes of the programs are greatest in central and eastern Europe, where American forces are helping to remake and arm military forces in countries that aspire to join the alliance. The U.S. military is also initiating military exchange programs in several recently independent states that border Russia, despite warnings from Russia that U.S. weapons transfers could trigger a conventional arms race in the area.

Current U.S. military policies are an important source of strains in U.S.–Russia relations. As Anatol Lieven notes in "Ham-Fisted Hegemon: The Clinton Administration and Russia," the current U.S. policy of rolling back Russian influence while offering Russia a subordinate role in an emerging American security system is an offer Russia cannot accept. According to Lieven, Russia's inconsistent foreign policies are a result of Russia's perception of this situation as being intolerable.

Continuing conflict with Iraq, Iran's efforts to obtain nuclear weapons capabilities, the bombings of the American embassies in Kenya and Tanzania during the summer of 1998, and the arrest of an Algerian with links to Muslim extremists, after he attempted to cross the U.S. border from Canada carrying explosives in 1999, underscore the importance of United States' policies towards the Islamic world. Increased number of analysts are now discussing the links between terrorist attacks at home and U.S. policies abroad. As Islam spreads throughout Asia and Africa, some analysts are calling for a retrenchment of U.S. military commitments abroad so that more resources and attention can be directed to homeland defense.

In contrast, other analysts stress that the spread of Islam and the linkages between events in Islamic countries and terrorist attacks abroad underscore the importance of the United States focusing more attention and formulating more consistent policies toward nation-states in the Islamic world. Augustus Norton represents this view in "Rethinking United States Policy toward the Muslim World," as he outlines the reasons why American policy can no longer afford to ignore the one-sixth of the world's population who are Muslims. Norton believes U.S. foreign policy toward Muslim states should emphasize the promotion of freedom, democracy, and human rights much like U.S. foreign policy toward other parts of the world.

A public opinion poll conducted at the end of 1999 found that Americans were feeling secure, prosperous, and confident about their future. The poll data reported in "Americans and the World: A Survey at Century's End," indicate that the American public see the United States as the world's most important and powerful country. However, Americans, anxious about the impact of globalism and the threat of terrorist attacks, support a "guarded engagement" in world affairs.

After the success of the U.S. air war against Serbia, many analysts claimed that Americans will no longer tolerate U.S. involvement in foreign conflicts if this involvement leads to the death of American soldiers. Many U.S. leaders now believe that Americans will lose their stomach for combat when the body bags come home. But the data presented by Peter Feaver and Christopher Gelpi in, "How Many Deaths Are Acceptable? A Surprising Answer" suggest that this view is wrong. Instead, they cite recent polls that suggest that Americans will accept combat deaths so long as the mission has the potential to be successful.

Despite its middle-level status, Canada has maintained an activist foreign policy while reducing military expenditures and increasing trade links. Canada maintains this profile by pursuing "niche" diplomacy that includes taking a leading role in sponsoring the international land mine treaty and participation in UN international peacekeeping missions. The approach permits Canada to play a large role in world affairs with limited resources.

Although the United States and Canada have managed to pursue peaceful relations throughout their history, water issues have always been a source of conflict between the two countries, especially among western provinces in Canada and western states in the United States. Water issues promise to continue to be a source of tensions between the two states in future decades. As writers for The Economist note in "Canada's Water: Hands Off," water is increasingly viewed as "blue gold" by federal officials in Ontario. As this abundant Canadian natural resource becomes more valuable to nation-states with water-scarce regions, the federal government is moving to regulate provinces' right to sell water to the United States and other customers worldwide.

Life after Pax Americana

Charles A. Kupchan

This decade has been a relatively easy one for American strategists. America's preponderant economic and military might has produced a unipolar international structure, which has in turn provided a ready foundation for global stability. Hierarchy and order have devolved naturally from power asymmetries, making less urgent the mapping of a new international landscape and the formulation of a new grand strategy. The Bush and Clinton administrations do deserve considerable credit for presiding over the end of the Cold War and responding sensibly to isolated crises around the globe. But America's uncontested hegemony has spared them the task of preserving peace and managing competition and balancing among multiple poles of power—a challenge that has consistently bedeviled statesmen throughout history.

The coming decade will be a far less tractable one for the architects of U.S. foreign policy. Although the United States will remain atop the international hierarchy for the near term, a global landscape in which power and influence are more equally distributed looms ahead. With this more equal distribution of power will come a more traditional geopolitics and the return of the competitive balancing that has been held in abeyance by America's preponderance. Economic globalization, nuclear weapons, new information technologies, and the spread of democracy may well tame geopolitics and dampen the rivalries likely to accompany a more diffuse distribution of power. But history provides sobering lessons in this respect. Time and again, postwar lulls in international competition and pronouncements about the obsolescence of war have given way to the return of power balancing and eventually to great-power conflict.

The foreign policy team that takes office in 2001 will therefore face the onerous task of piecing together a grand strategy for managing the return to multipolarity. The challenge will be as demanding politically as it is intellectually. Recognizing that new power centers are emerging and adjusting to their rise will meet political resistance after 50 years of American primacy. Politicians and strategists alike will have to engage in long-term planning and pursue policies that respond

Charles A. Kupchan is associate professor of international affairs at Georgetown University and a senior fellow at the Council on Foreign Relations. He is the author, among other works, of The Vulnerability of Empire.

to underlying trends rather than immediate challenges. But American elites must rise to the occasion. The coming decade represents a unique window of opportunity; the United States should plan for the future while it still enjoys preponderance, and not wait until the diffusion of power has already made international politics more competitive and unpredictable.

In the next section I explain how and why a transition to a multipolar world is likely to come about in the near term. The United States will not be eclipsed by a rising challenger, as is usually the case during transitions in international hierarchy. Instead, a shrinking American willingness to be the global protector of last resort will be the primary engine of a changing global landscape. The key challenge, I then argue, will not be in preparing for battle with the next contender for hegemony but in weaning Europe and East Asia of their excessive dependence on the current hegemon, the United States. Europeans and East Asians alike have found it both comfortable and cheap to rely on American power and diplomacy to provide their security. Americans have gone along with the deal for decades because of the importance of containing the Soviet Union and the profitability of being at the center of global politics.

But now that communist regimes are a dying breed and the Cold War is receding into the past, America's protective umbrella will slowly retract. If this retrenchment in the scope of America's engagement abroad is not to result in the return of destructive power balancing to Europe and East Asia, the United States and its main regional partners must start now to prepare for life after Pax Americana.

Benign Power

Most analysts of international politics trace change in the distribution of power to two sources: the secular diffusion over time and space of productive capabilities and material resources; and balancing against concentrations of power motivated by the search for security and prestige. Today's great powers will become tomorrow's has-beens as nodes of innovation and efficiency move from the core to the periphery of the international system. In addition, reigning hegemons threaten rising secondary states and thereby provoke the formation of countervailing coalitions. Taken together, these dynamics drive the cyclical pattern of the rise and fall of great powers.[1]

 From the *World Policy Journal*, Vol. XVI, No. 3, Fall 1999, pp. 20-27.

In contrast to this historical pattern, neither the diffusion of power nor balancing against the United States will be important factors driving the coming transition in the international system. It will be decades before any single state can match the United States in terms of either economic or military capability. Current power asymmetries are extreme by historical standards. The United States spends more on defense than all other great powers combined and more on defense research and development than the rest of the world combined. Its gross economic output dwarfs that of most other countries and its expenditure on R&D points to a growing qualitative edge in a global economy increasingly dominated by high-technology sectors.[2] Nor is balancing against American power likely to provoke a countervailing coalition. The United States is separated from both Europe and Asia by large expanses of water, making American power less threatening. Furthermore, it is hard to imagine that the United States would engage in behavior sufficiently aggressive to provoke opposing alliances. Even in the wake of NATO's air campaign against Yugoslavia, U.S. forces are for the most part welcomed by local powers in Europe and East Asia. Despite sporadic comments from French, Russian, and Chinese officials about America's overbearing behavior, the United States is generally viewed as a benign power, not as a predatory hegemon.[3]

The Rise of Europe

The waning of unipolarity is therefore likely to stem from two novel sources: regional amalgamation in Europe and shrinking internationalism in the United States. Europe is in the midst of a long-term process of political and economic integration that is gradually eliminating the importance of borders and centralizing authority and resources. To be sure, the European Union is not yet an amalgamated polity with a single center of authority. Nor does Europe have a military capability commensurate with its economic resources.

But trend lines do indicate that Europe is heading in the direction of becoming a new pole of power. Now that its single market is accompanied by a single currency, Europe has a collective weight on matters of trade and finance rivaling that of the United States. The aggregate wealth of the European Union's 15 members is already roughly equal to America's, and the coming entry of the new democracies of Central Europe will tilt the balance in the EU's favor.

Europe has also recently embarked on efforts to forge a common defense policy and to acquire the military wherewithal to operate independently of U.S. forces. The European Union has appointed a high representative to oversee security policy, is establishing a policy planning unit, and is starting to lay the political groundwork for revamping its forces. It will be decades, if ever, before the EU becomes a unitary state, especially in light of its impending enlargement to the east, but as its resources grow and its decision-making becomes more centralized, power and influence will become more equally distributed between the two sides of the Atlantic.

American Reluctance

The rise of Europe and its leveling effect on the global distribution of power will occur gradually. Of more immediate impact will be a diminishing appetite for robust internationalism in the United States. Today's unipolar landscape is a function not just of America's preponderant resources but also of its willingness to use them to underwrite international order. Accordingly, should the will of the body politic to bear the costs and risks of international leadership decline, so too would America's position of global primacy.

On the face of it, the appetite of the American polity for internationalism has diminished little, if at all, since the collapse of the Soviet Union. Both the Bush and Clinton administrations have pursued ambitious and activist foreign policies. The United States has taken the lead in building an open international economy and promoting financial stability, and it has repeatedly deployed its forces to trouble spots around the globe. But American internationalism is now at a high-water mark and, for three compelling reasons, it will begin to dissipate in the years ahead.

First, the internationalism of the 1990s has been sustained by a period of unprecedented economic growth in the United States. A booming stock market, an expanding economy, and substantial budget surpluses have created a political atmosphere conducive to trade liberalization, expenditure on the military, and repeated engagement in solving problems in less fortunate parts of the globe.

Yet, even under these auspicious conditions, the internationalist agenda has shown signs of faltering. Congress, for example, has mustered only a fickle enthusiasm for free trade, approving NAFTA in 1993 and the Uruguay Round in 1994, but then denying President Clinton fast-track negotiating authority in 1997. Congress has also been skeptical of America's interventions in Bosnia and Kosovo, tolerating them, but little more. When the stock market sputters and growth stalls (and this is a matter of when, not if), these inward-looking currents will grow much stronger. The little support for free trade that still exists will dwindle. And such stinginess is likely to spread into the security realm, intensifying the domestic debate over burden sharing and calls within Congress for America's regional partners to shoulder increased defense responsibilities.

Second, although the United States has pursued a very activist defense policy during the 1990s, it has done so on the cheap. Clinton has repeatedly authorized the use of force in the Balkans and in the Middle East. But he has relied almost exclusively on air power, successfully avoiding the casualties likely to accompany the introduction of ground troops in combat. In Somalia, the one case in which U.S. ground troops suffered significant losses, Clinton ordered the withdrawal of U.S. forces from the operation. In NATO's campaign against Yugoslavia, week after week of bombing only intensified the humanitarian crisis and increased the likelihood of a southward spread of the conflict. Nevertheless, the United States blocked the use of ground forces and insisted that aircraft bomb from 15,000 feet to avoid being shot down.

Congress revolted despite these operational constraints minimizing the risks to U.S. personnel. A month into the campaign, the House of Representatives voted 249 to 180 to refuse funding for sending U.S. ground troops to Yugoslavia without congressional permission. Even a resolution that merely endorsed the bombing campaign failed to win approval (the vote was 213 to 213). In short, the American polity appears to have near zero tolerance for casualties. The illusion that internationalism can be maintained with no or minimal loss of life will likely come back to haunt the United States in the years ahead, limiting its ability to use force in the appropriate manner when necessary.

Third, generational change is likely to take a toll on the character and scope of U.S. engagement abroad. The younger Americans already rising to positions of influence in the public and private sectors have not lived through the formative experiences—the Second World War and the rebuilding of Europe—that serve as historical anchors of internationalism. Individuals schooled in the 1990s and now entering the work force will not even have first-hand experience of the Cold War. These Americans will not necessarily be isolationist, but they will certainly be less interested in and knowledgeable about foreign affairs than their older colleagues—a pattern already becoming apparent in the Congress. In the absence of a manifest threat to American national security, making the case for engagement and sacrifice abroad thus promises to grow increasingly difficult with time. Trend lines clearly point to a turning inward, to a nation tiring of carrying the burdens of global leadership.

Bad News and Good News

The bad news is that the global stability that unipolarity has engendered will be jeopardized as power becomes more equally distributed in the international system. The good news is that this structural change

will occur through different mechanisms than in the past, and therefore *may* be easier to manage peacefully.

The rising challenger is Europe, not a unitary state with hegemonic ambitions. Europe's aspirations will be moderated by the self-checking mechanisms inherent in the EU and by cultural and linguistic barriers to centralization. In addition, the United States is likely to react to a more independent Europe by stepping back and making room for an EU that appears ready to be more self-reliant and more muscular. Unlike reigning hegemons in the past, the United States will not fight to the finish to maintain its primacy and prevent its eclipse by a rising challenger. On the contrary, the United States will cede leadership willingly as its economy slows and it grows weary of being the security guarantor of last resort.

The prospect is thus not one of clashing titans, but of no titans at all. Regions long accustomed to relying on American resources and leadership to preserve the peace may well be left to fend for themselves. These are the main reasons that the challenge for American grand strategy as the next century opens will be to wean Europe and East Asia of their dependence on the United States and put in place arrangements that will prevent the return of competitive balancing and regional rivalries in the wake of an American retrenchment.

Europe on Its Own

It is fortunate that the near-term challenge to U.S. primacy will come from Europe. After decades of close cooperation, Europe and North America enjoy unprecedented levels of trust and reciprocity. European states have gone along with U.S. leadership not just because they have not had the power and influence to do otherwise; despite cavils, they also welcome the particular brand of international order sustained by the United States. A more equal distribution of power across the Atlantic will no doubt engender increased competition between a collective Europe and the United States. But such conflict is likely to be restricted to economic matters and muted by the mutual benefits reaped from high levels of trade and investment. Furthermore, the underlying coincidence of values between North America and Europe means that even when interests diverge, geopolitical rivalry is not likely to follow. Efforts to preserve an Atlantic consensus may well lead to a lowest common denominator and produce inaction (as has occurred repeatedly in the Balkans). But it is hard to imagine the United States and Europe engaging in militarized conflict.

In this sense, the key concern for the coming decade is not the emergence of balancing between Europe and the United States, but the reemergence of balancing and rivalries *within* a Europe no longer under American protection. The European Union is well on its way to erecting a regional order that can withstand the retraction of American power. Through a steady process of pooling sovereignty, Europe has nurtured a supranational character and identity that make integration irreversible. Nevertheless, guaranteeing a self-sustaining and coherent European polity requires that Europe and the United States together pursue three initiatives.

A Window of Opportunity

To begin, Europe must follow through with the initial steps it has taken to create a military establishment capable of carrying out major missions without the assistance of U.S. forces. The United States should be far more forthcoming in welcoming this initiative, and stop worrying that an independent European military would undercut the transatlantic security link by fueling calls in Congress for the withdrawal of U.S. troops. NATO will be in much better shape five years hence if Europe is carrying a fair load than if Congress continues to see a Europe free-riding on American soldiers. Far from expediting a U.S. departure from the continent, a serious European military will only increase the chances that a mature and balanced transatlantic partnership emerges and that America maintains a presence in Europe.

Europe now has a window of opportunity to make serious progress on the defense front. A number of factors afford this opening: British willingness to take the lead on forging a collective defense policy; recognition within the EU of Europe's excessive dependence on U.S. capability (made clear by the campaign against Yugoslavia); and the appointment of a new European Commission, with Romani Prodi as its president and Javier Solana as its high representative for security policy.

The top priorities for EU members include moving to all-volunteer forces so that defense expenditures can go toward buying capability and force-projection assets, not paying poorly trained conscripts. Europe's defense industry must be consolidated to improve economies of scale, and more funding should go toward research and development and improving the technological sophistication of weapons and intelligence systems. Europe must also make tough decisions about an appropriate division of labor among its member states if it is to build a balanced and capable force structure.

Promoting a stable peace in southeastern Europe is the second key piece of unfinished business for Europe and the United States. The task of halting ethnic conflict in the Balkans repeatedly paralyzed both NATO and the EU throughout the decade. The European enterprise would have been set back grievously had NATO failed to act in Bosnia and Kosovo. Now that the fighting has stopped, the international community must take advantage of the opportunity to construct a lasting peace. That goal ultimately means drawing the Balkans into the European Union. Rapprochement between Greece and Turkey and resolution of the Cyprus problem are no less important if Europe is to avoid being engulfed in persistent crises in its southeast. In its quest to help ensure that Europe does not again fall prey to national rivalries, the United States should make southeastern Europe a top regional priority.

Embracing Russia in a wider Europe is the third step needed to prevent the return of rivalries and shifting balances of power to the continent. Russia in the years ahead will gradually reassume its position as one of Europe's great powers. If Russia is included in the European enterprise, its resources and influence will likely be directed toward furthering continent-wide integration. If it is excluded from the European project, Russia will likely seek a coalition to balance against Europe. Indeed, the enlargement of NATO has already increased the likelihood of such balancing by raising the prospect that Russia's entire western flank will abut the Atlantic Alliance.

Instead of using NATO to protect against a threat that no longer exists, its members should use the organization as a vehicle for anchoring Russia in Europe.[4] The EU is the more appropriate vehicle for this task, but its enlargement is lagging way behind NATO's because of the institutional changes and financial costs entailed in adding new members. Furthermore, the integration of Russia into the Atlantic community, in part because of European resistance on cultural grounds, will require considerable American influence and leadership—assets that NATO provides. While it is still Europe's chief peacemaker and protector, the United States needs to ensure that Russia is included in Europe's historic process of pacification and integration.

East Asia Estranged

Preparing East Asia to rely less on American power is far more complicated and dangerous than the parallel task in Europe. The key difference is that European states took advantage of America's protective umbrella to pursue reconciliation, rapprochement, and an ambitious agenda of regional cooperation and integration. Europeans have accordingly succeeded in fashioning a regional order that is likely to withstand the retraction of American power. In contrast, states in East Asia have hidden behind America's presence, pursuing neither reconciliation nor regional integration. East Asia's major powers remain estranged.

The United States therefore faces a severe trade-off in East Asia between the balancing provoked by its predominant role in the region and the intraregional balancing that would ensue in the wake of an American retrenchment. America's sizable military presence in East Asia keeps the peace and checks regional rivalries. But it also alienates China and holds in place a polarized political landscape.

As China's economy and military capability grow, its efforts to balance against the United States could become more pronounced. Were the United States to back off from its role as regional arbiter and protector, relations with China would improve, but at the expense of regional stability. Japan and Korea would no doubt increase their own military capabilities, risking a regionwide arms race and spiraling tensions.

If the United States is to escape the horns of this dilemma, it must help repair the region's main cleavage and facilitate rapprochement between East Asia's two major powers: Japan and China. Just as reconciliation between France and Germany was the critical ingredient in building a stable zone of peace in Europe, Sino-Japanese rapprochement is the sine qua non of a self-sustaining regional order in East Asia.

Primary responsibility for improving Sino-Japanese ties lies with Japan. With an economy and political system much more developed than China's, Japan has far more latitude in exploring openings in the relationship. Japan can also take a major step forward by finally acknowledging and formally apologizing for its behavior during the Second World War. The United States can further this process by welcoming and helping to facilitate overtures between Tokyo and Beijing.

Washington should also help dislodge the inertia that pervades politics in Tokyo by making it clear to the Japanese that they cannot indefinitely rely on American guarantees to ensure their security. Japan therefore needs to take advantage of America's protective umbrella while it lasts, pursuing the policies of reconciliation and integration essential to constructing a regional security order resting on cooperation rather than deterrence.

If overtures from Tokyo succeed in reducing tensions between China and Japan, the United States would be able to play a less prominent role in the region, making possible an improvement in its own relations with China. As it buys time for Sino-Japanese rapprochement to get underway, Washington should avoid the rhetoric and policies that might induce China to intensify its efforts to balance against Japan and the United States. Talk of an impending Chinese military threat is both counterproductive and misguided; the Chinese military is nowhere near world-class.[5] The United States should also avoid provocative moves, such as deploying antimissile defenses in the Western Pacific theater or supporting a Taiwanese policy of moving toward formal independence. China can do its part to strengthen its relationship with the United States by containing saber-rattling over Taiwan, halting the export of weapons to

rogue states, and avoiding actions and rhetoric that could inflame territorial disputes in the region.

A Global Directorate

If my analysis is correct, the most dangerous consequence of a return to multipolarity is not balancing between North America, Europe, and East Asia, but the reemergence of national rivalries and competitive balancing within Europe and East Asia as American retrenchment proceeds. It is for this reason that American grand strategy should focus on facilitating regional integration in Europe and East Asia as a means of preparing both areas to assume far more responsibility for managing their own affairs.

The ultimate vision that should guide U.S. grand strategy is the construction of a concert-like directorate of the major powers in North America, Europe, and East Asia. These major powers would together manage developments and regulate relations both within and among their respective regions.

Mustering the political will and the foresight to pursue this vision will be a formidable task. The United States will need to begin ceding influence and autonomy to regions that have grown all too comfortable with American primacy. Neither American statesmen, long accustomed to calling the shots, nor statesmen in Europe and East Asia, long accustomed to passing the buck, will find the transition an easy one.

But it is far wiser and safer to get ahead of the curve and shape structural change by design, than to find unipolarity giving way to a chaotic multipolarity by default. It will take a decade, if not two, for a new international system to evolve. But the decisions taken by the first American administration of the twenty-first century will play a critical role in determining whether multipolarity reemerges peacefully or brings with it the competitive jockeying that in the past has so frequently led to great-power war.

Notes

1. See Robert Gilpin, *War and Change in World Politics* (Cambridge: Cambridge University Press, 1981); Paul M. Kennedy, *The Rise and Fall of the Great Powers* (New York: Random House, 1987); and Christopher Layne, "The Unipolar Illusion: Why New Great Powers Will Rise," *International Security*, vol. 17 (spring 1993).
2. William C. Wohlforth, "The Stability of a Unipolar World," *International Security*, vol. 24 (summer 1999).
3. On the concept of benign power, see Charles Kupchan, "After Pax Americana: Benign Power, Regional Integration, and the Sources of a Stable Multipolarity," *International Security*, vol. 23 (fall 1998).
4. See Charles Kupchan, "Rethinking Europe," *The National Interest*, no. 56 (summer 1999).
5. See Bates Gill and Michael O'Hanlon, "China's Hollow Military," *The National Interest*, no. 56 (summer 1999); and Gerald Segal, "Does China Matter?" *Foreign Affairs*, vol. 78 (September/October 1999).

Ham-Fisted Hegemon:
The Clinton Administration and Russia

"A United States-Russia policy that attempts to operate simultaneously on the basis of the attitudes of Secretary of State Madeleine Albright and Deputy Secretary of State Strobe Talbott cannot help but be incoherent . . . and profoundly out of touch with the realities of post-Soviet Russia."

The United States has made Russia a geopolitical offer that it can neither accept nor refuse: a subordinate role in an American-dominated Eurasian security system. Forced to choose between these contradictory responses, Russian policy toward the United States and the West lurches back and forth in a manner that often appears illogical and unpredictable but in fact largely corresponds to the dictates of the trap in which Russia finds itself. This by no means necessarily makes Russia a committed enemy of the United States, but it certainly makes it a highly unreliable collaborator on many important international issues.

Russia's dilemma, and the oscillations it produces, were strikingly demonstrated over Kosovo. The NATO operation caused genuine anger in Russia, which was reflected in often hysterical rhetoric about "NATO genocide." The desire of the Yeltsin regime (and elements of the armed forces) to be seen as defying NATO and playing an independent role was reflected in the dash of the 200 Russian paratroopers from Bosnia to Pristina, the capital of Kosovo, in the days immediately after the air war's end.

But Russian policy overall was also helpful to NATO. Russia did not supply Yugoslavia with new weaponry by sea. It moved a symbolic force to Kosovo, not its entire Bosnia contingent, and in the end agreed to NATO's terms for its deployment. Its diplomatic influence, through former Prime Minister Viktor Chernomyrdin—above all, Russia's agreement to the Group of Eight peace plan—was evidently key in persuading Yugoslav President Slobodan Milosevic that his regime was internationally isolated and that he had no choice but to surrender. This was tremendously valuable to NATO; most military analysts agree that the Serbs could have gone on fighting for several more months. In the end, Russia's behavior was more that of a discontented United States client-state than that of an enemy.

The Russian position is striking because Kosovo gave Moscow the opportunity to try to inflict great damage on NATO. A Russian government as nationalist and anti-Western as many American commentators allege would have encouraged Milosevic to fight on, which would have forced NATO to accept a compromise or launch a ground offensive that would have widened existing splits in the alliance. If United States forces had led such an operation (as they necessarily would have) and suffered casualties while most European members refused to take part, the resulting bitterness between the United States and Europe would have been extremely dangerous for NATO's future.

That the Yeltsin regime did not take this chance says a great deal about its unwillingness to challenge the West seriously even when given the opportunity. Of course, Russia's failure to react also reflected economic dependence on the West, in particular the United States administration's threat to vote against IMF lending. However, this would not have stopped a truly determined government in Moscow, since IMF money is mainly used to repay past loans from the IMF itself.

This vacillation in Russian policy toward the United States has been attributed by most American commentators to Russia's Soviet or indeed pre-Soviet imperial legacy and general geopolitical situation. Of course, there is an element of truth in this. Equally important, however, has been the effect on Russia of the Clinton administration's Russia policy, which embodies wildly incompatible views of the nature of Yeltsin's Russia, Russia's future, and the proper American approach to Russia.

American policymakers have been unable to decide whether the United States should be more afraid of Russian weakness

ANATOL LIEVEN *is a specialist on the former Soviet Union at the International Institute for Strategic Studies in London. His latest book,* Ukraine and Russia: A Fraternal Rivalry, *was published in June by the United States Institute of Peace. His* Chechnya: Tombstone of Russian Power *(New Haven, Conn.: Yale University Press) was published in a new paperback edition in July.*

Reprinted with permission from *Current History* magazine, October 1999, pp. 307-315. © 1999 by Current History, Inc.

or Russian strength; whether Russia is to be treated as a useful and important (although irritable and uncomfortable) subordinate like France, or a species of rogue state; and whether therefore United States policy should be directed toward gaining Russian cooperation or containing and weakening Russia. To put it another way, a United States.–Russia policy that attempts to operate simultaneously on the basis of the attitudes of Secretary of State Madeleine Albright and Deputy Secretary of State Strobe Talbott cannot help but be incoherent. Moreover, these opposing views of Russia are in their different ways profoundly ideological–and profoundly out of touch with the realities of post-Soviet Russia.

As a result, while the Clinton administration has given some financial aid (for example, to Russia's space program) and has made a number of mainly symbolic gestures of partnership with Russia (membership in the Group of Eight, the Russia-NATO Joint Council, and so on), its policy toward the former Soviet Union has developed into something close to one of "containment," as laid down by Albright's mentor, former Carter administration national security adviser Zbigniew Brzezinski, although it does not go nearly as far as Brzezinski would have liked.[1] Thus Strobe Talbott himself now speaks of NATO expansion to the Baltic states as inevitable. American policy is also dedicated to building up Ukraine as a buffer against Russia (a process admittedly made extremely difficult by Ukrainian domestic mismanagement and corruption, as well as by the opposition of most Ukrainians to this policy). The United States is also openly working to "rollback" Russian influence in the Caucasus and Central Asia, a point to which we will return.

These policies are not part of a consciously worked out and coherent anti-Russia strategy. The expansion of NATO is more related to domestic politics in the United States and the pressure of the East Europeans themselves than to any consideration of Russia's position. United States support for the expansion of Turkish influence in the Caucasus and Central Asia—reflected in dogged advocacy of a Turkish route for Caspian oil—also reflects Turkey's importance to the United States and Israel in the Middle East rather than simply hostility to Russia.

Nonetheless, these policies do indicate a deep underlying hostility to Russia in much of the American policymaking elite. This hatred may well be considered implacable, since it has survived the end of the cold war, the end of the Soviet Union, the democratic euphoria of the early Yeltsin years, and the collapse of Russian economic and military power. It is fueled by the traditionally anti-Russian attitudes of various former Russian subject nations whose descendants are now United States citizens.

In an age when American foreign policy is increasingly a reflection of internal politics and electoral spending, Russia's lack of a consistent lobby in Washington is a crushing disadvantage. China, for example, also has implacable enemies, but thanks to successful economic reform it maintains the support of a strong United States business lobby. The only similar asset

held by Russia in Washington is indirect: the hostility of the Greek and Armenian lobbies to Turkey, which is even more steady and insistent than the Russophobes', and which does much to complicate United States policy in the Caucasus and eastern Mediterranean.

An interesting example of the Russophobe school among the policymaking elite (like Brzezinski, from the Democratic side of the party divide) is General William Odom—interesting because unlike many of the media Russia-haters, Odom is genuinely knowledgeable about aspects of Russia, especially the military. Yet for Odom, whenever Russian and United States interests clash, Russia is automatically to blame. He summarizes the whole of Russian history as follows: "The lesson is clear: liberalism in Russia prospers only after major defeats, and once the regime has regained its self-confidence and achieved détente with the West, Russia returns to domestic repression and imperialism."[2]

This historicism—bordering on racism—of summing up hundreds of years of immensely varied national history in this way should be apparent. Similarly, the notion that a United States that makes an ally of a dictator like Uzbekistan's Islam Karimov is by definition ethically in the right is morally and intellectually ridiculous. There is nothing necessarily wrong with a tough-minded foreign policy, but continually dressing it in moralizing rhetoric is nauseating.

It may be argued that this hatred of Russia is counterbalanced by the Russophilia of Americans like Strobe Talbott. But unlike Russophobia, the sympathy of these observers for Russia is not for Russia as a nation but for their own *idea* of Russia as a country "liberating itself from communism" and making "the transition to democracy and the free market."

These hopes have been reflected in the strong support the Clinton administration has given to the regime of Boris Yeltsin, which is very different from support for Russia. Two hundred years from now, a historian looking at the geopolitical picture at the end of the twentieth century may well attribute this policy to an intelligent and cynical desire to ensure that Russia was ruled by a weak and corrupt regime, one highly dependent on the West for aid: in other words, a policy to weaken Russia without running the risk of actually destroying it.

The truth, as we know, is much more complicated. Partly out of a misguided but genuine fear of a return of communism, not only the Clinton administration but most of the Western media and academic community genuinely came to hold a simplistic view of contemporary Russia: of good "democrats" and "young reformers" pitted against the assorted forces of evil. They believed this long after it should have become apparent that the Yeltsin regime itself had become the single greatest obstacle to a Russian recovery.[3]

In September 1999, with Yeltsin clearly considering the imposition of authoritarian rule and the cancellation of the June 2000 presidential elections, the fruits of this policy are turning

[1] See Zbigniew Brzezinski, *The Grand Chessboard: American Primacy and Its Geostrategic Imperatives* (New York: Basic Books, 1997).

[2] William Odom, "Russia's Several Seats at the Table," *International Affairs,* vol. 74, no. 4 (1998).
[3] See Dimitri K. Simes, "Russia's Crisis, America's Complicity," in *The National Interest,* Winter 1998–1999.

very bitter indeed. The risk is essentially that blind adherence to the policy of the past eight years will lead the Clinton administration into a repeat of October 1993, when it demonized the opposition and supported Yeltsin in his destruction of the Russian parliament. This time, however, the opposition is much stronger (and much more centrist), and Yeltsin's chances of success are much lower. The result would probably be a new Russian regime strongly resentful of the United States.

Already, not much is left of past American liberal hopes for Russia; and when these are disappointed, little sympathy for the country will remain. Furthermore, any United States official like Talbott accused of being pro-Russian is forced to prove the opposite (this helps explain Talbott's strong personal

> *America's frequent insistence that its national record is spotless and its national interests overarching and invariably moral is beginning to cause real anger.*

support for NATO membership for the Baltic states).

The element of deep-rooted instinctive hostility is even stronger on the Russian side—though as so often in the poorer parts of the world, and especially in those countries with a great past, it is counterbalanced by admiration for American wealth and American popular culture. The antagonism on the American side, however, may be more dangerous simply because most Americans are unaware of it. American officials and "experts" are genuinely surprised and angered by the hostility and "ingratitude" of Russia's response to United States policy. They are unable to see that what they are presenting to Russia is really an "offer" only in the sense immortalized by Don Vito Corleone in *The Godfather*. The terms of the deal that has been pressed on Moscow in the 1990s simply are not in Russia's national interest, if only because they do not commit the United States to Russia's defense. This is true not only of Yeltsin's Russia, but of any Russia, however led and constituted.

This does not mean that the United States should not press Russia to bow to American wishes and interests on a range of issues; a measure of ruthlessness will always have a place in the conduct of international affairs. But recognition that other countries have legitimately differing interests—the genuine recognition, not the lip service paid by United States officials—leads to certain conclusions. One is that every country has a hierarchy of interests. The whole trick of diplomacy—even hegemonic diplomacy—is to sacrifice lesser interests for the sake of greater ones.

The American public finds it difficult to argue coldly and coherently about the national interest, and the division of powers between executive and Congress makes it difficult to adhere

to a policy when it is opposed by powerful domestic lobbies. As a result, a hierarchy of interests has not been worked out regarding policy toward Russia. For example, if the United States could decide that what matters most is Russian cooperation against the proliferation of weapons of mass destruction, then Washington could try to gain this by abandoning NATO enlargement to the Baltic states (and instead guarantee their security though regional treaties).

A country that simply seeks to gain acceptance of all its interests is not engaged in diplomacy but bullying, and the response will be not a desire for compromise, but anger and resistance. The anger may be impotent and the resistance ineffective, but the portents for the long term will not be good.

The recognition that other countries have interests also tends to diminish hypocrisy, which obviously has a traditional and necessary role in international affairs, as does a certain forgetfulness of one's own national past. While too long and intense a contemplation of past sins leads to paralysis, such as has afflicted Germany for example, America's frequent insistence that its national record is spotless and its national interests overarching and invariably moral is beginning to cause real anger, not only in states such as Russia but also among United States allies. Successful hegemony requires military and economic strength and the willingness to employ it, but it is also helped by the occasional spell of good manners and self-awareness.

RUSSIA CONSTRAINED

But if for Russia full subordination to United States hegemony is senseless, outright revolt is hopeless. Since its defeat in Chechnya, Russia has been revealed to be militarily too weak even to intimidate most of its smaller neighbors, let alone the West. In the north Caucasus, the Russian republic of Dagestan appears to be slipping from Moscow's grasp as a result of Chechen guerrilla infiltration and Moscow's inability to subsidize the Dagestani government adequately. And as Kosovo demonstrated, Soviet-era military technology is no match for United States technological superiority.

The Communists and ultranationalists in Moscow may play with the idea of an alliance of "rogue states" against the United States, but such a league would recall the old saw about the Non-Aligned Movement: "ten drowning men holding on to each other." In Europe, Russia has no secure allies, with the potential exception of Greece. The one alliance that could threaten serious harm to the United States would be between Russia and China, and would involve an exchange of Russian military technology for Chinese consumer goods. These two states already cooperate diplomatically against American hegemony, especially at the UN Security Council—although this cooperation is of little significance since the United States increasingly ignores that body.

A full anti-American, Sino-Russian alliance, however, is far off. China's prospects for economic growth and prosperity are critically dependent on access to the American market, which vastly outweighs any possible economic advantages of links with Russia. And for Moscow the West, not China, is both the crucial market of Russia's exports of raw materials and the source of outside investment; an alliance that led to official United States hostility to Russia would foreclose any serious foreign investment in Russia.[4]

For Russia and China, an economic reorientation toward each other would require a fundamental restructuring of their domestic economies involving much greater state control, autarky, and the abandonment of mass prosperity in favor of national mobilization. The Russian state is simply no longer capable of such a transformation, nor, most probably, is China;

> *The United States essentially demands from Russia subjection and obedience without providing added defense and security.*

the Chinese people are reconciled to Communist rule precisely because of rising prosperity. An attempt to replace this with a program of nationalist austerity would almost certainly cause an explosion of public discontent.

Russia is also aware that, however infuriating and dangerous American policies may be, the United States does not have any potential claim on Russian territory, whereas the treaties of Argun and Peking, by which Russia acquired hundreds of thousands of square miles of Chinese territory north of the Amur River and east of the Ussuri River, are the last of the nineteenth-century "unequal treaties" to remain in force. Thus, if Russia were to become a junior partner in a Chinese-led anti-American alliance, it would be humiliating and dangerous. In the current circumstances, it would take exceptional foolishness on the part of Washington to drive Moscow and Beijing fully together.

Such an alliance is not impossible: some combination of NATO enlargement to the Baltic, war in the former Soviet Union, a formal Taiwanese declaration of independence, or a reunification of Korea on anti-Chinese terms would do the trick. This explains why those geopolitical thinkers most obsessed with containing or even destroying Russia, such as Brzezinski and former United States Secretary of State Henry Kissinger, tend to take a remarkably benign view of China, and oppose an American policy of containing Beijing.

A measure of Russian "cooperation" with the United States is not only dictated by a sober and patriotic assessment of Russian interests and Russian weakness. It is also implicit in

the nature of the contemporary Russian state, economy, and society, and above all in the composition and interests of Russia's ruling elites, interests now thoroughly tied to the Western economy and Western culture—not by productive economic relationships, but by the export of Russia's raw materials and investment of the proceeds in Western bank accounts, property, and luxury goods. Russia's elites therefore are loath to endanger their interests by allowing Russia to engage in a major clash with the West.

NOTHING WILL COME OF NOTHING

Even a regime as indifferent to Russian national interests as Yeltsin's cannot simply accept American terms for relations between the two countries, an attitude likely to be held by its successors. This refusal is partly because of nationalist feeling, but above all because the United States essentially demands from Russia subjection and obedience without providing added defense and security. Even Don Vito Corleone wouldn't have made an offer like that—he wouldn't have been so stupid. Any stable hegemonic system, whether feudal, geopolitical, or mafialike, depends on a reciprocal relationship in which the hegemon offers protection and advancement in return for service.

The United States is offering Russia a relationship in which Moscow is essentially bound by many of the constraints on its international behavior expected by members and would-be members of NATO without receiving NATO-style security guarantees in return. This means acceptance of NATO expansion to include those countries Washington decides shall become members; acquiescence to United States policy in Kosovo and Bosnia; acceptance of United States abrogation of the 1972 Anti-Ballistic Missile Treaty, thereby greatly diminishing the effectiveness of Russia's nuclear deterrent; acceptance of United States terms governing relations with Iran, Iraq, North Korea, and other American-declared rogue states, even when this means considerable trade losses for Russia; severe limits on Russia's arms trade, sometimes to the direct benefit of United States firms; acceptance of the United States as sole "mediator" in the Middle East peace process and as protector of Israel and dictator of terms to Moscow's former Arab allies; acceptance of United States decisions concerning various aspects of trade with other states; and acquiescence to a growing role for the United States and American protégés in other states of the former Soviet Union on terms set by the United States.

Finally, of course, it means a complete abandonment of the former Soviet role in Central America, Africa, and Southeast Asia. Herein lies part of the key to the utterly different perceptions by Americans and Russians of what ought to be Russia's international role. Americans frequently attribute Russian policies that displease them to "wounded pride," an immature and irrational refusal to come to terms with the reality of Russia's diminished powers (similar motives are attributed to inconvenient French Gaullist policies when these clash with American wishes). It is true that in the early 1990s the Russian expectation of the future relationship with the United States was one of equality, and it is true that it would be absurd to

---

[4] The United States and its allies have used the IMF as an instrument to gain Russian compliance with Western policies—most notably over Kosovo. An intelligent, strong, and determined Russian government might sensibly throw the IMF and its clapped-out nostrums overboard and pursue a program of protectionism and moderate inflationary spending modeled on the policies of Russian imperial Finance Minister Sergei Witte (and indeed on those of the nineteenth-century United States), but it could not possibly hope to succeed without massive foreign investment.

pretend that such equality is now possible, given the gross inequality in the two countries' power. Yet, for some time before the Soviet Union collapsed, Moscow under Soviet President Mikhail Gorbachev had already stopped trying to insist on an equal global role with the United States, and certainly Yeltsin's regime has never aspired to this. The last shadow of the old Soviet world policy is in the Middle East, and even this reflects far more the traditional commitments and hopes of old Soviet practitioners like former Prime Minister Yevgeny Primakov, and not those of the new Russian elite and the new Russian diplomacy. Where Russians are agreed is that Russian wishes should be respected in areas of vital interest to Russia.

But American involvement in these areas is being conducted according to the basic principle that American wishes ought to prevail over Russian desires. Clearly some of these wishes—the suppression of ethnic cleansing in Kosovo, the discouragement of nuclear proliferation—are in the wider interests of humanity in a way that most Russian policies are not. Also United States hegemony in general probably is "on the whole—and it is on the whole that such things must be judged—a beneficial and a kindly influence" (as Churchill once said of the British Empire), and that when American hegemony eventually vanishes, Russia will find itself in a harsher and more dangerous world.

Nonetheless, we can hardly expect Russians today to accept this hegemony, for except in the field of nuclear proliferation, Russia receives no direct added security in return for all the retreats and concessions it has made. And no nation on earth—the United States most emphatically included—would willingly agree to sacrifice its interests to those of humanity on terms dictated by another power in its own interests.

To understand the depth of Russian anger at recent American policies, it is important to remember that Russians believe they have already made an immense sacrifice in the name of general human interests, a new, civilized, and humane world order, and a "common European home." This sacrifice was called the abandonment of the Soviet bloc and the Soviet Union itself, a dissolution that was astonishingly peaceful when viewed against the expectations of most analysts and the experience of other European empires.

This Russian perception of what happened and why embodies considerable hypocrisy and self-deception. Nonetheless, it is not entirely false. The international behavior of Mikhail Gorbachev in particular is incomprehensible unless allowance is made for a measure of genuine idealism and faith in Western promises.

Thus, as was noted, Russia suffers many of the limitations on behavior dictated by membership in NATO or the European Union without the advantages of membership. Membership in the EU is impossible for the foreseeable future, if ever. The Russian economy is far too weak, chaotic, and criminalized to start on the path of European integration, and even if it were far stronger, Russia's size and history would make it wholly unfit to be an EU member.

The suggestion of future NATO membership (which former Defense Secretary William Perry used to wave about, to intense Russian irritation) is if anything even more grotesque.

In only two circumstances could this happen, neither of which is at all likely. One is if NATO were to abolish Article 5 (collective defense) and become a loose consultative body like the Organization for Security and Cooperation in Europe (OSCE), which would be equivalent to abolition. The second is if China were to become a clear, present, and serious danger to the vital interests of Russia, the United States, and Europe. But even if this were to occur, it is extremely unlikely that the United States would provide convincing guarantees of Russia's borders in Asia.[5]

"ROLLING BACK RUSSIAN INFLUENCE"

Security guarantees aside, the two areas in which United States policies toward Russia constitute a danger to Russia's security—not nearly as great as nationalist and communist Russians believe, but enough to give Russians genuine cause for concern— are the expansion of NATO and American ambitions in the Caucasus and Central Asia.

The bitter Russian reaction to NATO stems partly from a belief that the alliance has betrayed promises made when the Soviet government allowed the revolutions in Eastern Europe, and even more important, agreed to the reunification of Germany; these included a clear and implicit promise not to expand NATO to include the former Soviet bloc in Eastern Europe. If this were all, however, then Russia would have grumblingly agreed to enlargement, as indeed it has done with the expansion into Central Europe that took place last year with the accession of Poland, the Czech Republic, and Hungary.

The real danger from Russia's point of view is that NATO's eastward expansion will lead it to become embroiled in post-Soviet disputes, and on the side opposite Russia. Moscow might then find itself in a position where it could not help fighting and yet could not hope to win. This, rather than historical sympathy for the Serbs (which is felt by only a relatively small minority of Russians) explains the alarm and anger in Russia at the Kosovo operation. NATO had shown its willingness to intervene in other countries' conflicts, and the overwhelming technological superiority of American arms was made clear.

Potential conflicts on Russia's borders abound, although none of them (with the possible exception of the Georgian republic of Abkhazia) looks explosive in the short term. Although the chances of the United States becoming involved in these conflicts are small, they cannot be ignored: Azerbaijan, Georgia, and Moldova have suggested NATO's role in Kosovo as a possible model for NATO intervention in their own disputes with separatist regions.

The original scenario for the United States—Ukrainian "Sea Breeze" joint exercise of August 1997 was precisely that of the dispatch of United States troops to help Ukraine defeat a

---

[5] NATO officials still on occasion discuss possible future Russian membership in the alliance, but it is difficult to believe they take themselves seriously. See, for example, John Borawski, "NATO in the 21st Century: Into the Slipstream," in *Security Dialogue*, December 1998.

regional (that is, Crimean Russian) rebellion backed by a neighboring power (that is, Russia). This scenario was changed to a "humanitarian mission" after vehement protests by Russia and the Crimean Russian population—and, a realization in Washington of the great danger (not to mention the ethical issue) of making this kind of implicit promise without a real commitment to fulfill it. It is hardly surprising that Sea Breeze left a legacy of strong distrust in Moscow.

Russians thus have reason to fear that, in all but one case, they or the side they back in a dispute would not get a fair hearing in Washington—and that they would automatically be treated as the enemy. The exception is the Armenian-Azerbaijani conflict over the Azerbaijani enclave of Nagorno-Karabakh, where Russia's role in support of Armenia has indirectly been defended by the Armenian lobby in the United States. In all other regions of the former Soviet Union, United States policy is now directed to rolling back Russian influence.

This trend is openly acknowledged by American diplomats, and has been made explicit by United States sponsorship of the GUAM consultative grouping of Georgia, Ukraine, Azerbaijan, and Moldova, which informally links the members of the Commonwealth of Independent States whose interests are most opposed to those of Russia. GUAM is intended to function as a kind of counter-CIS, and has contributed to hastening the demise of that already moribund institution. American backing for GUAM became clearer than ever when the agreement by which Uzbekistan joined the group (making it GUAM) was signed in Washington in April 1999, a date deliberately chosen to coincide with NATO's fiftieth-anniversary summit in the same city.

WHICH THREAT FROM THE SOUTH?

Most worrying for Russia is American support for increased Turkish influence in the region, demonstrated by Washington's advocacy of an oil pipeline from Azerbaijan to the Turkish Mediterranean port of Ceyhan long after most Western (and United States) oil companies had decided that this route was economically unviable. American support for this option stems chiefly from Turkey's role as a key ally of the United States and Israel in the Middle East. United States policy was originally also motivated by a desire to keep a new main route for Azerbaijani oil exports out of Russia's hands. However, because of developments in Chechnya and Dagestan, a Russian route is simply no longer feasible, so United States support for Ceyhan now seems motivated more by a desire to favor Turkey for geopolitical reasons.

Russian fears of Turkey have their roots in the long history of conflict between the two nations. These concerns greatly increased with the appalling realization that hopelessly outnumbered Russian conventional forces in the Caucasus and Black Sea regions are now inferior to those of Turkey. In the event of a Turkish attack, the few thousand Russian troops in Armenia—stationed under a bilateral agreement intended to provide Armenia security against Turkey—would be overrun in a matter of hours.

Such an attack is hardly in the cards at present; Turkish policy in the Caucasus in recent years has been cautious. This restraint is especially commendable given Turkish sympathy for the Azeris (who are ethnically very close to the Turks) and the immense provocation to this feeling demonstrated by the Armenians during their successful offensives against Azerbaijan from 1991 to 1994, when nearly one-fifth of Azerbaijan's territory was captured and up to 1 million Azeris became refugees. It is also true that Armenia's victory was partly the result of Russian military aid, although the extent of this has never been clear (and most observers on the ground, myself included, attributed Armenian success chiefly to greater discipline and better morale).

Turkish restraint may not hold indefinitely if Russian military power continues to weaken and if violence resumes between Armenia and Azerbaijan. The presence in the Turkish ruling coalition of the Nationalist Action Party—a staunch advocate of stronger support for Azerbaijan against Armenia—can give little comfort to Russia or indeed most of Turkey's other neighbors. Over the past year, secure in the knowledge of United States and Israeli backing, the Turkish military has felt able to threaten Syria militarily to end Syrian support for the Kurdistan Workers Party and may be planning something similar against Iran.

The Crimea may also emerge as a Turkish-Russian flashpoint that could involve the United States. Crimean Tatars have returned, impoverished and embittered, to their ancestral homeland from their long Soviet-era exile in Central Asia, and now make up some 10 percent of the population of this contested Ukrainian peninsula. The Crimean Tatars resent the Russian (and Ukrainian) settlers who occupy their former homes, and also feel betrayed by the Ukrainian government, which has failed both to help them financially and to guarantee their political and constitutional position. The possibility of ethnic trouble between them and the Crimea's Slavic majority is a real one—and since they have close links to Turkey (which provides them with crucial financial support), Ankara could well become drawn in against its will.

United States policy in the Caucasus and Central Asia suggests that the Clinton administration has adopted a modified version of the program advocated by Henry Kissinger, Zbigniew Brzezinski, and others of containing and isolating Russia by creating a ring of buffer states around its borders.[6] In these circumstances, it would be illogical for Russia to accept "partnership" with the United States—a euphemism for full acceptance of United States domination of Russia's foreign policies.

Consider Russia's "Founding Charter" of 1998 with NATO—a face-saving device intended to limit Yeltsin's humiliation at having to agree to NATO expansion—that stipulates cooperation against "threats from the south." In an overwhelmingly empty document, this is the most ridiculous phrase of all. Admittedly, Russia and the West share a common fear of Sunni Islamist radicalism, and this threat to Russia has been underlined by the increasing destabilization of Dagestan by radical Islamist attacks from Chechnya. However, as far as Shia Iran, the

---

[6] See for example Zbigniew Brzezinski, Brent Scowcroft, and Richard Murphy, "Differentiated Containment," *Foreign Affairs,* May–June 1997.

West's other perceived threat from the Muslim world, is concerned, Russia regards Tehran not as a menace but as an important ally against radical Sunni Islam in Afghanistan and, even more important, against Turkey. How can there be NATO-Russian cooperation against "threats from the south" when one of the greatest threats to Russia comes from Turkey—a NATO ally?

FORGET RUSSIA?

If United States policy makes full Russian cooperation impossible, should the United States worry about this, given that a full Russian-Chinese alliance also appears unlikely at the moment? Does the prevailing United States attitude toward Russia, of hostility mixed with contemptuous indifference, not make a certain amount of sense, since Russia seems incapable of seriously harming American interests?

Although a certain geopolitical realism may justify this approach, the United States would do well to try to preserve working relations with Russia, even if this means modifying some current American goals. First, the United States cannot always rely on being able to fight its wars by means of aircraft at 15,000 feet. If United States troops become involved in another conflict on the ground—even a so-called low-intensity conflict—then a denial of weapon supplies to the other side will be of crucial importance. This is especially true given American sensitivity to casualties and the large number of deaths that can be caused in certain circumstances even by poorly equipped adversaries. Since Russia is by far the largest potential source of weaponry for countries outside the Western bloc, the need to conciliate Russia will then be all too obvious.

In Kosovo itself, NATO is now engaged in a mission the long-term official goal of which is impossible: the creation of a multiethnic state in which Albanians and Serbs will live in harmony. In a not-too-distant future, NATO troops either must rule Kosovo against the explicit wishes of the Albanian majority, or withdraw and let Albanians and Serbs fight it out. The future behavior of Serbia, Russia's influence on Serbia, and Russia's willingness (or not) to supply Serbia with weapons will all be of great importance.

Second, the policy of rolling back Russian influence and replacing it with that of the United States risks drawing America into a local conflict in the former Soviet Union or touching off a war between Turkey and Russia. This is of course not an American planner's scenario, but none of the states concerned can necessarily control the situation on the ground, especially in the Caucasus. It is also worth pointing out that if—as seems all too likely in Dagestan—the decline of Russian power leads to the ascendancy of radical Islam, it will certainly not be to America's advantage.

Finally, there is the question of the spread of technology and materials of mass destruction from Russia because of state policy or—much more probably—state weakness and the poverty and corruption of the armed forces and the scientific community. Terrorist attacks using nuclear, chemical, or biological weapons are the only way enemies of the United States can (potentially at least) strike directly at America itself.

If such an attack were to occur, the entire direction of United States foreign policy would change instantly. Issues that have been portrayed as "vital" United States interests—NATO expansion, Caspian oil—would be revealed as secondary compared to the critical issue of gaining Russian friendship and support against the proliferation of this threat. The catastrophic decline of Russia in the 1990s means that, in terms of a positive contribution to world developments, Russia and the rest of the former Soviet Union are now irrelevant. The region retains its importance only as a source of dangers, which the United States administration must diminish and not fuel.

"Muslims make up one-sixth the world's population, and for this reason alone no major government can afford to ignore the world of Islam, least of all the American government in its moment of undisputed power. . . .A more energetic promotion of central United States foreign policy themes—especially freedom, democracy, and human rights—would undermine Muslim critics of American policy and underscore that the future holds great opportunity for continued American cooperation with the Muslim world, rather than conflict."

Rethinking United States Policy toward the Muslim World

AUGUSTUS RICHARD NORTON

American and British warplanes bombarded Iraq in mid-December, just days before Ramadan, in a transparent but futile effort to foment dissension in the ranks of Iraq's military. State-of-the-art missiles once again proved to be poor implements for loosening the Iraqi president's grip on power. Saddam Hussein crowed victory and exploited the moment to proclaim an end to Iraqi cooperation with United Nations weapons inspectors. And despite strenuous denials by the Clinton White House and the Pentagon, suspicions linger that the eve-of-impeachment attack was a diversionary ploy.

If the American and British publics were equivocal, many Muslim voices were deeply cynical about Washington's agenda. While the air campaign was under way, Muslims protested the attacks. A mob sacked American Ambassador Ryan Crocker's residence in Damascus. Throughout South Asia and the Middle East, demonstrators rallied to express their anger at the victimization of the Iraqi people—but not solidarity with the Iraqi dictator. United States officials have argued that the sanctions regime put in place by the UN Security Council persists because of Saddam Hussein's obstructionism, but in the court of Muslim public opinion this is a hard argument to sustain. Reports of widespread malnutrition, soaring infant mortality rates, and general misery in Iraq have been sporadically published in the United States, but they are a staple of news reporting in the Muslim world.

Secretary of State Madeleine Albright has said (as have other former and current senior officials) that the United States will not permit the lifting of sanctions as long as Saddam

Hussein rules in Baghdad, which has only deepened Muslim cynicism about the sanctions' purpose. Underlying the suspicion of American motives is a widespread perception that the West, exemplified by the United States, applies a double standard when the rights of Muslims are threatened, whether in Bosnia, Somalia, Palestine, or Iraq. Muslims know that Saddam Hussein is no paragon of Islamic virtue and few people in the Muslim world have been fooled by his opportunism (which has included the addition, in 1990, of the *shahada,* the Muslim's profession of faith, that "There is no God except Allah, and Mohammed is the messenger of Allah" to the Iraqi flag).

THE MYTH OF MONOLITHIC ISLAM

Clichés about Muslims and their politics have taken on the standing of truisms, but virtually none—including the old standby that Muslims refuse to accept any distinction between the realm of religion and the realm of politics—stands up to serious reflection. Much Western commentary on the Muslim world draws heavily on classical writings as well as the rhetoric and ideology of contemporary Islamist movements. As a result, little attention is paid to the overwhelming majority of Muslims who do not support or join Islamist movements and who do not favor any single interpretation of Islam and its dictates.[1]

The rigidity or flexibility of Islam as practiced varies widely by social class, region, and political system. Muslims reside

---

[1] Nor has sufficient attention been paid to the reformist writings of Abdel Karem Sarroush in Iran, Fethullah Gullen in Turkey, Egypt's Hassan Hanafi, and Mohammed Shahrour in Syria, which are growing dramatically in readership, especially among the Muslim middle class. Each of these innovative thinkers emphasizes themes of tolerance and pluralism. Shahrour's book, *Al-Kitaab wa Quran* (The Book and the Koran), in which he argues that Islam must be interpreted as though the Koran were revealed yesterday, reflects a deep knowledge of Islam while espousing what amounts to a secular system of politics. Since its publication in 1990, *Al-Kitaab wa Quran* has been reprinted in 13 different Arabic language editions.

AUGUSTUS RICHARD NORTON, *a professor of anthropology and international relations at Boston University, is a* Current History *contributing editor. In 1997–1998 he headed the Council on Foreign Relations study group on the United States and the Muslim world.*

in a world of independent states, and these states are riven by competing interests on the international scene as well as by the pressures of domestic cultural diversity.

United States policymakers insist—sensibly—that the complexity of the Muslim world bedevils any attempt to create a grand strategy for dealing with it. American diplomats aptly note that the United States has no "one size fits all" policy for the Muslim world and that the United States conducts foreign policy with governments, not with religious institutions.

Even so, the "challenge" of Islam has been a persistent preoccupation for policymakers since the fall of the shah of Iran in 1979. While the political and social diversity of the Muslim world is hardly in debate, the fact remains that the United States is frequently viewed with skepticism, if not enmity, in the Muslim world. For their part, American officials have been at pains to emphasize that the United States government does not view Islam or Muslims in adversarial terms, except when Mulsims engage in terrorism or seek to undermine United States objectives, such as the successful shepherding of the peace process in the Middle East. America does have implacable foes in the Muslim world, but it would be dishonest to deny that in the United States there is a tendency to use the brush of extremism to paint those who simply oppose its policies, especially in the Middle East.

America's moment of global power and the spread of American economic culture offer an irresistible opportunity for Muslim politicians to mobilize support to thwart American hegemony and preserve the authenticity of Muslim societies. Thus, faced with the collapse of the Malaysian currency in 1998, Prime Minister Mahathir Mohamad assailed American influence in the International Monetary Fund as well as the chicanery of global financiers—notably George Soros, whose manipulation of the currency market, Mahathir asserted, was the root of Malaysia's ills. Mahathir's accusations have not, however, stifled the domestic dissent that was enlivened when he ordered the arrest of Anwar Ibrahim, the free market-oriented deputy prime minister, on charges of sodomy and corruption in September.

Not surprisingly, many Muslims aspire to surmount the divisiveness that afflicts humanity while simultaneously insulating themselves from the globalization of Western culture. Hassan Hanafi, a distinguished Egyptian Islamic scholar, describes globalization as the "new colonialism." Hanafi is deeply aware that globalization is not without its benefits, but like many other thoughtful Muslims he is committed to sustaining the "specificity" or uniqueness of his society. The puzzle is how to reap the benefits of the global marketplace without sacrificing a country's values on the altar of free market capitalism. There is no more a single "Islamic" solution to this dilemma than there is a Hindu or Christian one.

The world community of Muslims (the *ummah*) is an abstraction, not a coherent political force. In this sense, there is

no single Muslim world in which more than 1 billion Muslims make their home. Nonetheless, when Western governments are palpably insensitive to the suffering of Muslims, a momentary consensus can be catalyzed. But episodes in which anti-Western fury bubbles to the surface are rare, not least because Muslims states are often divided among themselves. Of course, there are small, if notorious, Islamist groups—such as the cabal led by Osama Bin Laden—that are ideologically committed to vanquishing Western influence from the Islamic world. Bin Laden has found sanctuary in Afghanistan, where the ruling Taliban enforce a draconian caricature of Islam that has been widely condemned by Muslims—including the Iranian government—as "extremist." (It is instructive to note the cooperation of leading Muslim states, following the bombings of the American embassies in Nairobi and Dar es Salaam, in apprehending suspected perpetrators for trial in the United States.)

> The source of the dissonance between official Washington and the Muslim world resides in the Middle East, where only 25 percent of all Muslims live.

ON A COLLISON COURSE?

Serious reflection on the realities of contemporary Muslim societies yields a clear picture of diversity and competition, rather than anything remotely resembling an Islamic behemoth, which is the image that drives Harvard University professor Samuel P. Huntington's "Clash of Civilizations" model. Fortunately, the idea that the West is destined to clash with Islam has found little support in the American foreign policymaking establishment.

In an important speech to the Jordanian parliament in 1994, President Bill Clinton strenuously repudiated the clash of civilizations thesis, noting that "there are those who insist that . . . there are impassable religious and other obstacles to harmony; that our beliefs and our cultures must somehow inevitably clash . . .America refuses to accept that our civilizations must collide." Other senior officials have followed suit. Notwithstanding such stunning high-level repudiation, the idea of an Islamic phalanx has proven remarkably durable, especially to members of the Western military establishment in the confusion of the post-cold war era. Willy Claes, then the secretary general of NATO, embraced the thesis in the mid-1990s when he pointed to the Islamic challenge as the major threat confronting the West (that is, NATO).

Despite official denials from Washington, even moderate Muslim intellectuals believe that the Huntington thesis defines United States policy. In the course of a series of meetings sponsored by the Council on Foreign Relations in 1997 and early 1998, one participant after another from the Muslim world voiced this view. At the same time, radical Islamic thinkers find the idea of Islam as a civilization in confrontation with the West congenial. The popular Turkish Islamist writer Mustapha Ozel has written extensively on the theme of the Islamic world as a great culture, along with China, Germany, India, Russia, and the (albeit declining) United States. Ozel is unabashed in his view of the United States as an adversary of Islam.

The source of the dissonance between official Washington and the Muslim world resides in the Middle East, where only 25 percent of all Muslims live. It is there that the contradictions of United States foreign policy appear most vividly. As the site for Islam's three holiest cities—Mecca, Medina, and Jerusalem—little happens in the region that is not magnified in global media. If the United States is prepared to subordinate the rights of Muslims to the flow of cheap oil from the Persian Gulf or to pursue a policy that is effectively blind to Israeli misbehavior, as many Muslim writers allege, it is frequently only a short leap to argue that the United States is anti-Islam. Equally important, there is no doubt that American foreign policy does adopt a separate standard for the Middle East when it comes to the espousal of values such as democracy and human rights.

THE DOUBLE STANDARD

The treatment of the Middle East as a special case becomes clear when contrasted with the American approach to Indonesia and Malaysia, both major Muslim states. Even veteran diplomats have an especially hard time seeing Indonesia as a Muslim country, even though it is home to 185 million Muslims—which is more than the Muslim populations of all the Arab countries combined. In general, American diplomats simply do not count religion as a significant factor in formulating policy for either country. No doubt this nonchalance about Islam in Southeast Asia partially reflects a lower profile of religion in public life, but it also is a measure of the degree to which America's relations with the region's states reflect economic interests rather than the dictates of domestic politics in America. The contrast became obvious when Indonesia and Malaysia were wracked by political crisis resulting from the collapse of their economies in 1998.

As his host fumed, Vice President Al Gore presented a courageous speech in Kuala Lumpur in November 1998 before Prime Minister Mahathir. Addressing the financial crisis confronting the states of East Asia, Gore linked democracy with economic reform and argued that "people will accept sacrifice in a democracy, not only because they have had a role in choosing it, but because they rightly believe they are likely to benefit from it. The message this year from Indonesia is unmistakable: People are willing to take responsibility for their future—if they have the power to determine that future . . . Among nations suffering economic crises, we continue to hear calls for democracy and reform in many languages—"people's power," "*doi moi*," "*reformasi.*" We hear them today—right here, right now—among the brave people of Malaysia . . . All who love freedom are obliged to redeem people's faith in self-government. Investments move in the direction of strong and deep democracy—and so, too, has our world history."

That Indonesia and Malaysia are overwhelmingly Muslim countries did not deter Gore from prescribing democracy. Yet in other parts of the Muslim world, and especially the Middle East, a search for comparable high-profile American statements espousing democracy and good government would prove futile. In contrast to the message in Kuala Lumpur, the focus of United States Middle East policy is not democracy and freedom but stability and control.

Consider the Israeli-Palestinian peace process. The October 1998 installment of United States–brokered negotiations between Prime Minister Benjamin Netanyahu and President Yasir Arafat took place at the bucolic Wye Plantation in rural Maryland. The resulting agreement, the Wye Memorandum, reveals no evidence of serious American (or Israeli) concern for the rule of law among the Palestinians. The now derailed memorandum engaged President Clinton for nearly 90 hours in the course of a week of negotiations. Clinton's astounding exertions may be less a measure of his commitment to Middle East peace and more a symptom of America's inability to do little more than coddle Israel. This distortion of American priorities in the region, for which credit may be shared more or less equally between the White House and the Congress, handicaps any United States negotiator, even the president. As agreed at Wye, so long as the Palestinian Authority corrals the alleged extremists of Hamas, thereby satisfying Israeli demands, it is clearly permissible to dispense with legal niceties. Justified or not, it is not difficult to see how charges of double standards arise.

Another case in point: an authoritative National Security Council document, "A National Security Strategy for a New Century," prepared in May 1997, avoids any coupling of the ideas of democracy or human rights with the Middle East. Although the document emphasizes United States interests in security in the region, it does not consider the "promotion of democracy" in the Middle East a particular aim. Rather, the regional goal is defined as "peace and stability." This omission stands in stark contrast to other areas such as Africa and Asia, where the promotion of democracy is a central focus on United States policy. But this is not a new phenomenon. During the 1990–1991 Persian Gulf War, White House press spokespeople were also instructed to avoid coupling the word "democracy" with references to the Arab world.

HOW TO THINK ABOUT MUSLIM POLITICS

In the two decades since the revolution in Iran, the idea of Islam as a resurgent force in world politics has captured the imagination of large numbers of Muslims, just as it has become an idée fixe of Western foreign policy establishments. There is little question that ideologies rooted in Islam can be a dynamic force for change. Yet Muslims and non-Muslims alike have often exaggerated the coherence of Islam as a political force. Consequently, more attention must be paid to the complex refractions of Muslim politics. There are three distinct but interrelated levels of Muslim politics:

- The interface of state and society, where governments often exploit Islamic or nationalist symbolism to maintain the consent of the governed, while opposition political movements often deploy competing Islamic or nationalist symbols to build support in society and undermine those in power. A number of authoritarian governments friendly to the United States face credible challenges from reform-oriented Islamist opposition movements, including Egypt and Saudi Arabia. In Indonesia, Jordan, Lebanon, Kuwait, and Yemen, Islamist opposition parties are considered legitimate participants in the political system. In sharp contrast, other governments—notably those of Egypt, Saudi Arabia, Syria, Tunisia, and, especially, Algeria—have opted for repression.

- The level of state-to-state relations, where realpolitik pragmatism is frequently camouflaged by idealistic Islamic rhetoric. The Islamic Republic of Iran is a case in point. In 1989, just before his death, Ayatollah Ruhollah Khomeini emphasized that the interests of the state precede the Interests of Islam. In the years since, Iran has tilted dramatically toward Christian Armenia in its conflict with Azerbaijan, even though the Azeri people are, like the Iranians, almost entirely Shiite Muslims. This reflects Iran's interest in curtailing any irredentist ambitions on the part of Azerbaijan toward the contiguous Azeri region of Iran, which is far more compelling than an ideal of solidarity among Muslims; it also reflects the larger point that the foreign policies of Muslim states are far more affected by geopolitics than by Islamic values.

- The transnational realm of pan-Islam, where diffuse Islamic themes reveal the complexity of the Muslim world. The transnational realm includes such forums as the Organization of the Islamic Conference, where Muslim governments periodically meet, as they did in December 1997 in Tehran. The 1997 meeting was not only marked by a dramatic juxtaposition of Iranian reformers and hard-liners, but also saw the Muslim states in attendance condemn any form of terrorism. Pan-Islam also includes the new media of global communications. Scholars are only beginning to explore the phenomenon of networks of Muslims communicating over the Internet, where new visions of politics and the fundamentals of Islam are actively debated.

These three levels of analysis are of varying significance for the United States. The state-society interface has a direct bearing on the future of a number of key Muslim states, and

In the two decades since the revolution in Iran, the idea of Islam as a resurgent force in world politics . . . has become an idée fixe of Western foreign policy establishments.

the inter-state dimension is the traditional province for diplomatists; these two levels are most significant to United States policymaking. As for transnational Islam, however fascinating it may appear, it has fewer policy ramifications at this time.[2]

INCLUSION OR EXCLUSION?

Those who argue that a rising level of popular dissatisfaction with government is a characteristic of the 1990s can find ample evidence in the Muslim world. Islamist opposition movements have established a foundation of popular support, particularly among the urban underclass, the lower middle class, and even the professional middle class. In reasonably fair elections, Islamist opposition parties have attracted between one-sixth and one-third of the vote in, for example, Jordan, Lebanon, Pakistan, and Yemen.

Islamist opposition movements often claim categorically that "Islam is the solution" to the ills plaguing their societies. Although this may prove to be a debatable proposition on examination, many Muslims prefer the untested promises of the Islamists to the demonstrated failures of their governments.

The meaningful question for United States foreign policy is not whether Islam is the answer, but whether political movements inspired by Islam are exempt from the political rules of the road by which non-Muslim political movements play. In other words, faced with the opportunity to share (not seize) power, to what degree does ideological commitment give way to pragmatic politics? The evidence from Indonesia, Jordan, Pakistan, and Turkey, to cite four interesting cases, seems to suggest that Islamist politicians demonstrate a considerable degree of flexibility in the interest of staying in the political game, even if that requires sacrificing their avowed goals.

The characteristic demand of Islamist politicians is the supplanting of secular norms of governance with the strictures of *sharia,* or Islamic law. Yet secular rule remains the norm in many Muslim states and structural constraints often bar all but minority participation in government by the Islamists. For example, in Lebanon, where parliamentary seats are allocated by religious sect, Hezbollah—the self-styled "Party of God"—would still hold only one-fifth of all seats if it were to win the 27 seats allocated to Shiites. Since elections resumed in 1992, Hezbollah has not won more than 8 seats because of the intense competition from rival Shiite parties and politicians.

There is, of course, wide disagreement over the wisdom of permitting the Islamists entrée to the political system. Skeptics have argued that the Islamists seek only to subvert the political system, while proponents of political inclusion emphasize the purported moderating effect of participation. Whatever the merits of the inclusion argument—which enjoys wide confirmation in non-Muslim cases—should the United States encourage the inclusion of Islamist movements in politics, even when key Muslim countries (and close friends of the United

---

[2] The most interesting question involves the role and significance of transnational Islam. This refers to a variety of phenomena, ranging from nongovernmental organizations such as the London-based Liberty, which promotes a model for a power-sharing Islam, to violent conspiratorial groups of former mujahiden ("holy warriors" in Afghanistan). The overwhelming majority of transnational players are committed to projects of reform and rejuvenation, not to violence. For example, the venerable Muslim Brotherhood, which originated in Egypt, has long had branches throughout the Muslim world. The Brotherhood and other transnational agents of change, including groups of Muslim women who boldly challenge the male-dominated interpretation of Islamic practice and custom, often appropriate a distinctively non-Islamic vocabulary, including the theme of democracy, the idea of civil society, and the question of pluralism. It remains to be seen to what extent transnational Islam poses a challenge or an opportunity for United States foreign policy.

States) appear bent on exclusion? Opinion within the American foreign policy establishment is mixed, but there does seem to be a growing appreciation of the importance of dialogue with groups that once were shunned. American diplomats have sustained a quiet dialogue with the Islamic Salvation Front of Algeria, the Muslim Brotherhood in Egypt, the former Refah Party in Turkey, and, until 1996, with Hamas, the Palestinian group.[3]

TAKING THE DEMOCRATIC GAMBLE

Although few Muslim governments qualify as democracies, some Islamic movements characterize themselves as democratic and have said they are willing to participate in free and fair elections. Given the declared United States policy of promoting the development of democracy, do the circumstances in the Middle East justify suspending the policy?

Washington has frequently been silent on the question of democracy in the Muslim world, especially the Middle East. Official statements proclaiming America's commitment to promoting democracy sound surreal when heard in that region. Even when friendly Muslim governments in the Arab world have been blatantly contemptuous of democracy, the United States has done little more than politely express its concern. This is precisely what happened in December 1995, when President Hosni Mubarak's government in Egypt made a mockery of free elections by permitting opposition candidates to win only 14 of 456 parliamentary seats. The election evoked no more than a perfunctory diplomatic démarche, to which the Egyptian government paid but passing notice.

There is a basic debate in democratic theory about whether it is possible to create a democracy without democrats. Some analysts argue that there are cultural preconditions for democracy, including individualism, civility, and a willingness to compromise in the interest of harmony, whereas others hold that democracy is a problem-solving solution, and that democrats evolve over time as people become habituated to the rules of the game. The terms of this debate define the controversy about bringing Islamists into the political game. On the one hand it is asserted that the preconditions for democracy are largely absent in the Muslim world, while on the other it is claimed that the key challenge is the construction of a system of guarantees that will preclude the Islamists, or any other opposition force, from using democratization to seize power and impose a dictatorship.

Seizing power is what some observers believed the Islamic Salvation Front (FIS) was about to do in Algeria in 1991 when it was on the brink of winning a commanding majority in parliament. Reflecting the apprehensions created by the potential electoral success of the FIS, Edward Djerejian, the United States assistant secretary of state for Near Eastern affairs, emphasized that a "democratic" system that permitted one man,

one vote, one time would find no support in Washington. Thus, when the Algerian army conducted a coup in January 1992, the United States only noted its "regret" about what had happened. After seven years of bloodshed, and 50,000 dead Algerians, the coup is no longer so easily rationalized.

Yet the evidence clearly suggests that when Islamist movements have been permitted to play within the rules of game, they adhere to them. The United States would defuse a considerable amount of criticism were it to adopt a clear stance in favor of freer, fairer, more responsive government in the Middle East. Moreover, where Islamist parties do demonstrate a willingness to play by the rules, permitting them a role in the system reduces the risk of polarization that breeds extremism. Middle Eastern rulers would obviously be no happier about this stance than was Malaysia's Mahathir as he listened to Vice President Gore's speech. Nonetheless, by tacitly supporting the categorical exclusion of Islamist opposition forces from politics, the United States provokes distrust and contributes to the fragility, not the solidity, of friendly Middle Eastern governments.

United States human rights policy intersects with the promotion of democracy. Few Muslim governments enjoy glowing assessments of their observance of human rights. A more vigorous promotion of human rights in the Muslim world would buttress liberal currents by opening up space for civil society. Some radical Islamist movements reject the human rights construct as an artifact of Western culture, but the discourse over human rights has increasingly become a global discourse. Of course, the fear is that promotion of human rights may have the effect [of] further eroding the legitimacy of friendly governments, as exemplified by the impact of President Jimmy Carter's advocacy of human rights on the shah of Iran. But the parable of the fall of the shah should not be read superficially, since his regime was weakened on many fronts, not least by a general deterioration in the Iranian economy and the monarch's penchant for surrounding himself with sycophants.

> *Muslims and non-Muslims alike have often exaggerated the coherence of Islam as a political force.*

IRAN AS A BELLWETHER

Five avowedly "Islamic" states now exist. Of these, Saudi Arabia is a close ally of the United States and a major consumer of United States arms exports, and strategically situated Pakistan has traditionally been friendly to the United States. In contrast, Iran and Sudan remain the persistent focus of a variety of American efforts to contain their purported radical objectives. Afghanistan, the latest addition to the club, is now dominated by the Taliban, a populist militia force that emerged in the Pushtun villages of the country.

Each country has, at times, demonstrated a missionary zeal for exporting its distinctive Islamic model of governance, and these efforts have sometimes posed a serious challenge to American and Western interests in the Muslim world. But relations between these five states are typically strained and they are hardly a prototype for an Islamic International. In this re-

---

[3] Although Hezbollah's entrance into the Lebanese political system would have been an unmitigated disaster in the 1980s, there is a growing appreciation in Washington that this group is in the midst of a dramatic and encouraging transition from terrorist organization to political party.

spect, former Turkish Prime Minister Necmettin Erbakan's fantasy of a global Islamic alliance quickly became a target for derision in Turkey, not least by Turkish Islamists.

No Muslim state is viewed with more suspicion in American policy circles than the self-styled Islamic Republic of Iran, which has succeeded in thwarting United States policy designs for nearly two decades. Despite continued United States attempts to contain its influence and restrain its power, Iran has not only maintained a flourishing trade with Europe and Japan, but has normalized its diplomatic ties with most states in the strategic Persian Gulf region. Although it confronts domestic economic difficulties, Iran's leadership continues to express suspicion of the United States and enmity for Israel. And, until recently, Iran had continued to stalk and murder adversaries around the globe, whether intellectual foes or political opponents. It has also maintained support for Hezbollah's war of resistance against the Israeli occupation of southern Lebanon, and it has vehemently condemned the United States-sponsored peace process in the Middle East.

Washington's efforts to isolate Iran have been, at best, a limited success. The United States–Iranian relationship is mired in mutual suspicion, and is plagued by a painful history in which neither side can claim a monopoly on virtue. The stunning presidential victory of Mahammed Khatami in 1997, however, may represent a new phase in the political history of Iran; it has already opened up new vistas for dialogue with the United States. In a much anticipated interview with CNN in January 1998, Khatami showed an impressive command of the history of colonial America, and especially the Puritans and their quest for religious freedom and liberty. Indeed, he emphasized that human beings deserve to have both religion and liberty. Khatami used the interview to call for a dialogue with Americans, including teachers, athletes, artists, and intellectuals, while foreclosing an official dialogue with Washington.

For its part, the United States recognized the potential for significant change in relations with Iran, and by the late spring and summer of 1997 the tone of official statements on Iran softened considerably. The nonofficial dialogue that Khatami espoused is also under way, including a 1998 visit by American collegiate wrestlers who were warmly received. By the time the World Cup qualifying match between Iran and the United States approached in July 1998, in Lyons, France, some senior Washington officials quietly said that they hoped Iran would win the match in the interest of improved relations.

Iran did win, but Khatami's domestic reforms have been fiercely resisted by regime hard-liners, and the time is certainly not propitious for a dramatic moment of peacemaking with the United States. Hatred of the United States government is a touchstone of the Iranian revolution. Thus, when Khatami made a relatively conciliatory speech at the December 1997 meeting of the organization of the Islamic Conference, he was followed by Sayed Ali Khamenehi, officially the Leader of the Revolution and the successor to Khomeini, who delivered a strident denunciation of the United States.

The flirtation between Khatami and the United States will no doubt continue to progress slowly; even Iranian intellectuals in favor of improved relations with the United States argue that the issue is so inflammatory domestically that it cannot be high on Khatami's list of priorities.

Iran's relationship with America may be a bellwether for Muslim opinion about the United States, since the distrust and animosity between the two states have become core elements of the foreign policy of each. Rightly or wrongly, many Muslims believe that hostility toward Iran stems from American unwillingness to accept Islam as the central premise of the Islamic Republic. But the slow two-way process of repairing relations with Iran is already bearing modest fruit.

THE CHALLENGE TO AMERICAN POLICY

Muslims make up one-sixth the world's population, and for this reason alone no major government can afford to ignore the world of Islam, not least of all American governments in its moment of undisputed power. Muslims form the majority population in more than 30 countries. Signal events, such as the crisis in the Balkans, the publication of the *Satanic Verses,* or, potentially, the bombing of a sacred site, such as the Dome of the Rock mosque in Jerusalem (which Jewish extremists plotted to blow up in 1982 and Christian cultists are suspected of targeting to mark the millennium), have served to inflame Muslim opinion against the West. Yet raison d'état seems to remain the dominant factor in explaining the foreign policies of Muslim states. Intergovernmental efforts to promote cooperation among Muslim states, such as the Organization of the Islamic Conference, have been modestly successful, but the participating governments have jealously guarded their own interests.

Arguably, bilateral relations between the United States and many Muslim governments are healthier today than during the cold war. America's ruinous policy toward Iraq is a major exception and is badly in need of renovation; the ramifications of that policy in the Muslim world have a deleterious effect on United States interests. In addition, the ability of the United States to do business with many of the present Muslim governments encourages an understandable affection for the status quo, with the result that the United States is often perceived, with some accuracy, as an opponent of political change. Unfortunately, a number of these friendly Muslim governments, particularly those in the Middle East, have failed to fulfill the social contract they have established with their citizens.

It is unrealistic to expect that the United States will jettison its desire for stability and predictable diplomatic relationships. The challenge is to imagine and foster a dynamic stability in which greater political and economic freedom blossom. This path is already being followed in significant parts of the Muslim world, as we have seen, but not in the Middle East. It is also foolhardy to expect the United States to be totally consistent in its relationships with any government, let alone those that are Muslim. But a more energetic promotion of central United States foreign policy themes—especially freedom, democracy, and human rights—would undermine Muslim critics of American policy and underscore that the future holds great opportunity for continued American cooperation with the Muslim world, rather than conflict.

Americans and the World: A Survey at Century's End

by John E. Rielly

As the twentieth century closes, Americans feel secure, prosperous, and confident. They see the United States as the world's most important and powerful country, with the fear of armed threats from a rival superpower diminished. In an era of increasing globalization, Americans view economic rather than military power as the most significant measure of global strength. Apprehension about economic competition from Japan or Europe has dissipated, as have concerns about immigration. Nevertheless, Americans are alarmed by violence at home and abroad. They support measures to thwart terrorists, prevent the spread of weapons of mass destruction, and keep defense strong, but shy away from deploying U.S. troops on foreign soil. American public and leadership opinion on foreign policy today reflects a "guarded engagement" by a largely satisfied superpower.

These are some of the most significant conclusions from the latest quadrennial survey of American public and leadership opinion sponsored by the Chicago Council on Foreign Relations. The survey was conducted during the last three months of 1998, the seventh in a series that has tracked foreign-policy opinions in the United States over two and a half decades. This is the third survey since the end of the Cold War.

JOHN E. RIELLY *is president of the Chicago Council on Foreign Relations. This article is adapted from a report titled* American Public Opinion and U.S. Foreign Policy 1999, *which was published simultaneously by the Chicago Council.*

A (MOSTLY) SELF-SATISFIED SUPERPOWER

As in all our previous surveys, support for an active role by the United States in world affairs remains strong, with 61 percent of the public and 96 percent of leaders in favor. On the question of the country's biggest foreign-policy problems, one of the responses chosen by the public, "staying out of the affairs of other countries," is down 12 points, from 19 percent in 1994 to 7 percent today. The American public is also more confident about the role of the United States in the world: Fifty percent believe it now plays a more important and powerful role as a world leader than it did 10 years ago, and only 19 percent (down seven points) foresee a lesser role. More than three-quarters of the public (79 percent) and 71 percent of leaders believe the United States will play a greater role in the world 10 years from now.

Reflecting other domestic polls finding record economic and personal satisfaction among Americans, the Chicago Council on Foreign Relations survey shows contentment on the foreign-policy front. When asked to list the two or three biggest foreign-policy problems facing the United States today, the most common public response (by 21 percent) was "I don't know." Though this might indicate a lack of interest in or attentiveness to foreign policy, the survey's findings suggest instead that Americans are feeling a sense of relative security.

President Bill Clinton has made a dramatic comeback from four years ago in approval ratings for his conduct of foreign policy. By one measure of the survey, he has risen from eighth to first place among postwar presi-

Ranking of U.S. Presidents on Foreign Policy
("Very Successful" in Foreign Policy)

1998	1994
1. Clinton	1. Kennedy
2. Kennedy	2. Nixon
3. Reagan	3. Truman
4. Bush	4. Eisenhower
5. Truman	5. Reagan
6. Eisenhower	6. Bush
7. Nixon	7. Carter
8. Carter	8. Clinton
9. Johnson	9. Johnson
10. Ford	10. Ford

tional terrorism, named by 84 percent of respondents, up 15 points from four years ago. This is followed by chemical and biological weapons (76 percent) and the possibility of unfriendly countries becoming nuclear powers (75 percent). Of the biggest foreign-policy problems that the public mentions, seven of the eleven most common responses relate to a fear of weapons, violence, and conflict. Although the terrorist bombings against U.S. embassies in Africa, and the subsequent retaliatory U.S. air strikes in Afghanistan and Sudan, were probably fresh in the minds of the public during this survey, these fears of international violence also mirror the survey's finding of crime as the biggest perceived problem at home.

dents considered "very successful" by the public in the conduct of foreign policy. Clinton's high overall approval ratings in this area suggest that Americans are giving him credit for the strong position of the United States in the world and for its apparent lack of foreign-policy problems. Moreover, Secretary of State Madeleine Albright ranks fifth among various world leaders on the survey's "feeling thermometer," behind the pope, former U.S. presidents George Bush and Jimmy Carter, and South African president Nelson Mandela.

Congress is perceived as playing about the right role in determining foreign policy vis-à-vis the president, despite concern over matters surrounding the president and the impeachment process (which the public listed second most frequently as one of the biggest problems facing the country). Forty-three percent of Americans say Congress' role in foreign policy is about right, the highest number since the surveys began in 1974—in other words, the public is the most satisfied it has been in 25 years with Congress' role in making foreign policy.

Despite the general sense of power, confidence, and contentment, there is some unease. A majority of Americans (53 percent) believe there will be more bloodshed and violence in the twenty-first century than in the twentieth century, with 19 percent saying less. Leaders disagree, with a plurality (40 percent) believing there will be less violence and only 23 percent believing there will be more.

The number one "critical threat" to U.S. vital interests in the minds of the public is interna-

GUARDED ENGAGEMENT

Perhaps reflecting this fear of violence, Americans show a degree of caution about becoming involved internationally. Overall public commitment to engagement coexists with reluctance to support the use of U.S. troops overseas.

In only one hypothetical case—if Iraq invaded Saudi Arabia—is there a plurality of public support for using U.S. troops in other parts of the world; otherwise, at least a plurality oppose military intervention. Because of their unlikeliness, possible attacks on Europe or Japan—cases that in the past have received the strongest support for intervention—were not included in the 1998 survey. Nevertheless, in the instances for which there is comparative data, the proportion of the public in favor of using troops has dropped and the percentage opposed has risen by four points to ten points from 1994.

By contrast, leaders generally favor the use of U.S. troops under hypothetical scenarios, with a majority supporting intervention in Israel, Kosovo, Poland, Saudi Arabia, South Korea, and Taiwan. The only exception is Cuba, where leaders overwhelmingly oppose intervention (80 percent against) in the case of a revolution.

The public's aversion to the use of troops may also reflect a lingering post-Vietnam "syndrome." Sixty-three percent of the public agree that "the Vietnam War was more than a mistake, it was fundamentally wrong and immoral," an increase of four points from 1994, but lower than in earlier surveys. Moreover, the survey's scenarios for using troops were

Ranking of U.S. Foreign-Policy Goals
(Percentage of Respondents Who Said "Very Important")

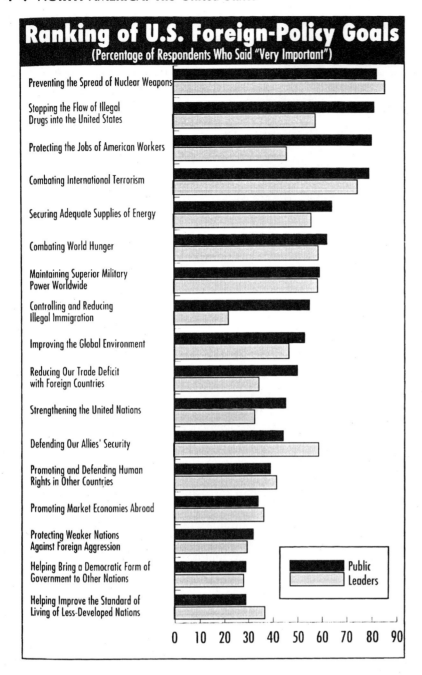

Preventing the Spread of Nuclear Weapons

Stopping the Flow of Illegal Drugs into the United States

Protecting the Jobs of American Workers

Combating International Terrorism

Securing Adequate Supplies of Energy

Combating World Hunger

Maintaining Superior Military Power Worldwide

Controlling and Reducing Illegal Immigration

Improving the Global Environment

Reducing Our Trade Deficit with Foreign Countries

Strengthening the United Nations

Defending Our Allies' Security

Promoting and Defending Human Rights in Other Countries

Promoting Market Economies Abroad

Protecting Weaker Nations Against Foreign Aggression

Helping Bring a Democratic Form of Government to Other Nations

Helping Improve the Standard of Living of Less-Developed Nations

■ Public
☐ Leaders

0 10 20 30 40 50 60 70 80 90

mostly traditional cases of defending allies, which as an overall goal of foreign policy is ranked relatively low by the public (but not by leaders). In a more economically and politically pragmatic world, the public may perceive fewer direct national or personal consequences from troubles overseas and hence be less willing to put U.S. troops in harm's way.

The picture changes dramatically, however, in the fight against terrorism, where Americans are prepared to use significant force. Seventy-four percent of the public favor U.S. air strikes against terrorist training camps and other facilities. Fifty-seven percent favor attacks by U.S. ground troops. Fifty-four percent of

the public even favor assassination of terrorist leaders, though only 34 percent of leaders. Among the public and leaders, diplomatic efforts to improve U.S. relations with potential adversary countries receive an even greater degree of support (79 percent for the public and 96 percent for leaders) than military measures to combat international terrorism. Since the survey began not long after the bombing of American embassies and the retaliatory U.S. air strikes, it is not surprising that concern about terrorism was high. Nevertheless, the responses clearly illustrate that Americans will support the use of force under certain circumstances.

Despite confidence in the U.S. position as a world power, Americans are not taking chances. While a plurality of both the public and leaders still favor keeping levels of defense spending the same (as they did in 1994), the number who would expand it has increased. Among the public, 30 percent would expand the defense budget (an increase of nine points from four years ago to the highest level since 1978), 38 percent would keep it the same, and 28 percent would cut it back. The percentage of leaders who would increase defense spending has risen from 15 percent in 1994 to 26 percent today, with 41 percent preferring to keep it the same and 32 percent still favoring a cutback. Support for expanding federal spending to gather intelligence about other countries is on the rise, jumping from 18 percent to 27 percent among the public and from 16 percent to 34 percent among leaders. The percentage of respondents who would cut it back has dropped from 29 percent to 22 percent among the public and 37 percent to 15 percent among leaders, with the remainder preferring to keep spending levels the same.

A PREFERENCE FOR MULTILATERALISM

An important aspect of the public's commitment to engagement abroad is support for a multilateral foreign policy. Fifty-seven percent

Perceived U.S. Vital Interests Around the World

"The U.S. does have a vital interest in . . ." (Percent)

Country	1998		1994	
	Public	Leaders	Public	Leaders
Japan	87	94	85	96
Russia	77	93	79	98
Saudi Arabia	77	88	83	94
China	74	95	68	95
Israel	69	86	64	86
Canada	69	89	71	93
Kuwait	68	-	76	-
Mexico	66	93	76	98
Great Britain	66	84	69	82
Iran	61	72	-	-
Germany	60	83	66	91
South Korea	54	82	65	90
South Africa	52	52	57	52
Taiwan	52	-	49	-
Bosnia	51	48	44	-
Cuba	50	-	67	-
Egypt	46	66	45	78
Afghanistan	45	-	-	-
France	37	57	39	59
India	36	-	31	-
Indonesia	33	50	-	-
Brazil	33	75	34	49
Turkey	33	-	-	-
Haiti	31	-	56	33
Poland	31	42	31	46
Estonia, Latvia, and Lithuania	27	30	29	34

1994) would keep support for NATO the same. Twenty-one percent would decrease it or withdraw from NATO entirely, down five points from four years ago, while the 9 percent in favor of increasing support represents a gain of four points. Among leaders, support for maintaining the current level of U.S. commitment to NATO has risen from 57 percent to 64 percent, and sentiment for decreasing commitment or withdrawing entirely has declined from 37 percent to 28 percent; only 7 percent want to increase U.S. commitment.

Although unilateral American initiatives continue, as in the peace process in Northern Ireland and the U.S. bombing of suspected terrorist facilities, preference for engagement through multilateral institutions and alliances suggests that Americans would rather share risks and build consensus. However, this inclination does not necessarily translate into support for engagement that would primarily benefit others. A continuing focus on national self-interest is clearly evident in the foreign-policy priorities of Americans.

Preventing the spread of nuclear weapons, stopping the flow of illegal drugs into the United States, and protecting the jobs of American workers top the list of goals that the public perceives as "very important." Of the 11 goals with at least plurality support as very important, only three do not stem strictly from self-interest: combating world hunger; improving the global environment; and strengthening the United Nations. The lowest priorities are all associated with other examples of altruistic internationalism: defending our allies' security; promoting and defending human rights in other countries; promoting market economies abroad; protecting weaker nations against foreign aggression; helping bring a democratic form of government to other nations; and helping improve the standard of living of less-developed nations. The findings suggest that Americans prefer a guarded engagement, becoming involved mainly to defend their interests and alleviate

agree that the United States should take part in UN peacekeeping efforts in troubled parts of the world, with only 20 percent preferring to leave the job to other countries. Seventy-two percent think the United States should not take action alone in international crises if it does not have the support of allies. Leaders are more evenly divided: Forty-eight percent prefer not to act alone and 44 percent are willing to take action without allied support.

Support for the principal military alliance of the United States, NATO, is solid. Most of the public (59 percent, up three points from

their fears rather than to foster change according to an American model.

ADJUSTING TO GLOBALIZATION

Economics in general has risen dramatically as an important dimension of international activity and U.S. engagement. When respondents were asked whether a country's economic strength or military strength is more important in determining its overall power and influence in the world, 63 percent of the public chose economic, compared with 28 percent who chose military. Leaders (89 percent) are even more overwhelmingly convinced of the power of economics. On the question of globalization, defined as the increasing connections of our economy with others around the world, 54 percent of the public believe that globalization is mostly good for the United States, with 20 percent saying mostly bad. Leaders are again more unified, with 87 percent believing globalization is mostly good.

The positive evaluation of globalization and the perceived economic strength of the United States coexist with concern about troubles in the global economy. While the United States has been largely insulated from financial turmoil in Asia and elsewhere, fears of instability persist, with the "world economy" appearing second only to terrorism on the list of foreign-policy problems mentioned by the public. Leaders are even more concerned, with 21 percent citing the world economy most often on the list of the country's biggest foreign-policy problems. An additional 13 percent of leaders specify "Japan/Asian Economy/Crisis" as a significant problem.

Despite concern about the global economy, the public is unsupportive of efforts to bail out other countries suffering from financial crises. To the question of whether the United States, along with other countries, should contribute more money to the International Monetary Fund (IMF) to meet world financial crises, 51 percent of the public respond no, 25 percent respond yes, and 24 percent do not

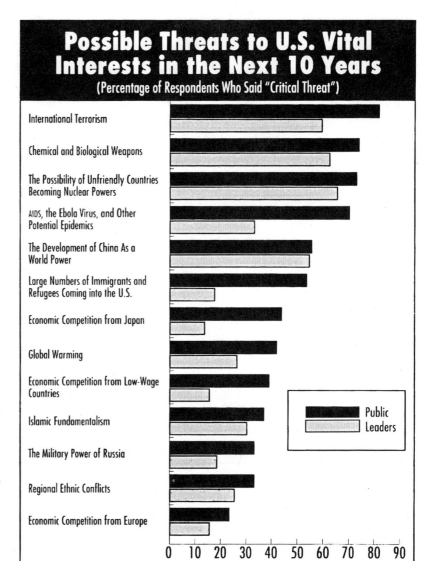

Possible Threats to U.S. Vital Interests in the Next 10 Years
(Percentage of Respondents Who Said "Critical Threat")

International Terrorism

Chemical and Biological Weapons

The Possibility of Unfriendly Countries Becoming Nuclear Powers

AIDS, the Ebola Virus, and Other Potential Epidemics

The Development of China As a World Power

Large Numbers of Immigrants and Refugees Coming into the U.S.

Economic Competition from Japan

Global Warming

Economic Competition from Low-Wage Countries

Islamic Fundamentalism

The Military Power of Russia

Regional Ethnic Conflicts

Economic Competition from Europe

■ Public
□ Leaders

0 10 20 30 40 50 60 70 80 90

know. A plurality of Americans (38 percent) believe Russia should solve its own economic problems, with 34 percent preferring Europe take the lead in providing assistance. Only 17 percent want the United States to do so. This finding is consistent with the long-term trend of low support for federal spending on economic aid to other nations. Forty-eight percent of the public want to cut it back, down 10 points from four years ago, and only 13 percent want to expand.

By contrast, 82 percent of leaders favor giving more money to the IMF, and 44 percent favor Europe taking the lead on assistance to Russia, with 34 percent wanting the United States to take the lead and only 17 percent believing Russia should solve its own problems. A plurality of leaders (43 percent) are happy with the current level of federal spending on economic aid to other nations, though

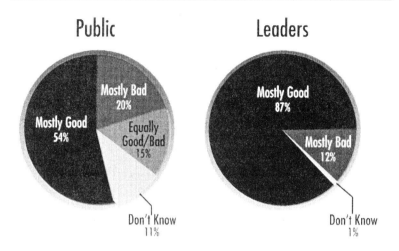

Attitudes on Globalization

"Do you believe that globalization, especially the increasing connections of our economy with others around the world, is mostly good or mostly bad for the United States?"

Public

Mostly Good 54%
Mostly Bad 20%
Equally Good/Bad 15%
Don't Know 11%

Leaders

Mostly Good 87%
Mostly Bad 12%
Don't Know 1%

a notable number (38 percent) favor expanding it, a significant 18-point increase from 1994.

Global economic turmoil may have led to the increase in the number of leaders who believe tariffs are necessary, from 20 percent in 1994 to 34 percent in 1998, although most still prefer to eliminate tariffs (62 percent). The public maintains its historic belief in the need for tariffs, though by a plurality (49 percent) and not a majority, as was the case prior to 1994.

OLD FRIENDS, NEW RIVALS

Europe: Increasing Comity

As in previous surveys, the public ranks European nations as America's closest friends and allies on the feeling thermometer. A plurality of Americans also believe that Europe is more important to the United States than Asia (42 percent to 28 percent). However, the gap has narrowed since 1994, with Asia's importance up seven points and Europe's down seven points, a trend that likely reflects the impact of Asia's financial crash last year. Among leaders, Europe's relative importance over Asia has increased from 42 percent to 51 percent, with those citing Asia as more important (37 percent) remaining largely the same as four years ago. Public concern about economic competition from Europe as a critical threat has lessened during the last four years from 27 percent to 24 percent. Although concern has increased among leaders (from 11

percent to 16 percent), it remains far below the 41 percent reported in 1990.

Russia: End of the Honeymoon?

The general optimism and goodwill that characterized U.S.-Russian relations in the immediate post-Cold War years appear to have dissipated somewhat, strained by Russia's economic woes, unstable domestic politics, dangerous nuclear arsenal, and bilateral foreign-policy tensions. As mentioned, although a plurality of Americans believe Russia should solve its own economic problems, a plurality of leaders want Europe to take the lead in providing assistance. Leaders rank dealings with Russia among the five biggest foreign-policy problems (tied with Japan/Asian Economy/Crisis), even though the public is less concerned. A solid, if lower, majority of the public (77 percent) and leaders (93 percent) still consider Russia a vital interest to the United States, even though there is relatively low concern about the military threat that it poses. Consistent with a greater general willingness by leaders to use U.S. troops, many more leaders (58 percent) than the public (28 percent) would favor the use of U.S. troops to counter a Russian invasion of Poland.

Japan: Declining Preoccupation

America's economic success and Japan's continuing recession have mitigated fears of economic competition from Tokyo. Although public concern about such competition has not disappeared, the 45 percent who perceive it as a critical threat is considerably less than the 62 percent of 1994. Even fewer leaders see economic competition from Japan as a critical threat, dropping from 63 percent in 1990 to 21 percent in 1994 and 14 percent in 1998. Although 55 percent of the public and 75 percent of leaders believe Japan practices unfair trade, the proportion thinking Japan practices fair trade is up from 17 percent to 31 percent among the public and from 18 percent to 22 percent among leaders. Declining public preoccupation with Japan is also reflected in the decreasing percentage of Americans who believe Japan will play a greater role in world affairs in the next 10 years (from 66 percent to 59 percent), while the opinions of leaders remain largely unchanged (from 47 percent to 46 percent).

Thermometer Ratings for Countries

"If you have a warm feeling toward a country, give it a temperature higher than 50°. If you have a cool feeling, give it less than 50°."

Country	Mean temperature — degrees				
	'98	'94	'90	'86	'82
Canada	72	73	76	77	74
Great Britain	69	69	74	73	68
Italy	62	58	59	58	55
Mexico	57	57	56	59	60
Germany	56	57	62	62	59
Brazil	56	54	54	54	54
Japan	55	53	52	61	53
Israel	55	54	54	59	55
France	55	55	56	58	60
South Africa	54	52	51	48	45
Taiwan	51	48	48	52	49
South Korea	50	48	47	51	44
Poland	50	52	57	54	52
Russia**	49	54	59	32	26
Argentina	49	47	-	-	-
China***	47	46	45	53	47
India	46	48	48	48	48
Saudi Arabia	46	48	53	50	52
Nigeria	46	-	-	-	-
Turkey	45	-	-	-	-
Pakistan	42	-	-	-	-
Cuba	38	38	-	-	27
North Korea	36	34	-	-	-
Iran	28	28	27	23	28
Iraq	25	24	20	-	-

Note: *Prior to the 1990 survey this was "West Germany"
**Prior to the 1994 survey this was "Soviet Union"
***Prior to the 1994 survey this was "People's Republic of China"

Japan's temperature rating on the feeling thermometer continues to be lukewarm (55 degrees), but it remains the country considered most vital to American interests by the public and is a close second to China among leaders, moving ahead of Mexico and Russia. A greater percentage of the public view Japan (47 percent) as more important to the United States than China (28 percent), while leaders are split evenly on this issue. A strong majority of leaders (75 percent) believe that reform of Japan's economic and financial structures is very important for addressing the Asian financial crisis.

China: Measured Concern

Public attitudes toward China reflect some concern about this Asian giant's changing role

in the world. Sixty-nine percent of Americans believe China will play a greater role in the next 10 years than today, while 97 percent of leaders hold that opinion. As mentioned, leaders are split on whether China (47 percent) is more important than Japan (48 percent). Leaders consider China to be the most vital country to the United States (95 percent), just ahead of Japan (94 percent), while the public puts China fourth (74 percent), behind Japan, Russia, and Saudi Arabia. A nearly equal percentage of the public and leaders consider the development of China as a world power to be a possible critical threat to U.S. vital interests, a moderate 57 percent and 56 percent, respectively.

Concern about China among leaders can also be seen in the 9 percent who consider relations with China to be among the biggest foreign-policy problems, compared with 3 percent of the public. On the subject of economic sanctions, the public (52 percent) is much more willing than leaders (36 percent) to impose such sanctions on China. Conversely, more leaders (51 percent) than the public (27 percent) support the use of U.S. troops if China were to invade Taiwan.

Israel: Qualified Support

Israel continues to rank high on the vital-interest scale for both the public and leaders, yet receives a lukewarm rating on the feeling thermometer (55 degrees) from the public. The Middle East situation is cited among the six most important foreign-policy problems by the public and the leaders. Nevertheless, public support for economic aid to Israel remains virtually unchanged from 1994, with a plurality believing aid levels should remain the same (42 percent) and substantially more favoring a decrease (23 percent) than an increase (10 percent). If Arab forces were to invade Israel, leaders strongly support intervention by U.S. troops. Although evenly divided on the issue in the past two surveys, a plurality of the public are now opposed to such intervention (49 percent opposed, 38 percent in favor).

On a key issue in Middle East relations—whether an independent Palestinian state should be established on the West Bank and Gaza Strip—leaders are overwhelmingly in favor (77 percent), with only 18 percent opposed. Support is much lower among the

Biggest Problems Facing the Country
"What do you feel are the two or three biggest problems facing the country today?"
(four most common responses)

Public		Leaders	
Crime	26%	Education	26%
The President/Bill Clinton	22%	Dissatisfaction with Government	14%
Drug Abuse	21%	Immorality	14%
Education	15%	Asian Economy	13%

public (36 percent), with 26 percent opposed and a plurality (38 percent) offering no opinion.

The most pressing perceived problems in the Middle East do not appear to include Islamic fundamentalism. This phenomenon is low on the list of perceived critical threats to U.S. vital interests for both the public and leaders. Yet, a plurality of 38 percent of the public now perceive it as a critical threat, a five-point increase from 1994.

Persian Gulf: Crisis Redux

A series of new crises involving Iraq raised the foreign-policy profile of the region during 1998, particularly at the end of the year. Since the U.S.-British attack on Iraq occurred after the public survey had been conducted but before the leadership survey was fully completed, leaders, not surprisingly, view Iraq as more threatening than do the public, ranking relations with this country as the second biggest foreign-policy problem. Leaders are significantly more supportive than the public of U.S. intervention if Iraq were to invade Saudi Arabia (79 percent vs. 46 percent). In terms of vital interests, Saudi Arabia remains high among both leaders (88 percent) and the public (77 percent).

BRACING FOR THE TWENTY-FIRST CENTURY

As the United States enjoys the strongest economic strength and military strength in decades, the survey findings point to some clouds on the horizon that warrant attention.

During a period when the United States has been acting unilaterally in response to some crises abroad, nearly three-quarters of

the public prefer that the United States act together with allies, not alone.

Despite the perception of many vital interests around the world, public support for using troops to defend those interests has declined.

Perhaps the most poignant finding in the survey is the dramatic difference in future outlook between the public and their leaders. Although leaders are optimistic about a more peaceful twenty-first century, the public fear more bloodshed and violence than in the present one, during which an estimated 150 million people have perished in conflict. At a time when most people believe increased global cooperation and strong leadership are needed to solve current problems and thereby prevent future violence and instability, continued public support for international involvement is encouraging. Nevertheless, the guarded nature of that engagement could prove problematic if global leadership requires the United States to make tougher choices in the next century than it has faced thus far as the post-Cold War world's only superpower.

WANT TO KNOW MORE?

Contact the Chicago Council on Foreign Relations for further information on the full report, *American Public Opinion and U.S. Foreign Policy 1999,* or visit the Chicago Council's Web site, **www.ccfrg.org.** The analysis for this study was prepared with the following collaborators: Arthur Cyr, Clausen distinguished professor at Carthage College; Stephen Del Rosso Jr., program director of the Chicago Council; April Kanne Donnellan, program officer of the Chicago Council; Catharine Hug, consultant; Benjamin Page, Fulcher professor

Biggest Foreign-Policy Problems Facing the Country
"What do you feel are the two or three biggest foreign-policy problems facing the United States today?"
(Five Most Common Responses)

Public		Leaders	
Don't Know	21%	World Economy	21%
Terrorism	12%	Iraq	18%
World Economy	11%	Arms Control	15%
Balance of Payments	10%	Japan/Asian Economy/Crisis	13%
Middle East Situation	8%	Dealings with Russia	13%

of decision making at Northwestern University; Richard Sobel, political scientist at Harvard University; and Jason Barabas, doctoral student in political science at Northwestern University.*

To understand how domestic public and élite sentiments on foreign policy have shifted since the Chicago Council's last nationwide survey, read John E. Rielly, ed., *American Public Opinion and U.S. Foreign Policy 1995* (Chicago: Chicago Council on Foreign Relations, 1995). Rielly's **"The Public Mood at Mid-Decade"** (FOREIGN POLICY, Spring 1995) provides a summary and an analysis of the 1994 survey's findings. For a contrasting view, see *America's Place in the World II* (Washington: Pew Research Center for the People & the Press, 1997). The most in-depth analysis of the Chicago Council's surveys was undertaken in Eugene Wittkopf's *Faces of Internationalism: Public Opinion and American Foreign Policy* (Durham: Duke University Press, 1990).

To find another recent surveys of American public attitudes on foreign-policy "hot-button" topics ranging from NATO enlargement to U.S. funding of the United Nations and the International Monetary Fund, consult the series of studies published by the **Program on International Policy Attitudes** (PIPA). A clearing-house for thousands of surveys, the **Roper Center for Public Opinion** is also an excellent resource for all students of the subject.

Much of the recent debate among academics has focused on the perceived disjoint between leaders and the American public on the issue of how prominent a role the United States should play overseas. Steven Kull, I.M. Destler, and Clay Ramsay contend that policymakers have mistakenly identified an isolationist impulse in the American people in their report. **The Foreign Policy Gap: How Policymakers Misread the Public** (College Park: PIPA, 1997). Kull summarizes his view on the topic in **"What the Public Knows That**

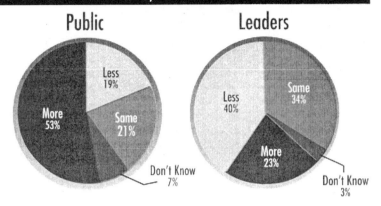

Bloodshed and Violence in the 21st Century

"Some have argued that the 20th Century has been the most violent in human history, with an estimated 150 million people having perished from war and other acts of violence. Do you believe that there will be less bloodshed and violence, more bloodshed and violence, or about the same in the 21st Century?"

Public
Less 19%
More 53%
Same 21%
Don't Know 7%

Leaders
Less 40%
Same 34%
More 23%
Don't Know 3%

Washington Doesn't" (FOREIGN POLICY, Winter 1996).

Across the Atlantic, an invaluable asset to understanding how Europeans view regional and global developments is the **Eurobarometer** series organized by the European Commission. The latest installments of the *Standard Eurobarometer* and the *Central and Eastern Eurobarometer* are available on the EU's official Web site, **Europa.** For public-opinion research in 25 countries ranging from China to Chile, an excellent source is the **Gallup Organization's** Web site.

The power of the American public over the conduct of foreign policy has been hotly contested over the years. A classic work on the subject is Gabriel Almond's *The American People and Foreign Policy* (New York: Praeger, 1954). A more recent assessment is Bruce Russett's **Controlling the Sword: The Democractic Governance of National Security** (Cambridge: Harvard University Press, 1990). Thomas Graham outlines the conditions under which public opinion shapes policy formulation in *Public Opinion and U.S. Foreign Policy Decision Making"* in David Deese, ed., *The New Politics of American Foreign Policy* (New York: St. Martin's Press, 1994). Eric Alterman's **Who Speaks for America: Why Democracy Matters in Foreign Policy?** (Ithaca: Cornell University Press, 1998) argues provacatively that the American Public has, at best, a muted voice in the making of U.S. foreign policy.

For links to relevant Web sites, as well as a comprehensive index of related FOREIGN POLICY articles, access *www.foreignpolicy.com.*

---

* The nationwide survey on which these findings are based was conducted by the Gallup Organization between October 15 and November 10, 1998. During that period, 1,507 men and women were interviewed in person. In addition, a total of 379 leaders were interviewed by telephone between November 2 and December 21, 1998. The leadership sample includes members of the Clinton administration, Congress, international business, media, labor, academic and religious institutions, private foreign-policy organizations, and special-interest groups with expertise in foreign affairs.

WHEN THE BODY BAGS COME HOME, *Americans lose their stomach for combat—or so U.S. leaders believe. A new study suggests that view is wrong.*

How Many Deaths Are Acceptable? A Surprising Answer

By PETER D. FEAVER *and* CHRISTOPHER GELPI

The good news is that we drove Serbian troops out of Kosovo without suffering any U.S. combat fatalities, a testament to American military professionalism and prowess.

The bad news is that the foreign policy community, both inside and outside the U.S. government, generally believes that Americans demand a casualty-free victory as the price of supporting any military intervention abroad.

These influential elites are wrong. They have bought into a powerful myth, born during the Vietnam War and cemented during the ill-fated Somalia action of October 1993, that Americans are casualty-shy.

Though the belief has become conventional wisdom, it is not well supported by public opinion polls. A careful analysis of surveys that we conducted last fall and winter shows convincingly that the general public is far more willing to tolerate combat losses than civilian policymakers—or senior military officers.

Peter Feaver is an associate professor of political science at Duke University, and co-principal investigator of the TISS Project on the Gap Between the Military and Civilian Society. Christopher Gelpi is an assistant professor of political science at Duke.

From the *Washington Post,* November 7, 1999, p. B3. © 1999 by The Washington Post Writers Group. Reprinted by permission.

The casualty-aversion myth has no doubt been exacerbated by President Clinton's awkward relations with the military and thus constitutes part of his troubled legacy in foreign policy. But our research suggests the issue will outlast this president. Coming to terms with it will be a major challenge for the next administration.

Defenders of the "we can't take it anymore" school of thought offer no concrete evidence for their position. Instead, they retreat to anecdotes about the Somalia debacle and the "CNN effect." They say televised images of starving Somalis moved Americans to demand the United States intervene in that country's civil war in December 1992, and images of a dead U.S. soldier being dragged through the streets of Somalia's capital just as rapidly moved them to demand a retreat 10 months later.

That is not what happened.

There was a CNN effect in Somalia, but it did not involve the American public; it involved government officials.

In a recent speech, former president George Bush described how the decision to commit U.S. troops to Somalia came after he and his wife, watching TV, saw "those starving kids . . . in quest of a little pitiful cup of rice." He said he phoned his national security team and said, "Please come over to the White House. I—we—can't watch this anymore. You've got to do something."

Different leaders but a similar dynamic precipitated America's humiliating withdrawal. As news of the disastrous Ranger raid—which left 18 American troops dead—came over the airwaves, members of Congress rushed to the floor to

What They Said

The question about casualty aversion was one of several in the survey done by the Triangle Institute for Security Studies (TISS) Project on the Gap Between the Military and Civilian Society:

WHO WAS POLLED The military elite, 623 officers whose promise for advancement has been recognized by assignment to attend the professional military education course appropriate for their rank; the civilian elite, 683 non-veterans selected from Who's Who in America and other directories of leading Americans, foreign policy opinion leaders, and civilians studying at professional military education institutions; the mass public, 1001 adults selected as a representative national sample by Princeton Research Associates.

WHEN THE SURVEY WAS DONE TISS collected data between September 1998 and June 1999.

THE QUESTION When American troops are sent overseas, there are almost always casualties. For instance, 43 Americans were killed in Somalia, 383 in the Gulf War, roughly 54,000 in Korea, roughly

demand that the mission be aborted. The White House, moved by the same images, began to shut down the operation.

The public can distinguish between suffering defeat and suffering casualties.

When asked by an interviewer about the gruesome TV footage, Clinton took pains to draw a parallel with Bush's reasoning. "I just think it's irresistible to show vivid images. . . . The same television power is what got the country and the world community into it in the first place."

One of us—Feaver—was on the National Security Council staff during this period. Though not privy to Oval Office counsels, the staff realized within 24 hours of the first ugly TV reports that the administration had lost its stomach for the Somalia mission.

Outside the Beltway, however, a majority of Americans were less queasy. Studies by foreign policy experts Eric Larson, James Burk, Steven Kull and I.M. Destler, re-analyzing polls taken during the crisis, demonstrate that even after the television reports, there was a reservoir of public support for the operation. If the sight of dead American soldiers somewhat undermined it, it was because the Clinton administration made no effort to frame the casualties as anything other than a disaster in a mission that had drifted dreadfully off course.

ILLUSTRATION BY DAVID McLIMANS FOR THE WASHINGTON POST

58,000 in Vietnam and roughly 400,000 in World War II. Imagine for a moment that a President decided to send military troops on one of the following missions. In your opinion, what would be the highest number of American military deaths that would be acceptable to achieve this goal?

A) To stabilize a democratic government in **Congo**_____.*
B) To prevent **Iraq** from obtaining weapons of mass destruction_____.
C) To defend **Taiwan** against invasion by China_____.

THE RESULTS

Military Mission	Military Elite	Civilian Elite	Mass Public
Congo	284	484	6,861
Iraq	6,016	19,045	29,853
Taiwan	17,425	17,554	20,172

* The survey did not specify the Democratic Republic of Congo (formerly Zaire) or the Republic of Congo

Had the administration chosen instead to galvanize public opposition to Somali warlord Mohamed Farah Aideed, our research suggests that Americans would have tolerated an *expanded* effort to catch and punish him.

We and two dozen fellow scholars have just completed an extensive analysis of the views of some 4,900 Americans, drawn from three groups: senior or rising military officers, influential civilians and the general public. It was part of a major investigation of American civil-military relations conducted by the Triangle Institute for Security Studies (TISS), a faculty consortium based at Duke University, the University of North Carolina at Chapel Hill and North Carolina State University. The study was prompted by concerns, expressed in 1997 by Secretary of Defense William Cohen and echoed elsewhere, about the possibility of a growing gap between the U.S. armed forces and American society as a whole—one that could harm military effectiveness and civil-military cooperation.

Our study confirmed that the myth of casualty aversion is entrenched at the upper levels of society. Overwhelmingly, both civilian and military leaders agreed with the statement, "The American public will rarely tolerate large numbers of U.S. casualties in military operations."

But a very different picture emerges from the citizens themselves. We asked respondents to consider how many American deaths would be acceptable to complete three plausible missions successfully: defending Taiwan against China; preventing Iraq from acquiring weapons of mass destruction; and defending democracy in Congo. We compared the answers from the general public with those from two groups of influential civilians and members of the military.

Regarding America's long-standing commitment to defend Taiwan against China, we found broad consensus: All three groups agree that this mission would be worth the sacrifice of a substantial number of American lives.

No such consensus exists, however, with regard to typical post-Cold War missions in Iraq and Congo.

First, the general public indicates that it is willing to accept not just hundreds but thousands of casualties to accomplish these missions.

On average, our sample of the public allowed even higher numbers of casualties to curb Iraqi weapons than to defend Taiwan. This may reflect lingering traces of successful Bush-Clinton efforts to demonize Saddam Hussein combined with Clinton's attempts to pursue a conciliatory policy toward China.

The public's estimates for the mission to restore democracy in Congo were much lower, but were nonetheless substantial. In fact, they were many times higher than the actual casualties suffered by the U.S. military in all post-Cold War military actions combined.

The numbers cited on this page are averages, of course, and it is important that they be interpreted in general terms. For instance, we would not predict that most Americans would stop supporting democracy in Congo the day the death toll reached 6,182. And certainly there is a difference between asking people to guess how they would feel about casualties and the reality of seeing actual body bags. But the sheer numbers, and the dramatic differences between our sample groups, are surely significant.

Collectively, these results suggest that a majority of the American people will accept combat deaths—*so long as the mission has the potential to be successful.* The public can distinguish between suffering defeat and suffering casualties.

By far the lowest acceptable casualty figures in our study came from the military. Regarding the "non-traditional" military missions, elite military officers responded with estimates that were one-fourth to one-half those of elite civilians. Of course, this aversion to casualties is, in part, a function of what might be called rational calculations. That is, one reason military officers give lower casualty estimates for non-traditional missions is that they do not believe those missions are vital to the national interest. It stands to reason, therefore, that they would not consider them worth extensive loss of American lives.

Likewise, respondents who have a friend or relative in the military are slightly more averse to casualties, although the effect appears to be marginal. (Data on this point are not broken down here, but like many other factors we studied, they are reported and analyzed in more complex ways in our complete report. More information can be found at our Web site: *www.poli.duke.edu/civmil.*)

Even after accounting for these "rational effects," however, the gap between the military and the other samples remains significant. Moreover, it exists despite the relatively low number of women and the lower average age in the military. (As a group, women and older people are substantially more averse to casualties.)

Significantly, the evidence indicates that casualty aversion is not simply a function of self-preservation. If that were the case, we would expect sensitivity to be highest among officers whose roles are combat-related. However, our data show virtually no difference in casualty aversion among the combat, combat support and other sub-samples of elite military officers. Even more telling, younger officers, who are more likely to see combat duty, are more tolerant of casualties.

Instead, we think several factors are at work. For one, officers certainly feel a special responsibility for their troops' welfare. Second, senior officers may lack confidence in the reliability of civilian leaders; thus they fear that the government will abandon the military if casualties mount. Finally, casualty aversion may be an aspect of a growing zero-defect mentality among senior officers, in which casualties are not only deaths—they are an immediate indication that an operation is a failure. If a zero-defect mentality is on the rise, then civilian leaders must share culpability for this problem.

There are at least three reasons to be concerned about our leaders' attitudes regarding casualty aversion. First, their planning could be hamstrung by the erroneous belief that the public will demand that they cut and run at the first American combat deaths.

Of course, it is important to prevent or limit American casualties as much as possible. But it would be a grave mistake to believe that we can wield influence around the world and use our military to defend national interests without risking casualties. It is also a mistake to believe that the American public is unwilling to take risks when its leaders say that risks are appropriate.

Casualty aversion creates a second and more subtle threat to national security: It is corrosive to the professional military ethic. As retired Army colonel and West Point professor Donald M. Snider has argued, our military is built on the principles of self-sacrifice and mission accomplishment. Troops are supposed to be willing to die so that civilians do not have to.

In the Bosnian peacekeeping operation, casualty aversion reached an unprecedented level. "Force protection," meaning the prevention of U.S. casualties, became an explicit mission goal, on par with, if not superseding, the primary mission of restoring peace to Bosnia. As a result, war criminals were not aggressively pursued and arrested, community-building activities were curtailed, and every stray movement of a U.S. peacekeeper was a mission-threatening event.

Finally, if American casualties are politically impossible, then citizens of other countries will be at greater risk. While NATO was arguably victorious in Kosovo without losing a pilot in combat, that was achieved by forgoing a ground invasion, using high-altitude bombing and otherwise shifting the costs of the conflict onto the people of Kosovo and Serbia. By our own actions, we turned the famous question on its head: How many Yugoslavs are worth the life of a single American?

Our study cannot say whether America ought to be intervening in conflicts around the world, or whether we ought to be willing to suffer casualties in order to do so. But we can recommend that policymakers start listening more carefully to the expressed—not mythical—views of the American people. A myth is hardly sound footing for American foreign policy in the 21st century.

NO-FIRST-USE FOR NATO?

*In December the House of Commons Standing Committee on Foreign
Affairs and International Trade issued a report recommending, among other
things, that NATO adopt a policy of no-first-use of nuclear weapons. Last month,
Policy Options editor* **William Watson** *asked the chairman of the committee, the
Hon.* **Bill Graham,** *and* **Frank Gaffney,** *founder and director of the Washington-based
Center for Security Policy and Deputy Assistant Secretary of Defense for Nuclear
Forces and Arms Control Policy in the Reagan administration, to discuss this
proposal by conference call. Here is an edited transcript of their conversation.*

Mr. Graham, last December your committee published a report recommending, among other things, that NATO consider adopting a policy of no-first-use of nuclear weapons. What's your reason for wanting to change NATO's current policy, which is that nuclear weapons are a weapon of last resort?

Bill Graham: Let me make two points. The report clearly says that for NATO to conduct a strategic review and not to review the nuclear component of its strategy just doesn't make sense, and, therefore, the nuclear review should take place as a part of the over-all strategic review by NATO. Others, particularly in the defense department in the United States, feel strongly that this subject shouldn't even be talked about. So, really, there are two conversations here. One is, is it appropriate to have a review as a part of NATO's review and, two, if you do, then what's your point of view of what the policy should [be]? Should it be no-first-use, should it be the status quo, or what? The committee's conclusion, and certainly my own, is that the important thing is that this be on the agenda for discussion, that the strategic review of NATO will lack credibility if it doesn't discuss this issue, even if, in the end, the allies together come to the conclusion that the status quo is the appropriate place to be.

That said, you can then go on and say, "Where would you be if you were in that debate?" and I personally would lean towards those that would say, "Well, I think there's a momentum now for NATO to consider a no-first-use policy," but that's another discussion and that was not the recommendation of the report.

Could you explain why you do lean in the direction of no-first-use?

Bill Graham: I want to make it clear that I am not a nuclear policy expert in any way. I came to this as someone whose job was to hear Canadians and try to understand their position *vis-à-vis* that of our allies and those others outside of Canada that we were able to talk to, in the context of considering this issue and then referring this matter to the government for a response, which they will give in the House of Commons to the recommendations of the report. So, with that caveat, what we heard was that the first-use policy of NATO first came about as a deterrence factor at a time when NATO forces in Europe had a conventional disparity *vis-á-vis* the Soviet Union. In fact, the Warsaw Pact had an enormous superiority. That is no longer the case and that in itself, I think, has changed one's views.

We heard the US National Academy of Sciences, and the Canberra Commission, and General George Lee Butler, commander of the United States Strategic Command from 1992 to 1994, and the Pugwash Conference, and statements by people like Paul Nitze and retired General Andrew Goodpastor and former Secretary of Defense Robert McNamara. Most of those highly qualified people are saying, "Now is the time to go for no-first-use." The persuasive thing for me is that it moves the agenda along in trying to persuade other countries that they have to give up the idea of developing nuclear weapons. We have to deal with a nuclear Israel, we have to deal now with a nuclear Pakistan and a nuclear India. I was just on a trip to

Iran. If the West doesn't have any credibility in bringing nuclear weapons down and reducing their availability and their usefulness, then the other states are going to be driven to acquiring them.

Frank Gaffney: I believe it's a bit disingenuous, frankly, to suggest that we're only interested in talking about it. People who are interested in having this idea on the agenda clearly have in mind bringing pressure to bear on the United States, and the NATO alliance more generally, to adopt a policy that NATO has for the better part of its 50 years of existence deemed unacceptable. I am among those supporters of NATO

If the West doesn't have any credibility in bringing nuclear weapons down and reducing their availability and their usefulness, then other states will be driven to acquire them.

who think that even in a post-Cold War world the NATO alliance is an important instrument for peace, both in its own immediate region and, to some extent, more generally. Anything which contributes to divisiveness and the perception that NATO is driven by internal strife in one form or another is counterproductive. And it's particularly unhelpful when the alliance is supposedly trying to celebrate its half century of success. So I would be opposed to talking about it unless people are serious about changing the policy. To suggest that the proponents of this are not serious about changing the policy is either misleading or suggests that the whole exercise would be counterproductive.

But the bigger problem is, why would you change this policy? I do consider myself something of a nuclear policy expert, even if Bill chooses to describe his credentials as otherwise. In 25 years of work in this field, I've seen a lot of ideas, nostrums and notions advanced. And one of the hoariest is that if only we behave in such and such a fashion, countries around the world like Iran will see the wisdom of eschewing nuclear weapons. This is, on the face of it, laughable. I must say with all due respect that it is laughable to suggest that Iran is motivated in its pursuit of nuclear weapons—or for that matter chemical weapons or biological weapons or the long-range ballistic missiles with which to deliver them or any form of weaponry—by what they think is the declaratory policy of the United States government or NATO or some other

country that might be setting some sort of high moral tone.

Finally, and I know this does not sit well with my Canadian friends, but in the interest of candour and a frank and therefore constructive relationship between our two countries I think it best to say: It is deeply distressing to me that in this area a country that is currently bearing very little of the share of the burden of providing for its own security, let alone anybody else's security, is insisting on dictating, or at least instructing, the country that is principally providing for its security as to the terms and conditions under which that security will be provided. As a case in point, I know that I'm wearing the scars of what I consider to be an extremely counterproductive and dangerous Canadian initiative on banning landmines. It is the height of irresponsibility, in my judgment, for the United States to be coerced, pressured, cajoled, intimidated, choose your verb, by its Canadian ally, among others of course, into giving up weapons that are deemed by our military to be essential to providing for the security of our own troops and those that they are in places around the world to protect, which I suggest includes Canadian interests broadly defined as well.

Bill Graham: I certainly don't mean to be disingenuous. What I do say, though, is that I believe strongly that this matter should be debated. But it is the governments in NATO that will debate it, so it is in no way Canada dictating anything to anybody, including the United States. We're talking about NATO here. The United States can keep any policy it wants. It has that sovereign right. Nobody is saying the United States should give up its no-first-use policy, that's its internal debate. But we are a participant in NATO, and Germany is a participant in NATO, too. If American strategists are concerned about NATO cohesion, well, I think the genie is out of the bottle, and to try to suppress it at this point would be much more dangerous. If you look at the vote in the United Nations on the new agenda, it was very clear that the majority of the United States' and our NATO allies abstained along with us on that resolution, clearly indicating that within NATO itself there's a strong push. Even if it were just Germany alone, but with Germany, Canada and various other countries dealing with this, I think it has to be debated in NATO.

If this ends up causing a change in policy, then we'd have to look at whether that change is desirable or not. But I would have thought that if Frank's position is as well-founded in policy as he puts it, he has nothing to fear from an open debate, and he can give the back of his hand to the National Academy of Sciences, the Canberra Commission, General Butler, General Goodpastor and everybody else and tell them they're out to lunch. But that will have to be a debate that takes place within that NATO context.

How about the argument that Iraq or Iran will not pay any attention to what the NATO declaration says?

Bill Graham: As I say I've just come back from Iran—that hardly makes me an expert on Iran—but one of the problems is that when you talk to people, they say, "Well, Israel's there, they've got the nuclear weapons, they haven't signed the non-proliferation treaty, we've signed the non-proliferation treaty." They say, "We don't trust you, we don't care what you say, you're going to do whatever you're going to do."

At some point, we have to work towards constraining people from access to nuclear weapons. We do that through our policies in the various forums where we control access to nuclear technology, and so on. But I think we have to try and draw people in as well where they believe there is some greater form of greater disarmament that is taking place by the major powers. I mean, India said, "Well, look we've developed a nuclear weapon because we will not be dictated to by the other countries as to whether we should have one or not, they themselves are making no serious disarmament moves." I disagree with that by the way. I think the United States and the Soviet Union have made some enormously serious moves in disarmament. So that's an exaggerated position, but it is a position we have to be able to deal with.

Frank Gaffney: It is a fraud. It is an excuse designed to induce, on the part of Westerners, a sense of responsibility for behaviour that these countries are pursuing for their own reasons that have nothing to do with policies or positions of the United States or others. You might argue that the Indians are pursuing it because of the Pakistanis or the Chinese, but the United States could become a zero nuclear weapons state and I daresay it would be an inducement to the Iranians and the Indians and these other characters to proceed apace because then they become bigger fish than otherwise.

But if I may come back to a point I didn't address in my initial response. We're hearing cited as authorities for a policy that NATO has consistently rejected over the years the Canberra Commission, the Pugwash Conference, the several distinguished former American generals and Secretary of Defense. I think it only fair to point out that these institutions and individuals have associated themselves with the idea of abolishing nuclear weapons. Now I don't know where the government of Canada is on abolishing nuclear weapons. They're certainly following the logic of abolishing landmines. If you believe you can abolish landmines, you certainly can abolish nuclear weapons. But since you can't abolish either, it is nonsense to even discuss it—unless what you really are about is taking huge risks by disarming the country that you know you can disarm, which is of course the United States, and letting the devil take the hindmost with respect to the others, who will not observe international

treaty obligations. We know this on the basis of historical experience. These countries will, to the contrary, see this as an opportunity to advance their national agendas, improving their relative positions *vis-à-vis* the United States or for that matter, the United States and its allies, like NATO. My point is that we must not lose sight of the agenda of at least some of the individuals whose advice the committee apparently has taken to heart.

I think it's time to call a spade a spade. They have embarked upon a loony left-wing disarmament agenda, the first step of which is a policy shift that seems relatively innocuous: announcing we no longer will use nuclear weapons first. Another step embraced by many of these organizations is to de-alert our nuclear weapons so they couldn't be used even if the policy were otherwise. But the desired end result is clear. And I think we ought to hear: Does the government of Canada or the parliamentary forces within Canada or Mr. Graham individually believe that in the world we are currently in or are about to enter we can safely abandon or abolish nuclear weapons—or not? And if not, you might want to distance yourself somewhat from the authorities who are now telling you it would also be a splendid idea to announce a no-first-use policy.

Bill Graham: I didn't, quite frankly, get the impression that the people who have been mentioned, while they are seeking to reduce nuclear weapons completely as a long-term goal, are in any way dewy-eyed crazies. They all were talking the language of extreme caution in moving towards that goal, which would be accompanied by appropriate surveillance and international controls. Our committee didn't espouse—and I cannot speak for the government of Canada, but I do believe that when the government of Canada responds to our report in the House of Commons, they will not adopt—some, "Yes, let's just go and get everybody to agree to get rid of everything" without any controls, without the usual steps that we're going through which take an extreme degree of caution and a great deal of surveillance and mutual reductions.

Frank Gaffney: As opposed to landmines.

Bill Graham: No, landmines as well.

If you think you can abolish landmines, you certainly can abolish nuclear weapons. But since you can't abolish either, it is nonsense to even discuss it.

Frank Gaffney: No, there were no controls on land-mines. There was none of this caution. It was "Let's go do it right now and make ourselves all feel better."

Bill Graham: We could discuss landmines, but I think that in fact the treaty has been extremely successful and I believe the time will come when the United States signs on.

Frank Gaffney: The landmine ban has not prevented the building or deployment of a single landmine any-where on the planet.

Bill Graham: I think that your comment about Canada bearing a small security burden really should not go unchallenged. Whether you want to talk about Mr. Axworthy's concept of human security, which a lot of people are very interested in, or whether you look at what Canada is doing in peacekeeping, we're making a contribution to security in a way which I believe helps the United States in its security. When we put our peacekeepers into Haiti and into Bosnia and contribute to these operations, these are coming at no little cost to us. When the allies are talking about the present Kosovo situation, the prime minister has said he will look very favourably at a Canadian contribution. I'm sure that when that matter is debated in the House, I would strongly speak in favour of it. I believe that is the type of operation where we must contribute and also recognize tremendous United States leadership. But that doesn't mean we have to agree on every other single item about where we're going, and nuclear weapons, landmines and a few others are clearly areas where we disagree. But I don't think we should get confused in that sort of debate and say that "You guys are doing nothing." That's an unfortunate exaggeration of the situation.

Frank Gaffney: As to whether people are dewy-eyed crazies who espouse the long-term abolition of nuclear weapons, you can use whatever qualifiers, adjectives, conditions, caveats, you wish. It is dewy-eyed crazy to believe that you can rid the world of nuclear weapons. It is fatuous nonsense. You cannot disinvent the technology. You cannot prevent it from proliferating further. You cannot dissuade people who now have either the means to buy this technology or make it available to themselves from proceeding to get it. I respectfully suggest that it is crazy and really misleading to think that people who can embrace that as a long-term goal are not impeaching their judgment on what seem to be less controversial or less radical but nearer-term steps. This is particularly true since they entail a real danger of increasing the possibilities of war through miscalculation rather than making the world a more peaceful place.

The problem with changing the policy of no-first-use—and the reason for my extreme reluctance to start a debate that, almost inevitably, will try to move NATO toward embracing that policy—is that it may create in the minds of potential aggressors a sense

that war is a more doable do, that it is less risky, that it is less deterred than it should be and then I think we have a responsibility to make it. That's the policy that has worked for us for 50 years and I believe it should be perpetuated.

A final point on this: I don't for a minute discount the fact that Canada is contributing to peacekeeping operations and thinks it is contributing to the security of the world by promulgating and promoting these kinds of arms control notions. I am simply saying that what history teaches us is that wars happen. Wars generally happen, certainly in this century, after people embark on this kind of nuttiness, this kind of self-delusion, that "human security" and arms control are going to provide for the physical security of their countries.

What Canada is doing to dissipate what is left of its armed forces and use what remains of those forces in places like Kosovo, which have precious little to do with Canada's security and certainly less with the larger international security than does the question of whether or not we are going to maintain a coherent, viable, credible NATO and a NATO nuclear deterrent. I would prefer to see Canada adopting a different set of priorities than the one which is obviously in place.

NATO has discussed its nuclear strategy in the past and has moved from a doctrine of massive retaliation to flexible response to, in the early nineties, a weapons-of-last-resort doctrine. Haven't we slid down most of the slippery slope already? Why is it that discussion of no-first-use would create an even greater danger? And in what circumstances these days could you imagine first-use?

Frank Gaffney: I believe, based on my study and my own personal involvement as a Defense Department official leading NATO's High Level Group, that nuclear weapons have always been something that American officials and NATO officials would be very reluctant to use. Even during the days when we were facing a great disparity between the armed forces of the Soviet Warsaw Pact and very little conventional capability on the part of the West, there was never any illusion on the part of Western leaders, certainly in the United States, that nuclear weapons would be a very, very unattractive option for the West to have to use in its defense. You'd wind up destroying a good part of the West to save the rest.

The steps that have been taken to this point to refine the kind of weapons we have, the kind of doctrine we have for their employment and the kind of circumstances under which they would be used, all was consistent with *enhancing* deterrence, not undermining it. Our concern and NATO's historical concern and the concern NATO felt even when Andy Goodpastor was SHAPE's commander was that you don't want to take steps that would encourage others to believe that nuclear weapons might not be used at all.

The circumstances under which they would be used, if at all now, would be ones in which vital security interests of NATO were clearly, imminently threatened and as a matter of last resort and in as discriminate a way as possible to try to prevent that threat from materializing. But I think it will help enormously to keep that threat from materializing if we refrain from increasing people's uncertainty as to what would be the consequence if such a threat, in fact, did get used.

Bill Graham: I totally agree that within the NATO circles and amongst the strategy experts, the essence of the debate will turn around the issue of deterrence, because that is the only justifiable use or possession of nuclear weapons. When you look at it, it's hard to imagine any circumstance in which they will be used or could be used. But the fact of the matter is it is a deterrent, and as Mr. Gaffney says, it has served the alliance well in a certain context. Now the question is whether we move into a new phase. Everything in life is a series of tradeoffs. Deterrence is one thing, but if in fact by keeping to the present policies we contribute to the instability of the world and encourage other countries to decide to acquire nuclear weapons because of the fear that they might be used against them first, then of course we've not created a climate of deterrence and security, we've increased the insecurity and created a much more dangerous place. We don't want another 50 nuclear states galloping around the world. I think that perhaps the difference between Mr. Gaffney and myself is that he thinks that anybody who wants to become a nuclear state will do it anyway, regardless of the world conditions because they're all evil and can't be controlled. My view is

that we have to set in place some form of international framework within which we can work on these issues and bring them to the position where they recognize that it's not worth their while to get them.

Pakistan and India today are not better off for each having nuclear weapons. Everybody agrees that they're both far worse off from a military and every other point of view. They've just moved it up to the point where a possible Kashmir could be far more destructive than it otherwise was. So this it seems is what we're trying to work toward, this is the debate I'd like to see in NATO.

Frank Gaffney: Well, it remains to be seen whether things are worse on the subcontinent. I think you may, in fact, now see a standoff that perhaps permits a resolution of the Kashmir problem because neither side can afford to have a nuclear exchange over it. We'll see. My point is not that every country in the world is evil but that every country that wants nuclear weapons can get them. It is illusory to think that we will prevent them by exercising restraint and particularly in saying that a policy we felt was critical to NATO's security position for 50 years now is somehow the engine for causing others to proceed in a nuclear armaments program of their own. It hasn't been, it won't be, and we will simply do ourselves harm. The kind of calculation or balance that Mr. Graham is talking about is right but his answer is wrong. The costs that he perceives are not, in fact, the result of the policy that he proposes to change. If we change it, I don't think the result will be a real diminution of the proliferation of nuclear weapons around the world.

Thank you very much for doing this.

Canada's water:

Hands off

OTTAWA

"BLUE gold" is the latest catch-phrase to gain currency in Canada. It refers to the country's abundant water resources, estimated to amount to one-fifth of the world's total supply of fresh water. Water, declared Terence Corcoran, editor of the Toronto-based *Financial Post,* will be "the oil of the 21st century". As such a well-stocked supplier, Canada would stand to gain handsomely from a boom in demand for fresh water. But the subject is prompting more controversy than glee.

On November 29th and 30th, David Anderson, Canada's environment minister, and his ten provincial counterparts, whose governments jointly own nearly all the country's water, met to discuss water policy. The biggest headache is the prospect of large-scale water exports, for which firms in several provinces are lining up with export applications. The governments are formally against the idea, partly for ecological reasons, and, under pressure from the federal government, each province has now declared a six-month moratorium on approving any licences. Moreover, protest groups have been rallying to the issue, and some gathered this week to block the road bridge to Kananaskis, in the Rocky Mountains, where the ministers were meeting.

The matter has touched a raw nerve in a country deeply protective of its natural environment. In a report on the global water shortage entitled "Blue Gold", published in June, Maude Barlow, who heads the country's big-gest pressure group, the Council of Canadians, called Canada's fresh water "our lifeblood". She argued that water should be left where it is wherever possible and called for a "local sources first" policy worldwide. In short: hands off Canada's water. In September, her council sponsored a "water watch summit" of 40 protest groups, which called on both tiers of government to ban the bulk removal and export of water.

The bogeyman, as so often for Canadians, is the United States. To meet the demands of farmers and the growing population of the south-western states, ambitious and hugely controversial schemes have long been floated for diverting Canadian rivers southward. One would divert the Yukon and Mackenzie rivers down the Rocky Mountain Trench; another, which would be equally damaging to the environment, would trap several Quebec rivers inside a dike across James Bay, and flush the water through the Great Lakes. Yet it is the recent flood of far more modest applications to ship out water by the tankerful, not these vast diversion schemes, that have prompted the present calls to ban bulk exports.

Only recently, the Ontario government approved and then rescinded one application to ship water by tanker from Lake Superior to Asia, while the Newfoundland government pulled back from approving a much larger shipment to the Middle East. A Vancouver company hopes to ship Alaska's glacier water to China for bottling, which would skirt the British Columbia government's own ban on bulk exports that dates from 1993. A would-be importing company in California is now suing the British Columbia government for losses under this ban, saying it violates NAFTA rules on free trade in North America.

Ahead of this week's ministerial meeting, the federal government announced changes it wanted made to the Boundary Waters Treaty in order to prevent bulk water exports, and referred the Lake Superior case to the International Joint Commission, which deals with boundary waters. But the Newfoundland and British Columbia cases are outside the commission's mandate. So the federal government has now invited the provinces to sign a deal to ban, for environmental reasons, the bulk withdrawal of water at its source—an attempt at an export ban by other means.

To the fury of the government of British Columbia, there is, however, no mention in this deal of an explicit, water-tight export ban—partly for fear that this might amount to a concession that water is a tradable good, and therefore that it does fall under NAFTA's free-trade rules. Quebec and the prairie provinces also refused this week to sign the accord. A decision is now delayed until May next year, leaving Mr. Anderson to grumble that "contrived indecision" will only make Canada's resources even more sought-after.

Unit 5

Key Points to Consider

❖ What are some of the costs and benefits of the North American Free Trade Agreement for America? Canada? Mexico?

❖ What else might the United States do to stem the tide of drugs and illegal immigrants from Mexico? Colombia?

❖ What can the United States, Canada, and European countries do to encourage continued democratic and economic reform in Latin America?

 **Links**   **www.dushkin.com/online/**

18. **Inter-American Dialogue**
    http://www.iadialog.org

These sites are annotated on pages 6 and 7.

For nearly two centuries, the United States viewed Latin America as being within its exclusive sphere of influence. But several countries in the region are developing independent international security policies. In "The International Relations of Latin America and the Caribbean: Defining the New Era," G. Pope Atkins describes recent regional trends and outlines the reason why democratic development and economic reform are the new overarching norms in hemispheric relations.

Few Americans appreciate that North American Free Trade Association (NAFTA) countries purchase 40 percent of U.S. exports. Today the state of the Canadian and Mexican economies is as important for the continued health of the U.S. economy as are economic trends in large states such as Texas. Growing economic interdependence throughout the western hemisphere increases the risk that international contagion may eventually spread to the United States through its closest neighbors and most important trade partners.

In the early 1990s, when free market reforms were adopted, the economic growth rate throughout Central America was approximately 3 percent. This growth plummeted to .8 percent in 1995 after Mexico's crash. The backlash against free trade and government corruption plagued Mexico. There was widespread discontent when the government announced a $62 billion bailout plan in 1998 to help the bankrupt banks. Critics argue that the plan is a public subsidy for those who created the 1994 banking crisis. Continuing government corruption blocks efforts to reform the political process, further erodes the legitimacy of the national government, and permits the continued flow of black market drugs into the United States.

Most analysts predict that Mexico will be able to avoid a social explosion as long as American aid continues and unemployed Mexicans can emigrate to the United States. Future American aid, however, will be contingent on how Americans perceive Mexico's role as a source of illegal drugs and immigrants. While only a fraction of the estimated 7 million Mexicans living in the United States are involved in drug operations, drug trafficking into the United States from Mexico is increasing antagonism toward Mexican immigrants in the United States.

Traditionally, Central American states were viewed as "coffee" or "banana republics" but the region's political economy is being reshaped by Asian growth processes. Maquila-produced goods and nontraditional agricultural products now comprise approximately 60 percent of all exports from Guatemala, El Salvador, and Costa Rica. Unfortunately, the small size and openness of Central America's economies means that Asia's economic slowdown adversely affected the region's economies at the same time that the countries struggle to recover from the storm-damage caused by Hurricane Mitch during the fall of 1998. Hurricane Mitch left at least 10,000 dead in Honduras and Nicaragua, and thousands more dead or missing in El Salvador and Guatemala. Flooding during 1998 was the worst in recent history because the droughts associated with El Niño left little vegetation to stop the flood water that accompanied the La Niña storms. It may take decades for the region to recover as the losses are estimated in Honduras to be equal to the annual GDP of $4 billion and in Nicaragua to about half of its GDP of $1 billion.

Illegal drugs rather than natural disasters increasingly concerned U.S. government officials working to implement the U.S.'s "war on drugs." As Michael Shifter explains in, "Colombia at War," America's drug policy and policy toward Colombia have become nearly indistinguishable. Although Colombia's President Andres Pastrana entered into peace talks with the leftist guerrillas, the Revolutionary Armed Forces of Colombia (FARC), FARC's demands for extensive agriculture reforms and the redistribution of wealth and a restructuring of the national economic and political systems are unlikely to be met. There are other formidable obstacles to peace. President Pastrana replaced a president who had accepted millions in campaign contributions from the Cali drug cartel. The Clinton administration has continued aid to help combat the country's rampant drug traffic. However, concerns about civil rights abuses by the police and military and the failure of the government to stop right-wing vigilantes has led to increased calls for a halt to U.S. aid.

President Clinton's week-long trip to Latin American in 1997 symbolized the growing importance of Latin America to the United States. While he was well received, many in South America worried that a rush to free trade could destroy significant but fragile gains under liberal economic reforms made throughout the region in the 1990s. Clinton's hopes for swift progress toward a Pan-American free-trade area were dashed when Congress refused to renew his administration's fast-track authority to negotiate further tariff and trade restrictions with Mercosur countries.

Although the major Latin economies weathered the initial shocks associated with the Asia crisis and the reduction in world demand for commodity exports, international confidence in the national currencies continued to decline in part because all countries in the region have balance of payments deficits. Large amounts of international capital withdrew from "emerging markets" worldwide after Russia devalued the ruble in August of 1998. Brazil was forced to devalue the national currency, the real, at the beginning of 1999 in response to pressure on it's currency even though the country's fundamental ecnomic position was sound. State workers who had not been paid in several months rioted in several areas in Argentina during 1999 as hard times reduced popular support for Carlos Menin's efforts to implement economic reforms. The recent economic slowdown effected economies throughout Latin America. There is a great deal of uncertainty now about whether the economic downturn will stop recent movement toward free markets and democracy. James Mahon in "Economic Crisis in Latin America: Global Contagion, Local Pain," describes how many Latin Americans today wonder if their region is the innocent victim of irrational forces associated with "asymmetric globalization."

The political fall-out from the economic slowdown has been mixed. The re-election of President Cardoso in Brazil in 1998 was interpreted as popular support for implementing a new painful austerity and continuing with privatization. In contrast, the newly elected president of Venezuela, Hugo Chavez, is a radical populist and former paratrooper who led a failed coup attempt in the early 1990s. His election was widely interpreted as a sign of increased discontent among the poor. Although the Chavez regime carried through on promised changes designed to reform the old order, the worst flooding in the history of Venezuela killed an unknown number of citizens.

Latin America

The International Relations of Latin America and the Caribbean: Defining the New Era

G. Pope Atkins

Dr. Atkins is a research fellow at the Institute of Latin American Studies, University of Texas at Austin and professor emeritus of political science, U.S. Naval Academy.

This article focuses on the structure and conditions of the international relations of Latin America and the Caribbean in the current international system. The end of global East-West conflict by the end of the 1980s was combined with Latin America's political and economic transformations away from authoritarian governance and state-dominated economies, which had begun earlier in the decade. The designation of "post–Cold War" indicates the understanding that the old analytic and policy frameworks were no longer valid. The United States abandoned its 180-year-old preoccupation with minimizing what it saw as hostile foreign intrusions in the Western Hemisphere. Consequently, the inter-American agenda was no longer encumbered with fears of Soviet encroachment and communist expansionism. A general consensus emerged that democratic development and economic reform constituted the overarching norms in hemispheric relations. They provided the subtext for the salient issues of human rights, state governance, and civil-military relations; economic integration, trade, and investment; illicit narcotics traffic; immigration and refugee problems; degradation of the physical environment and "sustainable" development; insurgencies, arms control, and demilitarization; and other matters. President Bush's Enterprise for the Americas Initiative proposed on June 27, 1990 called for a Western Hemispheric free trade area. It has been pursued in a slow and complex manner.

Questions arise about the appropriate "levels of analysis" in contemporary world politics. Many specialists on Latin America are impatient with overall regional parameters and highlight the major countries and subregions. Others emphasize the larger regional Inter-American System of all the states in the Western Hemisphere, and see inter-American cooperation as an important path to international problem-solving. Globalists say that the most important issues today are world-wide in scope and consequently analytic efforts should concentrate on that level, with a view to resolving current issues within global regimes. The debate has been further complicated by the revived importance of globalization and transnationalization—the intertwining of relations at all systemic levels and the elevating of the prominence of nonstate actors and transnational activities. In my view, an accurate picture of Latin America and Caribbean international relations requires that we acknowledge and link national, subregional, regional, hemispheric, and global and extrahemispheric levels of analysis. The nature of the issues and the high stakes involved compel action in all arenas.

THE LATIN AMERICAN-CARIBBEAN REGION

Latin America and the Caribbean comprises an area roughly two-and-one-half times larger than the United States. It is populated by almost 500 million people and mostly occupied by 33 independent states exhibiting great diversity in terms of culture, size, and other aspects. Among them are the 18 Spanish American states, with widely varying stages of development and international capabilities; huge Brazil, which is Portuguese in origin; and tiny Haiti, which has maintained its West African culture to a remarkable degree. These 20 states, all but two of which (Cuba and Panama) gained their independence during the first third of the nineteenth century, together account for some 97 percent of the region's territory and population. Since 1962 an additional 13 Car-

Original to *Annual Editions: World Politics 00/01.* © 2000 Dushkin/McGraw-Hill.

ibbean countries have gained independence; 12 of them had been British colonies and the thirteenth is Suriname, formerly a colony of the Netherlands. In order to recognize the emergence of these new states and distinguish them from the long- existing "traditional" Latin American states, the term "Latin America and the Caribbean" was adopted. This understandable effort is an inadequate adjustment, however, since older Spanish American states had already encompassed most of the Caribbean area's territory and population. Nevertheless, "Latin America and the Caribbean" has become a matter of general usage.

Despite the diversity, a Latin American regional subsystem has always exhibited to some degree an international life of its own. This has been partly reflected in Latin American self- perceptions. Latin Americans have always tended to band together when outsiders intervened or exerted other pressures. They have organized among themselves to achieve common purposes. A few examples illustrate the point. Latin American Groups were created within the United Nations, Third World associations, and the European Community (now the European Union), in order to caucus on a regional basis before confronting the outside world. The 11-member Latin American Free Trade Association (LAFTA), established in 1961 and reorganized in 1980 as the Latin American Integration Association (LAIA), includes all of the large regional economies so that it represents a broadly cross-regional association. The Latin American Parliament was created in 1964; although its decisions are not binding it serves as a focal point for the discussion of region-wide issues. Also in 1964 most Latin American states joined the Special Latin American Coordinating Committee (CECLA) as an informal regional caucusing group. In 1975 the permanent Latin American Economic System (SELA) was created with near-universal regional membership, superseding CECLA and broadening the agenda of purposes. Organized in 1986, the Rio Group expanded to include almost all of the Latin American and Caribbean states and became the leading voice on the new agenda of issues.

These organizations have taken on new significance in the post-Cold War era and given renewed impetus to inter-regional cooperation. Nevertheless, viewing Latin America only in terms of a single unit is insufficient. We also need to highlight those subregions where different conditions obtain.

MEXICO

Mexico stands apart as a large and important state that has intense bilateral relations with the United States. The current reality of the complicated Mexican-U.S. association, in contrast to much of the past, is the existence of a strong mutual dependency. Although the United States is clearly the stronger partner, Mexico has considerable say. Much of the relationship is essentially divorced from the broader Latin American arena. The issues have long been determined by territorial proximity and increasingly integrated economies and societies in terms of trade, investment, migration, tourism, the drug traffic, and a host of border issues.

Mexico and the United States recently reoriented their policies toward each other. Until the latter half of the 1980s, Mexico differed with the United States on such issues as Central American conflict, Cuba, and external debt. Then it began to abandon its historic protectionist investment and trade policies by privatizing government enterprises, liberalizing trade, and attracting U.S. investment. It pressed the United States for a free trade agreement; President Bush responded positively and in 1990 free trade negotiations began. Canada joined the process and the trilateral talks resulted in the North American Free Trade Agreement (NAFTA), which went into effect in January 1994.

The United States is by far Mexico's major trading partner; Mexico is the United States' third largest. Mexico's mutually exacerbating economic, political, and social crises complicated relations with the United States (and with Canada on a smaller scale) and eroded their smooth functioning. Other developments indicated, however, that the Mexican economy and NAFTA were weathering financial and commercial problems. In April 1996 Mexico signed an agreement with the European Union opening the possibility of a free trade arrangement between them.

THE CIRCUM-CARIBBEAN

The circum-Caribbean is a complex geographic and political region. It includes the islands of the Caribbean Sea and those nearby in the Atlantic Ocean, the Central American isthmus, and the north coast of South America extending into the Atlantic Ocean (thus including Colombia, Venezuela, and Suriname). It has its own further subregions, notably the Central American and the Commonwealth Caribbean countries. Throughout the twentieth century the United States pursued a hegemonic presence in the circum-Caribbean, with unilateral military interventions as late as 1983 in Grenada and 1989-1990 in Panama; in 1994 it led a United Nations force in the military occupation of Haiti. The Panama Canal historically loomed large in U.S. calculations; it is still of concern but the canal's strategic and commercial importance has sharply declined. A major challenge to U.S. hegemony arose after 1959 when Cuba became the Soviet Union's first high-priority Latin American interest. After the Nicaraguan Revolution of 1979 the Soviets supported the Sandinistas in Nicaragua and by extension the Farabundo Martí National Liberation Front (FMLN) insurgency in El Salvador.

The Nicaraguan Revolution precipitated general Central American conflict and the United States responded by making it a major Cold War arena. One of the casualties of the conflict was the effort to integrate the isthmian states. The Organization of Central American States (ODECA), made up of the five traditional isthmian states of Costa Rica, El Salvador, Guatemala, Honduras, and Nicaragua, had gone into effect in 1955. ODECA did not realize its purposes of both political and economic integration; it was unable to settle a variety of disputes between its members and its companion organization, the Central American Common Market (CACM) took the lead in economic integration. The CACM, composed of the same membership, began to function in 1960. The violent Central American conflict beginning in 1979 virtually dissolved the organization (as well as ODECA).

In 1983, Mexico, Venezuela, Colombia, and Panama organized the Contadora Group to offer a multilateral negotiating formula challenging U.S. policies; they were joined by the Contadora Support Group formed by Argentina, Brazil, Peru, and Uruguay. This was followed in 1987 by a multilateral peace plan agreed to by all five Central American states on the initiative of President Oscar Arias of Costa Rica that enjoyed considerable success. (In December 1986 the eight Contadora Group and Support Group met and created the Permanent Mechanism of Consultation and Political Coordination, known informally as the Rio Group. As Central American conflict faded the group expanded its agenda and membership in the context of growing Latin American unity and, as indicated above, became the most important and dynamic Latin American and Caribbean international organization.)

The Soviet role changed dramatically in the post–Cold War era as it ceased weapons transfers to Cuba and Nicaragua and pressured them to end deliveries to insurgents in El Salvador. The February 1990 elections in Nicaragua that ejected the Sandinista government also ended the by-then reluctant Soviet role. In the meantime, the Soviets joined the United States in the UN Security Council to create a peacekeeping force and other missions for electoral and human rights observation and verification that were sent to Central America. With the decline of Soviet power and then the breakup of the Soviet Union itself, commitments to Cuba were virtually canceled. Cuba itself became internationally isolated and increasingly inactive, absorbed with its own internal economic and social problems.

The Central American peace process revived subregional integration and then concentrated on expanding it. In 1987 the Central American presidents signed a treaty creating the Central American Parliament. In 1990 and 1991, as part of the Enterprise for the Americas Initiative, individual Central American states signed framework agreements with the United States committing to negotiations for a free trade agreement—processes that were stalled primarily by internal U.S. politics. Mexico initiated negotiations with Central America with the view of establishing a free trade area, implying the potential of their being a part of NAFTA. The Central American presidents continued to hold summit meetings and brought in Belize and Panama as participants. In December 1995 the presidents signed two treaties of particular significance and submitted them to the individual states for ratification. One of them extended the terms of the previously adopted Central American Alliance for Sustainable Development. The other, the Democratic Security Treaty of Central America, addressed legal systems, corruption, internationalization of organized crime, drug trafficking, terrorism, and arms smuggling; and stipulations concerning the reduction of national military forces. The European Union continued to hold high-level meetings with the Central American states, a practice begun early in the peace process.

The Commonwealth Caribbean countries are the 18 English-speaking entities in the circum-Caribbean. Of that number, 12 are no longer British dependencies and have become independent states—Antigua and Barbuda, Bahamas, Barbados, Belize, Dominica, Grenada, Guyana, Jamaica, St. Kitts-Nevis, St. Lucia, St. Vincent, and Trinidad and Tobago. One of them (Belize) is on the Central American isthmus, another (Guyana) is on the South American continent, and the remainder are islands in the Caribbean Sea. The non-sovereign countries have a constitutional status of "States in Association with Great Britain." They are self-governing but dependent on the United Kingdom for external affairs. They are Anguilla, Bermuda, British Virgin Islands, Cayman Islands, Montserrat, and the Turks and Caicos Islands.

A number of the Commonwealth Caribbean countries established the Caribbean Free Trade Association (CARIFTA) with an agreement that went into effect in 1968. In 1972 most CARIFTA members drew up a charter establishing the Caribbean Community (CARICOM) that went into effect in 1973 with 13 members (all but one a sovereign state). Three other local states—the Dominican Republic, Haiti, and Suriname, became permanent observers; the Dominican Republic later became a full member. In 1981, seven members formed the Organization of Eastern Caribbean States (OECS) within CARICOM in order to pool economic resources and coordinate foreign policy.

CARICOM was also stimulated by events in the new era. In 1991 it signed a framework agreement with the United States with a view to negotiating a free trade agreement. In 1991 and 1992 the member governments agreed to further elements of their integration structure but progress was slow. The Commonwealth Caribbean countries enjoy trade preferences with the European Community under the Lomé convention.

On July 24, 1994, the charter of the Association of Caribbean States (ACS) was signed and went into effect within a year with the purpose of forming a free trade area. The ACS members are divided into subgroups: CARICOM, Central America (including Panama but not Belize, a member of CARICOM), the Group of Three (a formal free trade agreement by Mexico, Colombia, and Venezuela), and Greater Antilles (the informal grouping of Cuba, the Dominican Republic, and Haiti). Provision was made for associate membership by non-sovereign entities. Anguilla, Turks and Caicos, and Guadaloupe joined as associate members; eligible were Bermuda, the Caymans, Martinique, the U.S. Virgin Islands, the British Virgin Islands, French Guiana, and Puerto Rico.

SOUTH AMERICA BEYOND THE CARIBBEAN

The third important subregion encompasses South America beyond the Caribbean, most of which are the countries of what is called the Southern Cone. The key states are Argentina, Brazil, and Chile; the others are Uruguay, Paraguay, Bolivia, and Peru. Brazil, like Mexico, can be singled out as forming its own subsystem. It stands apart with its Portuguese cultural heritage, large size, and potential to be a much more influential state in global politics.

The subregion has a number of characteristics that make it dramatically different from the northern half of Latin America. It has not been a sphere of influence of the United States or another state; no outside great power has had the function of international policeman enforcing the peace. The South American states have a broad array of external relationships. They represent a multilateralized trading area, with long-standing cultural and economic ties with Europe, and Japan an important economic actor. The transition away from militarism has been completed, although democracy has been under continuous stress and "partial democracies" more often than not characterize the current situation. Most of the subregion's traditional international rivalries have been muted. Brazil and Argentina have extended a rapprochement begun in 1979 to include extensive bilateral economic and other kinds of policy integration. Argentina and Chile settled their contentious Beagle Channel dispute in 1983. In 1990 Argentina and the United Kingdom reestablished relations broken in 1982 during their war over the Falkland/Malvinas islands.

When the Latin American Free Trade Association (LAFTA) was formed in 1961 it was widely perceived as the initial step toward formation of a Latin American-wide common market. A universal regional organization was not created, however. In fact, both LAFTA and its successor Latin American Integration Association (LAIA) were fragmented by South American-led reform movements. In 1969 certain dissatisfied LAFTA members formed the Andean Common Market, usually known as the Andean Group. They did not withdraw from LAFTA but hoped eventually to reform it. The charter members were Bolivia, Colombia, Chile, Ecuador and Peru; Venezuela joined in 1973 and Chile dropped out in 1976. Thus the Andean Group, with South American Caribbean states in its membership, in fact bridged two Latin American subregions. The Andean Group was able to undertake important reforms but it also suffered from its own political and economic divisiveness. In the new in-

ternational era the organization managed to overcome much of the differences and in 1995 converted itself to the Andean Community. In 1996 it signed a framework agreement with the European Union opening the possibility of free trade.

In 1991 another new organization was organized within LAIA—the Common Market of the South (MERCOSUR), made up of Argentina, Brazil, Paraguay, and Uruguay. In that year MERCOSUR signed a framework agreement with the United States with a view to negotiating free trade. The organization sought to expand its membership to other South American States. In 1996 Bolivia signed a complementation agreement and Chile became an associate member, preludes for both states to join as full members. In December 1995 MERCOSUR and the European Union signed a framework agreement for free trade and negotiations continued in 1996. MERCOSUR also commenced negotiations for reciprocal trade preferences with a wide range of other countries.

The world outside Latin America and the Caribbean is also differentiated so far as the regional states are concerned. They are essentially divided into relations with (1) the other Americas and (2) global and extrahemispheric actors.

INTER-AMERICAN SYSTEM

The Inter-American System (IAS) refers to formal multipurpose regional (Western Hemisphere-wide) organization among the American states that originated in 1889 and evolved thereafter to the present day. The designation denotes not a centralized institution overseeing subordinate organizations, but an "umbrella" concept covering an uneven yet uninterrupted history and current network of institutional principles, policies, procedures, and organizations. Today the IAS largely consists of the separate but coordinated Organization of American States (OAS) and Inter-American Development Bank (IDB). Other elements include a scattered system for the peaceful settlement of disputes and a once vigorous but now moribund Inter-American Treaty of Reciprocal Assistance (Rio Treaty) regime. In 1991 the OAS achieved universal membership of all 35 sovereign states in the Americas—the 33 Latin American and Caribbean states, the United States, and Canada. (Cuba is technically a member since sanctions imposed in 1962 deny participation, not membership, to the Castro government.) IAS activities evolved over the years to promote economic, social, and cultural cooperation, conflict resolution, nonintervention and sovereign equality, codification of international law, mutual security, and representative democracy and human rights. In recent years the problems of the narcotics traffic and environmental degradation were added.

Latin Americans were increasingly dissatisfied with U.S. efforts to transform the IAS into an anti-communist alliance, especially after the United States intervened militarily in the 1965 Dominican Republic civil war and then insisted on its conversion to an inter-American problem for settlement. The IAS became virtually impotent in the field of mutual security; it continued economic development activities but was not an important arena for addressing the external debt difficulties.

In the latter 1980s the OAS became an important actor in the Central American peace process, at the invitation of the Central American presidents who were leading the efforts. The revitalization continued with the emergence of a more positive Latin American nationalism and the return of the United States to a multilateral orientation, elements of the political changes in Latin America and the end of Cold War. Member states again perceived the IAS as an appropriate problem-solving forum. The promotion of democratic governance and human rights and economic well-being were the main principles that defined the new era, with other issues subsumed under them. The IAS has been highly active in terms of developing these principles, with resolutions, declarations, and OAS charter amendments, and engaging in policy action. The end of the Cold War did not alter the reality of asymmetrical inter-American power relations. Nevertheless, the nature of the issues, with their high domestic content, seemed to mute the consequences of asymmetry inasmuch as they required multilateral resolution.

THE GLOBAL SYSTEM AND EXTRAHEMISPHERIC ACTORS

Latin American and Caribbean governments seek to be active participants in the evolving global system. Latin Americans were instrumental in shaping the United Nations system at its inception. They later took leadership roles in the New International Economic Order (NIEO), a formal Third World association pursued especially in the serial United Nations Conference on Trade and Development (UNCTAD) and in the General Assembly. Beginning in 1961 many of them also joined the Nonaligned Movement. Latin American military regimes reduced their active interest in extra-regional affairs during the 1970s and into the 1980s but the succeeding democratic governments sought to reintegrate.

The end of the Cold War challenged the identity of both the Nonaligned Movement and the NIEO; alignment was no longer an issue in the former instance and the demise of the Soviet Union reduced the leverage of the latter. Latin American interest in both movements consequently declined. The United Nations presence increased in the Americas, however, in the broad and critical arena of conflict resolution for peace and security—matters in which the UN had formerly deferred to the IAS. Beginning in 1987, the two organizations developed a division of labor as highly active participants in the ongoing Central American peace process. The UN continues as the sponsor of the external peacekeeping presence in Haiti.

As a general matter, Latin American and Caribbean leaders seek to maintain and expand their relations with the European Union (EU) and other international associations, Japan and other states, and transnational political parties and nongovernmental organizations. In the critical area of international trade and investment, they were fully aware that hemispheric free trade would link their integration organizations more closely to the U.S. economy. To ensure they would not become a U.S. dominated economic preserve, they acted to expand extrahemispheric connections to parallel hemispheric arrangements. The EU responded positively and a number of significant actions occurred. In 1991 the EU and the Rio Group began to hold regular annual meetings of their foreign ministers. At the Sixth Institutionalized Meeting of Rio Group-European Union Foreign Ministers in April 1996 in Bolivia, initial agreements were signed opening the possibilities of free trade between the EU and Andean Community, Mexico, and Chile. The EU also held meetings with the Central American states. By the time of the Bolivia meeting the array of issues discussed had expanded dramatically. The foreign ministers addressed economic integration, inter- regional trade and investment, and strengthening economic and commercial relations, and sustainable development; democracy and human rights, women's rights, and respect for ethnic diversity and indigenous peoples' cultural heritage; and the international drug traffic. On December 15, 1995 the EU and MERCOSUR signed a wide-ranging Inter-Regional Framework Agreement as a first step toward progressive liberalization of trade (if realized the free trade area would constitute the largest in the world with some 600 million people). In 1996 MERCOSUR began negotiations for reciprocal trade preferences with some developing countries, among them Mexico, Colombia, India, Korea, the Philippines, and Egypt, and scheduled talks with Japan and Russia.

GLOBALIZATION AND TRANSNATIONALIZATION

The ideas of globalization and transnationalization have been increasingly adopted as key concepts for understanding current Latin American and Caribbean international relations. Globalization refers to the expansion of those relations at all systemic levels in the context of the new democratization and agenda of issues. Transnationalization elevates the prominence of non-nation-state actors and intensifies phenomena that evolve in a largely autonomous manner parallel with interstate relations. Thus, in the globalization process, states are joined by multinational corporations, nongovernmental organizations, international political party and labor associations, churches, communications media, immigrants and refugees, artists and entertainers, athletes, educators, and tourists, as well as narcotics traffickers, and others. They engage in transnational activities having immense political, economic, social, and cultural consequences. Goods, money, people, ideas, and images flow across and transcend state boundaries, creating overlapping but distinct political, economic, ethnic, and cultural patterns. Although little prospect exists that the states will cede sovereignty to other actors, globalization and accompanying transnationalization limit their ability to exercise political, economic, and social-cultural authority.

Some phenomena are of particular significance in the American arena. With the rise to prominence of neoliberalism and economic reform in the current international era, and the decline of traditional security concerns and their connection to Latin American and Caribbean stability, the actions and influence of private sector business and commercial influence have increased. They are led by U.S.-based multilateral corporations (MNCs), but Japanese and European MNCs are also of considerable consequence.

At another point on the spectrum, international trafficking in illicit narcotics has created its own culture. The United States provides the major market and many dealers, and people from Latin American and the Caribbean, both at home and in the United States, participate in the production, transporting and marketing of drugs.

More diffuse, less organized social-cultural elements have also had a major transnational impact. The principal phenomena are the proliferation of the U.S. communications and entertainment media, and the millions of Latin Americans resident in the United States with many of them moving back and forth between there and their homelands. This has been particularly true in the Caribbean area, as analysts refer to the consequences of U.S. influence as the "Northamericanization" of the Caribbean and the reciprocal impact as the "Caribbeanization" of the United States. While these transnational linkages have been growing since the 1950s and 1960s, in the early 1980s they began to increase rapidly. The process of North Americanization has resulted in divided Latin American views, and often ambivalence, about the United States. While these phenomena are not a consequence of overt U.S. government policies, those Latin Americans who resent or fear foreign influences see them as continuing cultural imperialism extended in a new international context, objecting to U.S. popular culture, materialism, and secularism. A large number of Latins, many of whom have adopted English as a second language, have welcomed or accepted U.S. ideas, values, products, and life-styles and equate North Americanization with modernization. Others see it as an inevitable consequence of societal proximity, migration, commerce, and cultural contact. In the United States, Caribbeanization has changed the political, social, and popular cultural scenes in several cities, notably New York and Miami. And it has fueled the debate about future immigration policy.

President Andrés Pastrana's peace effort, "if it goes forward at all, will do so only by fits and starts, with inevitable setbacks and countless frustrations. Its success or failure will depend ultimately on Colombians and their sense of exhaustion with unremitting violence; they will need to bring sustained political and social pressure to bear on the government and the insurgents to produce a settlement."

Colombia at War

Michael Shifter

W hat's important for now is not peace, but to be making it." It was early January, and Colombian Nobel laureate Gabriel García Márquez was trying to put the best face on an inauspicious start to peace talks between the Colombian government and the country's principal insurgency, the Revolutionary Armed Forces of Colombia (FARC). Only days before, FARC's undisputed leader, Manuel "Sure Shot" Marulanda, had failed to show up at the remote jungle town of San Vicente del Caguán for the opening ceremony of the much anticipated talks, citing alleged death threats from paramilitary groups.

Colombia's new president did show up, however. Andrés Pastrana, seated alone, was ready and waiting, along with an array of government and FARC representatives, journalists, invited guests—and an expectant nation. After nearly four decades of internal armed conflict that has claimed at least 35,000 Colombian lives, Pastrana—just five months into his term—was to have begun conversations with the country's chief guerrilla leader, with the presumed aim of preparing the way for a negotiated settlement.

The moves toward peace talks, however halting, have held out some promise to Colombians. The recent vicissitudes of Colombia's bewildering politics have been striking by any measure. At times the country appears on the verge of implosion; at others it evinces remarkable resilience. To many, however, the imagination of a García Márquez is required to believe that the array of formidable obstacles in the way of a serious peace process can be overcome.

MICHAEL SHIFTER *is a senior fellow at the Inter-American Dialogue in Washington, D. C., and teaches Latin American politics at Georgetown University's School of Foreign Service.*

COLLAPSED INTO CONFLICT

Colombia has defied the conventional predictions about a relatively peaceful Latin America in the post-cold war era. Central America's conflicts may have ended, and Peru's insurgencies may have been crippled, but guerrilla war continues unabated in Colombia. The government controls only roughly half the country's territory. Colombia's leftist guerrilla and rightist paramilitary forces have significantly expanded, which is reflected in their greater numbers, extended geographical reach, and uncommon ferocity; militarily and financially, they have never been stronger.

The violence in Colombia is not attributable to the kinds of intense ethnic and tribal conflicts that have consumed so many other countries since the cold war's end. It is instead the product of the intersection of three distinct tendencies: the crucial political role of violence, the development of the criminal drug economy, and the weakening of the state's capacity and effectiveness. The first is expressed today in the country's two main leftist insurgencies, FARC and the National Liberation Army (ELN). This political function of violence has a long history, and was part of the creation of Colombia's two main political parties, the Liberals and Conservatives, in the mid-1800s. In the contemporary period, the fierce pattern continued in the late 1940s and 1950s with the notorious land battles known as *La Violencia,* which took more than 200,000 lives.

FARC traces its origins to this latter period. At one point an intensely ideological, hard-line group with links to the Communist Party, FARC has over time become increasingly pragmatic. The late 1980s proved to be a turning point. After forming a political party, the Patriotic Union, and successfully competing in the 1986 elections—and after undergoing near extermination by paramilitary forces as a result—FARC began to take advantage of the country's burgeoning drug economy.

The insurgency increasingly relies on a "tax" levied against coca producers to fuel its operations. Though estimates vary widely, FARC is believed to have approximately 15,000 soldiers, organized in some 80 "fronts," with a presence in roughly half of Colombia's municipalities; the group is especially strong in rural areas.

The ELN is Colombia's second guerrilla force. Founded in the early 1960s chiefly as a student movement, with links to the Roman Catholic Church, it, too, has undergone important changes. Today the ELN is a significant insurgency, with some 3,000 to 4,000 troops that are concentrated in the oil-rich northeast of the country. Indeed, the ELN derives the main source of its financial resources from the oil industry, through extortion and kidnapping.

There are varied interpretations of precisely what FARC and the ELN are seeking, and what they would—or would not—be prepared to negotiate at some future point in a peace process. Though analysts differ about whether they chiefly seek to gain control of territory or to influence national policies, most agree that the guerrillas should be viewed neither as rigid ideologues, resistant to reason, nor as common criminals or drug mafias, devoid of agendas. They are, however, well endowed; estimates indicate that they have revenues of roughly $800 million a year, some $500 million of which is derived from the tax on coca producers and the rest from kidnapping and extortion.

The expansion of Colombia's two main guerrilla groups has been nourished by—and has coincided with—the two other national tendencies: the development of the criminal drug economy and the weakening of the state.

Colombia's elaborate infrastructure geared for narcotics (mainly cocaine and heroin) production and trafficking did not emerge in a vacuum. The country has a long history of similar activities with other commodities, including emeralds. But for the past two decades Colombia has become one of the main engines driving the international drug trade (albeit an engine fueled to a great extent by the demand originating in the United States). Narcotics has penetrated nearly all spheres of Colombian society, politics, and economics. Over the last 15 years, drug trafficking proceeds have grown to equal 25 to 35 percent of the country's total legal exports. By any measure, the dimensions of the trade are staggering.

THE STRESSED STATE

The third tendency—the progressively deepening political and institutional crisis—has only exacerbated the growth of guerrilla activity and the drug trade. For many years, through political pacts between the Liberal and Conservative Parties and well-oiled, clientelistic politics, the country has been able to manage its affairs reasonably well. But recently institutional problems have become far more acute; the system shows every sign of having reached its limit, with the political parties, courts, Congress, and security forces unable to adapt to growing demands and pressures. Colombian sociologist Alejandro Reyes has underlined the close association between the development of guerrilla activity and the absence of state activity

in some parts of the country. In such areas, the guerrilla groups have nearly become a surrogate state.

Colombia's insurgencies have operated within the context of a politically and militarily ineffective state. Over the past year, a succession of humiliating military defeats has dominated the news—and demoralized the country's security forces and most Colombians. These circumstances have helped give rise to an exponential growth in the country's paramilitary forces, now estimated to number roughly 4,000 to 5,000 combatants. Like the insurgencies, these groups are symptomatic of an underlying authority crisis.

Paramilitary groups have evolved from self-defense units, or civilian militias, established by the army and landowners in the 1980s to more sophisticated operations that in some cases have developed right-wing political identities and agendas. Many have a keen interest in participating in Colombia's political game, and are pressing to do so. Carlos Castaño, a prominent leader who has demanded a place at any peace talks, heads the United Self-Defense Forces of Colombia, the country's most substantial and well-organized paramilitary organizations. Some groups, including Castaño's, support their activities through sizable contributions collected from local ranchers and businessmen. There is also evidence linking Castaño to drug-trafficking operations in Antioquia and Cordoba. Finally, some paramilitary operations have links to government security forces, and the state has certainly been guilty of looking the other way when paramilitary units have committed atrocities.

Colombia's three intersecting tendencies have contributed to the most dire human rights situation in the hemisphere. Approximately 10 Colombians are killed in politically related violence each day. All the country's violent forces commit abuses, in clear violation of human rights and humanitarian standards, although both credible human rights groups and the United States State Department reported that the paramilitary units accounted for some 70 percent of all political killings in Colombia in 1997 (and an estimated 73 percent for the first half of 1998). Colombia is the only Latin American country where the office of the United Nations High Commissioner for Human Rights has a national operation, which was opened in April 1997.

The main victims of the country's human rights drama tend to be poor noncombatants. They figure disproportionately among the more than 1 million Colombians who have been displaced by violence since the mid-1980s. According to the New York–based group Human Rights Watch, Colombia has the fourth-largest internally displaced population in the world. The poor are also the main victims of Colombia's pervasive criminal violence, which accounts for some 85 percent of the country's yearly 30,000 homicides. Even in a disturbingly violent region, Colombia stands out.

THE PEACE CONSTITUENCY

President Pastrana's emphasis on peace builds on the country's resources—some long-standing, others more circumstantial. Colombia has been ruled by civilian constitutional governments longer than any other country in South America. The last round of elections, in which Colombia held four nationwide contests in less than nine months under progressively more secure conditions, underlined this exemplary tradition. In the first round of the presidential election in May 1998, Colombians resoundingly rejected Harold Bedoya, a former general whose recipes for Colombia's ills—he was the only candidate who did not advocate peace negotiations with the guerrillas—broke with the country's political practices.

Colombians have paid an immeasurable cost in all respects of the drug trade—in financial, political, and human terms. The record of the government in the past several years in passing money-laundering legislation and eradicating coca fields has been noteworthy (last year coca cultivating in the Guaviare region declined by 25 percent). In addition, Colombian administrations have periodically undertaken peace efforts to resolve the conflicts with insurgent groups. The country's capacity for political reform also stands out. Its constitution, which was modernized in 1991, contains a number of innovative features that are intended to make the political system more open, responsive, and representative.

Perhaps more than in any other area, Colombia's success in managing its economic affairs has been impressive. Colombia was the only major Latin American country unaffected by the debt crisis that gripped the region during the 1980s, and it has earned an unusually favorable reputation in international financial circles. A propensity for decentralized politics and a relatively vibrant private sector have also distinguished Colombia from many other Latin American countries.

In the last several years, however, the political and security crises have, for the first time, translated into mounting economic difficulties. At the end of the administration of President Ernesto Samper in August 1998, Colombia's fiscal deficit had reached 4 percent of GDP, and its inflation rate, at 20 percent, had become one of the highest in the region. Unemployment has been on the rise, climbing from 8 percent in 1993 to 12 percent in 1997. And the unrelenting violence has put a substantial dent in foreign investor confidence.

Toward the end of the Samper government, the violence—coupled with the more recent economic decline—helped awaken key elements of Colombia's civil society to the country's predicament. Prominent among them were select business and church leaders, a number of whom assumed an active role in the National Conciliation Commission, a church-linked group dedicated to finding a peaceful solution to the conflict.

The involvement of significant civilian elements distinguishes the current political moment from previous periods. Reinforcing the grounds for optimism was the overwhelming public "mandate for peace" reflected in the support of more than 10 million Colombians in a nonbinding plebiscite in October 1997. This mandate has assumed various organizational forms, such as the Permanent Assembly of Civil Society for Peace, which has brought together diverse sectors of Colom-

Even in a disturbingly violent region, Colombia stands out.

bian society. The main impetus behind the growing pressure for peace has come less from the insurgents or the government than from these recently energized, highly influential sectors.

REACHING OUT

Another factor that has changed is the role of the international community. Two key shifts can be discerned. The first, in evidence during the Samper administration, is that growing numbers of Colombians have concluded that some form of international support for a peace process is not only appropriate, but indispensable—a sentiment that would have drawn considerable resistance not so long ago.

Second, the Pastrana government enjoys substantial goodwill in the international community, and a willingness to back, both politically and economically, a viable peace plan. In an October 1998 visit to Washington, Pastrana was able to secure generous pledges of support from the World Bank and the Inter-American Development Bank. A number of governments—European, Latin American, and the United States—have also offered to help advance the process. Although a group of "friends" (Venezuela, Mexico, Costa Rica, and Spain) was formed toward the end of the Samper administration, Pastrana has yet to determine how and when to mobilize international political resources on behalf of his peace effort. Still, analysts agree that the most impressive accomplishments of Pastrana's government to date have been an improved image in the international arena and more fluid, constructive relationships with key actors.

Even before Pastrana took office in August, two dramatic moments illustrated the more hospitable environment for peace in Colombia. The first was a startling encounter on July 9 between President-elect Pastrana, Victor Ricardo, his principal adviser on peace (and currently high commissioner for peace), FARC's Marulanda, and Jorge Briceño, FARC's main military strategist. The second was a meeting that took place in mid-July in Mainz, Germany, between some 40 civil society representatives and ELN leaders.

Although both events generated considerable hope that the country could move toward peace, they also underlined the immense obstacles to making progress. The differences between the nationally and rurally rooted FARC and the more internationalist and fluid ELN are marked. While FARC plainly preferred to deal with prospective government representatives on national territory, the ELN opted to meet with church and business leaders—and in Europe.

There is tremendous fragmentation both among and within Colombia's violent forces. There are questions, for example, regarding the extent to which Marulanda commands authority and exercises discipline over all of FARC's fronts. Similarly, the country's paramilitary groups are far from monolithic. Whether, in the event of an agreement, they would defer to Castaño's negotiating posture is not altogether clear.

In addition, the almost simultaneous July meetings revealed that both insurgencies are in strong positions and drive hard bargains. The understandings that emerged from Mainz were minimal—to some, even laughable (the ELN agreed not to kidnap anyone over 65). And the main result of the discussions between Pastrana and Marulanda was an agreement— a good faith, confidence-building gesture—by the incoming administration to demilitarize five zones already heavily controlled by FARC guerrillas in the southern part of the country. The *despeje* (clearing out of security forces) of an area roughly twice the size of El Salvador started on November 7, 1998.

The temptation to allow domestic politics to drive United States policy—and to "get tough" in fighting either drugs or rebels—may be difficult to resist.

AMERICA'S CREEPING INVOLVEMENT

For United States and Colombian government officials, such stumbling blocks have been of some concern. But of even greater worry for many in the United States has been the possibility that Pastrana's confidence-building gesture would result in a slackening in counternarcotics efforts in the demilitarized area. This concern was explicitly incorporated into an October 1998 law the United States Congress passed that tripled counternarcotics assistance to Colombia to $289 million (the amount had already doubled each of the previous two years).[1]

Both the Pastrana administration and FARC have stressed that the talks are preliminary and that what fundamentally matters is that a process is under way (separate talks are scheduled to begin with the ELN). To the parties in conflict, the fact that the agendas, which concern agrarian reform and a host of other issues, are constantly shifting and often exceedingly vague is not of particular concern. It is hoped that the proposals will be modified and refined as the talks proceed, and will ultimately yield the basis for concrete, serious negotiations. Still, in an instructive document produced in 1998, the National Conciliation Commission and the International Red Cross pointed out that the agendas advanced by the different parties in conflict—paramilitary groups included—were remarkably similar to one another.

The government's task is particularly daunting. The insurgencies and the paramilitary forces have demonstrated enormous strength, and any meaningful process must of course deal with them. But dealing simultaneously with mutually hostile forces is a tough balancing act, requiring great political skill. In January, FARC broke off the initial talks with the government, insisting that the paramilitary forces—which had killed at least 140 people in the first part of that month—be reined in. It is unclear whether the Pastrana administration will be able, first, to develop an effective strategy to do this, and second, to bring along key military and civilian constituencies. In the meantime, as the process unfolds, a war logic prevails, taking a tremendous toll in Colombian lives and severely testing morale.

Colombia's experience with the despeje illustrates a critical problem. Although the Pastrana administration complied with the terms of the agreement and withdrew its security forces from the zone, FARC insisted that approximately 100 military personnel who performed essentially administrative tasks also leave the area. In the end, the government acceded to this demand. But the second sticking point has proved far more problematic. FARC has pressed for a hostage swap that would free some 450 jailed rebels, in exchange for the 326 police and soldiers FARC holds as prisoners. This demand, which would have to be approved by Congress, remains unmet.

The condition restricting counternarcotics assistance highlights a fundamental difference in approach and instinct between Colombian and United States policymakers. Pastrana and his team are seeking to regain some measure of authority and improve the security situation as a way of addressing Colombia's serious drug problem. United States policy, in contrast, tends to be politically driven, and fails to acknowledge a trade-off in dealing with the drug and security challenges. Any trace of softened anti-drug efforts is, from this perspective, unacceptable.

Since the end of the cold war, United States drug policy and policy toward Colombia have been nearly indistinguishable. The bilateral relationship, historically close and friendly, reached its lowest point during the Samper administration, prompted by accusations that the Colombian president had accepted some $6 million from the Cali drug cartel in his 1994 presidential campaign. Samper's visa was revoked, and, under a 1986 law, the United States "decertified" Colombia in 1996 and 1997 for failing to cooperate in the fight against drugs. Decertification, which made Colombia subject to sanctions, did little to bolster the Colombian government's credibility or capacity, and may have enabled the country's violent forces— paramilitaries, guerrillas, and drug traffickers—to advance.

At the same time, human rights concerns have also figured prominently in American policy toward Colombia. Assistance to the Colombian military was suspended in 1996, and has been restricted since, because of its human rights record; support was instead given to the national police for fighting drugs. In addition, the United States rescinded the visas of several generals credibly charged by human rights groups of committing grave abuses.

---

[1]According to the section on counternarcotics assistance in the Western Hemisphere Drug Eradication Act (H.R. 4300, approved on October 21, 1998): "United States counternarcotics assistance may not be provided for the Government of Colombia under this Act or under any other provision of law on or after the date of the enactment of this Act if the Government of Colombia negotiates or permits the establishment of any demilitarized zone in which the eradication and interdiction of drug production by the security forces of Colombia, including the Colombian National Policy antinarcotics unit, is prohibited."

American officials were undoubtedly relieved, and pleased, with Pastrana's election in June 1998, which prepared the way for a less punitive-minded policy. Pastrana visited Washington on three occasions in less than four months.

Yet despite the recent improvement in United States–Colombian relations, problems are bound to emerge. The two governments give different priority to the goals of addressing security and fighting drugs. Pastrana has emphasized the importance of providing incentives for coca growers to pursue alternative development strategies. Washington, however, wants to keep eradication a central element of its counternarcotics approach. Many in Colombia are not merely skeptical of this policy but adamantly opposed, believing that it is counterproductive and often results in increasing the number of both coca producers and guerrillas.

It may, of course, be misleading to generalize about "Washington." United States policy toward Colombia involves a multitude of actors and agencies, with competing interests and agendas, that include the Defense, State, and Justice Departments, the Office of National Drug Control Policy, and key congressional representatives and their staffs. As a clear expression of backing for Pastrana's peace effort, several State Department officials met in Costa Rica with FARC representatives in December 1998, and United States Ambassador to Colombia Curtis Kamman was present when talks with FARC began.

Still, with a threefold increase in counternarcotics assistance approved for 1999, it is unclear to what extent the United States will be prepared to provide sustained high-level support to the Pastrana government as it pursues its peace strategy. That Washington policy discussions about Colombia are often filled with references to Vietnam ("avoiding a quagmire") and El Salvador ("leveling the playing field")—and even laced with questions like "Who lost Colombia?"—raises serious concerns. The temptation to allow domestic politics to drive United States policy—and to "get tough" in fighting either drugs or rebels—may be difficult to resist. As a White House official acknowledged to the *Washington Post* on December 27, "Co-

lombia poses a greater immediate threat to us than Bosnia did, yet it receives almost no attention. So policy is set by default."

Of course, with such a sharp increase in United States assistance for counternarcotics efforts (which includes support for a special elite military force), major human rights concerns will undoubtedly be raised. This is especially so in light of growing concerns that counternarcotics and counterinsurgency operations are increasingly blurred, making it difficult for the United States to aid one without aiding the other. The Leahy Amendment, a human rights law sponsored by Senator Patrick Leahy (D-VT) and passed in 1996, prohibits the use of United States funds for units of foreign security forces that have committed human rights violations. As this law is applied, it is likely to make United States policy toward Colombia even more complicated and ambivalent.

HOPES AND FEARS

Pastrana's peace effort, if it goes forward at all, will do so only by fits and starts, with inevitable setbacks and countless frustrations. Its success or failure will depend ultimately on Colombians and their sense of exhaustion with unremitting violence; they will need to bring sustained political and social pressure to bear on the government and the insurgents to produce a settlement. Ironically, the country's dim economic prospects may help spur the peace effort. At the same time, United States backing for the Pastrana administration may be helpful, but myopia about drugs and a "good guy/bad guy" optic could have harmful results.

The obstacles to progress are formidable; the incentives for negotiation may not be fully developed and the moment may not be ripe. Mistrust is at every turn; any process of building confidence will be difficult and painstakingly slow. The photo of Pastrana, alone, at San Vicente del Caguán powerfully dramatized the problem. Yet that the historic meeting took place, even without Marulanda, offers reason for hope. The country of García Márquez may yet be able to summon the imagination needed to make the process now under way work.

"The late 1990s were supposed to be the years in which the long period of austerity and adjustment to world market norms would pay off for the majority of Latin America's people. The post-Russia crisis has shaken this faith. Like [Brazilian President Fernando Henrique] Cardoso, many Latin Americans again wonder if the region is the innocent victim of irrational forces."

Economic Crisis in Latin America: Global Contagion, Local Pain

JAMES E. MAHON, JR.

At a small luncheon on January 4 in honor of his second inauguration, Brazilian President Fernando Henrique Cardoso spoke extemporaneously to a crowd that included four other regional leaders and about a hundred VIPs from Brazilian business and diplomatic circles. Criticizing "asymmetric globalization," Cardoso argued that free financial markets imply a "protectionism of the strongest" in which "perverse processes" can "turn markets into casinos." Although globalization is "a fact of our times," he said, and although "it is useless to oppose it, it would be irresponsible not to seek ways to guarantee economic and social growth." Only nine days later, what Cardoso would have called "perverse processes" forced an unscheduled depreciation of the Brazilian currency and created a new round of worries about the regional economy.

Although the regional fallout from Brazil's financial crisis may turn out to be less severe than the August 1998 Russian debt default, many Latin American countries continue to suffer from important weaknesses, especially the growth of fiscal and current account deficits. At a time when global investors have become selective about emerging markets, these deficits will make new inflows of portfolio capital scarce and expensive in large part because the region now needs them badly. This implies another round of domestic "adjustment," which will entail additional burdens on debtors and the poor in a region whose income distribution is the most unequal in the world. Political opposition to liberal economic policies may also grow

JAMES E. MAHON, JR., *is an associate professor of political science at Williams College and author of* Mobile Capital and Latin American Development *(University Park: Penn State Press, 1996).*

even as financial markets, and governments' dependence on them, seem to foreclose other policy options.

FLOATING RATES, FLEEING CAPITAL

Global economic conditions have affected Latin American economies in several ways. First, the recession in Asia has further depressed commodity prices, especially for copper and oil, which has hurt export prices across the region. Second, Asian firms, many desperate to cover debts and operating with sharply devalued currencies, have become more formidable competitors for Latin American manufacturers in home and third-country markets. Finally and most important, financial crises in Asia and Russia triggered the big stampede out of Latin American securities, mainly in the third quarter of 1998.

The first two phenomena have negatively affected trade balances, and thus current account balances, which provide one measure of the need for capital inflows. According to preliminary estimates by the IMF and the UN Economic Commission for Latin America and the Caribbean (ECLAC), the regional current account deficit (that is, trade in merchandise and in services, including interest payments) rose from just over 3 percent of GDP in 1997 to more than 4 percent in 1998. The largest deficits were in Bolivia and Ecuador (both around 9 percent), Chile (just under 7 percent), Colombia (6.6 percent), and Peru (6.5 percent). Brazil's deficit declined slightly, due to the government's austerity efforts, to equal the regional average. The steep drop in oil prices helped double Mexico's deficit to 3.5 percent and turned Venezuela's 1997 surplus into a small deficit. The oil decline, of course, has also had a strong negative impact on government budgets in oil-exporting countries.

The third phenomenon—flight of capital from emerging markets—has had various effects. Equity markets in Latin America had their worst year since 1987. Latin American funds were the weakest of all stock fund categories tracked by Lipper, Inc., for 1998, with average losses of over 38 percent. (Emerging market funds worldwide lost almost 27 percent, with those specializing in the Asia-Pacific region falling 9 percent.) More important, the withdrawal of foreign money forced up local interest rates as governments sought to defend the "credibility" of their currency regimes and avoid massive, Indonesia-style depreciation. This took place even in countries (for example, Chile, Colombia, and Mexico) whose floating exchange-rate regimes gave them more flexibility in choosing a response.

Devaluations of fixed or programmed exchange rates (the latter included Brazil's) were avoided until the Brazilian crisis in January of this year. But the rise in interest rates has also raised government borrowing costs at the same time as slowing economies have reduced tax revenues—thus knocking budgets further out of balance. Conditions improved in the last quarter of 1998, thanks in large part to the IMF agreement with Brazil negotiated in October and November. Yet even before the Brazilian shock of mid-January, interest rates were much higher than they were before August.

THE AUSTERITY CURE

Combined, the deterioration of the current account and the continued reluctance of global investors create gloomy prospects for Latin America for 1999. Risk-averse international investors may now be inclined to shy away from precisely those countries whose needs for external financing are greatest—and whose needs they were willing to meet until August 1998. As the IMF noted in its interim December 1998 *World Economic Outlook,* "the spillovers from Russia were felt with most severity in those Latin American countries perceived as having the largest financing needs . . . Asian emerging markets were less affected, since their external financing needs were regarded as relatively small in view of large current account surpluses." Looking toward the coming year, Charles Clough, chief investment strategist for Merrill Lynch, said in *The New York Times* on December 6 that "the theme for 1999 is that money will gravitate toward economies and markets that are running current account surpluses and are not heavily dependent on inflows of foreign capital."

What will fill the gap? There will be more lending by multilateral official sources other than the IMF: the World Bank and the Inter-American Development Bank. The latter doubled its lending in 1998 and is preparing to do so again in 1999. Beyond this, there are some reasons for optimism. The Russian crisis has forced global speculators to retreat from extreme levels of leverage, which means that the markets may be more selective and that Brazil's problems may not pull down every country in the region. Investors may then notice that current

account deficits have been shrinking since late 1998 in several countries, Chile and Peru among them.

Moreover, many Latin American companies with strong balance sheets began the year trading at less than eight times their projected 1999 earnings—a fraction of the bubble-inflated ratios among United States blue-chip stocks. Global conditions could change favorably, too. An Asian recovery or a euro boom would firm up commodity prices. And although emerging markets have often followed Wall Street in its downward swings, their present weakness might insulate them (though probably not Mexico) from a correction in American stock markets. Such a correction would bring on a recession in the United States, but it would first push down American interest rates and the value of the dollar. These conditions might permit Latin American interest rates to decline substantially.

> *In 1998 governments in Latin America were not yet ready to embrace policies unfriendly to international capital.*

However, these outside remedies are uncertain or, where not uncertain, probably insufficient. Most likely, Latin American governments will continue to mollify international capital by taking its prescribed medicine internally—that is, first, another dose of "adjustment," meaning fiscal austerity and the persistence of high interest rates, and second, new openings to foreign direct investment through accelerated and extended privatizations of state assets, or through the sale of locally owned private firms at bargain prices. Why this mix of policies?

FORCED TO CHOOSE

Despite the coalescence of some left intellectuals and politicians around an *alternativa latinoamericana* or Latin American alternative, there remains a widespread perception that there is little choice about major economic policies, at least under the present circumstances of moderate indebtedness and rising fiscal and current account deficits.[1] Instead, the crisis has pushed the region's governments to adopt policies even more in line with the preferences of international financial markets.

Consider the recent events in Venezuela. Hugo Chávez, the newly elected president, entered 1998 as the worst nightmare of his country's economic and financial establishment: not only was he a vitriolic opponent of the traditional political parties, he had also advocated, among other "populist" measures, a moratorium on foreign debt payments. During the presidential campaign he equivocated on economic policy as his opponents called him a fascist, a Stalinist, and another Castro. Some of the nervous rich took their families and a lot of their assets to Miami. Yet at the same time, many international investors were voicing confidence that, given the country's difficult situation, Chávez would have to "come to terms" with the IMF and international finance. Some Wall Street hands, citing the examples of other "populists" who changed their spots upon election

[1]See Lucy Conger, "A Fourth Way? The Latin American Alternative to Neo-liberalism," *Current History,* November 1998.

(Argentina's Carlos Saúl Menem, Peru's Alberto Fujimori, and Venezuela's Carlos Andrés Pérez himself), counseled investors to buy on the preelection panic and sell when Chávez came around. And they were right. After his December 6 election, Chávez rejected devaluation and exchange controls (both of which had been tried by his predecessor) while promising spending cuts, a revival of the widely hated value-added tax, stricter tax enforcement, and a welcome mat for foreign investment. Prices of Venezuelan bonds rose.

Controls on capital flows are another area in which financial market preferences have been adopted. The Asian meltdown led many well-known liberal economists to part company with the orthodox camp on capital controls, repeatedly pointing to Chile as an example of their wise use. But just as they were doing so the Chilean government, under pressure from market conditions, first reduced and then, during the September chaos, eliminated the most important barrier, the *encaje* (an obligatory, noninterest-bearing deposit equal to a set proportion of a capital inflow that was held at the central bank). Although the authorities say they intend to raise it again as conditions allow, and thus it may again serve (however effectively) to moderate currency fluctuations, their responses to financial contagion have been in the direction of more orthodoxy, not less.

Finally, consider the approval of Mexico's controversial bank-bailout legislation. The bill proposed to make tradable sovereign debt obligations, totaling $65 billion, out of the IOUs the government had given bankers in exchange for their bad loans during the crisis of 1994–1995. Building on suspicions that fraud and cronyism were being rewarded with taxpayers' money, the opposition Party of the Democratic Revolution turned this bill, and banking generally, into a mount-the-barricades issue for the Mexican left. The obvious unpopularity of a public dole for rich and sometimes shady bankers stalled negotiations on the bill until late September, when talks resumed after several weeks in which Mexican markets were roiled by the global storms. As Felipe Calderón, leader of the opposition National Action Party, told the October 7 *Financial Times,* "I see an international panorama that is serious and very delicate and it's better to hurry up and put things in order."

Hence, while the terms of the debate may have shifted somewhat in the wake of the Asian and Russian crises, in 1998 governments in Latin America were not yet ready to embrace policies unfriendly to international capital.

THE ORTHODOX CURES

Let us consider the current adjustment policies in more detail. We can begin with the last policy response noted: accelerating privatization in the pursuit of fiscal and current account balance. Brazil is likely to be the largest privatizer in the coming year, since it still has considerable good state-owned assets

> *What kind of capitalism do we get when interest rates suddenly double or triple, bringing bankruptcy and unemployment, because global asset-holders have taken fright of events on the other side of the world?*

to sell and because its large projected debt-amortization costs demand that something be done quickly. According to UN estimates, Brazil could gain between $40 billion and $50 billion from sales of state assets in 1999. Across the region, privatizations will likely include firms in electrical generation and distribution, airports, banking, and telecommunications. There may also be strong pressure to look at important natural resource companies, perhaps those producing coal in Colombia or aluminum in Venezuela, or even parts of Ecuador's state oil operations.

The trend toward greater foreign ownership will be accentuated by purchases of local private firms by bargain-hunting multinationals. As Doreen Hemlock reports in the Fort Lauderdale, Florida, *Sun-Sentinel* of January 4, "global companies with a foot in The Latin region are taking advantage of today's tough times to boost their market share at discount prices. They are snapping up low-priced stock and buying debt-strapped rivals at a discount." Latin American economies will probably be significantly more foreign-owned at the end of 1999 than they were at its beginning.

Since privatization will not suffice, additional fiscal stringency is also in the cards. Public-sector deficits are a major determinant of a country's ongoing financing needs (and thus of bond market opinion), so resolute action to cut spending and increase tax revenue can often calm the markets at relatively little cost to the real economy (or, if conditions are right and markets respond enthusiastically, at no net cost at all, as President Bill Clinton has found out).

But as Brazil has shown, the fiscal road to adjustment is slow and slippery because of the political implications of taxing and spending. Mexico has followed it most ably, with three major budget cuts in 1998 and an austere budget approved for 1999. Brazil, Ecuador, and Venezuela, with the largest projected deficits, now face some rough patches. Like most countries, they do not have pro-austerity legislative majorities in place. Anxious investors can find a lot to worry about in the open democratic politics of fiscal policy. Every step in the progress of Brazilian budget legislation and every revelation of the country's fractious federalism has been enough to spook markets around the world.

As was noted, the dominant policy response to international financial contagion has been tight money. Part of the reason is that presidents can raise short-term rates immediately in reaction to market slumps without consulting anyone outside a small circle of technocrats. But although this option is quick and clean, in recent Latin American experience it has generally taken punishing levels of interest rates to persuade nervous investors. This has immediate effects in the real economy. In October 1997 and September 1998, for example, Brazilian debtors, generally in floating-rate contracts, saw their obligations triple almost overnight. Credit scarcity choked off growth in interest-rate-sensitive sectors.

Large currency devaluations used to be part of adjustment packages, but Latin American countries have shied away from them recently. Why? Until a few years ago, received wisdom held that countries faced this trade-off: either slow the economy with tight money or cause some inflation, through rising import prices, with currency depreciation. This reasoning would imply that exporters and import-competing firms favor depreciation because it improves their competitiveness, even though it may later require fiscal or interest-rate adjustments to forestall an inflation-depreciation spiral. By the same token, government budgets could gain from depreciation where state-owned firms sell oil into the world market in dollars (for example, Ecuador, Mexico, and Venezuela) since depreciation would reduce government expenditures denominated in the local currency while not affecting revenues earned from the sale of oil.

But this picture gets complicated when a variety of financial connections link the domestic and the international economy. Holders of domestic-currency bonds dislike depreciation because it erodes the value of their asset in terms of dollars (or another reference currency). Domestic firms owning debts in dollars fear depreciation insofar as their revenues are in local currency, since these are thereby reduced relative to expenses. (They may hedge against it but where markets are poorly developed this may be expensive.) Holders of dollar-denominated bonds may not mind it unless they see in it a willingness to violate the trust of all creditors. In general, however, the old formulas of the gold-standard era usually apply: financial interests want currency stability while manufacturers and exporters prefer to keep credit loose and the economy growing.

The difference today is that financial interests now have a stronger hold on more of these economies. The Mexican crisis showed that a sudden depreciation of the currency scares the markets so much that stratospheric interest rates are required to stop a downward spiral. Mexico and Asia showed the dangers of systemic crisis arising from a devaluation's damage to big domestic firms with unhedged foreign debts. Hence Latin American governments have been more receptive to insistent voices coming from the IMF and Wall Street.

As Brazil has lately shown, the tight-money policy concentrates the initial damage among highly indebted or interest-rate-sensitive businesses with few international financial ties, as well as among the consumer-debt-loving urban salaried class. The greatest and most persistent damage is to employment. According to ECLAC, regional unemployment reached 7.9 percent in 1998, well above the 6.3 percent that was seen in 1994 just before the Mexican crisis forced an increase in interest rates.

One consequence of long periods of tight money is to make the political divide between debtor and creditor, and between domestically focused industry and internationally connected finance, more salient than that between capital and labor. In Brazil, for example, the leader of the Federation of Industries of São Paulo State, the country's most powerful employers' organization, sought in December 1998 an unprecedented alliance with the radical labor confederation, the Unified Workers' Central, against the "monetarist" policies of the Cardoso government.

The debtor-creditor conflict may get even worse if tight money leads to a banking crisis. At high real interest rates, banks opt increasingly for the easy profits of high-coupon government debt and the private sector becomes starved for credit. Banks' existing portfolios deteriorate. Old fixed-rate assets will become losers, while floating-rate contracts will squeeze the borrowers and lead to a rise in defaults. Banking systems are only as solid as the people and firms making the interest payments, and not many borrowers can remain solid if real interest rates exceed 15 or 20 percent for a year. In 1998, banks in Colombia and Ecuador saw their portfolios weaken considerably. The crisis set back the recuperation of Mexico's ailing banks, too, and it has already begun to affect Brazil's in 1999.

Some political consequences of a banking crisis can be seen in recent Mexican experience. Massive defaults can on consumer and business loans create the potential for organized action on the part of debtors, as in the movement called El Barzón (The Yoke). Seeing their numbers, debtors become aware of the larger causes behind their plight and they lose their shame. If the crisis requires government intervention, further polarization may ensue as taxpayers—who under the now common consumption taxes include everybody, even the poorest—are forced to bail out rich and sometimes dishonest bankers.

A final, more subtle issue relates to the magnitude of the interest-rate spikes that have been imposed on these countries. Over the last few years, with liberal economic policies firmly in place, Latin Americans have been urged to pursue a second, more fundamental kind of reform, aimed at strengthening institutions and deepening the rule of law. It is true that the rule of law can bring predictability to economic life. It might contracts easily enforceable, secures property rights, and reduces the arbitrariness of the state. It is thus a necessary ingredient for a rational and just capitalism.

Necessary, but maybe not sufficient. In another part of his luncheon speech, President Cardoso argued that "the market ought to reward effort, work, technical innovation, and the entrepreneurial spirit, and not speculation." But what kind of capitalism do we get when interest rates suddenly double or triple, bringing bankruptcy and unemployment, because global asset-holders have taken fright of events on the other side of the world?

ASYMMETRY AS A FACT OF LIFE

Over the course of the 1980s, most Latin American opinion leaders accepted the idea that the largest portion of blame for the decade's debt crisis lay with the bad policies pursued by their governments. By the mid-1990s the bad policies were mostly remedied, and in the last few years many Latin American governments have become accustomed to receiving praise for their achievements in free-market reform. Indeed, after the Asian crisis broke, Mexico's response in 1995 to its crisis was taken as a model for others to emulate. The late 1990s were supposed to be the years in which the long period of austerity and adjustment to world market norms would pay off for the majority of Latin America's people.

The post-Russia crisis has shaken this faith. Like President Cardoso, many Latin Americans again wonder if the region is the innocent victim of irrational forces. Not that problems are absent: the commodity price declines are real, as are the daunting schedule of Brazilian debt amortization and the slow, narrowly confined progress on legal and institutional reform. But Latin Americans are now less ready to agree that these sins are enough to make them deserve the financial purgatory of recession, unemployment, bank bailouts, and denationalization of the productive structure.

What can they do? The crisis has helped to clarify a few of the structural problems associated with Latin America's insertion into the world economy, and with the world economy itself.

For the region, four problems stand out. First, a still significant dependence on commodity exports; second, a tendency for the import bill to increase quickly with GDP growth; third, in most but not all countries, weak tax structures with high rates of evasion; and fourth, national savings that are probably too low and are relatively globalized in their disposition. The first makes export receipts and thus the current account balance (and in some places the fiscal balance) vulnerable to the wild price swings of these goods. The second tends to make growth dependent to an unusual degree on capital inflows, while the third means that government finance often shares this dependence. And the fourth implies that a great proportion of Latin American countries' national savings has a global view, and thus is as unstable as foreign capital in the event of a crisis.

Of these problems, only two have straightforward solutions. For commodity price shocks, stabilization funds (as Chile has

in place for copper) save hard currency during commodity booms in order to spend it during busts. And tax evasion could be reduced. In addition, policymakers should use periods of rapid growth and capital inflow to build net fiscal surpluses and large defensive stocks of foreign exchange reserves, which would help insulate the economy from an unpredictable and unforgiving global financial environment. Capital controls are best applied when flows are abundant; they should be eased, as in Chile, when they are scarce. While the events of the past year have provided a good argument for reducing dependence on foreign finance, there are obvious problems with a government unilaterally doing so immediately after it has sold (and encouraged local firms to sell) many billions of dollars of debt into the world market.

Until good times return, "asymmetric globalization" will be a painful fact of life. Some governments are discussing the abolition of their central banks and the adoption of the United States dollar. This would soothe investor worries about exchange rate risk, but it would also mean renouncing the benefits of a local lender of last resort and a monetary policy that helps moderate global shocks. Other countries will have to accept that they need to regain the "confidence" of international finance by following another old recipe: making bankers and other asset-holders lots of money for a long time.

This leads us to the world economy. Keep in mind the Merrill Lynch strategist quoted earlier, who wanted to see current account surpluses before committing funds in 1999. Insofar as this reasoning holds sway, the present situation resembles that of the 1930s, when a joke then popular in Eastern Europe compared international bankers to people who are happy to lend you an umbrella as long as it is not raining. Well, it's raining again in Latin America, and a lot of people are getting wet.

Unit 6

Key Points to Consider

❖ Explain why you agree or disagree with the assessment that 1989 marked a turning point in European history and an end of the balance of power politics in Europe.

❖ What types of changes do you expect to see in Europe during the second post–cold war decade?

❖ Explain why you do or do not expect to see a separate European defense force in your lifetime. What about a common European foreign policy in your lifetime? Why do you agree or disagree with analysts that the current peace settlement will bring lasting peace to Northern Ireland?

❖ Describe what you believe are the most important and most lasting effects of the Revolutions of 1989 for three Central or Eastern European countries.

 **Links**   # www.dushkin.com/online/

These sites are annotated on pages 6 and 7.

Nineteen eighty-nine marked the end of cold war and a break in European history as the old balance-of-power system in Europe came to an end. The first decade of the new century promises to be just the start of breathtaking changes throughout the Continent. A new security system and way of thinking about foreign affairs is emerging. As other parts of the world become more disorderly, Europe faces the twin challenge of making its own new model of security work while living with a world operating on the old balance-of-power rules.

The North Atlantic Treaty Organization (NATO) air campaign against Yugoslavia and subsequent deployment of 50,000 peacekeepers to Kosovo revealed the huge military disparity between the United States and other members of NATO. The United States carried 90 percent of the load in the 47-day air campaign in which the weapons, planes, and pilots were all Americans. Many allies found that they lacked the equipment necessary to gather detailed intelligence, to strike targets with precision, and sustain forces during 78 days of high tempo operations. European countries had to struggle to get some 40,000 troops together to serve in Kosovo. Most analysts believe that Europeans are not investing enough in military capabilities even though Europe spends over 60 percent of what the United States spends on defense.

Since Kosovo, European allies have initiated a spirited defense debate. Most European governments now support the creation of a regional defense structure, the European Security and Defense Identity, that would make it possible for Europeans to operate in situations in which NATO itself is not engaged. The dilemma is that most European governments currently lack the military capability to sustain such a force, which would require European countries to move forces rapidly, to sustain them outside their national territories, and to equip their military with modern technology. Serious discussions are now underway between smaller countries about how to pool resources and rationalize capabilities with neighbors in order to be able to contribute to a regional mobility command and proposed rapid-reaction force to be called the Eurocorp.

Establishing a separate European defense identity will not be easy. France is downsizing and shifting to a smaller, more professional military. Large majorities in most other Western European countries favor additional defense cuts. The new left-of-center German government favors upgrading the role of the 52-nation Organization for Security and Cooperation in Europe (OSCE) while reducing NATO's role.

The successful NATO campaign in Serbia and the combined efforts of NATO, the European Community, OSCE countries, and the UN to help an autonomous Kosovo recover from the war has convinced most Europeans, at least for the moment, that continued participation in NATO is in Europe's interest. However, a number of basic questions must still be answered about the alliance's future as an expanded alliance. As Europeans move towards establishing a truly European security system they must decide "whether," and if so, "why," "when," "where," and "how much," the organization should expand and where it should eventually stop.

A European military force will also require greater coordination of European national foreign policies. A common foreign policy has been a long-term goal of the European Union. Reginald Dale explains how European countries currently are pursuing this goal in "The Search for a Common Foreign Policy." The principle of "constructive attention" is now used to assure member governments that their national policies will not be overruled. The war in Kosovo, the need to stabilize southeastern Europe, and recent political trends are fueling public support and government efforts to implement long-dormant efforts to develop European military capabilities.

Another integration milestone for the European Union (EU) occurred on January 1, 1999 with the introduction of a new single currency, the euro. This historic venture agreed to in the Maastricht Treaty was implemented much more smoothly than many analysts had predicted. If all goes as planned, the gradual phase-in of the European Monetary Union (EMU) and use of the euro as a common currency will be completed by 2002 except in Britain, Denmark, Sweden, and Greece, which did not join in 1999. The euro is expected to transform every level of European business and society as travel and commerce for millions across the continent is eased. The euro has also stimulated a spate of mergers within Europe and between European and American companies The new currency and trade block has a population larger than the United States and a GDP that is 77 percent of the United States'. The general expectation is that the euro will create a more efficient economy, increase the volume of trade with major trading partners, provide another currency that may soon rival the dollar, and stimulate further cultural and political integration in Europe.

Sustaining progress toward greater economic integration will not be easy. Historically, Germany paid a disproportionate share of the costs of the European Union. Germany plans to work to achieve a rebate on Germany's net EU annual contribution by cutting the Union's farm-support program, which consumes 70 percent of the EU's budget. Germany is also pushing for other EU countries to accept more political refugees. At present, nearly half of all political refugees settle in Germany.

The European Union continues plans to expand membership to eligible countries in central and eastern Europe. The Czech Republic, Hungary, Poland and Slovenia remain leading candidates while the six countries in the second flight—Bulgaria, Romania, Slovakia, Russia, Ukraine, and Belarus currently are beyond the pale. Peter Rutland, in "The Revolutions of 1989 Reconsidered," describes how some countries turned out to be capitalist while some capitalists turned out to be crooks. For many in Eastern Europe, revolutions have meant a return to ethnicity and a realization of the high cost of freedom.

NATO extension and European integration are more complicated today due to the continuing cost and complexity of issues involved in continued peacekeeping in Bosnia and Kosovo. NATO ministers want to reduce the NATO peacekeeping force as soon as possible in both regions of the former Yugoslav Republic. While some cite NATO's victory in Kosovo as a harbinger of a new type of humanitarian intervention, Ivo Daalder and Michael O'Hanlon, in "Unlearning the Lessons of Kosovo," explain why a closer look at the conflict reaffirms old truths rather than offers new lessons. It is now clear that post-reconstruction of an autonomous Kosovo will require costly and long-term commitments by all parties involved in the military victory.

The Search for a Common Foreign Policy

By Reginald Dale

The Past

As the great enterprise of European integration has struggled forward over the past half century, its grandest ambitions have always attracted skepticism. Sometimes the skeptics have been right, more often they have been wrong, or at least behind the times.

But perhaps no project has engendered more doubts and disbelief than the attempt to create a common foreign policy, in which the member states of the European Union would ultimately speak with a single voice in world affairs.

Those doubts have hardly been alleviated by the EU's plans, first officially formulated in the early 1990s, to include security policy in the search for common positions.

The skeptics ask how fifteen proud nations with such different cultures, histories, and interests could possibly reach common ground on the vital issues of foreign and security policy that lie at the heart of national sovereignty.

Some American commentators have confidently stated that the European Union will never have a common foreign and security policy, still less the single telephone number that former secretary of state Henry Kissinger used to say he wanted for his diplomatic dealings with Europe.

But "never" is a dangerous word to use in politics, and experience suggests it is also unwise to apply it to the tortuous process of European integration. Although the unification process often moves crabwise and sometimes backward, it has consistently reached most of its objectives, though admittedly not always on time. Now, from an unexpected quarter, the war in Kosovo has suddenly injected a new sense of urgency into the efforts to create a common foreign and security policy.

European leaders have been shocked by the inadequacy of their disparate armed forces in the crisis and by the extent of their dependence on uncertain US leadership.

That painful awakening led to big steps forward. At their summit meeting in Cologne in early June, the EU's leaders took a series of ambitious decisions intended to bring foreign and security issues into the framework of the EU institutions and approved plans for combined, if limited, EU military operations in future emergencies in Europe.

Underlining their new found readiness to press ahead, they appointed a high-profile international official, Javier Solana of Spain, the NATO secretary general, to the new post of European high representative for foreign and security affairs.

There are good reasons why progress in foreign and security policy should have lagged behind most other fields of cooperation. The integration strategy adopted by the European Union's founding fathers called for economic unification to precede political union.

In the EU's formative years, the importance of that sequence was dramatically demonstrated by some bad experiences in the field of common foreign and defense policy—after which the very words "common foreign policy" remained taboo for almost forty years.

The first unhappy experience came in the early 1950s, even before the establishment of the original six-nation European Economic Community, when the French parliament rejected plans for a European Defense Community.

The plan had been hatched by the six countries that would subsequently go on to found the EEC—France, Germany, Italy, Belgium, the Netherlands, and Luxembourg—in the hope of creating a common European army under the aegis of a European political community with federal institutions.

Against the background of the beginning of the cold war and the Korean War, the aim was to create a framework that would allow German rearmament without rekindling the fires of German militarism. German rearmament, of course, eventually went ahead, but the call for a common European army was far ahead of its time.

The next attempt—the so-called Fouchet Plan launched by France under President Charles de Gaulle in 1961–2—was equally ill-fated, for virtually the opposite reasons. This time France's partners rejected proposals designed to lead to a unified foreign policy and coordinated defense policies.

While the French parliament felt the proposed defense community went too far in a federal direction, France's partners thought the Fouchet Plan did not go far enough. They found the plan too intergovernmental, leaving too much power in the hands of national capitals, especially Paris. They also feared it might threaten defense links with the United States in NATO.

Following those two failures, the next attempts were more modest. In 1970, the six began cooperation on foreign policy, by means of closer links between their diplomatic services, in order to strengthen their solidarity on major international issues. The process was known as European political cooperation (EPC).

But the process yielded few spectacular results in the 1970s. It was not until ten years later that the political and economic (not military) aspects of security were included in EPC, and it was not until the mid-1980s that steps were taken to give EPC a formal structure, including a secretariat.

From 1970 to 1986, European diplomacy was harmonized through informal agreements, with France insisting on keeping the process intergovernmental, not subject to normal Community disciplines that would have reduced the influence of national capitals.

Foreign policy cooperation finally began to get serious in the mid-1980s, when the Single European Act relaunched economic and political integration after years of near-stagnation. In addition to setting up the EU's single market, the act, which came into force in 1987, formalized the EPC system.

The act provided for meetings of foreign ministers at least four times a year, regular meetings of the political committee (composed of the political directors of the national foreign ministries) and a separate EPC secretariat. A reference to closer cooperation on security questions was included for the first time in an EU treaty.

Foreign policy cooperation remained a matter for national governments, outside the regular EU institutional framework. Nevertheless, both the Commission and the European Parliament were drawn somewhat closer into the process, with provisions for the Commission to be "fully associated with the proceedings," and the Parliament to be kept regularly informed.

The member countries undertook to work toward "the convergence of their positions and the implementation of joint actions." But it was not until the Maastricht Treaty on European Union, which came into force in 1993, that a more solid structure was built on these foundations. That treaty is the basis for most of today's foreign policy and security cooperation.

The Present

The early 1990s, with the Gulf War and the beginning of hostilities in Yugoslavia, gave the EU countries plenty of reasons to believe that common policies were increasingly necessary. The idea that the time was ripe was also fostered by the end of the cold war and German unification, both of which seemed likely to boost the international role of the EU, in Europe if not beyond.

At the same time, the move to a single European market at the beginning of 1993, and the Maastricht commitment to economic and monetary union later in the decade, was giving a new dynamism to political as well as economic integration.

With the cold war over, many Europeans also assumed that the US military presence in Europe would be wound down, making a stronger European defense and foreign policy capability both more necessary and more achievable.

At the start of the troubles in Bosnia, the then Luxembourg foreign minister Jacques Poos gained widespread notoriety by announcing that the "hour of Europe" had arrived. It turned out that it had not—the EU lamentably failed to resolve the Bosnian crisis.

Nevertheless, the EU's efforts to present a common front to the world intensified. The Maastricht Treaty set one of the Union's objectives as "the implementation of a common foreign and security policy, including the eventual framing of a common defense policy."

European political cooperation had been implemented by means of consultations, information exchanges, and the issuing of joint declaration.

Now, following Maastricht, the EU governments are actively pursuing the more demanding aims of agreeing "common positions" and implementing "joint actions." The Amsterdam Treaty, which came into force in May, added a loosely defined concept of "common strategies."

CFSP activities have included moves to encourage the settlement of border disputes among Central and East European countries, monitoring elections in Russia and South Africa, dispatching humanitarian aid to Bosnia, administrating the Bosnian city of Mostar, and supporting the Gaza-Jericho agreement in the Middle East.

Special envoys have been appointed to represent the Union in the Middle East peace process and to help resolve crises in Africa's Great Lakes region and in the countries of former Yugoslavia.

None of these activities has had a huge impact on the course of world events. Even the most ardent supporters of the CFSP would admit that the EU has not proved terribly effective in the major areas in which it has sought to play a role, especially Bosnia and the Middle East.

In Bosnia, the key diplomatic and military players turned out to be the United States, NATO, and the United Nations, not the European Union. In the Middle East, Israel and, to a lesser extent, the US has successfully kept the EU at a safe distance from the heart of the peace process, correctly assuming that the EU is more sympathetic than Washington to the Arab point of view.

The EU's policymaking has suffered from a lack of clear definition of the EU's interests and objectives, as opposed to national interests. Some

Europeans fear a pattern is emerging in which the United States makes the main geopolitical decisions and Europe pays for them.

The EU is by far the main provider of humanitarian assistance to the former republics of Yugoslavia and of economic aid to Russia, the countries of Central Europe, and the Palestinians. It is the main source of international development aid and will inevitably have to bear most of the cost of rebuilding Kosovo.

That is at least partly a reflection of the fact that the EU is much more credible as a commercial and economic power on a world stage than as a political player.

The EU's efforts to assume a political role have been handicapped by awkward institutional arrangements, designed to separate the CFSP from the usual EU decision-making process with its greater limits on national sovereignty.

Those arrangements have now been simplified: The general principles of the CFSP are defined by EU leaders meeting in the European Council. Decisions are taken in the Council of Foreign Ministers, who must act unanimously except in the implementation of some joint actions.

However, the aim is still to prevent national governments being overruled on sensitive foreign policy issues—the consequence of which, in the past, has been to give every and any member state a veto over the formulation of a common position.

The Amsterdam Treaty seeks to resolve that problem with the introduction of the concept of "constructive abstention." Henceforth, a member state that does not like a proposal can abstain and not be obliged to apply the resulting decision. But the abstaining government must accept that the decision commits the Union and must refrain from doing anything that would conflict with the EU action.

The Future

The war in Kosovo has injected a sudden note of reality into some of the more abstruse discussions of the common foreign and security policy. Many European leaders are making clear they see the crisis as a decisive test of their ability to purge Europe of its old nationalistic demons and present a common front to the world in the coming century.

Joschka Fischer, the German foreign minister, has gone so far as to describe the hostilities over Kosovo as a "unification war" that will lead to a much more united Europe. The war will oblige Europeans to grasp the need for a common defense, as well as for the expansion of both NATO and the EU to incorporate most or all of Central and Eastern Europe, he says.

Romano Prodi, the president-designate of the European Commission, has even revived calls for a European army.

Work is underway in Brussels on a new pact aimed at stabilizing southeastern Europe by drawing the countries of the Balkans closer to the EU, with the possibility of membership in the distant future acting as an incentive for the hostile ethnic groups to learn to live together.

It is a huge task, involving the creation of civilized market democracies in the region virtually from scratch. It will be a major test for the CFSP, as will the efforts to create a more integrated and more independent European defense capability that many European leaders are now urging. Rudolf Scharping, the German defense minister, says that Europe must acquire its own major military assets, such as satellite reconnaissance and airlift capacity, for which it is currently obliged to turn to the United States. The same proposal has been made by other leading Europeans, although few of them have yet begun to tackle the issue of how such grandiose plans should be paid for—and whether European taxpayers are prepared to foot the bill.

Nevertheless, there is no doubt that Kosovo has given a big boost to proposals for integrating defense policies more closely into the EU structure. Plans are afoot to fold the Western European Union, the long-dormant European defense cooperation forum, into the EU, thus giving the Union a formal defense dimension.

Another consequence of Kosovo is likely to be that cooperation on defense policies will now take over the lead from foreign policy coordination as the driving force of the CFSP.

After a May meeting in Bremen, northern Germany, the WEU's defense and foreign ministers said they were now committed to "the development of an effective European defense and security policy."

Scharping, who chaired the meeting, stressed that the aim was not to replace or compete with NATO but to "strengthen Europe's voice" within the transatlantic alliance.

At their Cologne summit meeting, the EU leaders took these ideas a step further. In addition to appointing Solana as high representative, a post created by the Amsterdam Treaty, the leaders agreed that the EU should have its own military capabilities to tackle regional crises in Europe, backed by adequate intelligence and strategic planning capacities. They agreed on a number of possible ways for bringing defense into the EU's traditional decision-making process, including the participation of defense ministers in meetings of the Council of Foreign Ministers.

Other proposals include the creation of an EU military committee, composed of military personnel, that would make recommendations to a permanent new political and security committee in Brussels.

Until now, such ideas would have been dismissed as fantasy, implying as they do a central control over defense policies, which is unacceptable both to major member states, like France and the United Kingdom, and to the EU's neutral countries.

Prospects for closer defense cooperation had already begun to improve before the bombing in Kosovo started. Last fall, the United Kingdom dropped long-standing opposition to merging the WEU with the EU and agreed to a joint declaration with France at St. Malo calling for a stronger European defense policy.

Germany, shedding lingering inhibitions stemming from World War II, has been showing growing readiness to play an active European security role—an evolution dramatically underlined by the inclusion of German combat troops in the peacemaking forces in Kosovo.

The United Kingdom, anxious not to undermine NATO and US leadership, has traditionally resisted efforts to create an independent European defense capability. But Prime Minister Tony Blair is now keen to find new areas of cooperation with Europe in order to assert his leadership on the international stage.

With the United Kingdom not among the eleven nations that have adopted the single European currency, the euro, defense is the most obvious field for cooperation, and stronger defense links with Europe are surprisingly popular with British public opinion.

Surveys suggest that the British public is more in favor of defense and foreign policy cooperation with the rest of Europe than it is of the trade and economic cooperation that is the bread and butter of EU membership.

The trend long predates Kosovo. Polling by the United States Information Agency shows that the British have long been highly supportive of European defense cooperation, somewhat less supportive of foreign policy cooperation, and much less favorable to the single currency.

A similar pattern exists in Germany, where public opinion favors foreign policy cooperation most of all and prefers defense cooperation to membership in the single currency. In France, there is much more support for the euro but still higher levels of support for defense and foreign policy cooperation.

For all these reasons, optimists believe it will finally be possible to take big steps forward in foreign policy and defense cooperation. However, it remains easy to be skeptical. Cynics might point out that the climate has been propitious before—as it was at the beginning of the 1990s—and the EU failed to take advantage of it.

But it would be wise not to be too cynical. Only a year or two ago, skeptics on both sides of the Atlantic were predicting that European economic and monetary union would never happen and that the euro would be indefinitely delayed. That was to underestimate the forces driving Europe toward closer integration. Those forces have now been reinforced by Kosovo.

"Kosovo could be our military euro," Ulrich Beck, a professor at Munich University, told the *New York Times* in April. The Balkan crisis, he argued, could create "a political and defense identity for the European Union in the same way as the euro is the expression of economic and financial integration."

That may be a little overambitious. But at least, with Javier Solana's appointment as 'Mr. CFSP', the EU now has someone to answer the telephone when Washington calls.

Reginald Dale is a columnist for the International Herald Tribune.

BRITAIN

Enemies and colleagues

The ministers in Northern Ireland's new government have a long history of mutual hatred. But they will work together all the same

THE peace process in Northern Ireland, never smooth, has this week made dramatic and historic progress. The province's new government includes the former IRA commander, Martin McGuinness, as minister for education. It also includes ministers from the Democratic Unionist Party (DUP), led by the Reverend Ian Paisley, which has all along denounced the province's peace deal as a surrender to terrorism.

Peter Robinson, the deputy leader of the DUP, has been put in charge of regional development. He swears that he will not sit down with Mr McGuinness, and that the DUP is in government only to "thwart the IRA". But the extremes in Northern Ireland's politics are now corralled into a coalition government, and will share the power devolved from Westminister at midnight on Wednesday December 1st.

The arrangements for decommissioning weapons remain shrouded in deliberate ambiguity. However, as *The Economist* went to press, the IRA seemed poised to appoint a representative to deal with an international decommissioning body. There may never be a single moment when fear

of failure finally disappears. But this week's developments provide ballast for the peace deal.

The IRA has delayed discussions on decommissioning until the last possible moment, clutching at the residual mystique of a secret army's "right to bear arms against an occupying power." It regards itself as the heir to 800 years of resistance to British rule in Ireland. But centuries of struggle have ended, not in the long-demanded British withdrawal, but with agreed Irish-British arrangements for the government of Northern Ireland. Mainstream republicanism—minus an unreconciled fringe—has settled for a constitutional path towards its goal. And a change in the constitution of the Irish republic—dropping its constitutional claim to the north—should assuage unionist fears of annexation by an Irish state.

Britain has also altered its legal relationship with Northern Ireland, by dropping the claim in the Government of Ireland Act to be the "sovereign power". The two governments are now pledged, in a new British-Irish accord signed on December 2nd, to facilitate

change in the status of Northern Ireland only when a majority there wishes it.

A British-Irish council, important to unionists, will bring representatives from the new devolved assemblies in Belfast, Edinburgh and Cardiff, to discuss shared concerns with British and Irish MPS. A North-South council, a nationalist enthusiasm, will see ministers in Belfast and Dublin working to increase cross-border co-operation. Its first meeting took place on November 30th, with Northern Ireland represented by the unionist and nationalist joint heads of the executive: David Trimble of the Ulster Unionists and the SDLP's Seamus Mallon.

The raft of new structures rapidly slotted into place once Mr Trimble secured approval from his Ulster Unionist Party's policymaking council on November 27th. His party has been torn from the start on the merits of the 1998 Good Friday Agreement package, in part because it is terrified of losing voters to the hardliners led by Mr Paisley. Mr Trimble's most vulnerable point has always been the fraught business of decommissioning.

A brief history of strife

1921: Ireland is partitioned. Southern Ireland becomes an independent country. The north gets its own parliament and remains within the United Kingdom.
1922: Proportional representation abolished in local elections in Northern Ireland.
1939: IRA bombing in England.
1949: Ireland Act passed at Westminster guaranteeing that Northern Ireland will remain within the United Kingdom unless its parliament decides otherwise.
1967: Catholic civil-rights movement gets going in Northern Ireland.
1969: Rioting in Belfast and Londonderry. Sectarian clashes. Troops arrive.
1970: IRA mobilises. 28 deaths.
1971: 184 people die as IRA shoots soldiers and bombs Protestant districts, and loyalists bomb Catholic pubs. Internment introduced; 374 arrests in Belfast.
1972: The worst year with 497 deaths. "Bloody Sunday" in Londonderry in January, when soldiers fire on a banned march and kill 13. "Bloody Friday" in July, when 22 IRA bombs explode within 75 minutes. Northern Ireland's Stormont parliament replaced by direct rule from London.
1973: Attempt to devise new power-sharing political structure for Northern Ireland through the Sunningdale agreement.

1974: Sunningdale brought down by protests by Protestant unions, paramilitaries and politicians. Direct rule from London resumed. Loyalist bombs kill 33 in Ireland.
1979: IRA kills 18 soldiers at Warrenpoint.
1981: IRA hunger strikes. Ten republican prisoners starve themselves to death in support of their demands for political status. One, Bobby Sands, had been elected as Sinn Fein's first MP.
1984: IRA bombs Grand Hotel in Brighton during the Conservative Party conference.
1985: Britain and Ireland sign the Anglo-Irish agreement giving Ireland consultative rights in Northern Irish affairs.
1991: IRA launches mortar bombs at 10 Downing Street.
1993: Gerry Adams of Sinn Fein and John Hume of the Catholic nationalist SDLP begin talks to find a political way forward.
1994: First IRA ceasefire announced. Loyalist paramilitaries also declare a ceasefire.
1995: Tories and unionists demand the IRA "decommission" weapons before peace talks can begin. Senator George Mitchell invited in to try to end the deadlock. He proposes decommissioning should be "addressed" during talks.

1996: The IRA breaks its ceasefire and bombs Canary Wharf and Manchester.
1997: Tony Blair elected. IRA renews ceasefire and Sinn Fein enters talks.
1998: The talks conclude in April with the Good Friday Agreement. Sinn Fein accepts that Northern Ireland will remain part of the United Kingdom, as long as a majority of the population are in favour. Under the agreement, power will be devolved from Westminster to a new assembly and Northern Ireland executive, structured to ensure cross-community participation. There will be "North-South" bodies linking northern and southern Ireland and a British-Irish council, linking Ireland with Britain. The deal is approved in referendums staged in Northern Ireland and in the Irish republic.

In August, IRA renegades set off a bomb in Omagh killing 28 people.

In October, John Hume and David Trimble, the leader of the Ulster Unionists, are jointly awarded the Nobel Peace Prize.
1999: Endless haggling over decommissioning appears to threaten the peace deal. But the Unionists eventually drop their demand that decommissioning must precede Sinn Fein's entry into government. Martin McGuinness, a former IRA commander, becomes minister for education.

All told, more than 3,600 people have died during the Troubles.

In 1995 his party's position was that peace talks could not start before decommissioning. Then it became that the issue of weapons had to be dealt with during the course of the talks. Once the talks concluded Mr Trimble's party said that no government could be formed until decommissioning took place.

But a ten-week negotiation chaired by a former American senator, George Mitchell, produced the formula of Sinn Fein entry into government to be followed immediately by the appointment of an IRA "interlocutor" on decommissioning. The Mitchell talks at last convinced Mr Trimble that republicans could not deliver the decommissioning of weapons before a government was set up, alongside the other structures set out in the Good Friday Agreement.

Having hoped for 60% plus support from the Ulster Unionist council, he won 58% backing from the 829-strong attendance. The narrow win was bought at the expense of a promise to recall the council in February, when he and the other three Ulster Unionist ministers say they will resign, if they judge that insufficient progress has been made on decommissioning. Gerry Adams and Mr McGuinness promptly condemned this "precondition". But neither they, nor a later IRA warning that Ulster Unionists had stepped back from the deal agreed by the Mitchell review, showed real anger.

The other pro-agreement parties—the SDLP, Sinn Fein, the small cross-community Alliance Party, the tiny loyalist Progressive Unionists and the Women's Coalition—recognise that the future of the new government depends on sustaining Mr Trimble's leadership. Pro- and anti-agreement unionists have equal numbers inside the devolved assembly. The agreement provided careful checks and balances to protect the narrow pro-agreement unionist block from being undone by the anti-agreement DUP.

It is clear to all that Mr Trimble is still dogged by unionist critics inside and outside his party and will have difficulty each step of the way ahead. But he must be cheered by the realisation that his own waverers stood firm on the day that ministers were nominated, despite Paisleyite theatrics designed to shame them into opposing the nomination of Sinn Fein ministers.

There may also be some promise of stability in the fact that even the Paisleyite DUP's behaviour is much more cautious than its rhetoric. Unionists of all shades reacted with anger to the appointment of Mr McGuinness, personification for many of IRA terror, to take charge of primary and secondary education, with Sinn Fein's other appointee taking over health and public safety. But Mr. Trimble's Ulster Unionists noted acidly that the DUP could have blocked Mr McGuinness's appointment to such a sensitive job, by choosing that portfolio themselves.

Many see the Paisley strategy as a prolonged attempt to tar the Ulster Unionists as traitors, rather than a genuine attempt to bring the government down. Over the past year assembly committees, with Sinn Fein and DUP members, including Mr Paisley, have had a total of 180 meetings preparing for devolution. The DUP's two ministers, Peter Robinson and Nigel Dodds, say they will have no dealings inside the executive with the Sinn Fein pair. But Sammy Wilson, the DUP's vice-chair of the assembly committee which will monitor Mr McGuinness's stewardship, promises to harry Mr McGuinness on the assembly floor with his questions.

This combination of public posturing and quiet co-operation is already well-established in local government in Northern Ireland. When Sinn Fein took dozens of council seats in the early 1980s, the DUP swore never to sit with them. In Cookstown, County Tyrone, they placed their chairs some distance away from the rest of the council. But over several years, the chairs have crept towards the table. In another council a DUP member sprayed republicans with deodorant.

In the assembly's public gallery, one protester became so overwrought that he vomited on people sitting next to him as the Sinn Fein ministers were named. But sullen resignation has largely displaced violent obstruction. The year's delays and stumbles have helped acclimatise people to change. Those still unsure about republicans' commitment to democracy may even concede in time that there could be evidence of serious intent in Sinn Fein's choice of two demanding ministries, at the heart of Northern Ireland's daily life: education and health.

Disposing of guns has preoccupied unionists. The republicans, representatives of some of the poorest sections of society, will soon face other tests imposed by democratic politics— when Bairbre De Brun has to close hospitals and Martin McGuinness cannot end Northern Ireland's selective education system. Everything about their acceptance of the posts suggested an eagerness to face the challenge. Mr McGuinness's paramilitary credentials helped Mr Adams reroute republicans away from violence towards politics. His installation as a minister was the seal on that policy.

One ex-prisoner watching this week's ceremony has voiced the growing acceptance among republicans that decommissioning will not be allowed to block progress. "If it comes to walking away from the institutions, or walking away from the guns," he said, "there's no doubt about it. We'll walk away from the guns."

The Revolutions of 1989 Reconsidered

"The unease about the true significance of the events of 1989 is only reinforced by developments since then. No one expected that so many former communist managers would quickly shed their socialist colors and embrace the capitalist path.... As in all revolutions, ideas and assumptions were overturned and events developed in unexpected directions. Some communists turned out to be capitalists, and some capitalists turned out to be crooks."

PETER RUTLAND

It hardly seems possible that 10 years have already elapsed since the breakup of the Soviet empire in Eastern Europe. The passage of time was brought home to me recently when a student mentioned the "postwar period," and I realized that he was referring to events since the end of the cold war, not those after the Second World War.

The collapse of communism in 1989 happened so quickly that it left us not with a rich store of memories, but with a blur of CNN images and a trail of still unresolved questions. Two scenes capture that miraculous year. The defining picture was that of delirious Germans chipping away at the Berlin Wall. A month later and a thousand miles south, grainy footage taken by a Romanian army cameraman recorded the execution of Nicolae and Elena Ceausescu in front of another, less celebrated wall.

The unresolved questions seem to grow more acute with each passing year. Why did the collapse occur so quickly? Was it part of a plot by groups in the ruling elite to cling to power and loot their countries' wealth? Were all those societies really ready for such an abrupt transition from state socialism to market democracy? Will they stay democratic, or will they revert to their authoritarian ways?

A CURIOUS REVOLUTION

Events in 1989 gathered pace so quickly that they seemed beyond human control, almost beyond human comprehension. That summer, for the first time in 70 years, Russian coal min-

ers stood up to the Soviet state—and the state backed down. These were the first large-scale public protests in Russia since 1962, when dozens of striking workers in Novocherkassk had indeed been shot down. In 1989 Soviet leader Mikhail Gorbachev still had the power to order the police to shoot the miners, but he chose not to use it. That same summer, China's leaders came to a different conclusion, and sent the army to clear protesters from Tiananmen Square. A "Chinese variant" was still possible in Eastern Europe, and could perhaps have bought another decade of socialism. That would have been the option selected by leaders such as East Germany's Erich Honecker—if Gorbachev had not been in the Kremlin to order the troops back to the barracks.

The speed of communism's collapse in Europe left little time for heroic acts and resolute bravery. Things moved too fast. One minute the people were powerless and the situation seemed hopeless. The next moment everybody was in the streets. The Poles were the first to test the limits of Gorbachev's "socialism with a human face," following the traditions they had established through uprisings in 1980, 1970, 1956, and for that matter 1863. An unsung genius came up with the idea of "roundtable" discussions, a concept presumably borrowed from the legend of King Arthur's knights. Poland's pragmatic communists, led by General Wojciech Jaruzelski, and the idealistic intellectuals and trade unionists sat down together and forged a political compromise.

The communists gambled that their best shot at staying in power was to introduce partly free elections, hoping that they would be able to claim the credit for liberalizing the regime. Hungary's ruling Socialist Party followed a similar logic. Unlike Poland, Hungary had a land border with the capitalist West, and hence in May had the privilege of being the first country to dismantle the Iron Curtain. Poland's elections in

PETER RUTLAND *is a professor of government at Wesleyan University. An earlier version of this essay appeared in the Prague journal* Transitions *in January 1999.*

June saw all the free seats snapped up by candidates backed by the Solidarity trade-union movement. The communists were caught by surprise: perhaps they had not realized that in a democracy people can actually vote against their rulers.

Meanwhile, increasing numbers of East Germans were escaping through Hungary. Others, wanting to stay at home but under a different regime, boldly took to the streets. The numbers steadily grew at the protests staged every Monday evening (outside business hours, in respect of the work ethnic) in Leipzig, Dresden, and other cities, culminating in the crowds that breached the Berlin Wall on November 9.

Then it was the turn of the Czechs and Slovaks. A student demonstration was called for November 17 to mark, in the Eastern European tradition of historical resonance, the fiftieth anniversary of a student march repressed by the Nazis. The 1989 demonstration yielded a telling anecdote, which a student-participant related to me in 1991.

"Pavel" said that he was near the head of the march, arms locked with his friends, when the demonstrators were attacked by police. Militia came down the line systematically beating people—the boy to the right, the girl to the left. Much to his surprise, Pavel was left unscathed and was able to run off. A lucky break, or so he thought at the time. A year later he read the report of the parliamentary commission of inquiry into the police action, which revealed that young secret policemen had been planted among the students. To identify themselves they all wore identical black woolen caps—precisely the sort of cap that Pavel happened to be wearing that night. His lucky escape was clouded with widespread speculation—which continues to this day—about the role of secret police provocateurs in organizing the march and perhaps the downfall of the communist regime itself.

Such doubts hung heavier over the stage-managed revolutions of Romania and Albania. Still more so in the Soviet Union itself, where the regime imploded as a result of a failed coup at its apex. Only in a few corners of the Soviet Union could one talk of a large-scale popular movement for change—in the Baltics, the Caucasus, western Ukraine, and inside the Moscow beltway. In many of the 15 new states that emerged from the Soviet Union, the existing communist leaders stayed in power. They simply changed their titles ("president" instead of "first secretary") and traded in the rhetoric of socialism for the rhetoric of nation-building.

Nineteen eighty-nine was a curious, one-sided revolution. The people rose up against the state, but the state refused to fight back. At the time, no one knew that Gorbachev, Jaruzelski, and the rest would throw in the towel. Now, with the double-edged benefit of hindsight, we "know" that the socialist state was doomed. What at the time seemed inconceivable, in retrospect appears to have been inevitable. Nobody quite understands why it happened so quickly. A degree of ambiguity, rather than heroism, hangs over the events of 1989.

Western observers seemed to be taken by surprise ("shocked, shocked") to discover that capitalism could turn out to have a rotten core.

AFTER THE DELUGE

The unease about the true significance of the events of 1989 is only reinforced by developments since then. No one expected that so many former communist managers would quickly shed their socialist colors and embrace the capitalist path. The countries of the region have seen the rise of "crony capitalism" in which former members of the communist nomenklatura have converted their pre-1989 connections (what sociologists call "social capital") into capitalist business empires. As in all revolutions, ideas and assumptions were overturned and events developed in unexpected directions. Some communists turned out to be capitalists, and some capitalists turned out to be crooks.

Western observers seemed to be taken by surprise ("shocked, shocked") to discover that capitalism could turn out to have a rotten core. During the cold war there was only one type of capitalism (good) and one type of communism (bad), and a blind eye was turned to the crony capitalism found in South Korea, Indonesia, and elsewhere.

The ancien régime of the socialist states had run on ideology. Citizens and leaders alike were obliged to adhere to the official ideology, at least in public. What they thought (and did) in private was largely their own affair. The ruling ideology was the glue holding the communist system together—that, and the implicit threat of coercion. With the collapse of the Berlin Wall, this official ideology disintegrated instantly.

Paradoxically, the rapid demise of ideology, which was greeted with such joy at the time, turned out to be an obstacle to the construction of capitalism. After 40 years of communism people were so suspicious of political leaders, and of political life in general, that they refused to follow any movement, including the newly founded liberal and democratic parties. In most of Eastern Europe and the former Soviet Union, capitalism has actually been built by transitional teams of technocrats with no solid domestic political movement to back them up. More often than not, from Lithuania to Hungary, the job of introducing a market economy has been completed by none other than reformed communist parties. They managed to maintain more of a social base than the newly formed democratic parties, and were therefore able to win the second round of elections in a majority of countries of the region from 1994 onwards.

THE POVERTY OF POSTCOMMUNIST NATIONS

The construction of capitalism in the former socialist countries was not solely a domestic affair. The international community rallied to the cause. First off the plane in the wake of the 1989 revolutions were salesmen. With them came cheap consumer goods: chewing gum and chocolate, followed by alcohol and tobacco, and later the big-ticket items, from washing machines to autos. In almost every country, the first Western corporation to set up a local production facility was a tobacco company. Eastern Europe represented (along with China) tobacco's last frontier.

Western capitalists were cautious. They were keen to find new markets for their products, but less willing to invest in new manufacturing capacity in the region. The advantage of cheap labor was outweighed by political uncertainty, the legal vacuum, and poor transport links. Only Hungary, Poland, and the Czech Republic received substantial foreign direct investment.

International financial institutions were also active in the region. The International Monetary Fund and the World Bank leapt at the chance of a new mission to justify their continued existence. The IMF had been created to manage the foreign exchange controls introduced after World War II. That system was dismantled in the 1970s, but the IMF lived on. Similarly, the World Bank had been set up to channel development loans to the third world. Decades later, much of that world remained mired in poverty. Hence these agencies eagerly turned to the new task of turning decrepit planned economies into capitalist engines of growth and prosperity.

Unfortunately, the box of tools at their disposal, which had been developed to tackle inflation crises in Latin America and infrastructure projects in Africa and Asia, did not really fit the job at hand. Nonetheless, the IMF was able to devise a formula for the creation of a capitalist economy: liberalization (the removal of controls on domestic and international business activity); stabilization (a tough monetary policy, a balanced budget, and a convertible currency to control inflation); and privatization (the lifting of restrictions on private business and transfer of property from state to private ownership).

The IMF and World Bank remain convinced that this formula is a recipe for success. A number of countries that bit the bullet and introduced such measures ("shock therapy") experienced a couple of years of economic decline, but their economies started to grow earlier, and faster, than countries that tried to delay the necessary reforms: contrast the success of Poland with the sorry state of Romania or Ukraine. Indeed, there are virtually no examples of countries finding a successful alternative to the IMF recipe. China is an exception—and an important one—in that it has maintained many state controls over the economy, including a nonconvertible currency (which shielded it from the Asian financial meltdown). But none of the Eurasian economies have the attributes necessary to emulate the Chinese model, such as a vast internal market and underutilized peasantry.

Radical reform has proved to be a necessary but not a sufficient condition for economic success. Not all the countries that tried to introduce reform have succeeded in building a functioning capitalist economy. Plucky Moldova and Kyrgyzstan followed the recipes of the IMF cookbook to the letter, but their economies continue to sink. In economic reform, as in real estate, everything seems to hinge on location. The countries of Central Europe and the Baltic can easily sell their goods in the nearby markets of the European Union. For distant Ukraine, and still more for landlocked Central Asia, it will never be profitable to ship manufactured items to Europe. These countries can only hope to sell their raw materials and semiprocessed goods (iron and steel, gold, cotton, and oil).

Russia itself is extraordinarily disadvantaged by the legacy of the Soviet economy. For 75 years the country was developed through a central plan based on military-strategic considerations rather than market prices. Most Soviet-era factories are in the wrong place, and producing the wrong things, from the point of view of the market economy. There is nothing to do but close them down. But what will happen to the people who work there? What will happen to the 8 million Russians the Soviet planners, in their wisdom, sent to live in giant cities north of the Arctic Circle? And how can one introduce, in the space of a few years, the institutions of law and civic trust that have matured over centuries in the established capitalist economies, and that were systematically destroyed in the Soviet Union?

The reform formulas of the IMF will not provide an answer to these questions. The trouble is that the Russian government does not have a clue what to do either. After 1992 it tried, intermittently, to adopt the IMF approach, but that proved unworkable. The IMF attributes the failure of reform in the former Soviet Union to a lack of political will. Eventually, the fund says, the Russian elite will see the error of its ways and will introduce competitive capitalism. This may take several decades (as it did, for example, in Argentina). In the meantime, the Russian economy shows no sign of pulling out of its nosedive. And the economies of the other newly independent states (with the exception of the Baltics) are in even worse shape. Ukraine and Belarus lack Russia's wealth of natural resources, and those countries that do have oil and gas deposits (Azerbaijan, Kazakhstan, and Turkmenistan) are still almost totally dependent on the Russian pipeline network to export their products.

ETHNIC REVANCHISM

While political identities were quick to change in the former socialist bloc, national self-images were more enduring. For the peoples of Eastern Europe, the most important single achievement of 1989 was, after all, liberation from Soviet occupation and the restoration of national sovereignty. In terms of ethnic identity, in 1989 the region saw a reversion to the past rather than the birth of a new order. It is true that many people, especially in Central Europe, eagerly embraced the prospect of a new, pan-European identity. But at the same time it is striking that all three of the multinational federal states in the region—Czechoslovakia, Yugoslavia, and the Soviet Union—disintegrated along national lines. In Prague, already by 1990 some cars were optimistically displaying "EU" bumper stickers alongside the "CS." Soon they were joined by tongue-in-cheek stickers advertising Prague city districts ("Zizkov," "Krc"), a small sign that global and local identities can grow in parallel, and are not necessarily mutually exclusive.

In the former Yugoslavia, Tajikistan, and much of the Caucasus region, ethnic antagonism drove society over the edge into violent civil war. Liberals tell us that these conflicts cannot, must not, be attributed to "ancient hatreds." They note that the various ethnic groups in those countries had lived in peace for decades, and that intermarriage rates were often high. It is also true that ethnic conflicts were often triggered and manipulated by unscrupulous political leaders. But the fault lines along which these societies fractured were ethnic identities that predate the communist era. Revolutions invariably involve to some extent the completion of a circle, a return to the past. For many in Eastern Europe, it has been a return to ethnicity.

The international community has been understandably reluctant to confront this reality. It is striking that since the wave of recognitions that followed the collapse of the three socialist federations into their component parts in 1991 and 1992, not a single new state has been internationally recognized. After winning a two-year war during which more than 40,000 people were killed, Chechnya is still not recognized as an independent state by the international community, which pretends that it is part of the Russian Federation (even though no Russian official dares set foot on Chechen territory). Similarly, the Armenian enclave of Nagorno-Karabakh has been detached from Azerbaijan and is a de facto part of Armenia, but no diplomat will say as much. The refusal to confront the right of nations to self-determination also clouds the ongoing peace efforts in the Serbian province of Kosovo. The most that the international powers are willing to grant the Kosovo Albanians is autonomy, and no talk of independence for at least three years.

Alongside Chechnya, Karabakh, and Kosovo are a number of other rump statelets no government can control—Transdniester in Moldova, Abkhazia and South Ossetia in Georgia, and large tracts of Tajikistan. These territories exemplify what some scholars call "neo-medievalism," since they provide a base for international criminal groups dealing in drugs, guns, and other nefarious activities.

THE COST OF FREEDOM

History will no doubt record that the twentieth century, which began with the cataclysm of 1914, ended with the collapse of European communism in 1989. The shock waves of 1989 spread far beyond the countries of the socialist bloc. The end of the cold war brought an end to the old international balance of power system, thereby triggering a wave of armed conflicts from Yugoslavia to Zaire and Ethiopia. It also, less obviously, undermined the cohesion of political regimes from South Africa to Italy. The collapse of the Soviet regime was taken by the rulers of apartheid as a signal that the days of their own oppressive system of rule were numbered; in Italy, the Soviet collapse made the Communist Party eligible to join a coalition government and before long the corruption that had flourished among Italy's postwar rulers was exposed.

Freedom has a price, and it seems to be measured in dollars and cents.

Francis Fukuyama drew considerable attention—and some ridicule—for his 1989 essay predicting "The End of 'History' "; rereading Fukuyama's essay 10 years later one is impressed by the perspicacity of his vision. Fukuyama was writing early in 1989, months before the collapse of the Berlin Wall and two years before the breakup of the Soviet Union. He was one of the first—and one of the few—to accurately predict the political, economic, and moral bankruptcy of the socialist system. Moreover, the central argument of his essay has often been misunderstood, in part because of ambiguities in his original article. Fukuyama was predicting the end of "History" in a Hegelian sense: History as a process with an inner meaning, with a beginning, a middle and an end. It is this sort of History (with a capital H) that ended with the death of the socialist project. Daily life, with all its attendant problems and disappointments, would continue after the end of History. Liberal democracy, with its ambivalence over final ends, and with its agreement to disagree over practical solutions, would be the only game in town.

In this Fukuyama has surely been proved more right than wrong. Since 1991 there has been no resurgence of communism, nor the appearance of any ideology or philosophy that comes close to mounting a universal challenge to liberalism. (Fundamentalist religious movements in Islamic and Hindu societies are important phenomena, but do not have much of a constituency in Europe.) The people of Eastern and Central Europe may be forgiven for thinking that History has passed them by. Ten years on, most countries of the region are living under liberal democracy and a market economy. And yet something is missing; there is a pervasive sense of hopes unfulfilled and sacrifices betrayed.

A general feeling of anxiety and disappointment can be found among those countries and social groups that are moving ahead, and an air of resignation and despair among those that have fallen behind. Capitalism has brought inequality and it has brought uncertainty. It is not that socialist societies were completely egalitarian; but at least the communist elite were obliged to hide their privileges. And the rigid bureaucratism of state socialism brought a high degree of predictability and security to people's lives with respect to education, career, and livelihood (at least until the region's economies started to falter in the 1980s, led by Poland and Romania).

Despite the new economic uncertainties, 1989 stands tall as a victory for the individual over the state, a reaffirmation of people's rights to live their own lives as they wish, for good or ill.

Yet what sort of individual is important in the modern world? The individual as citizen? As voter? As religious believer? As worker? Over the past century, any one of these roles might have been an answer to this question. But in Europe since 1989 there can be only one answer: the individual as consumer.

Late-twentieth-century capitalism is above all consumer capitalism. Workers (that is, people who actually make things) make up a small and diminishing share of the population of developed economies, 20 percent at best. Farmers, the relic of long-dead economies, make up another 10 percent. The rest of us belong to the amorphous "service sector." At the low end that means physically bringing products to consumers; at the high end, those former American Labor Secretary Robert Reich calls the "symbolic manipulators" explain to consumers what the products mean, and why we need them.

Western Europe has had 40 years to get used to this sort of economy (the United States even longer); but the Eastern Europeans found it brought to their living rooms, courtesy of television, within months of the revolution. The rapid and pervasive spread of television culture in postcommunist Europe, from salad-shooter ads to inane homegrown game shows, has been truly breathtaking. It would be a mistake to imagine that this consumer world was foisted on a reluctant and resistant Eastern Europe by the evil machinations of global corporations. This was a willing embrace. The East German demonstrators back in 1989 got it right when they used the humble banana as one of their revolutionary symbols. (Bananas, it seems, grow in reactionary capitalist climates, and they were one of the consumer goodies that the Honecker regime was hard-pressed to supply to its population.)

There is a snake, however, in this televisual consumer Eden. It turns out that the new postsocialist world is divided into the rich and poor, the haves and have-nots, both within and between countries. The emissaries of the free market that flooded Eastern Europe after 1989 did not mention the uncomfortable fact that one-third of the population of the world's market economies gets by on less than $2 a day. Even after 40 years of intense international efforts, Western development economics is still unable to deliver on liberty and prosperity for all.

Whole nations seem condemned to marginalization and exclusion from the global economy. This is true also for the former socialist bloc. Some countries are clearly going to make it into the club of the fortunate, others are not. This apparently has a lot to do with simple geography, and relatively little to do with the policies a country's leadership adopts. Slovenia has been slow to privatize, but because of the accidents of history and location it enjoys the highest living standard in the region (about $8,000 per capita per year) and is on the fast track for entry into the European Union. To be sure, the Slovenians are hard-working and diligent people; but is that not also true of Ukrainians, Uzbeks, and all the others?

Nineteen eighty-nine was not only about consumption. It was also about freedom: freedom of speech and thought, freedom of worship, freedom from arbitrary treatment by the state, freedom to live one's life as one chooses. But freedom is a curious thing. Like physical health, its value is only really appreciated when it is absent. Now that they have it, the Eastern Europeans hardly notice it. They are literally free to worry about other things, such as finding a better job, or looking out for their children's future.

Of all the freedoms Central and Eastern Europeans won in 1989, freedom of religion and freedom of movement may be the most valued. The latter is also probably the freedom most overlooked by Westerners, since it is hard to imagine, or believe, the extent to which most of the socialist countries used to control the international movement of their peoples. The right to travel where one wants, when one wants, is soon taken for granted. The peoples of Eastern Europe step faster on the treadmill of work, so as to earn more money to travel further, for longer: the $50 overnight coach trip to Paris of 1992 has now given way to a $300 fortnight vacation in a Turkish beach resort. So even the main achievement of the 1989 revolution, personal freedom, itself turns back into the realm of consumption. Freedom has a price, and it seems to be measured in dollars and cents.

Unlearning the Lessons of Kosovo

by Ivo H. Daalder and Michael O'Hanlon

First, the mea culpas. Like many of the analysts looking at the war in Kosovo, we were (fortunately) wrong in several of our predictions. The air campaign succeeded. NATO achieved its objectives without launching a ground invasion or changing its demands. All Serbian forces have left Kosovo, some 50,000 NATO troops have entered in their wake, and more than 1 million refugees and displaced persons have returned home. This success is a testament to NATO's remarkable unity and perseverance, to the lethality of its military power, and to the prowess of American, European, and Russian diplomats.

What are the lessons and the legacy of Operation Allied Force? President Bill Clinton emerged from the war confident that Kosovo set a new precedent—a "Clinton Doctrine"—for humanitarian intervention: "I think there's an important principle here that I hope will be now upheld in the future.... And that is that while there may well be a great deal of ethnic and religious conflict in the world— some of it might break out into wars—that whether within or beyond the borders of a country, if the world community has the power to stop it, we ought to stop genocide and ethnic cleansing."

Yet the failure of many (including not just ourselves, but the Clinton administration and other NATO governments) to predict the course

IVO H. DAALDER AND MICHAEL E. O'HANLON *are senior fellows at the Brookings Institution and authors of* Kosovo: Anatomy of a Crisis *(Washington: Brookings Institution Press, forthcoming).*

of the war should give appropriate pause to those now quick to draw lessons from NATO's success. As Clinton's own secretary of state, Madeleine Albright, warned just a few days after the president's pronouncements: "Some hope, and others fear, that Kosovo will be a precedent for similar interventions around the globe. I would caution against any such sweeping conclusions. Every circumstance is unique. Decisions on the use of force will be made by any president on a case-by-case basis after weighing a host of factors." A month later, National Security Advisor Sandy Berger added another hurdle to humanitarian intervention, suggesting that in cases of genocide the United States needed to weigh its national interest in a country before deciding to employ military power.

The Clinton administration's internal confusion about the meaning of NATO's Kosovo war is hardly surprising. On closer inspection, the verities that emerge from wars often need revision. Immediately after the Gulf War, for example, many analysts believed that the Patriot system had offered a robust defense against incoming missiles, the hunt for Iraqi president Saddam Hussein's Scud missiles had been successful, the allied ground campaign had been little more than a mopping-up operation after the overwhelming success of the air war, and Saddam's days were numbered. Each of these assumptions turned out to be wrong.

THE "LESSONS" OF KOSOVO

The results of the current rush to judgment on the lessons of Kosovo may fare no better.

In that spirit, and mindful of our past mistakes, we offer a skeptical assessment of five of the most popular post-Kosovo truths: that NATO won; that airpower alone was responsible; that the Powell Doctrine of decisive force is dead; that the United Nation's role in such conflicts is marginal at best; and that Europe cannot pull its military weight. Seekers of a new doctrine of humanitarian intervention will be disappointed: The overall verdict on Kosovo is less likely to offer new lessons than to affirm old truths.

1. NATO Won

The conflict in Kosovo was two wars in one. NATO lost the first, but decisively won the second. The war it lost pitted more than 40,000 Serbian military, police, and paramilitary forces armed with more than 1,500 tanks and heavy weapons against a few thousand lightly armed Kosovo Liberation Army (KLA) fighters. Drawing on the words of Chairman Mao and draining the water in which the fish swim, Belgrade forcefully expelled the ethnic Albanian populations from Kosovo's villages, towns, and cities. Within weeks, Serbian forces were successful—if not in completely defeating the KLA, then certainly in removing 1.3 million people from their homes and thus radically altering the demographic make-up of Kosovo.

Had NATO not bombed, Yugoslav president Slobodan Milosevic still would have moved

against the Albanian population (as he had the previous year), but the Serbians might not have accelerated the killing or expanded their deadly reach to so many communities for fear of provoking NATO intervention. In that ironic sense, NATO's decision to launch the air campaign while ruling out the use of ground forces lifted a key constraint on Milosevic. As a result, the allies utterly failed to achieve two of the three objectives Clinton listed the day the bombing started: "to deter an even bloodier offensive against innocent civilians in Kosovo and, if necessary, to seriously damage the Serbian military's capacity to harm the people of Kosovo."

The other war was fought to achieve Clinton's third objective: "to demonstrate the seriousness of NATO's purpose so that the Serbian leaders understand the imperative of

reversing course." The alliance won this war without question, securing an outcome that improves markedly on the deal Milosevic rejected during the negotiations that took place in February of this year in Rambouillet, France. No Serbian forces remain in Kosovo. A larger and more capable NATO force has been deployed, with robust rules of engagement. Backed by NATO, the UN transitional administration is establishing control of the entire area. As a result, life in the province is much better for Kosovar Albanians than it was prior to the use of force. Compared with the situation in Kosovo before, these are major achievements that in our judgment outweigh the tragedies that befell the ethnic Albanians over the 78 days of air war.

But if the outcome of the war against Serbia was positive, what accounts for its success? Was NATO's reliance on airpower decisive? Was it wise? These questions are important, not only for understanding this particular war, but for discerning its lessons for the future.

2. Airpower Alone Worked

Considering both its effectiveness and relatively low cost, NATO's air campaign was probably the most successful use of strategic bombardment in the history of warfare. NATO airpower proved capable of eliminating virtually all of Serbia's oil-refining capacity, reducing its military oil stockpiles by half, seriously disrupting its transportation arteries (although 50 percent of all roads into Kosovo survived), and turning out the lights in most of Belgrade. Airpower also proved successful against the mainstays of Yugoslavia's military machine—its modern weaponry, logistical infrastructure, and military-industrial base. Immediately after the war, the Pentagon announced that half of Serbia's armor in Kosovo had been destroyed. That estimate now appears too high. But even if the allies actually destroyed only one-quarter of Serbia's Kosovo-based heavy equipment, it would have been enough to send Milosevic a clear signal that things could get even worse.

However, the case for airpower can easily be pushed too far and often is these days. NATO could not have achieved its success against Serbian armor from the air without the support of the KLA. In late May, a revitalized KLA launched ground offensives that forced Serbian units to concentrate and expose their armor and troops, making them acutely vulnerable to NATO airpower for the first time during the war. As a result, according to the Pentagon's June estimates, 40 percent of Serbian armor losses were suffered in the last week of NATO's 11-week war and fully 80 percent in the last two-and-a-half weeks. (Although the absolute numbers are likely to be lower, these ratios may hold up even when final reports on the air war are released.) The fact that fewer than 20,000 KLA troops were enough to act as NATO's ground force against 40,000 Serbians is an impressive testament to NATO airpower. But airpower alone could not have won the war.

In addition, it is now clear that the growing drumbeat for ground forces convinced Milosevic that, even if he withstood the intensified air campaign, there was no way out of the conflict short of accepting NATO's conditions to end its military action. A series of calculated actions and statements in the second half of May 1999 were designed to move the United States and NATO away from Clinton's initial statement that he had "no intention" of using ground forces in combat. On May 18, Clinton pointedly said that "we have not and will not take any option off the table." Three days later, NATO announced it would deploy 50,000 troops on the Kosovo border in order to ensure rapid implementation of any agreement that might be reached and—in General Wesley Clark's eyes at least—to present an implicit threat of invasion as well, a point Clark wisely made public. On May 27, Secretary of Defense William Cohen secretly flew to Europe to meet with his key counterparts to discuss ground force options, a trip that was promptly leaked to the *New York Times.*

Milosevic was well aware of the pending decision to use ground forces. Not only was speculation rife within the Western press, but Russian

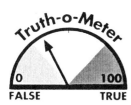

peace envoy Viktor Chernomyrdin apparently told Milosevic in late May that NATO would use ground forces if the air campaign failed and that Russia would not stand in NATO's way. Milosevic's one way out, the Russian suggested, was to settle now before a ground war raised the stakes. On June 3, the day that Clinton was to meet with his Joint Chiefs of Staff (JCS) to discuss various ground force options, Milosevic did just that.

Airpower has punitive uses, and perhaps even coercive utility, if the pain inflicted is high enough. But in Kosovo, it could neither prevent the murder and forced expulsions that served as NATO's justification for intervening nor win the conflict on its own.

Moreover, in many of the worst civil and ethnic wars around the world there are few strategic and armored targets ripe for air attack. Coercive bombing is also unlikely to be of much use, since atrocities are often committed by militias or rebel forces that do not have clear dependencies or vulnerabilities that can be targeted by airpower. Consider Africa, the site of three-fourths of the world's worst civil wars in the 1990s—the most lethal taking place in Angola, Burundi, Liberia, Somalia, Sudan, and of course, Rwanda. (In Europe, only the Bosnian war made the top ten list of the decade's most deadly conflicts, and it was less lethal than any of the African conflicts mentioned above, with the possible exception of Liberia's.) A B-2 bomber simply is not a very effective instrument to stop genocide committed largely with machetes or even machine guns. That task calls for ground troops—and usually more rather than less. And once troops are deployed, the aim must be to achieve the objective decisively in order to minimize risks to U.S. and allied forces. To do so requires decisive force, rather than gradual escalation.

3. The Powell Doctrine Is Dead

NATO's success in using limited means to achieve decisive ends has led senior officials in the Clinton administration to welcome the demise of the so-called Powell Doctrine: the notion that the United States should use military force only after exhausting all other alternatives and then only decisively to achieve clearly defined political objectives. NATO's strategy, one White House official noted, was the "anti-Powell Doctrine." Its success, said another, meant that "you won't see Colin Powell on TV today talking about the Powell Doctrine."

The Powell Doctrine is often mentioned in the same breath as the Weinberger Doctrine. However, even though General Colin Powell had a hand in drafting both, they are not the same. Caspar Weinberger, secretary of defense under President Ronald Reagan, insisted that force should be used solely in defense of vital U.S. interests. Powell was less concerned

Defense Visual Information Center

Is the Powell Doctrine on hold?

wisdom has had it that Americans have a low tolerance for casualties. But Americans are much more willing to use force than the zero-casualty shibboleth suggests. After the Mogadishu tragedy, for example, as many Americans were inclined to retaliate and prevail as wanted to withdraw. The U.S. public also supported the Bush administration's 1989 intervention to shore up democracy in Panama even though it cost more than 20 American lives. Americans rightly insist that if they are to intervene to save lives, the costs should be contained, victory should be assured, and the burden of intervention should be shared with others when possible. Under these conditions, casualties, though always tragic, are both expected and accepted.

In addition, many who favor the use of force to support diplomacy reject General Powell's supposed dictum for using overwhelming force, believing that there must be a place for its more limited employment. However, even in Kosovo, NATO did not prevail until it tripled its air armada, bombed for many more weeks than originally planned, and talked convincingly about deploying ground forces. In other words, it succeeded as its military strategy became increasingly muscular and decisive—or to put it differently, increasingly Powell-like. Perhaps not a textbook case of what the former JCS chairman and national security advisor would have recommended, but not its antithesis either.

4. The UN Is Nice, But Not Necessary

NATO went to war in March 1999 by attacking a sovereign country. It did not do so to uphold the inherent right of individual or collective self-defense or with explicit authorization from the UN Security Council. Neither did it justify its action under the 1948 Genocide Convention.

However, these facts do not mean that the alliance's action was illegitimate. The Security Council had identified the crisis in Kosovo as a threat to international peace and security in 1998. NATO did not request the council's

with limiting the objectives than with defining them clearly and using force decisively to achieve them. He vigorously defended the Bush administration's uses of force to remove Manuel Noriega from power in Panama and to protect democracy against coup attempts in the Philippines. He also supported humanitarian relief missions in Bangladesh, Bosnia, Iraq, Russia, and Somalia, as well as the Clinton administration's later intervention in Haiti.

What Powell rejected was the idea of using force without clearly defined and achievable objectives or ample means for accomplishing them. "Decisive means and results are always to be preferred, even if they are not always possible. So you bet I get nervous when so-called experts suggest that all we need is a little surgical bombing or a limited attack. When the desired result isn't obtained, a new set of experts then comes forward with talk of a little escalation. History has not been kind to this approach." In other words, Powell objected to coercive uses of force in which the achievement of the objective depends on the adversary crying uncle.

Opposition to the Powell Doctrine has come from those who believe that decisive force tends to be costly, especially in terms of casualties. Since the October 1993 debacle in Mogadishu, Somalia, when 18 U.S. Army Rangers died in a single battle, conventional

authorization to use force in 1999 because Russia (quietly supported by China) indicated that it would veto any such resolution. Yet Moscow and Beijing also failed to offer any promising alternative strategies for stopping the carnage. That left the NATO countries with a choice between not acting in response to the humanitarian emergency or acting without the Security Council's explicit backing. After much debate, the allies chose the latter option, justifying their decision with reference to the urgency of the situation.

Did NATO's action set a precedent—that a UN imprimatur on intervention for humanitarian ends is nice, but not necessary? Perhaps. But Kosovo ultimately says more about the UN's continued strength than its weakness. The United Nations proved to be a central character in the intricate diplomatic minuet danced by the Americans, the Europeans, and the Russians in the weeks leading up to Belgrade's surrender. It was the prospect of agreement on a UN Security Council resolution reflecting NATO's demands that finally convinced Milosevic he stood all alone. Once Belgrade gave in, the United Nations was given political control of Kosovo and charged with managing the mammoth task of building a stable, peaceful, and hopefully democratic Kosovo. Its responsibility in Kosovo is akin to a 1920s League of Nations mandate for a protectorate and exceeds anything the organization has done before.

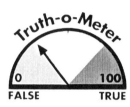

Not only does the United Nations dominate Kosovo's present, it also will have the decisive role in determining the territory's political future. The UN's administration of Kosovo is open-ended and can only be terminated by a vote of the Security Council, requiring that all five permanent members agree on what will replace it. That in turn means that both Beijing and Moscow have a veto over any Kosovar Albanian aspirations to independence, any schemes for partitioning Kosovo, or any attempts to link Kosovo's fate to a future Balkans conference that might also redefine Bosnia's status.

If the United Nations has emerged strengthened from the war, it has done so only in a limited way. It may legitimize action by states, but it cannot conduct military operations itself. As the war over Kosovo once again tragically demonstrated, humanitarian interventions are harder than they look, and initial estimates of their military requirements are often understated. The UN is not equipped to handle these types of operations; indeed, Kosovo shows that it is not even well prepared to handle the postconflict civilian side of interventions. Actual military interventions are best left to regional organizations, such as NATO, or to coalitions of the willing that, for now at least, will generally have to have the United States at their core.

5. In Military Terms, Europe Is a Dwarf to America's Giant

The mediocre job that most U.S. allies have done to reconfigure their militaries showed in Kosovo. The war was run and largely conducted by Americans. Two-thirds of the strike missions were flown by U.S. aircraft. Virtually all the targets were identified using U.S. intelligence assets and nearly every precision-guided weapon was launched from an American aircraft. Had the war turned out to be more expensive in blood and treasure, the repercussions would have been significant. A vigorous debate on burden sharing would have ensued, potentially triggering American resentment of its relatively free-riding allies.

That said, many of the charges made against the NATO allies are unfair. Consider the matter of NATO's war strategy against Serbia. Some blame NATO for micromanaging General Clark's war plans and hampering his ability to hit Milosevic hard in the first days of the war. But the strategy of gradual escalation and the decision to publicly rule out the deployment of ground forces were both devised in Washington. Reflecting a conviction on the part of President Clinton, Secretary of State Albright, and others that Milosevic was bound to cave quickly, NATO planners were instructed to generate only three days' worth of targets for the air campaign. Fear of casualties also drove the strategy toward minimalism—whether by limiting early air strikes to attacks unlikely to cause civilian casualties, or by mandating that U.S. aircraft fly above 15,000 feet to reduce the risk to American pilots.

All in all, the Kosovo war was a peculiarly American show. But thankfully, and promisingly, it made many European allies distinctly uncomfortable. As German foreign minister Joschka Fischer reflected after the war, "The Kosovo war was mainly an experience of Europe's own insufficiency and weakness; we as Europeans never could have coped with the Balkan wars that were caused by Milosevic without the help of the United States. The sad truth is that Kosovo showed Europe is still not able to solve its own problems." In military terms, Kosovo underscored that Europe is a dwarf to America's giant. This imbalance is not just for lack of spending—the European NATO countries spend about two-thirds as much as the United States on defense—as for how such spending is allocated. With the exception of Great Britain and, to some extent France, Europeans still emphasize conscription-based armies for territorial defense, rather than modest numbers of deployable high-tech professional forces for use beyond the alliance's borders.

Europe's realization of its large—and growing—military inferiority has had two salutary effects. First, America may have run the war, but Europe is running the peace. The EU envoy, Finnish president Martti Ahtisaari, played a crucial role in devising the diplomatic strategy and in delivering the word to Milosevic that his time had run out. At 85 percent of the troop total, moreover, the European contribution to KFOR, the NATO-led force in Kosovo, is larger and (and will be far more costly) than the U.S. contribution to the air war. The European Union has also taken the lead in devising a strategy for Kosovo's reconstruction and the region's stabilization and is responsible for the vast bulk of the financial resources necessary to bring about both. As a result, Europeans head both the military and civilian implementation efforts in Kosovo.

Second, the Kosovo crisis and war has produced a sea change in European attitudes on things military. Most noteworthy is Germany's continuing emergence as a normal military power. If prior to Dayton, Germany's military contribution to missions in the Balkans was virtually nil and after Dayton it was tentative at best, in the Kosovo war German combat aircraft participated fully. Berlin's KFOR contribution of at least 5,500 troops is comparable to that of the United States; only Great Britain's contribution is significantly larger.

Equally significant has been the change in attitude toward European defense in London. Concerned that Europe had been forced to defer to an American military and diplomatic strategy he found wanting, British prime minister Tony Blair became convinced that Europe's diplomatic weakness was linked to its relatively feeble military capability. Ever since, Blair has lobbied his European partners to increase their combined military capacity. In the process, he has been willing to abandon long-standing British opposition to increasing Europe's voice on defense matters, for fear that this would undermine the transatlantic partnership.

The growing consensus on the need for a European defense capability is a direct consequence of the Kosovo crisis. To date, it has been translated into a commitment to give Europe a voice in foreign and security policy, in the person of Javier Solana, who leaves his job as secretary general of NATO to become responsible for Europe's Common Foreign and Security Policy.

The difficulty, as always, will be to translate this consensus into concrete action. Still needed are tangible steps—including enhanced mobility for a larger number of forces, better sustainability of forces operating at large distances, and greater intelligence gathering and strategic transport capabilities—necessary to provide European countries individually, and as a whole, with the military capacity to act on their newfound common policies. Great Britain has already done much of what is required, and France is committed to follow suit. The key to success lies in Berlin—and to a lesser, but important, extent in Rome as well.

Europe's challenge is real. If after their demonstrated military weakness in Kosovo, the Europeans fail to get their house in order and adopt a coherent plan for military modernization, the consequences for the alliance will be serious. With U.S. armed forces working hard from the Korean Peninsula to the Taiwan Straits to the Persian Gulf to the Balkans, Americans may soon get fed up doing much more than their fair share in relatively thankless work. What much of the rest of the world sees as hegemony, many Americans see as a burden—and an increasingly unsatisfying one at that. If Europe lacks the capacity to do its part in responding militarily to the next Kosovo, the alternative could easily be no intervention at all rather than one led by the United States.

WHICH CLINTON DOCTRINE?

So what does all of this mean for the future? President Clinton's conviction that the United

States and other members of the world community have an obligation to stop genocide and other mass-casualty wars wherever they might occur is admirable. However, this rhetorical commitment does not match Clinton's own record in dealing with these types of conflicts. Ever since the Somalia debacle of 1993, the United States has intervened decisively only when humanitarian crises occurred near U.S. territory or in Europe, only when extremely few U.S. casualties were expected, and only when the president's own rhetoric had essentially forced the administration to do something. Kosovo, like Haiti and Bosnia before it, reaffirms the central validity of these tenets and suggests that the president's rhetoric outpaces likely action in the future.

Far from heralding a new age of humanitarian interventionism, the war in Kosovo highlights the difficulty of pursuing such a course. The single most important lesson of the conflict is that there is no cheap, easy way to prevent genocide or mass killing. Airpower alone will not generally determine what transpires on the ground. Only when paired with ground forces—and only if used decisively—can airpower be expected to work. That, of course, raises the cost of using force, making it more important that operations enjoy international legitimacy and that allies and others bear their full share of the burden. But even if the European allies undertake major initiatives to improve their military capacity, they will not be able to take over the lead responsibility for humanitarian intervention from the United States anytime soon. In most cases, politics aside, they will simply not have the requisite physical tools—and neither will the United Nations.

Nonetheless, if the United States is clear about the costs of intervention and if its allies are willing and able to team up, it can use force in a timely and effective way in the future. A sure sign of success will be when, in the next war, Washington can prepare to use ground forces before intervening rather than a month or two into the conflict. Had the United States been politically willing and militarily able to do so, what was an imperfect win might well have been an unblemished victory—quite possibly a victory in which the allies would not have needed to see Kosovo destroyed in order to save it.

WANT TO KNOW MORE?

The post–Cold War era has seen a resurgence of interest in humanitarian interventions in ethnic and other internal conflicts. Notable literature on the subject includes Michael Brown's *Ethnic Conflict and International Security* (Princeton: Princeton University Press, 1993) and *The International Dimensions of Internal Conflict* (Cambridge: Massachusetts Institute of Technology Press, 1996), as well as Richard Haass' *Intervention: The Uses of Military Force in the Post–Cold War World,* second edition (Washington: Brookings Institution Press, 1999). For a skeptical view of the rise of ethnic conflicts in the post–Cold War world, see Yahya Sadowski's **"Think Again: Ethnic Conflict"** (FOREIGN POLICY, Summer 1998). As yet, there has been little in-depth analysis on the causes and conduct of the Kosovo war. Until these are completed (including a Brookings Institution study by Ivo Daalder and Michael O'Hanlon, *Kosovo: Anatomy of a Crisis,* to be published in early 2000), consult Michael Ignatieff's **"The Virtual Commander"** (*New Yorker,* August 2, 1999) and Anthony Cordesman's *The Lessons and Non-Lessons of the Air and Missile War in Kosovo* (Washington: Center for Strategic and International Studies, July 1999), which is available on the center's Web site. On the utility of airpower in war, see especially Robert Pape's *Bombing to Win: Air Power and Coercion in War* (Ithaca: Cornell University Press, 1996) and Thomas Keaney and Eliot Cohen's *Gulf War Air Power Survey Summary Report* (Washington: Government Printing Office, 1993). The Powell Doctrine is elaborated most fully in Colin Powell's **"U.S. Forces: Challenges Ahead"** (*Foreign Affairs,* Winter 1992/93). On the United Nations and its role in peace operations, consult William Durch, ed., *UN Peacekeeping, American Policy, and the Uncivil Wars of the 1990s* (New York: St. Martin's Press, 1996). Europe's evolving military capacity is examined in John Peters and Howard Deshong's *Out of Area or Out of Reach?: European Military Support for Operations in Southwest Asia* (Santa Monica: RAND Corporation, 1995) and Michael O'Hanlon's **"Transforming NATO: The Role of European Forces"** (*Survival,* Autumn 1997).

For links to relevant Web sites, as well as a comprehensive index of related FOREIGN POLICY articles, access **www.foreignpolicy.com.**

Unit 7

Unit Selections

27. **Life with Boris: Rousing, *Infuriating*, Always Surprising—Yeltsin the Singular,** *Andrew Higgins and Steve Liesman*
28. **Still Soul Searching,** Konstantin Eggert
29. **The Baltics: Between Russia and the West,** James Kurth
30. **Chaos in the Caucasus,** *The Economist*

Key Points to Consider

❖ What factors do you believe will be the most important in determining the future direction of Russian foreign policy?

❖ Should the European Union and the United States support the integration of Estonia, Latvia, and Lithuania into the West despite Russian views of this region as a buffer zone of the Russian Republic? Why or why not?

❖ Explain why you do or do not agree that conflicts in the Caucasus and Central Asian region indicate that a more political brand of Islam, rather than Islamic militancy, is now a major factor in understanding politics in this region.

 **Links**   # www.dushkin.com/online/

23. **Russia Today**
    http://www.russiatoday.com

24. **Russian and East European Network Information Center, University of Texas at Austin**
    http://reenic.utexas.edu/reenic.html

These sites are annotated on pages 6 and 7.

160

The former USSR is a region composed of 15 independent nation-states, with each state trying to define separate national interests as it experiences extreme economic problems. Today many ex-Soviet citizens share a sense of disorientation and "pocketbook" shock as their standard of living is lower today than it was under communism. About half of these states are experiencing political instability and growing discontent. Ukraine was the only state to peacefully transfer power from one elected president to another during the early post–USSR era, but its economy remains highly interdependent with the Russian economy. Consequently, it and most other former Soviet states suffered with the devaluation of the ruble.

Uncertainty is the principal characteristic of the current Russian political system. The Russian government was disintegrating after having failed in attempts to impose austerity measures and collect taxes when the IMF approved a $22.6 billion IMF-led rescue loan for Moscow in July, 1998. Shortly afterwards the Russian government devalued the ruble, defaulted on domestic bonds, and placed a moratorium on paying overseas creditors. The actions triggered the worst economic crisis in Russia since the collapse of communism and increased fears worldwide that the IMF was powerless to prevent "contagion" effects from spreading worldwide.

Most observers hailed Russia's parliamentary election at the end of 1999 as a step toward democracy. These optimistic assessments were made despite the fact that these elections were characterized by widespread mudslinging, dirty tricks at the polls, and corruption. While the Communist Party remains a powerful force in the State Duma, the lower house of parliament, two pro-government parties won surprisingly large percentages of the vote. The widespread support for these recently formed parties that lack political platforms was interpreted as a strong nationalistic desire to support the current government's military offensive in the breakaway province of Chechnya. The vote was also viewed as an endorsement of Prime Minister Vladimir Putin, the sixth prime minister to be appointed to Yeltsin's government during the past 2 years. At the same time the International Monetary Fund (IMF) delayed releasing an installment loan to Moscow. This action was at least in part a reaction to the military offensive directed at civilian areas used by the Russian military as they fought to retake the capital city of Grozny in Chechnya.

Boris Yeltsin, who abruptly stepped down as president in January 2000, named Prime Minister Vladimir Putin as his successor. One of Putin's first acts was to grant Yeltsin blanket amnesty from any future investigation of his family finances. Putin is now the favored candidate to win the 2000 presidential elections. His hard line and willingness to use military force in Chechen is widely popular and his future popularity is believed to hinge on how well he handles the military campaign in the rebellious region.

Putin, like other recent Russian prime ministers, is critical of Russia's reliance on foreign capital and Western advice. Few Russians benefitted from privatization or other free-market reforms. Instead, the country turned toward oligarchic capitalism, dominated by a few wealthy tycoons and giant conglomerates that enjoy special privileges and a cozy relationship with the state. This "tycoon model" is also found in regions outside Moscow where local governors and magnates mirror the Moscow tycoons. Thus, 10 years into reform

in Russia, many considered U.S.–backed economic reforms as being wealth confiscation rather than wealth creation measures.

The magnitude of the economic crisis is so great that the Russian state is shrinking. Nowhere is this more apparent than in the Russian military-security complex where a breakdown of cohesion and morale in the Russian military reflects a general loss of stability in Russian society. With the Russian military bordering on collapse, Russia shifted to a greater reliance on nuclear weapons and a "launch on warning" strategy. Many observers doubt the reliability of antiquated radar systems and deteriorating armed forces to protect the country from either domestic or foreign military threats. These doubts increase the pressure on the current Russian government to demonstrate that conventional Russian forces can crush the rebel offensive in Chechnya.

Konstantin Eggert notes in "Still Soul Searching" that it is not possible to know the domestic and international consequences of the current period of instability on Russia's future leaders or how Russia will define her national interests. The popularity of Russia's initial defiance of NATO's orders in deploying troops in Kosovo and concerns about the status of states bordering Russia suggest that nationalistics tendencies will be an important force guiding future Russian foreign policy. James Kurth explains in "The Baltics: Between Russia and the West" how most Russians view the Baltic states of Estonia, Latvia, and Lithuania as part of a natural western frontier. The potential for future conflicts exist as most Balkan citizens consider their countries to be a part of the West. The distinctive characteristics of these countries will require western states to use wise diplomatic skills in order to continue to support Baltic independence and security while also maintaining peaceful, cooperative relations with Russia.

Some analysts interpret recent fighting in the Caucasus as further evidence of a "clash of civilizations" between the Islamic world and other geopolitical blocks. In "Chaos in the Caucasus," writers for *The Economist* reject this view. Instead they view conflicts in the Caucasus and Central Asia as underscoring the fact that Islam exists in many different forms. They suggest that as Islamic militancy recedes in the Middle East, poltiical Islam is spreading to the periphery.

A thorough understanding of the cultural trends is important because the Central Asian states bordering the Caspian sea are poised to undergo dramatic changes as their oil and gas reserves, estimated to be worth between $2.5 and $3 trillion dollars, are developed. These untapped resources have stimulated a growing web of recent deals in Central Asia and increasingly make the area appear to be a new kind of post–cold war battleground pitting the interests of three former military rivals—China, Russia, and the United States—and a variety of multinational corporations against each other. Some analysts have compared the future consequences of this coming oil boom to the fate of OPEC whose members squandered their 1970s windfall. No one knows yet whether the Caspian states will be able to resist the temptation of petromania in their quest to go quickly from rags to riches. Optimists construct rosy scenarios in which the countries with the biggest resources use their mineral wealth to become the future economic hub of Central Asia. Cynics argue that a darker scenario of wasted resources, economic stagnation, and ethnic strife is an equally plausible one.

Life With Boris

Rousing, Infuriating, Always Surprising— Yeltsin the Singular

An Apparatchik With Vision Pushed Russia Around, But in the Right Direction

Grand Finale: Picking Putin

Andrew Higgins and Steve Liesman led The Wall Street team that was awarded a Pulitzer Prize last April for coverage of Russia. Between them, they have covered Russian continuously since 1991, throughout the Yeltsin era. Here, they discuss where Russia has been, where it is going— and Mr. Yeltsin's legacy.

It makes your neck hurt.

Boris Yeltsin gave up tennis years ago, but watching him rule Russia for the better part of a decade has left the world with a case of whiplash worthy of Wimbledon.

Swinging back and forth on political and economic reform, Mr. Yeltsin created a blur of late-night government sackings, capricious presidential decrees, impulsive policy reversals and siren-screeching cavalcades to and from the hospital.

The score sheet is staggering: seven prime ministers, six national elections, a quintuple heart-bypass operation, four loan agreements with the International Monetary Fund, three ruble crises, two vicious wars in Chechnya, and a stunning grand finale: a millennium-eve resignation.

What to focus on? It's a contrarian theory born partly of exasperation, but through the muddle stretches an unbroken, though often tangled, thread.

Russia is ultimately lurching toward democracy, capitalism and integration with the world. It will be a particularly Russian brand of all three that will never sit quite right with Western sensibilities. Progress will be slow, marked by sometimes frightening fits and starts. But on balance, the outcome should be far better than what Russians have had for most of the their thousand-year history.

The same holds for President Yeltsin's abrupt resignation Friday and his

appointment of Prime Minister Vladimir Putin as acting custodian of the Kremlin. It sets up an early presidential election in March, quashing speculation that Mr. Yeltsin would somehow stay on in the Kremlin despite a constitution requiring his departure no later than next summer. But it effectively pre-empts the ballot box by entrenching a single candidate.

His resignation also shifts power to a new generation born after World War II—Mr. Putin is 47 years old—but does so by vesting the future in the hands of a man nurtured by the KGB, the "sword and shield" of the Communist past. It's pure Yeltsin. Always reaching backward in an attempt to prod Russia forward.

It's another big gamble, probably positive on balance, but with plenty of reasons for skepticism and doubt. To arrive at that conclusion, it's necessary to ask two questions: What is the legacy that Mr. Yeltsin, 68, leaves for Mr. Putin? And what is known about Mr. Putin that tells us what he will do with that legacy?

Perhaps nothing defines Mr. Yeltsin's political life better than the manner of his leaving it. He wrong-footed Russia and the world on New Year's Eve without a whiff of what was coming, just as he defied the pundits and some of his own closest aides by putting his fate in the hands of voters in 1996 rather than calling off an election he initially seemed doomed to lose.

Anatoly Chubais, architect of Mr. Yeltsin's odds-defying re-election campaign three years ago, had this to say after the Friday announcement: "Once again, Boris Nikolayevich proved himself beyond all predictions including—in this case, my own."

Why did Mr. Yeltsin do it?

To exit on terms that he dictated. (He never did anything that could give the slightest impression that he was being pushed around.) To ensure his own survival by hand-picking a successor. To all but guarantee that Mr. Putin, a former KGB spy who has never held an elected office, would take over through a democratic election stacked in his favor. (It always seemed that Mr. Yeltsin wanted to be a democrat, if only to secure his place in history. But the legacy of his own past as a Communist Party baron in the Siberian city of Sverdlovsk kept him from trusting any election fought and won on an entirely even playing field.)

And perhaps, finally, to prove that he wasn't the same as the enfeebled, entrenched party bosses he derided in a 1994 autobiography: "Leaders have never voluntarily parted with power in Russia. . . . Once you have scrambled to the top, the altitude is so dizzying you cannot step down."

Mr. Yeltsin's motives are clear. The legacy they yield is less so. Consider the Russian economy. Mr. Yeltsin took a wrecking ball to Communist central planning. He created corporations out of Soviet-era factories. He privatized hundreds of thousands of businesses. But he allowed a coterie of cronies to enjoy the lion's share of the Soviet spoils.

Mr. Putin's most zealous fans are the beneficiaries of this system. This winter, Valentin Yumashev—a close confidant of Mr. Yeltsin and his daughter Tatyana Dyachenko—traveled to New York and Washington to sell Mr. Putin to U.S. policy makers and media poohbahs. With him on the trip was a public-

relations consultant from OAO Sibneft, an oil company linked to two of Russia's best-connected tycoons, Boris Berezovsky and Roman Abramovich.

Mr. Berezovsky used to boast of how he played tennis with Mr. Yeltsin. But he never talked much about how he secured control of much of the cash stream from the sale of Avtovaz cars. He talked often about how he was a close friend of the family, but was reluctant to explain how he came to own shares of Aeroflot, the national airline. He regaled, in talks in his gilded baroque private club in Moscow about how he was an adviser to the president. He was quieter about how he bought a chunk of Sibneft for a song in 1995.

So there is the first piece of the legacy: Mr. Putin inherits an economy that's largely in private hands but anchored less in a spirit of free and fair competition than in a very Soviet mechanism of connections and the favors they bring.

To be fair, that's what Yeltsin inherited from the Communists, who inherited it from the czars. But he let a cancer of insider deals and corruption vitiate his greatest asset: an ability to rally ordinary Russians to make a radical break with the past.

When he clambered atop a tank to defy a hard-line Communist putsch in August 1991, Mr. Yeltsin gave voice to a profound popular yearning for an end to rule by cabals of courtiers and commissars. By the time he shuffled out of the Kremlin into a black Mercedes limousine on Friday, the cabal was back in charge. Mr. Yeltsin appeared lonely and remote, in command of little but his ability to leave office.

"I ask forgiveness for not justifying some hopes of those people who believed that at one stroke, in one spurt, we could leap from the gray, stagnant, totalitarian past into the light, rich, civilized future," he said in a melancholy farewell address on New Year's Eve. "I myself believed in this, that we could overcome everything in one spurt."

Mr. Putin, by contrast, has no ambitions to turn the system upside down. "Russia has used up its limit for political and socioeconomic upheavals, cataclysms and radical reforms," he says. His first acts as acting president confirm this. He signed a decree guaranteeing immunity for Mr. Yeltsin. He reappointed Mr. Yeltsin's chief of staff, Alexander Voloshin. Mr. Putin's "main

features are decency, reliability and loyalty," says Alexander Sobchak, former mayor of St. Petersburg and Mr. Putin's former law professor at Leningrad University.

Hardly the qualities he will need to take on the vested interests that did so much to discredit the cause of free-market reform in the eyes of the public. The hope is that his loyalty is only tactical. He needs the help of Mr. Yeltsin's circle of business and political cronies to fight a presidential election in March: They control the money and the media. After that, all bets are off.

When Mr. Yeltsin came to power in 1991, he inherited an economy in ruins. The oil fields were running dry. The military had lost the arms race. The nation had been growing poorer for more than a decade. It was a system without cash or controls. Moscow ordered factories to produce and shops to stock the paltry result. Cash was nothing more than window-dressing in empty stores where prices were set by committee.

Russia's first democratically elected president created a cash economy, though one in which barter often blunted market discipline. He did it impetuously—maybe there was no other way—resulting in inflation that clocked 2,506% in 1992. He quickly made enemies of the people whose enthusiasm had swept him into power.

As his political fortunes waxed and waned with the intensity of economic change, Mr. Yeltsin shuffled ministers and policies with abandon, tilting one month toward free-market reformers, the next toward stolid apparatchiks. He wanted to believe the former, but often felt more comfortable with the latter, veterans like himself of the party system. Along the way, relations with the IMF, with billions of dollars at stake, rode a roller-coaster: agreement, disappointment, revision and, ultimately, mostly failure. In 1998, the train flew off the tracks: The ruble collapsed, Russia's domestic and international debt crumpled, and the IMF, badly bruised along with Western investors, staggered away.

This is the second piece of Mr. Yeltsin's legacy: Mr. Putin inherits a Western-style, cash-based economic system that has many of the same tools that other industrialized nations use to control growth and inflation. And it's not an economy in terrible shape, either. After its nose dive in 1998, the economy grew last year by about 2%—only its second increase since Mr. Yeltsin came to power. Investment in fixed capital rose for the first time in a decade.

The question is what lessons Mr. Putin draws from Mr. Yeltsin's push-me-pull-you record. He could decide that retrenching is a quick way to gain political points when reform starts to bite, especially if, like Mr. Yeltsin, he lets others take the blame for the policies. Or, he could decide that stopping and starting a reform program only prolongs people's agony and ultimately erodes political support.

So far, Mr. Putin has defined himself through war in Chechnya. He greeted the new millennium aboard a military helicopter in the battle zone with his wife, Lyudmila, his third visit to the Caucasus region in as many months. He has prosecuted the war with brutal zeal. But his energetic, hands-on style marks a break from Mr. Yeltsin, who traveled just once to Chechnya during Russia's disastrous 1994-96 war there: He flew into the airport, declared victory and then left. Russian troops retreated in defeat a few months later.

Mr. Putin's no-nonsense manner and physical vigor—he is adept at judo and a form of wrestling that involves throttling neck grips—have made him hugely popular. A Moscow tabloid calls him "Russia's Bruce Willis." Other nicknames are more sinister. He was known in St. Petersburg, where he worked after returning from duties as a KGB lieutenant colonel in East Germany, as "the gray cardinal" and "stasi," after the East German secret police.

His true identity will become clearer in how he chooses to interpret Mr. Yeltsin's political legacy. At its heart is a baffling contradiction: To preserve democracy, Mr. Yeltsin frequently compromised it. Confronted with a mutinous parliament elected under the Soviet Union, he tore up a Soviet-era constitution in 1993 and sent tanks onto Kalininsky Bridge in the center of Moscow to hurl shells at rebellious and armed legislators holed up inside the Russian White

House. It had been the scene of his own defiant stand against a Communist coup two years earlier.

Less visible, but just as important as an illustration of the contradictory forces tugging at Mr. Yeltsin, was the fat man with a red face, red beard and red pencil who arrived at Moscow's biggest printing press on Pravda Street soon after the showdown at the White House. Armed with decree No. 1578, signed by Mr. Yeltsin, he commandeered a room and taped a hastily printed sign on the door: Committee for the Control of Newspaper Publication. His job: to censor newspapers.

Across Russia, the machinery of control Mr. Yeltsin had himself done so much to dismantle spluttered back to life. But just as the gears were beginning to grind, Mr. Yeltsin shifted direction again. Tanks pulled out; censors vanished, and Mr. Yeltsin ordered elections to choose a new parliament and endorse a new constitution, putting his military victory on the line.

This constitution is the cornerstone of the Yeltsin era. It enshrines a panoply of democratic rights and freedoms, many of which are flouted by bribe-taking police, venal officials and often corrupt courts. It clearly delineates powers between the president, the government and the legislature, but vests overwhelming authority in the Kremlin and fairly mocks the notion of checks and balances.

Russia now has a democracy that allows leaders to rule only with a mandate from a popular, competitive election. In 1996 and early 1997, voters threw out of office about half of the incumbent governors.

But, as in the economy, the political playing field is slanted. No one enforces rules governing candidates' spending. Television stations and newspapers controlled by the Kremlin or local governors bludgeon foes and flatter friends. During the 1996 election campaign, two Kremlin aides were detained outside the government's headquarters with a box containing $500,000 in cash. No charges were ever brought.

Vladimir Gussinsky, a mogul who helped mobilize money and media for Mr. Yeltsin in 1996, now has second thoughts about a precedent he helped set: "These people observe no rules because they are reformers and they are carrying out a revolution."

Mr. Putin is their masterpiece. Plucked from obscurity just five months ago as head of the country's revamped KGB, now known as the FSB, and lavished with hagiographic coverage by state-controlled media, he now looks unbeatable as a presidential candidate in March. But if he is ever to drain the swamp of corruption, he must eventually take on some of the people who put him in office. These could include the man who first gave him a job in Moscow, Pavel Borodin, overlord of the Kremlin's vast property agency and the focus of a Swiss bribery investigation. Mr. Borodin denies any wrongdoing.

Mr. Putin shows no inclination, at least not yet, to dilute the power of the elite that run the show. His watchword is stability, not upheaval. Russia, he says, will never be a "second edition of, say, the U.S. or Britain, in which liberal values have developed historic traditions. . . . For Russians, a strong state is not an anomaly that should be eliminated."

Ultimately, however, Mr. Putin seems a likely candidate to continue the Westernization of Russia. Here he is an heir of not only Mr. Yeltsin, but of a much longer tradition stretching back, with many interruptions, to Peter the Great.

With a career in international espionage, some of it spent monitoring Western technology, a daughter in a German school in Moscow and a stint in the early 1990s alongside St. Petersburg reformers, Mr. Putin clearly looks beyond Russia's borders. He is a nationalist, but he has already come to the same central conclusion about his country's best course that Mr. Yeltsin did:

"Russia has entered the highway by which the whole of humanity is traveling," Mr. Putin declared in a manifesto posted last week on the Internet. "There is no alternative to it."

STILL SOUL SEARCHING

Konstantin Eggert

This has been a tough year for Russia watchers. President Boris Yeltsin has sacked two governments for reasons ill-comprehended by Westerners, who are used to more predictable political behaviour. NATO's operation in the Balkans whipped up anti-Western, and especially anti-American, feeling to a frenzy comparable to the days of the Cold War. Although the IMF bailout package arrived just in time to avert sovereign default, more than a few questions remain as far as the economic future is concerned. And now a series of bombs in Moscow has left hundreds dead and produced a state of high anxiety.

WHAT ARE RUSSIA'S PROSPECTS? WHAT KIND OF consequences both domestically and internationally is the current period of instability likely to have? These are the questions, which are frequently asked these days, adding up to the all time favourite: who will be the next master of the Kremlin?

There is still no definite answer to the question of the Kremlin succession, except maybe that a communist party candidate is highly unlikely to win. Some analysts have already proclaimed the two most likely victors—Moscow Mayor Yuri Luzhkov or former Prime Minister Yevgeny Primakov. Their chances look bright indeed—for now.

But in Russian terms there is still a long time left before the vote is due to be held in the summer of 2000. Political careers are made and wrecked sometimes literally overnight. By the time the race for the Kremlin is on in earnest, most of today's favourites will have been on track for too long—and the public may well take a liking to some fresh face.

Vladimir Putin, an ex-KGB officer who was appointed prime minister in August, was discarded by most analysts from the outset as a potential front-runner. But in May, the same people were writing off Sergei Stepashin, who had just been appointed premier. Now he is setting his sights on the Duma contest and is considered to be a potentially strong contender for the presidency. The fact that his ratings shot from zero to eight percent in less than three months is a good example of what a determined politician can do—especially if given sufficient power—and how wrong hasty judgements can be in Russia.

It's futile to try and predict all the twists and turns of politics. But it is possible to draw some wider conclusions. To achieve this it is necessary to understand that at the core of most significant events in the country is a search, probably even a struggle, for the new face of Russia—its domestic and international identity.

DIFFERENT AND SPECIAL

In most countries of Central and Eastern Europe, strong cultural links to Western civilisation encourage a general acceptance of liberal democracy and the market economy. This is put into practice by ruling elites, who—irrespective of party affiliation—pursue the policy of integrating former Warsaw Pact and COMECON nations into the web of Euro-Atlantic institutions.

KONSTANTIN EGGERT is a senior correspondent and analyst with the BBC Russian Service in Moscow. He was previously Diplomatic Correspondent of *Izvestia*.

From *The World Today*, October 1999, pp. 6-9. © 1999 by The World Today, a publication of the Royal Institute of International Affairs. Reprinted by permission.

Russia is still hesitant and confused about the road the country should take. There is a strong perception that Russia is different from both East and West, although few would be able to describe what exactly makes the country so special. The fact that Russia had never existed within its current borders only adds to the confusion. Nostalgia for lost superpower status creates an emotional climate where reasonable policymaking becomes difficult if not impossible.

There is a widespread opinion in the West that the 1990's were a time of liberal if painful and bungled—(but still liberal) reform. But the main features of the decade were quite different. It was rather an *époque* when the former Soviet bureaucracy transformed itself into the new Russian bureaucracy, breaking the shackles of Communist party control.

It was also an age of the greatest redistribution of state property history has ever known. There is still plenty of argument as to whether privatisation in Russia was derailed or intended to be what it eventually became. In the end it led to a perfect marriage between state bureaucracy, selected big businessmen—usually former bureaucrats or party functionaries and, in some cases, organised crime.

Whatever was achieved in terms of liberal reform in economics, politics and society looks like a by-product of this process rather than vice versa. The textbook liberals—such as Prime Ministers Yegor Gaidar and Sergei Kiriyenko—held power for less than eighteen months of the eight years since the break-up of the Soviet Union.

ON THE SIDELINES

Society in general is largely left on the sidelines. Poorly directed socio-economic policies overlap with hurt feelings about the demise of what is seen by the majority of the population as a mighty Soviet state. And there is nobody around to offer any kind of new vision—the crisis of leadership is evident among Russia's politicians.

The necessary—if painful—decisions on bankruptcy, selling off the sizeable remaining state assets, opening the doors wide to foreign investors—don't have much chance of being resolutely implemented as the country's political class feels the increasing power of regional governors.

Not all, but the majority, of these people are former local communist party bosses. They are mostly supportive of enhancing what they call 'the regulatory function of the state'. They are strongly protectionist and highly authoritarian with no great attachment to democracy or the free market. Sometimes they are outwardly hostile to them. Corruption, cronyism and strongarm tactics against critics are widespread.

So is it all hopeless? The answer is probably not. But the transformation of Russian society may take much longer than many people, both in Russia and in the West,

expected. Still there are positive signs. The slow but steady growth of civic society institutions, the increasing number of non-governmental organisations, charities, activist groups and an increasingly self-assured and independent lawyers' community. All this may be seen not only in Moscow and St Petersburgh but also in provincial towns. A decade of electoral experience has left its mark too—people tend to vote more responsibly now.

It is safe to assume that two trends in mass thinking will dominate: one is a generally conservative philosophy, which still relies a lot on state support and interference in day-to-day economic and social life. This is within a non-communist state organised along democratic lines with a market economy. This kind of thinking distinguishes two presidential front-runners, Messers Primakov and Luzhkov. The latter has famously summed up his attitude in the slogan 'Let's work like capitalists and distribute like socialists'.

But the reverse tendency will, no doubt, manifest itself too. After a series of setbacks, the liberally minded minority has come of age. The achiever community of the last decade feels the growing need for political representation. This is especially true after the August 1998 financial crash found the Russian middle class practically defenceless against corrupt bankers and the omnipowerful state bureaucracy.

It seems that the Union of the Forces of the Right—the centre-right coalition, created by Russia's arch-reformers Yegor Gaidar and Anatoly Chubais, and supported by some reform-minded regional leaders, has a chance of making it into parliament—the State Duma. In the 1995 elections, the liberals failed to breach the necessary five percent vote barrier.

It looks as though the new Duma will be more representative of political trends in Russia, and probably more responsible, than the current one. But the big question remains—what kind of state and what kind of society will Russia eventually become?

The lines for the next—but by no means last—stage of the battle for the future. of Russia will be drawn during next year's presidential campaign. Paradoxically, a victory for Yuri Luzhkov or Yevgeny Primakov might galvanise liberal public opinion and serve as a catalyst for new ideas and new centre-right leaders.

INTERNATIONAL IDENTITY

That events at home have a direct impact on Moscow's international behaviour is only natural. But here the unfinished search for a new identity has an even stronger influence on decision-making and decision-makers. The crisis over Kosovo highlighted some underlying factors behind foreign policy. And although some of them are bound to have long term negative effects on Russia's relations with the West, it's conceivable that others may provide a more sober, realistic and predictable, if not more open and co-operative, foreign policy in future.

The biggest lesson of the whole Russia-NATO stand-off over the former Yugoslavia is the most vivid proof of what lies at the heart of many a disagreement between Moscow and the West. It could be termed incompatibility of values. Neither ordinary citizens nor politicians were able to comprehend the Western alliance's desire to intervene in Kosovo. The notion of individual rights preceding those of the state is still quite alien. Many Russians would concede that the Yugoslav President, Slobodan Milosevic, is not exactly an angel, but as long as he defends the territorial integrity of his state he's in the clear.

This majority view probably has roots not in the much-discussed ethnic and religious links between the Russians and the Serbs, but rather in recent history. The collapse of the USSR is a vivid and hurtful memory for many Russians, and in the fate of Yugoslavia they find a lot in common with what happened to their former country.

The fact that most Kosovars are Muslims and that the Kosovo Liberation Army resembles the Chechen fighters who defeated the Russian army only three years ago, ensures that ill feeling towards NATO's Kosovo operation will linger. Every time the defence of human rights is invoked by the West as a reason for tough action somewhere, it is bound to be met with mistrust if not animosity by politicians and public opinion alike.

ANTI-AMERICANISM

Another relatively long-term factor is the anti-Americanism of public opinion. NATO's operation in the Balkans was seen by Russians primarily as an American one. While at the beginning of the decade Russia's Westernisers were pro-American, today a great number of those who wholeheartedly support democracy and free enterprise have nothing but scorn for the US.

Anybody who advocates good relations with Washington risks marginalisation and even vilification. It took a lot of courage for former Prime Minister Sergei Stepashin to say that Moscow should stop the policy of 'what's bad for America is good for Russia'. The fact that this was said in Washington and not in Moscow made some experts suspicious of his sincerity.

However, there was nothing spectacular about these statements for, as long as Boris Yeltsin remains in the Kremlin, the basics of sound relations with the West in general, and the US in particular, will remain. Russia's first president prides himself on two essential—and indisputable achievements: political freedoms at home and established (and close) relations with the Western world. He is not going to sacrifice these for reasons of political expediency.

But Yeltsin is on his way out. His policies are increasingly under attack. Military and industry kingpins, as well as some top generals, don't make a secret of their desire to do away with what they see as a soft approach towards the West. And the majority of the public applaud their actions.

The maverick take-over of Pristina airport was cheered by ordinary Russians as a blow to American prestige—and a return of Russia's military glory. It was all the Moscow taxi drivers could talk about for days. The fact that British Gurkhas soon had to supply the Russian force with mineral water did not count—and was hardly reported by the ever jubilant media.

HARDER LINE

Yeltsin's successor and his team may start by pursuing a more anti-Western line, at least in public. Both the military industry barons and some elements in the general staff will no doubt try to press the president-elect whoever he may be—to stick to a harder line in dealing with Washington. Attempts at increased defence spending and a reassesment of the nuclear posture—such as a return to the first strike option—are possible.

As for diplomacy, it will probably develop its favourite idea of recent years—driving a wedge between the US and Europe. Befriending China and India will remain an international priority.

But there are certain limits to this kind of policy change. First, there is no way to achieve a significant increase in military spending—there is simply no money around, at least not a sufficient amount of it. To try and provide more would mean either printing worthless banknotes or reneging on the sovereign debt and isolating the country. Both options were studiously avoided even by a left-leaning Primakov cabinet. There is no reason to believe that any future president will change his mind on this.

Secondly, trying to play on US-European differences demands a much more subtle and finely tuned diplomacy than that which has characterised Moscow's European effort recently. The problem of Russian foreign policy is that for half a century it has been isolated from the process of creating the transatlantic relationship, which was perceived by Moscow only in the context of Cold War block-building.

That's why Russian politicians rarely understand the complexity and deep roots of the US-European link. As one high ranking and supposedly liberal member of Duma defence committee put it at a recent meeting with British MPs: 'We need European investment instead of IMF money. In return, Europe can rely on Russia to help her check American ambitions, because today Europe is totally subjected to the USA'.

Many decision-makers in Moscow think of Europe only as a partner in arms against the US. They are cheered by talk of the Old World's newly discovered assertiveness vis-à-vis Washington. Policy planners in Russia don't seem to realise that even if there were some deep rethinking of the transatlantic partnership, it would be because the Europeans judge it to be in their own interest and would have nothing to do with the kind of inferiority complex that Russia still suffers from in dealing with the US.

The same goes for European—especially German and Scandinavian—attitudes to Russia. If they stretch out a hand to Moscow it's because they find the American way of dealing too abrasive and counterproductive for their own interests not because they want to upset the US.

Still, Moscow's effort to build ties with Europe may in itself prove very useful. Russia will become more adept at modern European consensus building and will learn to take into account—if not necessarily agree with—a multitude of views. It may help Russians to shed the habit of measuring their country exclusively against the United States—and by doing so take a few steps towards defining the nation's new foreign policy.

Finally, getting pally with Beijing and New Delhi has its limits too. For once, Russia's economic needs cannot be limited to selling arms and nuclear powerplants, important though they may be. Russia will eventually need massive investment and technological input. This is not going to be achieved by courting anti-Western elements in India and China. Cultural differences and geopolitical divisions also count.

ALL IN THE HEAD

Even the staunchest nationalists in Russia hardly believe that an invasion from the West remains a possibility. On the contrary, the vulnerability of the Russian Far East to Chinese attack is still a strategic consideration. As the Chinese armed forces gradually modernise, it is not inconceivable that Russia will curtail its arms sales to China and start seeing NATO as a rather useful partner in off-setting Beijing's ambitions.

'It's all in the head', one of Russia's top defence reporters, Igor Korotchenko, once remarked. 'The Russian generals were planning armoured thrusts through Germany to the Channel. They just cannot change their minds quickly enough—if at all. We'll have to wait for another generation to take over that will start to treat the Alliance as a reality one cannot avoid, and probably as a partner too'.

In the end it all boils down to the question, what really is Russia's national interest? Is it what the army's top brass, military industry bosses and some corrupt businessmen think—suspiciously facing the West and beefing up the imperial muscle at the expense of the people? Or is it building a free, prosperous and secure society—respected but not necessarily feared by the world? The answer may seem obvious to those living in Western democracies. But it will take time before the Russians themselves accept it as the only viable alternative.

The Baltics: Between Russia and the West

"For 800 years, the distinctive character of the Baltic countries has been shaped by their peculiar and precarious position between the East and the West. That position has generated for these countries both great creativity and great tragedy. It is also a position that will not soon change."

JAMES KURTH

On the northwestern frontier of Russia lie three small nations whose cultures are very different from that of Russia and very similar to those of the West. These are Estonia, Latvia, and Lithuania, which collectively are known as the Baltic states. Seen by the Russians, the Baltic countries are a natural extension of Russia. Seen by the Baltic nations themselves, they have all too often been in Russia, but they have never been of it.

The Baltic countries were the westernmost extension of the Russian Empire of the czars and the Soviet Union of the Communists. Earlier they had been for several centuries the easternmost extension of German rule and culture. The German presence in the Baltic countries was so pronounced that it made the Baltics permanently a part of the civilization of the West. This Western character, so different from the Russian, would survive two centuries of czarist rule and a half-century of Soviet repression, and it still distinguishes the Baltic states today.

The Baltic countries can properly be seen as both the East of the West, and the West of the East. The Baltics were first, in the thirteenth and fourteenth centuries, the object of the Germans' drive to the East and later, in the eighteenth and nineteenth centuries, the object of the Russians' drive to the West. Then, in the First and Second World Wars, they had the great misfortune to be the object of both.

THE VIEW FROM RUSSIA

From the Russian perspective, the Baltic countries are obviously a part of Russian geography. Russia reaches its natural western frontier with the distinct geographical feature of the Baltic Sea. Conversely, no pronounced geographical features on the eastern borders of the Baltic countries establish a natural frontier between themselves and Russia.

The principal reason Peter the Great became great was that he understood this reality and acted on it. He did so through his military victories over Sweden in the decisive Great Northern War of 1700–1721, which saw him conquer the Baltic lands and extend Russian power to the Baltic Sea. Peter culminated his and Russia's drive to the Baltic by building a new city and new capital, St. Petersburg, which he envisioned would become Russia's gateway to the West. For more than two centuries thereafter, the Baltic countries were under the political authority of the Russian czars, and they guarded the military approaches to the Russian capital.

Peter had intended that St. Petersburg would be Russia's window on the West, serving as a conduit of Western ideas and ways that would enter, and progressively modernize, the vast Russian hinterland. To a degree, his new city did come to serve this role. However, it was Peter's other acquisition, the Baltic countries, that performed the Westernizing role even more clearly and consistently. This was especially the case with the old city of Riga, which became a busier and more successful port for the Russian Empire than did St. Petersburg.

The Baltic countries performed this Westernizing role so well because they were already a part of the West, not just a window on it. Although they might be geographically the westernmost extension of Russia, that is, the West of the East, the Baltic countries were culturally the easternmost extension of Germany, or the East of the West.

Five centuries before Peter the Great conquered the Baltic countries from the east, the Teutonic Knights had invaded them from the west. Henceforth, the Germans held the economic and social power in the Baltic countries. Most of the Baltic countryside was owned by German nobles, and most of the Baltic towns were dominated by German merchants, especially the cities of Riga and Tallinn. Although the successive military victories of the Poles, the Swedes, and finally the Russians

JAMES KURTH *is a professor of political science at Swarthmore College.*

enabled these peoples to succeed the Teutonic Knights as the political authorities in the Baltic countries, the economic achievements of the Baltic Germans continued to give them the social power.

THE "BALTIC SPECIAL ORDER" . . .

The Russian political authorities found it in their interest to preserve and protect the economic position of the Baltic Germans because they provided educated officials, tax revenues, and Western connections for the czar's regime. This preservation of an economic and social part of Germany within the political and military realm of Russia was known as the "Baltic Special Order" (*Baltisches Sonderrecht*).

Beneath the political power of the Russians and the economic power of the Germans could be found the original Baltic peoples, most of whom were peasants. When, in the nineteenth century, these peoples began to develop their own distinct national identities—as Estonians, Latvians, and Lithuanians—they followed the German models of national development at the time.

One dimension of national development was the recovery of national culture, or more accurately, the invention of national tradition. The Baltic national movements placed great emphasis on the establishment of a distinctive national language, literature, music, and artistic style. The other dimension of national development was the construction of a modern society. The Baltic national movements emphasized the creation of a society that adhered to and operated under Western, especially German, standards in such areas as education, public health, civic associations, and economic enterprise. By the beginning of the twentieth century, the national movements had largely succeeded in achieving the cultural goals, and they were well advanced toward achieving the social goals.

. . . AND ITS DEMISE

The Russian Empire and the Baltic Special Order within it collapsed in the course of World War I and the Russian Revolution. The Baltic peoples, through their military achievements against both the Russian and German armies in 1918 and 1919, overthrew the Russian authorities, expropriated the German landed estates, and established themselves as independent national states. From the Estonian, Latvian, and Lithuanian perspectives, it was the natural fulfillment of their decades-long period of national development.

Russia saw the political and military independence of the Baltic countries as the unnatural consequence of temporary Russian weakness, brought about by the world war, the Russian Revolution, and the ensuing Russian civil war. With time, Russia would regain its natural and rightful power and status. Then, the two-century norm established by Peter the Great would resume, replacing the two-decade anomaly of Baltic independence.

This resumption occurred in 1939 and 1940 with the beginning of the next world war and the Soviet annexation of the three Baltic states, which were forced to become Soviet republics within the Soviet Union. Soviet leader Joseph Stalin clearly saw himself as restoring or realizing anew a large aspect of the understanding of Peter the Great and the succeeding czars: that the Baltic countries were the natural, westernmost extension of Russia.

Stalin did not see himself as restoring the other aspect of that understanding: the idea that the Baltic countries were a window on the West, which had underlain the Baltic Special Order. Quite the contrary. Stalin's methods in the Baltic countries were exceptionally brutal and destructive. His secret police murdered or deported to Siberia more than 5 percent of the general population and more than 50 percent of the professional classes in each of the three countries. Anything and anyone connected with the West was liquidated.

Stalin's successors followed this line during the 1950s and 1960s. Thus, in the first three decades of their rule in the Baltics, the Soviet authorities repressed every expression of Western ideas and ways. There seemed to be nothing left of a Baltic Special Order.

THE SOVIET WINDOW OF VULNERABILITY

In the last two decades of Soviet rule, the Baltic countries once again became Russia's window on the West. During the 1970s and 1980s, the Soviet Union began to allow local Baltic initiatives in some cultural, social, and economic areas, and these initiatives quickly emulated Western models. Western cultural innovations and economic practices often first entered into the Soviet Union through experiments within the Baltic republics, from which they then spread to Russia and beyond. Although this was hardly a robust version of a Baltic Special Order, a common view in the Soviet Union was that the Baltic republics were clearly the most European of the Soviet republics, and they were known as the "Soviet West."

In August 1989, on the occasion of the fiftieth anniversary of the Nazi-Soviet Pact that had consigned them to Soviet rule, the three Baltic republics took the lead among the Soviet republics in demanding freedom from Soviet rule. Their demand for autonomy soon became one for full independence. In August 1991 the three Baltic countries succeeded in gaining this independence, and in December 1991, when the other republics also broke away, the Soviet Union disintegrated entirely. The window on the West had let in a political hurricane.

A decade later the Baltic nations are still, in several senses, a window on the West for Russia. First, a large part of the Russian underground economy connects and operates with Western economies through the Baltic countries, especially through the port cities of Riga and Tallinn (the capitals of Latvia and Estonia, respectively). Second, large Russian minorities reside in Latvia (33 percent of the population) and Estonia (28 percent); Russians also form a majority of the population in Riga and in Tallinn. Russian demography, as well as Russian geography, still reaches to the Baltic Sea. Third, the Baltic countries form a military and strategic buffer between Russia and the recently expanded NATO (especially its easternmost member, Poland).

Most Russians see the political and military independence of the Baltic states as the regrettable consequence of an abnormal Russian weakness, brought about by the collapse of the Soviet Union and the confusion and disorder of succeeding Russian governments. They view this kind of full independence for the Baltic countries as unnatural and unhistorical. And the efforts of the Baltic states to become political and military allies of the West—that is, to become members of NATO—are seen as threatening and insulting.

For Russia, reasonable and acceptable independence for the Baltic states should follow the model of Finnish independence: to be economically and culturally part of the West, politically independent of the West and Russia, and militarily neutral and unthreatening to Russia. When Russia regains its natural and rightful power and status, some version of the norm established by Peter the Great should once again resume, replacing the recent anomaly of Baltic full independence. With this resumption, however, and unlike that of Stalin, some new version of Russia's window on the West and the Baltic Special Order may arise.

Russia sees several possible models for this new Baltic Special Order. First is the Finland-like status, with economic, cultural, and political—but not military—independence. Next would be a status like that of the Baltic Germans under the czars, with economic and cultural independence, but not political and military independence. Next would be a status like that of the Baltic republics in the later Soviet Union: no real independence but still a conduit of selected Western ways, a window on the West.

Finally, there would be the low status and dreary specter represented by what is another Baltic territory, although its population is now completely Russian. This is the geographical anomaly that is the Kaliningrad region of Russia, which, before World War II, was the East Prussian region of Germany. Here the Russians have demolished virtually everything Western. Kaliningrad, to the immediate south of the Baltic states, is the total opposite of Finland, to the immediate north.

THE BALTIC PERSPECTIVE

The Baltic peoples view themselves as distinct from other nations, and from each other. But their conceptions of what a proper nation should be have always been defined by the conceptions of the nations to the West. Although this has been especially the case with Germany, the Balts have also been attentive to the ideas of other nations, especially if they were the leading Western powers of the time (Britain after World War I and the United States since World War II).

During their first period of national independence in the 1920s and 1930s, the Baltic states were among the smallest nations in Europe. Their populations at that time (Estonia, 1.1 million; Latvia, 1.9 million; Lithuania, 2.9 million) were even less than that of Denmark. But these new and miniature nation-states adhered to and operated under the cultural and economic standards of those that were the largest and most advanced (Estonia, for example, had one of the highest literacy rates in the world, and Latvia was not far behind).

The Baltic nations have always believed, therefore, that they should and could learn from the West. Conversely, they have almost always believed that the Russians have nothing to teach them. (An exception was some elements of the Latvian industrial workers at the time of the Russian Revolution.) The Baltic nations fear and loathe the Russians, even more after the Soviet period than after the czarist. They also fear and loathe the very thought of sinking to Russian standards. Even when the Germans oppressed and exploited the Baltic peoples, they provided the Balts with many of their models. In contrast, the Russians under both the czarist and Soviet regimes oppressed and exploited the Balts and provided no models. In contrast again, the British and the Americans, who have been too distant from the Baltic countries to pose a threat to them, have provided only models. From the Baltic perspective, the United States—both Western and remote—is the perfect great power.

THE RUSSIAN QUESTION

In this Baltic conception of the region as the East of the West, the Russian minority in the Baltic states has a special, and unstable, place. It is seen as an alien body, a form of East in the West.

The Russian minority in the Baltic countries is largely a product of the Soviet occupation. In the interwar period, Russians comprised only 8 percent of the population of Estonia, 9 percent of Latvia, and 3 percent of Lithuania. During the Soviet period, authorities brought in vast numbers of Russians (and also Belarusians and Ukrainians) to work in the new factories in heavy industries (known as "black work"), which the regime built according to Soviet concepts of industrialization. They also brought in large numbers of Russians and other Soviet nationalities to serve as soldiers and sailors in the great network of military bases that the regime built. Many officers in the military and security services found the Baltic republics so congenial that they retired there. These included officers of the KGB, the Soviet secret police.

By 1959 these two processes of industrialization and militarization, Soviet style, had greatly altered the ethnic structure of the Baltic countries. In that year the Russians comprised 20 percent of the population of Estonia, 27 percent of Lativa, and 9 percent of Lithuania. The Sovietization and Russification continued, especially in Estonia and Latvia. In 1989, on the eve of Baltic independence, the Russians comprised 30 percent of the population of Estonia and 34 percent of that of Latvia (and it remained at 9 percent of Lithuania).

After almost a decade of independence, the Russian minority is only slightly smaller: 28 percent in Estonia, 33 percent in Latvia, and 8 percent in Lithuania. Despite being the objects of Baltic political discrimination, the Russians are often the beneficiaries of Baltic economic growth. They have concluded that it is better to be a second-class citizen in a Baltic country than a first-class citizen in Russia.

The Russians largely live in vast and ugly working-class suburbs. Most are not citizens of the new states. The granting of citizenship is closely tied to knowledge of the national language, and most Russians are unwilling or unable to learn these obscure and difficult tongues.

The Russians in the Baltics have the same social attitudes and behavior as the Russians in Russia: many are conspicuously sullen, surly, and self-pitying. The Russian young men are especially antisocial. Their behavior in public places typically is crude, mean-spirited, and drunken. And then there are the wannabes of the Russian Mafia, dressed in black. The Russian minority is *in* the Baltic countries, but not *of* them.

From the perspective of the Baltic nations, the Russian minority is a legacy of Soviet colonial occupation, a collaborator with the Soviet totalitarian regime, and a product of the worst excesses of Soviet industrialization and militarization. Like the abandoned industrial factories and military bases, the Russian minority is thought of as something like a toxic waste dump. It represents the nightmare of the past rather than the promise of the future, Eurasia rather than Europe, the East rather than the West, and, in the minds of many Balts, even barbarism rather than civilization. As the Baltic nations see it, the more Russian their countries remain, the less Western they will become.

The characteristics of the Russian minority and the attitudes of the Baltic nations toward it create a serious problem for democracy in the Baltic states. For the Baltic nations, to grant full citizenship and equal rights to the Russians would be to reverse their epic journey toward the West and to stumble back toward the East. This problem for Baltic democracy is compounded by differences in political culture. The political culture of the Baltic nations, especially the Estonians and Latvians, is like that of the Scandinavians: democratic, rationalist, and legalist. The political culture of the Russian minority is like that of Russia itself: authoritarian, ethnocentric, and populist.

If democracy is defined by adherence to democratic values, a substantive definition, then Baltic democracy will best operate if it is limited to the Baltic peoples themselves; it will be in danger of ceasing to operate if it is extended to large

RUSSIANS IN THE BALTIC STATES

▨ Russian-populated areas
⊙ National capitals

0 25 50 75 100 Miles

TALLINN

ESTONIA

BALTIC SEA

RUSSIA

LATVIA

Riga

LITHUANIA

KALININGRAD (RUSSIA)

Vilnius

BELARUS

POLAND

© Current History, Inc.

[Stalin's] secret police murdered or deported to Siberia more than 5 percent of the general population.

numbers of Russians. This substantive conception of democracy is the one held by the Baltic nations. Yet if democracy is defined by adherence to democratic procedures, a formal definition, then Baltic democracy must be extended to include all or most Russians. This formal conception appears superficial and frivolous to the Baltic nations.

It is this formal conception, however, that is advanced by political and intellectual elites in Western Europe and especially in the United States. These elites are now largely believers in the ideologies of multicultural diversity and universal human rights. To them, the idea that the Baltic countries might better be seen as cases of bipolar division rather than multicultural diversity, and of historic communal identities rather than universal human rights, is politically incorrect.

The governments of Western Europe and the United States, along with the European Union (EU) and the Organization for Security and Cooperation in Europe (OSCE), have pressured the Baltic states to loosen their citizenship requirements and open their political processes to the Russian minority. From the perspective of the Baltic nations, this would have the paradoxical result that, in order for them to become more Western in form, and as members of Western international organizations (the EU, OSCE, and perhaps NATO), they must become less Western in substance.

In response to this pressure from Western governments and international organizations, Estonia and Latvia in 1998 liberalized their citizenship requirements; Russian children born in these countries after 1991 (the date of independence) will become citizens almost automatically, and the number of Russians who can be certified for the national language requirement has been increased. But this year the Latvian parliament has moved to have government business conducted only in the Latvian language, setting off another round of criticisms from Russia and the West. The conjoined issues of the citizenship rights and the language rights of the Russian minority will continue to trouble both the national identity and the international relations of the Baltic states.

FROM THE BALKANS TO THE BALTICS

The NATO air war against Serbia in the spring of 1999 could establish an ominous precedent for future Russian actions against the Baltic states. The United States and NATO argued that the Serbs were engaging in gross violations of the human rights of the Albanian majority in Kosovo, a region of Serbia. This justified NATO military operations, including the bombing of Belgrade and other Serbian cities outside Kosovo. The bombing continued until the Serbs accepted NATO's demands for the autonomy (and de facto independence) of the Albanians in Kosovo, backed up by the occupation of the region by NATO military forces.

During the Kosovo campaign Russia saw itself as the historical ally of Serbia. Although in its current weakness it could do nothing substantial in military terms to help the Serbs, it did engage in many symbolic actions, including the preemptive occupation of Kosovo's Pristina airport by a small contingent of Russian soldiers. In any event, Russia never considered the NATO arguments and actions to be legitimate.

Russia may now consider these arguments to be a precedent, for it can see potential parallels between recent NATO interpretations of the situation in the Balkans and its own interpretations of the situation in the Baltics. From the Russian perspective, the Estonians and the Latvians are engaged in the extensive denial of the human rights of the Russians. Although the Russians are a minority of the total population of Estonia and Latvia, they constitute a majority in the eastern districts, which border on Russia. They are also a majority in the capital cities of Tallinn and Riga. And although the extensive denial of human rights is not the same as their gross violation through murder and expulsion, as in Kosovo, the Russian security agencies have long experience in inflating incidents (or even provoking them) for purposes of propaganda within Russia itself.

Further, although the NATO intervention in Serbia was legitimated by the approval of two major international organizations (the EU as well as NATO), and a Russian intervention would have no chance of gaining the approval of any international organization, in Russian eyes this lack of international legitimacy could be compensated by demographic affinity and geographic proximity. Russians would be coming to the aid of Russians, a far more compelling calling than Americans coming to the aid of Albanians. And they would be doing so in territories that, for most of the past three centuries, Russians have ruled and have seen as a natural extension of Russia itself. (In 1998 the Russian military conducted maneuvers on the border of Estonia, which were code-named "Operation Return.")

NATO'S NEWEST MEMBERS?

The potential Russian threat to the Baltic states poses the question of NATO's further expansion to the east. Should NATO's recent admission of Poland, the Czech Republic, and Hungary be followed by a "second round of enlargement," which would include the Baltic states? The Baltic nations certainly think so. For them, NATO membership would be a full and formal recognition by Western Europe and the United States that they are indeed the East of the West, and also a full and formal deterrent against Russia, making them once again the West of the East. Further, the Clinton administration has made statements that have encouraged the Baltic nations to think they will be included in the next round of NATO expansion.

It is not clear, however, that a political base within Western Europe and the United States is sufficient to support a full NATO commitment to the Baltic states. In particular, are the United States Senate (which must ratify a treaty) and the United States Army (which must compose a strategy) likely to assume an obligation to guarantee the military security of these three small countries that border Russia, are within 150 kilometers of Russia's second-largest city, St. Petersburg, and contain large and alienated Russian minority populations? What would be NATO's military strategy? If it were conventional defense, how would this be possible? If it were nuclear deterrence, how would this be credible? Finally, even if American congressional and military leaders should agree to a guarantee given the current weakness of Russia and its military, what would this guarantee look like if Russian strength should revive a decade or two from now?

The Baltics see membership in NATO as desirable, even essential. For the United States it may seem impractical, even impossible. This contradiction suggests the need to search for a new version of a Baltic Special Order.

CREATING A NEW BALTIC SPECIAL ORDER

The old Baltic Special Order was designed by Russia and saw the Baltics as the West of the East. While giving primacy to Russian security interests, it also preserved Baltic economic and cultural autonomy. The new Baltic Special Order could be designed by the United States, along with Western Europe, and would see the Baltics as the East of the West. While giving primacy to Baltic economic, cultural, and political independence, it would also preserve Russian security interests. One possible model for this combination, as was noted earlier, is Finland. Before the Soviet period, Finland often followed a path similar to that of Estonia, Latvia, and Lithuania, and it was often defined as a Baltic country. Perhaps in the future the four countries can be similar again, all in a special Baltic way.

For 800 years, the distinctive character of the Baltic countries has been shaped by their peculiar and precarious position between the East and the West. That position has generated for these countries both great creativity and great tragedy. It is also a position that will not soon change. The task of the West, and especially the United States, is to bring its strategic vision and diplomatic skills to support Baltic independence and security, while maintaining and strengthening peaceful and productive relations with Russia. It will take the best of the West to preserve and protect this easternmost part of itself.

Chaos in the Caucasus

No, the fighting in the Caucasus is not evidence of a "clash of civilisations" between the Islamic world and other geopolitical blocks

AT LEAST until recently, the main enemy of Islamic terrorism seemed to be the United States. However diverse and quarrelsome its practitioners, they knew what they hated most: the global policeman whom they accused of propping up Israel, starving the Iraqis and undermining the Muslim way of life with an insidiously attractive culture.

Anti-Americanism, after all, has been a common thread in a series of spectacular acts of violence over the past decade. They include the bombing of the World Trade Centre in New York in February 1993; the explosion that killed 19 American soldiers at a base in Saudi Arabia in June 1996; and the deadly blasts at the American embassies in Kenya and Tanzania in August 1998.

In many of the more recent attacks it has suffered, the United States has discerned the hand of Osama bin Laden, the Saudi-born co-ordinator of an international network of militant Muslims. In February last year, he and his sympathisers in Egypt, Pakistan and Bangladesh issued a statement declaring that "to kill the Americans and their allies—civilian and military—is an individual duty for every Muslim who can do it." Such blood-curdling talk was inevitably seized on by believers in the "clash of civilisations" described by Samuel Huntington, a Harvard professor who said in 1993 that cultural or religious fault-lines were the most likely source of conflict in the post–cold-war world.

Now, it might appear, Russia's turn has come to do battle on a new front in this many-sided conflict. The Russian government has blamed terrorists from the country's Muslim south for a series of bomb blasts in Moscow and other cities which have claimed over 300 lives. And it has launched a broadening land and air attack against the mainly Muslim republic of Chechnya,

where the terrorists are alleged to originate.

In their more strident moments, officials and newspaper columnists in Moscow say that Russia is in the forefront of a fight between "civilisation and barbarism" and is therefore entitled to western understanding. "We face a common enemy, international terrorism," Russia's prime minister, Vladimir Putin, told President Bill Clinton last month. As evidence that anti-Russian and anti-American guerrillas have at least one common source, officials in Moscow have pointed to the alleged involvement of Mr bin Laden and his fighters, both in the Caucasus and in the urban bombing campaign.

In most of their comments, President Boris Yeltsin and his lieutenants have been careful to distinguish between their current adversaries and Muslims in general. "Terrorists are an enemy with no faith or nationality," Mr Yeltsin has said. Russian diplomats are stressing the support they have received from many Muslim governments—particularly Iran's, which is seen in Moscow as an important strategic partner and counterweight to western influence in the Caspian.

Whereas western countries have chided Russia (mildly) for its military operation against Chechnya, Iran has been much more supportive. Kamal Kharrazi, Iran's foreign minister, has promised "effective collaboration" with the Kremlin against what he has described as terrorists bent on destabilising Russia. Russia, for its part, has thanked Iran for using its chairmanship of the Organisation of the Islamic Conference to present the Russian case.

Perhaps because of Russia's friendship with certain parts of the Muslim world, Mr Putin has firmly rejected the view that the "bandits" Russia is now fighting could properly be described as Islamic. "They are international

terrorists, most of them mercenaries, who cover themselves in religious slogans," he insists.

But ordinary Muslims in the Moscow street—whether they are of Caucasian origin, or from the Tatar or Bashkir nations based in central Russia—fear a general backlash. "Politicians and the mass media are equating us, the Muslim faithful, with armed groups," complains Ravil Gainutdin, Russia's senior mufti. Patriarch Alexy II, the head of the Russian Orthodox church, has been urging his flock not to blame their 18m Muslim compatriots for the recent violence. "Russian Christians and Muslims traditionally live in peace," he has reminded them. His senior bishops—probably with a nod of encouragement from Russian officialdom—are engaged in a set-piece theological dialogue with Iran's spiritual leaders.

Clash, or conspiracy?

But even if Russia's southern war is not yet a "clash of civilisations", might it soon become one? And if so, would that bring Russia closer to the West, or push it farther away?

Islam is certainly one element in the crisis looming on Russia's southern rim, but it is by no means the only one. The latest flare-up began in August in the wild border country between Chechnya—which has been virtually independent since Russian troops were forced out, after two years of brutal war, in 1996—and Dagestan, a ramshackle, multiethnic republic where a pro-Russian government has been steadily losing control.

Two factors came together to set the scene for conflict. One was the long-running feud between Aslan Maskhadov, Chechnya's elected president, and Shamil Basaev, a younger and more militant figure with a history of

Action replay in Chechnya?

MOSCOW

SO FAR, the Russians have had the easiest part of their new war against Chechnya. Since the ground offensive started on October 1st, the Kremlin's forces, some 30,000 strong, have moved from the neighbouring republics of Dagestan and Ingushetia, and from Russia's Stavropol region, to seize the most accessible and least-defended part of Chechnya, its northern third. The Russians have also shown their ability to bomb civilian and economic targets (such as oil refineries) in the capital Grozny at will. These achievements are not surprising, given Russia's huge superiority in men, armour and aircraft.

The big question is what happens next. Russia's first claim to be establishing just a buffer zone, seems not to be the full story. By mid-week, Russian forces had taken up positions along the Terek river, and some were within artillery range of Grozny. But a Russian attempt to stop the war by declaring victory now would not work. It would give the Chechens a chance to regroup and harry the occupying soldiers. That in effect would repeat the history of the 1994–96 war, when Russian soldiers bloodily conquered Chechnya, only to see guerrillas stealthily retake the country once victory had been declared.

Pushing the offensive further—which Russian officials do not exclude—looks unattractive too. The Chechens are already celebrating the shooting down of at least two Russian aircraft, and claim to have destroyed half a dozen armoured vehicles and captured several Russian soldiers. Russia says only two of its men have been killed, and 22 wounded. Even if true—and the Chechens claim to have killed dozens of Russians—that total would rise sharply should the fighting become hand-to-hand in Chechnya's towns, let alone mountain warfare. In that sort of conflict, the gritty Chechens excel. The riskiest part of Russia's immediate plan will be to establish control over Chechnya's border with Georgia. This has yet to begin.

Both sides seem to think time is on their side. Russia is backing up its military offensive with economic warfare—for example, by cutting back gas and electricity supplies. It has also indicated that it will resettle refugees in the Russian-controlled sector of Chechnya, whether or not they came from there originally. This zone will presumably be well supplied with energy and utilities, to make the point that life under Russia is better.

On the Chechen side, internal squabbles have been set aside. Shamil Basaev, the best-known Chechen warlord, has sarcastically said he is "very grateful" to Russia for creating a new sense of unity among his people. His erstwhile rival, President Aslan Maskhadov, has called on Chechnya's religious leaders to rally the nation to holy war, "to defend the [country's] sovereignty and integrity in the name of Allah the benevolent and merciful." Martial law has been declared in Grozny, although it is not clear who will enforce it.

Over the next few months, it is likely that the combination of winter and Russia's endemic military disorganisation will hurt the invading forces more than the defenders, although the greatest misery is now borne by the 120,000 refugees.

So far there is no sign of a political compromise between Russia and Chechnya's leadership. Russia has dusted down the collaborationist Chechen parliament which it used in the previous war, and partly withdrawn its grudging recognition of the Chechen government and president. The Russian side has so far provided no evidence of the terrorist training camps that the war is meant to destroy.

The most worrying thought is that the war may be a prelude to a wider conflict. Russia has denied Azerbaijani claims that its air force bombed a village in Azerbaijan on October 1st, although it has admitted bombing villages in Georgia last month, and has increased the number of soldiers based there. Russia has warned Azerbaijan not to allow aid to Chechnya to cross its territory. In Shia Muslim (but not very devout) Azerbaijan, and in Orthodox Christian Georgia, people are united in hoping against hope that their hard-won modicum of stability, and independence from Russia, are not about to be forfeited.

involvement in spectacular acts of violence. The other factor was the emergence, in the morass of lawlessness and poverty that has engulfed both republics, of a new and more zealous form of Islam, mainly imported from Saudi Arabia.

A few weeks ago, Mr Basaev and his militant Dagestani friends (who, at least so far, have been a small, unpopular minority among their compatriots) proclaimed a sort of mini-state inside Dagestan. They spoke of creating a Russia-free zone stretching at least from Chechnya to the Caspian Sea. In its biggest show of force for three years, the Russian high command blasted the rebels with fighter-bombers and artillery. By early September, it claimed to have forced them to retreat from Dagestan into Chechnya.

The story took an entirely new turn with a series of bomb attacks in Russian cities in September. The worst, on September 13th, claimed 119 lives. The authorities were quick to blame the explosions on Chechen terrorists, though they did not provide evidence, and Chechen leaders denied involvement.

Many people in Russia did not need any evidence; the government's allegations simply confirmed the anti-Chechen, and generally anti-Caucasian, prejudice they already harboured. Other Russians take a more cynical view. They believe the bomb attacks are somehow related to the power struggle raging in Moscow as the "courtiers" of President Yeltsin try to cling to their power and privilege in the face of looming electoral defeat.

Even those who believe that Chechens, and only Chechens, are responsible for the bombs have had their faith tested at times. In the town of Ryazan, the security services were caught virtually red-handed after placing a quantity of explosives in an apartment building. They claimed it was part of an exercise to "test the readiness" of the population.

Such incidents are grist to the mill of Moscow's conspiracy theorists. Some believe that the bombs were indeed the work of Chechen extremists, but insist that the fighting in the south is mainly the result of Russian provocation; some say it is the other way round. Whatever the truth, the crisis has certainly played into the hands of the most hardline elements in Russia's leadership. But there are also signs that people from outside Russia have been stirring the pot.

Mark Galeotti, a British lecturer on Russia's armed forces, says there is evidence that Mr bin Laden, while not the instigator of the urban bombing campaign, has offered financial help to its perpetrators. And fighters under the influence of Mr bin Laden have certainly been active in Chechnya and Dagestan—though their presence is probably not the main reason why war is raging now.

With or without some mischief-making by dark forces in Moscow, Russia would have a problem in the northern Caucasus. Hostility between Russians and Chechens goes back to the north Caucasian wars of the 19th century, when the tsar's forces took more than 50 years to bring the Chechens under control. As well as strong family loyalties, part of the glue that held the Chechens and other north Caucasian people together was Sufism, the mystical strand of Islam.

Although Sufism is often associated with contemplation, among the proud mountain clans of Chechnya and Dagestan it acquired a strongly anti-Russian flavour. The Sufi sheikhs, or holy men, preached that a true Muslim could not tolerate the rule of foreign infidels. There were two acceptable forms of *jihad*, or holy war. A Muslim could serve Allah as a fighter or as a scholar. The Chechens became famous for their warrior prowess, the Dagestanis for their Koranic learning.

The Bolshevik revolution of 1917 promised to liberate all the subject peoples of the tsarist empire. As civil war loomed, Lenin and Stalin made a cynical bid for Muslim support by promising the creation of semi-independent Islamic states in Russia and Central Asia, saying: "All you whose mosques and houses of prayer have been destroyed, whose beliefs and customs have been flouted by the tsars and the oppressors of Russia—from now on your beliefs and customs, your national and cultural institutions are free and inviolable."

The reality of Soviet rule was, of course, very different. Periods of repression alternated with periods of relative toleration, but repression was the norm. In 1944, the Chechens (along with seven other ethnic groups) were deported en masse to Kazakhstan as part of Stalin's policy of punishing "untrustworthy" ethnic groups. But Chechen culture, in particular, proved remarkably hard to destroy.

By the 1980s, there were estimated to be 50m Soviet citizens of Muslim ancestry. For most of them, Soviet rule had had a powerful secularising effect. Out of cultural habit, many still circumcised their baby boys and buried their dead according to Muslim custom. But the closure of all but a handful of mosques, and the virtual end of religious education, meant that knowledge of Islam had nearly evaporated.

Among the few places in the Soviet Union where Islam remained fairly strong was the northern Caucasus. The Sufi tradition was well able to survive in semi-clandestine conditions. Even without mosques, the Chechens were able to go on venerating the memory of their local sheikhs and performing traditional dances and chants. Anna Zelkina, a Russian expert on Islam, says the KGB knew a lot about the Sufi brotherhoods, but found Sufism too deeply rooted to be eradicated.

Enter the Wahhabis

Since the collapse of the Soviet Union in 1991, the Sufi tradition has faced a challenge of a very different type. Emissaries from the Arab world, especially Saudi Arabia, have flooded into the Caucasus and Central Asia, seeing an opportunity in the spiritual and economic wasteland left by Marxist ideology.

Financed by Saudi petrodollars, these preachers have begun propagating a new form of Islam, which has become known (through a slight over-simplification) as Wahhabism: in other words, the austere form of Islam dominant in Saudi Arabia. The new version of Islam strives to be as close as possible to the faith's 1,400-year-old roots. It opposes the secularism of Russian life. Its universalising message aims to transcend ethnic and linguistic barriers, and it has no place for the local cults of Sufism.

Many Chechens and Dagestanis find the new form of Islam alien and uncomfortable, and some actively oppose it. It has caused division, and even violence, within families. But by building mosques and establishing scholarships, the Wahhabis have won a following, especially among the young—often impatient with what they see as a corrupt official religious establishment left over from Soviet times. Moreover, in the confusion of post–Soviet Russia, the new creed offers disillusioned and unemployed young men money and weapons and a sense of purpose which they cannot find anywhere else.

"For the disenchanted," writes Nabi Abdullaev, a journalist based in Makhachkala, the Dagestani capital, "Wahhabism has become a spiritual refuge." At first, the Wahhabis acted peacefully. They took over a few villages in Dagestan and established new communities where their strict interpretation of Islam was followed. But they gradually began to arm themselves and set up semi-autonomous enclaves where they enforced the *sharia* (Islamic law).

They claimed they needed weapons for self-defence because of harassment by the police and the local authorities. But local officials became convinced they were dangerous foreign-backed fanatics. In 1997, the Dagestani authorities outlawed "Wahhabism" and a number of the movement's leaders were arrested. Some escaped, with or without their followers, into neighbouring Chechnya. With its long tradition of warrior prowess, Chechnya became the military base of the "new Islam", and Mr Basaev its military leader.

A daredevil hijacker and hostage-taker, Mr Basaev took part in the Russian-backed war against Georgia in 1992–93, and then fought ruthlessly against Russia in the Chechen war of 1994–96. Trained in the Soviet army, he now says his life's mission is to wage holy war against Russia and avenge its crimes against his people. He is not himself a Wahhabi, but he seems to have decided that the new Muslims would make useful recruits for his *jihad*, even though he does not share their extreme puritanism.

Mr Basaev is both a Muslim and a Chechen patriot; the two qualities are inseparable. But despite his bushy beard and talk of holy wars, he does not quite correspond to the image of a single-minded fundamentalist. His heroes, after all, include Garibaldi and Abraham Lincoln. There is, however, another member of the Basaev camp who comes closer to fitting the bill: a young Arab fighter known as Khattab, whose trademark is a mane of long black hair.

Educated in Saudi Arabia, Khattab fought the Russians in Afghanistan before settling in Chechnya. In other words, he is one of the "Afghanis"—the 15,000 or so volunteers from all over the Middle East (particularly Saudi Arabia, Yemen, Egypt and Algeria) who did battle, with strong American support, against the Soviet occupiers of Afghanistan. Since the war ended, these fighters have returned to their homelands, or moved to other countries, in search of new Islamist causes to fight.

It is the existence of the Afghanis (of whom the most notorious is Mr bin Laden himself) which helps to explain why Russia regards its own Islamic adversaries as Frankensteinian monsters created by western governments and their friends in Saudi Arabia and Pakistan. The Afghani connection also helps to explain why Russia and Iran see eye-to-eye on the question of Islamist violence. As well as loathing the West and all its works, some of the Afghanis—as zealous practitioners of Sunni Islam—are sworn enemies of the Shia Muslim faith, of which Iran is the main bastion.

Ramzi Youzef, the Afghani (and protégé of Mr bin Laden) who was convicted of bombing the World Trade Centre, has also been linked with the June 1994 bombing of a Shia holy place in Iran. From Iran's point of view, both the Afghanis and the Taliban movement that now controls most of Afghanistan are manifestations of the Sunni fundamentalism that has been called into existence by the United States and its friends.

Iran has always been resentful of America's connections with Saudi Arabia and Pakistan, even though its own relations with those two countries have been improving. Russia sympathises, to put it mildly, with that resentment. America, for its part, is highly suspicious of Russia's friendship with Iran.

The many faces of Islam

If there is a geopolitical stand-off involving Russia, America and the Islamic world, it is not a simple triangle. If anything, Russia and America have each identified different bits of the Islamic world as friends, and each is suspicious of the other's partnerships.

Although Russian diplomacy has been quite adept at manipulating the geopolitical divisions within the Muslim world, there is a real possibility that its own clumsiness and brutality could create a Muslim enemy within its borders, as well as alienating Muslims farther afield. Already, the Kremlin's heavy-handedness has galvanised the Chechens to mobilise for a new war against Russia. The neighbouring Ingush people, related to the Chechens but hitherto willing to accept Russian authority, may now be drawn into the conflict—along with at least four or five other north Caucasian peoples who have until now been content to let Russia run their affairs.

If Russia found itself at war with half a dozen Muslim peoples in the Caucasus, the effects would certainly be felt in places farther north, such as Tatarstan. Tatarstan's leader, Mintimer Shaimiev, has trodden a careful line between co-operation with the Kremlin and indulging the anti-Slavic feelings of local Tatar nationalists and Muslims. In recent days, he has insisted that no conscripts from his republic will fight Russia's war in the Caucasus.

But if some sort of common Muslim front ever emerges in Russia, resentment of Moscow will be the only factor that holds it together. In the Caucasus and elsewhere, Muslims are fragmented; there is not even a united or coherent Wahhabi movement.

Nor is there any natural unity between Chechnya and Dagestan. Chechnya (a bit smaller than Wales) is ethnically homogeneous. Dagestan (the size of Scotland) is a mosaic of 34 distinct ethnic groups. The two also differ over their relations with Russia. The Chechens still feel the scars of their last war with the Russians, and so the secessionist impulse is much stronger than in Dagestan, which has little sense of a common national identity and is economically heavily dependent on Russia.

Nor is it inevitable that Islamic militancy in the northern Caucasus and in other parts of the Muslim world will reinforce one another. Rather than being proof that political Islam is spreading, the fighting in the Caucasus is a reminder that Islam exists in many different forms. In the heartland of the Muslim world, the Middle East, the wave of Islamic militancy appears to be receding. In the early 1980s, the years immediately after the Iranian revolution, the Arab countries and Turkey felt themselves most vulnerable to political Islam.

Those expectations are now subsiding. Egypt, Tunisia, Saudi Arabia—all countries that experienced serious Islamic opposition—have survived, bruised but intact. Even Algeria, where Islamism took the most violent form and was suppressed with particular harshness, seems to have entered a more hopeful phase.

Olivier Roy, a French expert on Islamic movements, believes that the phenomenon has moved from the centre to the periphery—from the Middle East to the fringes of the Muslim world. In the Middle East, the main promoter of political Islam (the Iranian revolution) came in 1979, so the movements which imitated the Iranian experience have had two decades to play themselves out.

In the Caucasus and Central Asia, as in former Yugoslavia, the moment of opportunity for political Islam came a decade or so later, with the collapse of communism, and so the new Islamic movements are younger and still developing. They are a powerful and potentially destabilising force, but they are no more destined to win power than their equivalents elsewhere.

There is, however, a form of "peripheral" Islam which ought to be giving Russian policymakers food for thought: the impressive strength of the Muslim faith, sometimes accompanied by political radicalism, in western cities that lie thousands of miles from the heartlands of Islam. From Detroit to Lyons, young Muslims have been rediscovering their beliefs and identity—often as a reaction against the poverty, racism and (as they would see it) sterile secularism of the societies around them. This phenomenon owes nothing to geopolitical calculation, or to the policies of any government, either western or Middle Eastern; nor can it be restrained by government action. If radical forms of Islam can flourish in places like Glasgow and Frankfurt, there is no reason why they cannot do so in Moscow and Murmansk—particularly if the Russian government seems to be fighting a brutal, pointless war at the other end of the country.

Unit 8

Key Points to Consider

❖ Pick an Asian country, describe recent economic and political trends, and explain why you believe this country is or is not likely to continue recovering from the economic crisis within the next few years.

❖ Is it in the United States' interest to promote economic reforms in China? Why, or why not?

❖ What types of political changes do you expect to see in Southeast Asian countries over the next decade?

❖ What are some of the advantages and disadvantages of Japan playing a more activist role in world affairs—for Japan? Asian neighbors? The United States?

 **Links** **www.dushkin.com/online/**

These sites are annotated on pages 6 and 7.

Conventional wisdom about economic development was shaken by the economic instability experienced by the Asian "tigers" and by a prolonged recession in Japan. Analysts now worry about the political fallout from the economic downturn on domestic political stability. Jonathan Lemco and Scott MacDonald in "Is the Asian Financial Crisis Over?" describe how most Asian economies were recovering by the end of 1999. They note that the financial crisis will have a lingering impact on the region and present three possible future scenarios that will determine whether the current reform process will be successful. The economic slowdown crisis occurred at the same time as a relatively unstable Pacific Basin security environment experienced a series of shocks. Indian and Pakistani nuclear tests and North Korea's continued development of missiles raised new security concerns.

The slowdown started during 1997 in Thailand's supercharged economy, when a run on the local currency burst the speculative bubble. Thailand was the first of several Asian tigers to devalue its currency and to accept harsh austerity measures as a condition for an IMF bailout package. The Thai crisis triggered a wider regional slowdown. By early 1998 local stock markets had lost two-thirds of their value, unemployment was rising, prices skyrocketing, living standards were falling, and recession spread throughout the region.

Some analysts now view the Southeast Asian currency crises of 1997 as part of a pattern of financial instability that often accompanies rapid economic growth. These analysts predict that Asian economies will continue to grow and account for over half the world's income by 2025. However, as David Martin Jones and Mike Smith explain in "Tigers Ready to Roar?" debates continue about whether recent economic recovery is a meaningful upswing fueled by consumer demand in the United States or a temporary recovery. Most analysts agree that sustained economic recovery will require growth in the economies of both Japan and China.

Although its economy has also slowed, to date China has managed to avoid a currency devaluation. The downturn of Hong Kong's stock market was another blow. Although the transition from Great Britain to China went smoothly, Hong Kong experienced a dramatic drop-off in tourism and a sell-off of property stocks after the island reverted to Chinese control.

China is struggling with the dislocations caused by government efforts to reform its "iron rice bowl" economy based on socialistic principles. Economic reforms are eliminating many of the subsidies for food, housing, and jobs that have been promised to all citizens under socialism. China is also eliminating nonperforming state entities and halving the number of state workers. The result is massive unemployment, growing resentment with increased disparities, and a fundamental change in the relationship between the state, the Communist Party, and workers.

Zhu Rongji, Prime Minister since March 1998, is implementing these reforms in a cautious, piecemeal fashion over a 3-year period. Inefficient state enterprises must close. State banks must eliminate bad loans from their books and only make loans on commercial terms. The government is supporting a housing and investment boom in the hope that private business will be able to employ millions who are being released from state enterprises and the military. As the military downsizes and shifts to a volunteer force, millions of demobilized former soldiers are joining the ranks of the unemployed. The government is also trying to reform and dismantle the huge corporate complex of over 1,500 businesses currently run by the military.

The Chinese government celebrated the fiftieth anniversary of Communist rule with a massive military parade in 1999. The celebrations followed a widespread crackdown on the now banned spiritual sect Falun Gong. The government views this growing spiritual movement as a potential threat to communist rule and has detained hundreds of followers.

Despite continued repression at home, China's foreign policies increasingly resemble those of a status quo power. China works closely with the United States, Japan, and other major powers to cope with regional problems. Most analysts predict that China will continue to cooperate with the United States and other major powers as long as it believes it is regaining its rightful place in the world after a century of "humiliation." Concern mounted during 1999 when China threatened to use military force against Taiwan if Taiwan moved toward independence. The Chinese government was reacting to statements made by President Lee Teng-Hui that viewed Taiwan as a separate sovereign state. In "Does China Matter?" Gerald Segal goes further than much of the conventional wisdom in discounting the importance of China as an emerging power. Segal outlines the reasons why China is overrated as a market, a military or political power, and a source of ideas in international relations.

Spreading economic problems throughout Southeast Asia threaten three decades of political stability. The economic crisis in Asia wiped out the gains of a large proportion of middle class citizens. The economic upheaval that has occurred to date is fueling major political changes in Thailand, Malaysia, Singapore, Vietnam, Indonesia, and the Philippines. Many analysts believe that major political change has only just begun. The reaction of a government-backed militia to an independence vote in East Timor in 1999 seemed to confirm these predictions.

Japan's continuing recession and banking crisis has had a major effect on the region. The government's several reform packages, introduced since 1997, failed to restore confidence in Japan's shaky financial system initially. However, the government is now moving slowly to stimulate the revamping of the Japan's economy. Economic reforms that are not politically popular are being implemented.

Japan is trying to cope with economic recession at the same time that it is redefining its role in world affairs. A more activist role for Japan is supported by a majority of the public. In "Tokyo's Depression Diplomacy," Yoichi Funabashi describes how Japan now faces its biggest foreign policy challenges since World War II. Funabashi warns that Japan's current pessimism threatens world prosperity.

Policymakers worldwide focus on the instability of the North Korean government because there is continuing uncertainty about what foreign policies the leader of this isolationist nation-state is likely to pursue. In "Toward a Comprehensive Settlement of the Korea Problem," Bruce Cumings explains why the ongoing humanitarian emergency and the needs of the North Korean economy provide opportunities to transform the security stalemate on the Korean peninsula. Cumings predicts that there will be movement toward eventual reconciliation and reunion.

Although a number of arguments have been advanced to explain Asia's turnaround, they "do not take into account another, deeper cause for Asia's recovery—one that also leads us to recommend caution about the extent of that recovery."

Is the Asian Financial Crisis Over?

JONATHAN LEMCO AND SCOTT B. MACDONALD

By the end of 1998, much of Asia had fallen victim to a severe economic reversal. Currencies were in free fall, growth had stalled, foreign investors were either fleeing or sharply reducing their commitments, and joblessness was increasing. Before the crisis, Asian economies had been among the most dynamic in the world. Now it appeared that growth in South Korea, Indonesia, Thailand, Malaysia, the Philippines, and Hong Kong would be negative. Even the well-managed Singaporean and Taiwanese economies suffered slowdowns related to the collapse of regional markets. Japan, the world's second-largest economy, was also mired in a steep recession and its banks were hit hard by a wave of nonperforming loans at home and elsewhere in Asia. China was expected to devalue its currency, which would enhance its export competitiveness but diminish that of the region's other major exporters. Pronouncements about the dawn of the Asian century became distant echoes.

JONATHAN LEMCO *is senior international research analyst at KWR International. He previously was the director of sovereign risk research at Credit Suisse First Boston and a professor of political science at the Johns Hopkins University Paul Nitze School of Advanced International Studies.* SCOTT B. MACDONALD *is the chief economist and director of investor relations at KWR International. He is the former director of sovereign research at Donaldson, Lufkin and Jenrette and served as international economic adviser at the Office of the Comptroller of the Currency from 1988 to 1993.*

One year later the picture appears far less bleak. Improved growth forecasts, less onerous unemployment numbers, and increasingly positive trade balances are the norm throughout the region. International investors are cautiously bringing their money back; according to the Washington-based Institute of International Finance, private capital inflows to Asia are expected to rebound from a low of $8.6 billion in 1998 to $39.3 billion in 1999. Asian households are consuming again. The perception in the region is that the worst of the crisis is over.

What led to Asia's seemingly quick turnaround? Regional specialists offer a number of interrelated factors, including the fiscal prudence demonstrated by many Asian governments before and during the worst of the crisis; the apparent commitment by many Asian leaders to meaningful private sector reform (especially in South Korea, Japan, and Thailand); the sudden confidence-building interest-rate cuts in the United States; continued evidence of new economic growth in Western Europe; and the IMF's insistence that Indonesia, South Korea, and Thailand raise interest rates to bolster their currencies (although we have strong doubts about the viability of this suggestion).

These arguments, however, do not take into account another, deeper cause for Asia's recovery—one that also leads us to recommend caution about the extent of that recovery. The Asian nations were never the economic basket cases as some portrayed them in 1998. Most Asian states, unlike their Latin American counterparts in the 1980s, did not run budget deficits, managed their public sectors, and maintained low-inflation environments. Thus, when the crisis broke, the public sector side was able to rebound (with the assistance of the IMF)—hence

Reprinted with permission from *Current History* magazine, December 1999, pp. 433-437. © 1999 by Current History, Inc.

Asia's rapid recovery. Although Asian political leaders may speak in glowing terms of their reform agendas, especially the modest government pressure to reform that has been exerted on domestic financial institutions and the largest industrial enterprises, the evidence of meaningful private sector reform throughout the region is mixed, with some nations faring better than others. Furthermore, greater progress has been made with regard to financial sector reform than to corporate reform. Let us put this discussion into context by addressing briefly the root causes of the financial crisis.

"A RECIPE FOR DISASTER"

The Asian financial crisis surprised many analysts and economists. Most of the economies in the region had pursued prudent fiscal policies. Public sector debt was fairly low. Trade and current account balances were in surplus or in only mild deficit (with the exception of Thailand). Foreign direct investment was on the rise. Inflation and unemployment levels were negligible. Savings rates were among the highest in the world. Most important, growth rates were extraordinary. For example, Thailand's real GNP average growth rate was 7.3 percent between 1965 and 1996, and South Korea's was 8.9 percent. These positive economic conditions were coupled with an almost unprecedented degree of political stability in the region.

The onset of the crisis was surprising because it originated primarily in the private sector. A surge of private capital inflows in the form of bank loans and portfolio investments led to asset-price inflation that fueled a speculative bubble. A considerable amount of foreign-borrowed money was channeled into problematic real estate and other projects throughout Southeast Asia and South Korea. In 1996 Thailand, for example, received the equivalent of 3 percent of its GDP in short-term capital inflows, and its foreign debt stood at 50 percent of GDP.

This debt was critical. Much of the external debt of countries such as South Korea, Indonesia, and Thailand was short-term and concentrated in the private sector. In addition, wage costs throughout the region were rising while foreign demand for Asia's high-tech exports was declining. But the failure of many regional governments to delink from the dollar after it appreciated against their currencies in 1996—which meant that the debt denominated in dollars began to rise—was the critical factor in exacerbating the debt burden.

As exports stagnated and with foreign lending diverted into risky real estate ventures, there was a substantial risk that Asia's banks and finance companies would be unable to service their debts if exchange rates weakened. Governments' fixed exchange rates reduced their capacity to react to the crisis quickly. Foreign currency debt loans were high relative to the private sector's ability to finance repayments as well as to the availability of foreign exchange (foreign exchange reserves were falling throughout the region, with the notable exception of China). These factors, taken together, were a recipe for disaster. Once Thailand devalued its currency on July 2, 1997, panic-stricken international investors, seeking total security, began to move their money out of Asia and other emerging

markets to United States Treasury bonds. It was an old-fashioned bank run.

Banks, currency speculators, and hedge funds discovered that when they lost money in one Asian country, they had to pull money out of another one to successfully manage their risk exposures in emerging markets. Institutional investors followed suit, and this aggravated the panic.

Other culprits were at work also. Crony capitalism was pervasive in many Asian economies. Government contracts were awarded unfairly and on the basis of personal connections. Bankers, especially in Thailand and South Korea, were too close to senior government officials. Bank debt was rolled over and insolvent banks allowed to continue to operate. This encouraged many bankers to take inappropriate risks, overextending credit as well as concentrating it in a few sectors, such as real estate. Heavy foreign investment, combined with weak financial regulation, had allowed lenders throughout the region to rapidly expand credit, often to high-risk borrowers, thereby making the financial system even more vulnerable.

The IMF has been criticized, sometime scathingly, for offering the wrong advice during the worst of the crisis. Some analysts insisted that urging the Asian nations to raise interest rates in an effort to stabilize their currencies was exactly the wrong approach. This critique has some merit. Credit-rating agencies also played a role in exacerbating the crisis; their rapid downgrading of South Korea's and Thailand's creditworthiness accelerated the dramatic outflow of capital from those countries. But it is too easy to blame the IMF, the rating agencies, and the Asian governments for the crisis—investors were not blameless either.

From the mid-1980s through 1997, investors were quick to put money into a region that seemed to be doing everything right. They ignored the evidence of crony capitalism in favor of large returns. Indeed, conducting business with cronies often was preferred. This could be seen in investor relations with the family and close associates of Indonesia's President Suharto.

At the same time, many investors did not subject Asia markets to the same stringent tests they applied to United States corporate bond issuers. Investors relied too much on the opinions of the credit-rating agency analysts, who were investigating only part of the story, and investment bankers, who had a vested interest in selling Asian bonds and equities.

RECOVERY BEGUN . . .

This emerging understanding of the financial crisis's causes has led to a rethinking of the economic policymaking environment in Asia. It is here that the critical battle to reform Asia's economies will likely be won or lost.

Before the crisis the economic policymaking environment was dominated by a broad regional consensus on the need for economic growth. Government and other key political actors made economic growth their focus. Now the focus has changed. Technocrats are under considerable pressure to demonstrate their effectiveness; gone is the senior bureaucrat's ability to implement sometimes harsh economic programs without public discussion. Politicians have shifted from building consensus to accommodating political change. This includes a new environment where social and ethnic differences are more politically salient than before and where demands are articulated for greater accountability in the political process.

For the domestic business elite the shift in focus may mean an end to the opaque nature of business and the unhealthy coziness with the public sector and a dominant bank. In their place are newly established independent regulatory agencies, demands for greater financial transparency and disclosure, and a revised, arm's-length relationship with the banks. For the banks, it also means adoption of a credit culture that emphasizes sound business practices over personal relationships.

The business sector is where the greatest battles are being fought to create a new competitive Asia—and their outcome will have an enormous impact on the last group involved in the economic policymaking environment: the broader public. Before the crisis, many Asian citizens were focused on economic growth and the attainment of a better standard of living. In the wake of the crisis, Asian publics are demanding greater accountability and new skills from not just the government, but also the bureaucrats, the politicians, and the business community.

The objective of this new economic paradigm is to create an Asia that is more transparent, efficient, and responsive to the public's needs through more market-driven policies. This implies a major overhaul of old political and economic relationships, the discarding of bad habits, and an embrace of things new and difficult. Although the current recovery of economic growth rates helps move the process along, pitfalls remain.

...AND SUSTAINED

Several events must occur to maximize the chances that Asia's recovery will be sustained. First, it is vital that the United States economy continue to prosper and that American and other international consumers continue to import Asian products. In this regard, the yen-dollar exchange rate is key, for if the yen continues to strengthen, Japanese products will become prohibitively expensive for Americans. The Japanese central bank may have to intervene to weaken the currency in coordination with other G-7 countries, such as the United States and Germany.

In addition, since Japan is the most important economic power in Asia, it is urgent that the island nation reduce its large public debt, currently a staggering $5.4 trillion, approximately 100 percent of GDP. Debt at this level could lead to higher interest rates. Should this occur, long-term interest rates would likely rise elsewhere in the world, further stifling growth.

Macroeconomic policymaking in non- Japan Asia must also remain fiscally prudent, and economic indicators must remain

> *The financial crisis in Asia may be over, but the new era is one fraught with exceedingly difficult decisions.*

positive. Here the news is largely upbeat. Inflation is low and declining. Domestic savings throughout the region remain among the highest in the world. There is a large pool of workers and high potential productivity gains through technology transfer. Exports are gradually increasing and consumers are spending again. Most notably, many analysts expect better policymaking to continue to improve economic growth rates.

During the financial crisis, Asian governments adhered to orthodox monetary and fiscal policies and kept their markets open (Malaysia partly excepted), and this has maintained the region's attractiveness for foreign direct investment. Regarding monetary policy, the region's central-bank governors have stressed the importance of price stability. They did not print money to deal with their banking crisis and seem prepared to raise interest rates when necessary. The cost of this tight monetary policy was a deep recession and a collapse in private sector investment. But the payoff has been a spectacular turnaround in trade and investment performance. Asia is earning its way out of the crisis and paying down its bank debt.

Another key to sustaining growth in Asia will be the ability to raise capital in the world's equity and bond markets, and to develop local currency fixed-income markets. To this end, some Asian nations are making efforts to improve the performance of their financial systems by enhancing the degree of transparency, enforcing stricter auditing procedures, and granting more rights to minority shareholders. The nations of Asia also must continue to secure bank loans when necessary, but developing their domestic stock and bond markets will be even more vital.

One recent positive sign has been the performance of some of these equity markets. The South Korean and Singaporean stock markets are now ahead of where they were before the beginning of the financial crisis in 1997, despite a slower pace in October 1999. Also, in just the past year, the stock markets of Thailand and Malaysia have doubled in value. Most of the region's other stock markets—including Japan's—have also improved. This phenomenon has occurred much more quickly than virtually all analysts had predicted, and reflects, in part, some of the fundamental strengths of these economies. Most notable is the benign mix of low interest rates and stronger export performance.

If the nations of Asia are to compete effectively in increasing exports or attracting more foreign direct investment, they must look at nonfinancial issues as well, especially telecommunications infrastructure. Although Asia has become the world's information-technology hardware factory, the adoption and application of these new technologies has been uneven. Capturing the productivity gains from technology will require high levels of investment both in manufacturing hardware and in raising education levels. Given the high debt of some Asian nations, it remains to be seen how willing they will be to invest in the technology training required.

Another nonfinancial concern is the need to contain strategic threats if growth in the region is to be sustained. If these economies must devote scarce resources to their military capabilities, then economic growth will decline. The intensification of conflicts between China and Taiwan, South and North Korea, and growing internal strife in Indonesia would hamper a full economic recovery for these nations.

THE CHALLENGES

Clearly, sustaining economic growth in Asia will be a challenge. Obstacles to overcome include the difficulties of implementing financial sector and corporate reform, as well as dealing with high debt and growing levels of economic inequality.

The region's banking systems are especially in need of changes. For many years, banks in China, South Korea, and Thailand especially lent money to problematic companies with little regard for the credit risks. Many banks were tied to large conglomerates, and consequently there was minimal independent regulatory supervision. (Singapore, Malaysia, Taiwan, and the Philippines were notable exceptions to this regional trend.) In general, progress in banking reform has been slower than in other areas. This will remain the case until the importance of credit risk and reward within the financial services sector are more fully appreciated. Malaysia is overhauling its banking system by reducing its 58 financial institutions into 6 superbanks. Korea has sold some poorly managed and unprofitable banks, merged many, and closed others. Thailand has sold 2 banks to foreign entities. But in general, the relationships among banks, governments, and corporations remain too cozy.

A related problem for many of these economies is the weak or nonexistent enforcement of bankruptcy laws. Too many insolvent financial institutions are government-supported, and the courts choose not to make the hard decisions to close them. Yet the quick recovery has removed the sense of political urgency that forced the positive changes that have occurred. The reform process has slowed, but many problems remain and could worsen.

Still, most Asian economies are likely to witness a continuing reduction of government involvement in the private sector. In an effort to attract foreign investment, Asian nations will have little choice but to permit greater market liberalization, especially in the financial sector. At the same time that governments are reducing their economic roles, they may increase their presence in other ways, including establishing more government regulatory powers and providing stronger social safety nets. Systems of corporate governance are likely to change, and provisions for more transparency in corporate accounting and reporting practices will become evident. In the long run, pressure will mount for the overhaul of large, highly diversified industrial conglomerates in South Korea, Thailand, Indonesia, and Malaysia.

The economic shakeout might also accelerate the process of political change in the region. This is most obvious in Indonesia and possibly Malaysia, but we are likely to see an intensification of pressures for more competitive political party systems in other Asian economies as well. As economic inequality in Asia increases, and as popular awareness of this inequality becomes more pervasive, the economic underclasses are likely to demand a greater role in the political process. In the medium to long term, new parties may emerge to challenge the established ones.

THREE PATHS TO THE FUTURE

The financial crisis in Asia may be over, but the new era is one fraught with exceedingly difficult decisions that will pull the region either into the globalized international economy or doom it to regressing into a second-rate manufacturing zone, vulnerable to external shocks. Three scenarios for Asia in the post-financial crisis era are briefly described.

The first is a boom scenario in which external factors continue to be positive: moderate to strong economic growth continues in the United States, Canada, and Europe; commodity prices firm up; and interest rates in key markets remain relatively low. Within Asia, governments continue to support reform programs, forcing local corporate sectors to become more competitive by focusing on core areas of expertise, adding to shareholder clout, and overhauling banking sectors. Under this scenario, foreign direct investment increases, and as foreign companies enter local markets they help reinforce and accelerate change. Although initially difficult to implement and often increasing unemployment, these changes ultimately will strengthen Asian economies and businesses. The reforms should put the region back on track with rapid growth, improved living conditions for the majority of its citizens, and a stronger concept of the rule of law and the need for a just society. This scenario also envisions a reduction in regional political tensions, with a desire to resolve issues by diplomacy or through the ballot box. By 2001 Asia is once again riding high. This is a highly optimistic outlook, and it has only a small chance of occurring.

The second scenario is one of gloom and doom. A number of governments slow the pace of structural reform as economic growth initially returns, indicating that the crisis is over and the hardships endured were indeed short-lived. However, this is a false dawn. After a couple of years of strong economic growth, another crisis hits the region because politicians, senior bureaucrats, and corporate leaders are not fully committed to the reform process. The half-reformed corporate and banking sectors cannot withstand the new round of troubles, and the crisis is worse than in 1997 and 1998. Adding to this, Asia's political situation has only worsened. China, Indonesia, and Malaysia are marked by political tensions. China's leaders, hard-pressed by domestic unrest over the stagnation in economic growth, decide to play the nationalist card and are increasingly aggressive in pursuing their claims to Taiwan and the South China Sea. They also become much more forceful with their Central Asian neighbors, which results in a sharp increase in unrest among China's Muslim population in the northwest. Japan is in no condition to counter Chinese actions since its political system has spawned further political fragmentation and a rapid rotation of weak and ineffective coalition governments, marked by an inability to create, let alone implement, any lasting policies. By 2002 Asia is once again mired in economic crisis. This scenario also has little chance of coming to fruition.

The last scenario is more gradual and probably the most realistic. Growth is up, inflation remains low, and unemployment falls below crisis levels. Local equity and debt markets develop as well as more sophisticated financial systems. Significantly, a credit culture is developing within the banking systems that screen good loans from bad. Additionally, the central banks become more independent, and political party systems become more competitive. However, the recovery will remain tenuous and a number of factors, most internal, but some external, can lead the region back to crisis.

This scenario will be characterized by more short-term hardship in terms of high unemployment, corporate up-heaval in the form of mergers and acquisitions, and the evolution of democratic government. Under this scenario, the economic growth many Asian countries began to enjoy in 1999 will continue in 2000 and 2001, but at a more moderate pace than in the past two decades. Yet the recovery will not be across the board. Simply stated, those countries making the reforms will benefit the most from foreign direct investment and achieve a more sustainable recovery than those that do not.

Whichever scenario comes to pass, clearly Asia's financial crisis will have a lingering impact on the region's economic development. But although considerable damage was done, the potential exists for a new, stronger Asia. For all the nations of Asia, the reform process will encounter significant obstacles. Their eventual success will depend on the ability of regional leaders to make the tough but necessary policy choices.

TIGERS READY TO ROAR?

David Martin Jones
Mike Smith

Have the Asian economies, so recently in terminal decline, bounced back to miraculous recovery? Or are we seeing a short-term upswing fuelled by consumer demand in the United States? And is it international financial arrangements that need reform, rather than crony capitalism?

OVER THE PAST TWO YEARS students of East Asian political economy will have been struck by the rapid mood swings in their area. A wander through a Singapore bookshop in 1997 would have offered titles like *Negotiating the Pacific Century,* or *The New Rich in Asia: Mobile Phones, McDonald's and Middle-Class Revolution* or *The New Asian Renaissance.* A year on, these volumes, if not on special offer, gave way to titles like *Asia Falling* or *The Downsizing of Asia,* often by the same authors.

From being miracle economies demonstrating a variety of good practices long-term technocratic planning, high domestic savings rates, good basic education, low or non-existent welfare costs and close government-business links—they had been transformed into basket cases.

Former virtues had become structural defects. Far-sighted planning became market distortion, hiding cronyist relations between government and business conglomerates. In the deep recession, even high savings rates looked like a drag on consumption, whilst good basic education appeared like initiative stifling rote learning.

Between 1997 and 1998, Asian values turned into Asian vices and the Asian miracle looked about as authentic as the Turin Shroud. Stock exchanges from Seoul to Jakarta took an uninterrupted journey south.

DR DAVID MARTIN JONES is Senior Lecturer in Government at the University of Tasmania.
DR MIKE SMITH is Lecturer in the Department of War Studies, King's College, London.

Then something curious happened. In the first quarter of this year, Japan awoke from its decade-long recessive slumber, Asian economies returned to pre-crisis growth rates, trade balances swung back into surplus and the recession if not just a blip, looked like something that could be shrugged off.

WHAT WENT WRONG?

There are two explanations for the crisis, which began in Thailand in June 1997 with what Paul Krugman describes as an outbreak of 'bahtulism'. On the one hand, the less fashionable and market unfriendly school, led by Malaysian Prime Minister, Mahathir Mohamad, backed by an otherwise unsympathetic bunch of supporters ranging from Paul Krugman and George Soros to Gordon Brown and former Indonesian dictator Suharto, believe that it was a product of deregulated global capitalism.

Having opened their markets to global trade in the 1990s, the new boys on the international currency trading block—South Korea, Malaysia, Thailand, Indonesia and even financially streetwise Singapore and Hong Kong—were the innocent victims of a brutal mugging by a gang of spivish hedge funds and futures traders from New York, Chicago and London. From this perspective there was little wrong with Asian development that a few lessons in central banking and sovereign bond floating wouldn't fix.

The alternative, and until recently more popular hypothesis, held that it was the structural features of the Japanese sponsored Asian economic model that caused meltdown. In this view, cur-

From *The World Today,* October 1999, pp. 17-19. © 1999 by The World Today, a publication of the Royal Institute of International Affairs. Reprinted by permission.

rent account deficits, a speculative property boom, short-term borrowing to fund long-term investment and poor banking and financial regulation, that ran the spectrum from the inept and opaque to the fraudulent and corrupt, were major structural faults.

In 1997, world markets severely punished these defects. By mid-1998, currency contagion had left the region in turmoil with little to show for its vaunted developmental path apart from a profusion of under-patronised high rise hotels, unfinished office blocks and golf courses.

This academic disagreement has important political and economic ramifications because the cause of the crisis affects how state and international organisations like the International Monetary Fund (IMF) deal with its consequences. If Dr Mahathir's diagnosis is correct, and the medically trained doctor informs us that he is rarely wrong,[1] the prescription is a bit of rest and recuperation behind a wall of currency controls until the market returns to reason. The cure lies not in the reform of the Asian model but the building of new global financial architecture.

The IMF diagnosis, by contrast, requires a rigorous examination of the body politic, the excision of the cancer of corruption inherent in the intimate nature of business-government dealings, and the oxygen of rule-governed transparency supplied through the machinery of public accountability.

Ultimately, this implies a political and economic makeover rendering the rule of strong men and single parties accountable to the constitutional rule of law. Indeed, those most entranced by the prospect of the imminent demise of the Asian model have argued that the economies that successfully weathered the crisis were those that had made some strides along the apparently endless path of democratisation.

Let us briefly examine the apparent easing of the crisis and consider its implications for future economic and political developments.

SCENARIO 1: MIRACULOUS RECOVERY

Between 1997 and 1998, according to the World Bank, $115 billion fled the Asia-Pacific region. This was equivalent to eighteen percent of the region's Gross Domestic Product (GDP). Significantly, Japan, the pioneer of the Asian model, was both the major creditor of the ailing tiger economies and sent forty percent of its exports to Pacific Asia. Moreover, between fifteen and twenty-five percent of the exports of the meltdown economies went to a deflating Japan.

As regional trade accounted for almost a quarter of the total trade of these export oriented economies, lower consumer confidence in each receding tiger affected the export performance of its neighbour. After the currency panic of the summer of 1997, what seemed like a virtuous Asian circle of high savings and state engineered growth, turned into a recessionary spiral.

Remarkably, by the second quarter of this year, currencies had stabilised and growth had returned. Even the region's weakest economy, Indonesia, was showing some signs of life whilst the most successful Asian bounce back economies have grown by over five percent.

If the overused epithet 'miracle' has to be applied to the tiger economies, it should surely refer to this remarkable rise from the dead rather than the unsustainable growth in the 1980s. Regional stock markets have surged ahead, in the case of Singapore and Taiwan, surpassing pre-crisis levels.

Meanwhile, business confidence in Japan has risen sharply after a decade in the doldrums. South Korea's banks have posted $500 million in profits—compared with losses of $600 billion the previous year—and future growth is forecast at six percent.

From the perspective of Mahathir and his favourite economist, Paul Krugman, the recovery can be attributed to re-imposed monetary stability. With the exception of the Hong Kong dollar and the Chinese yuan, all the regional currencies were devalued as a result of hedge fund speculation and capital flight. Once the speculative dust settled and illiquid conglomerates and banks re-hydrated courtesy of the IMF, these economies could revert to the classic growth path.

Consequently, from Japan through South Korea to the Malay peninsula, imports have declined and exports grown because of their increasing affordability. Thus, Malaysia, Thailand, South Korea and Indonesia have all seen their ballooning trade deficits for 1993-97 reversed in the fiscal year 1998-99. At the same time, budgets have been balanced and investor confidence restored, foreign investment funds have even returned.

From this monetary perspective, severe alterations to Pacific Asian economic fundamentals are unnecessary. Here, the Malaysian case is salutary. In September 1998, Mahathir sacked his market friendly deputy, Anwar Ibrahim, and imposed both currency controls and restrictions on the movement of foreign investment funds from the Kuala Lumpur Stock Exchange.

To a chorus of international disapproval including Amnesty International, Presidents Habibie of Indonesia and Estrada of the Philippines, *The Business Times* (Singapore), *The Economist* as well as Al Gore—Malaysia's National Economic Action Council used the state apparatus to impose currency controls to restore financial stability and address foreign debt without recourse to the IMF.

Malaysia 'looked East' for liquidity.[2] Japanese loans, together with judicious raids on the state pension fund, provided the capital necessary to re-float faltering conglomerates linked to UMNO, Malaysia's ruling party.

Furthermore, in August, the Malaysian Central Bank announced plans to restructure Malaysia's indebted financial sector, combining fifty-eight banks and finance companies into six financial groups. Interestingly, this compulsory restructuring only reinforced the corporatist links between party and business. For the terms upon which banks were amalgamated depended not upon their bottom line but their ties to politically favoured UMNO patrons.[3]

Fuelled by a cheap currency and external demand for electronics, the Malaysian economy rebounded strongly in the second quarter of 1999. Moreover, when investment restrictions in Malaysia were lifted in September, foreign investors seemed happy to remain.

Malaysia's exceptionalism did not see it reduced to a regional pariah. Indeed, Mahathir maintains that those economies that had recourse to the IMF received inappropriate treatment. For alongside a necessary infusion of liquidity, Thailand, South Korea and Indonesia had to accept contradictory and often humiliating strictures on interest rates and debt restructuring. These made the recession and its political consequences far worse than it need have been. If little else, the Malaysian case demonstrates that, structural weakness notwithstanding, the developmental model could survive the challenges of globalisation.

SCENARIO 2: RATIONALISE NOT REFORM

Those less enamoured of Asian development argue by contrast that although Asia is certainly recovering from the very deep recession of 1997-98, structural problems continue. In this view, the initial panic was justified because of the undisclosed debt, cronyism, unaccountability and corruption from Japan to Jakarta.

The concern is that the recent 'bounce back' is unsustainable and obscures the urgent need for fundamental financial and political reform such as the restructuring of economies to ensure their long-term viability.

Short-term currency depreciations may give the likes of Thailand and Indonesia a renewed, but brief, lease of life as low cost manufacturers, but thorough supply side reforms in areas like education, training and financial regulation are absent.

Radical economic restructuring requires the break up of the crony capitalist relationships between businesses and their political friends in government. In the heady days of rapid economic growth, it was sometimes maintained that the cosy arrangements of informal deal making, preferential loans and *guanaxi* works were the lubricant of the Asian miracle. A recent survey by Harvard University's Center for International Development challenges this, arguing that the most significant feature of 'Asia's spectacular growth over the past several decades' was that it had been able to hide a 'host of inefficiencies.'[4]

Despite the shock of the meltdown, and the strictures of the IMF, there has been little fundamental change in local business culture and practice. In Thailand, the inadequacy of bankruptcy provisions permits technically insolvent businesses to continue trading. The courts are unable to enforce foreclosure and indebted companies refuse to repay loans.

In Indonesia, the most financially and politically damaged economy in the Asia-Pacific, IMF loans uncannily end up in the accounts of banks linked to the party of incumbent President Habibie.[5]

Even in South Korea, reform minded President Kim Dae Jung has been compelled to investigate the country's five main *chaebols*—business conglomerates—on suspicion that they are extending illegal preferential loans to their subsidiaries.

Meanwhile, the bureaucratic restrictions placed on western banks or companies taking over ailing South Korean concerns raise continuing doubts about commitment to reform. The fact that the government permits conglomerates like Hyundai and Daewoo to sustain debt levels exceeding $50 billion and debt/equity ratios over 350 percent indicates that the latest variant of the South Korean economic model is not driven by market considerations.[6] The Asian model has been rationalised rather than reformed.

Interestingly, then, whether we diagnose the causes of the Asian crisis from the perspective of Mahathir or the IMF, we can show that apart from some judicious financial tinkering, the basic Asian model and its export oriented character have not changed. Does this lack of structural reform matter?

Clearly, the Asian model was not quite the basket case it seemed in 1997. Problematically, however, the surge in exports from the region, whilst masking structural faults, is also causing new problems.

The pattern of Asia-Pacific trade has always been unbalanced. Japan has always assumed that it can protect its domestic markets while exporting high value-added technology. Since the 1980s, Japanese firms transferred labour intensive manufacturing to countries like Thailand and Malaysia.

The market for all this manufacturing continues to be the United States. Indeed, the strength of the US economy and the openness of its market has been central to Asia's recent recovery. The unexpectedly high demand there has single handedly revived the flagging electronic industries on which Thai, Malaysian and Indonesian growth depends.

Asian currencies are reviving along with their trade surpluses. Japan achieved a trade surplus of $118 billion to the end of March. To sustain this, the Japanese Central Bank intervenes in the foreign exchange markets to keep down the value of the yen. Other countries, like Singapore, have intervened in money markets. However, the US no longer accepts that 'manipulating currencies' can produce long term prosperity.[7] Given that the American economy has recently incurred record trade deficits and its growth is likely to slow, this could threaten the basis of Asian recovery and be a precursor to new trade disputes.

Moreover, in the meltdown, Japan lost its regional economic influence. Japanese banks were the first to take flight at the Asian contagion and their *sogoshosas*—trading companies are reluctant to return:[8] Mahathir's continuing infatuation with a 'look East' policy notwithstanding, Southeast Asian economies have become increasingly dependent on America and Europe for new foreign investment. This will ultimately alter the economic and political character of Southeast Asia.

In fact, meltdown and recession have already dramatically altered the international perception of Southeast Asia. Prior to the crisis, it was plausible to speak of common development patterns with export oriented growth dependent on Japanese investment, technocratic planning, single party rule and a governed labour and domestic market. Since 1997, the strategies adopted to deal with the meltdown have created distinctive differences in the region's political economies.

Thus, whilst Singapore reformed its banks, Thailand and then Indonesia invited the IMF to sort out their finances, Malaysia imposed currency controls and prohibited the repatriation of foreign funds invested on its stock exchange.[9]

Whilst Thailand moved tentatively to open its government as well as its domestic market, Malaysia witnessed acrimonious factionalism in the ruling party, culminating in the trial and imprisonment of Mahathir's erstwhile successor Anwar Ibrahim. Indonesia imploded politically as well as economically.

The fact that the largest country in the region, after China, is politically fragmenting as a consequence of its uncertain democratisation has exposed the incoherence of Asia-Pacific regionalism and much extolled multilateral security approaches. The Association of South Eastern Nations (ASEAN) is notable only by its absence from the anarchy. One of the few areas in which President Bill Clinton and Mahathir seem to agree is the irrelevance of the once heralded Asia-Pacific Economic Cooperation (APEC) and its vision of a regional free trade area.

There are signs of East Asian economic rejuvenation. However, with a number of its key elements punctured by the crisis, the direction in which the Asian model moves can no longer be as smoothly interdependent and export oriented as it was in the growth era.

Ironically, the failure to develop internal or external rule-governed procedures during the good times, has left Asian states and the regional arrangements they formed weak, unstable and increasingly vulnerable to the machinations of the global marketplace.

Notes

1. Mahathir Mohamad *A New Deal for Asia* (Kuala Lumpur Pelanduk, 1999) p.7

2. Malaysia borrowed $5 billion from the Miyazawa Fund and $1 billion from the Exim bank. Japan also sponsored the successful launch of a Malaysian government bond in May 1999.

3. Thus Hong Leong, a well-regulated financial group, but part of a conglomerate linked to Anwar, found itself forcibly merged in a financial institution dominated by Bank Bumiputra, an indebted bank patronised by Daim Zainuddin.

4. Sara E. Sievers and Wei Shang-Jin, 'The Cost of Crony Capitalism', *The Straits Times,* 4 July 1999.

5. 'The Bank Bali Scandal', *Business Times* (Singapore) 30 August 1999.

6. *Financial Times,* 1 September 1999.

7. Quoted in *International Herald Tribune,* 10-11 July 1999.

8. Exim Review, Vol. 19, No. 1 1999, p21 cited in *Australian Financial Review,* 1 June 1999.

9. The move froze approximately $10 billion in foreign emerging market funds in Malaysia and left $2 billion of shares in limbo on the Singapore CLOB (Central Limit Order Book). It also led to Malaysia being removed from the Morgan Stanley Capital International Index and the International Finance Corporation Index.

Does China Matter?

Gerald Segal

MIDDLE KINGDOM, MIDDLE POWER

DOES CHINA matter? No, it is not a silly question—merely one that is not asked often enough. Odd as it may seem, the country that is home to a fifth of humankind is overrated as a market, a power, and a source of ideas. At best, China is a second-rank middle power that has mastered the art of diplomatic theater: it has us willingly suspending our disbelief in its strength. In fact, China is better understood as a theoretical power—a country that has promised to deliver for much of the last 150 years but has consistently disappointed. After 50 years of Mao's revolution and 20 years of reform, it is time to leave the theater and see China for what it is. Only when we finally understand how little China matters will we be able to craft a sensible policy toward it.

DOES CHINA MATTER ECONOMICALLY?

CHINA, UNLIKE Russia or the Soviet Union before it, is supposed to matter because it is already an economic powerhouse. Or is it that China is on the verge of becoming an economic powerhouse, and you must be in the engine room helping the Chinese to enjoy the benefits to come? Whatever the spin, you know the argument: China is a huge market, and you cannot afford to miss it (although few say the same about India). The recently voiced "Kodak version" of this argument is that if only each Chinese will buy one full roll

GERALD SEGAL is Director of Studies at the International Institute for Strategic Studies in London and co-author, with Barry Buzan, of *Anticipating the Future*.

of film instead of the average half-roll that each currently buys, the West will be rich. Of course, nineteenth-century Manchester mill owners said much the same about their cotton, and in the early 1980s Japanese multinationals said much the same about their television sets. The Kodak version is just as hollow. In truth, China is a small market that matters relatively little to the world, especially outside Asia.

If this judgment seems harsh, let us begin with some harsh realities about the size and growth of the Chinese economy. In 1800 China accounted for 33 percent of world manufacturing output; by way of comparison, Europe as a whole was 28 percent, and the United States was 0.8 percent. By 1900 China was down to 6.2 percent (Europe was 62 percent, and the United States was 23.6 percent). In 1997 China accounted for 3.5 percent of world GNP (in 1997 constant dollars, the United States was 25.6 percent). China ranked seventh in the world, ahead of Brazil and behind Italy. Its per capita GDP ranking was 81st, just ahead of Georgia and behind Papua New Guinea. Taking the most favorable of the now-dubious purchasing-power-parity calculations; in 1997 China accounted for 11.8 percent of world GNP, and its per capita ranking was 65th, ahead of Jamaica and behind Latvia. Using the U.N. Human Development Index, China is 107th, bracketed by Albania and Namibia—not an impressive story.

Yes, you may say, but China has had a hard 200 years and is now rising swiftly. China has undoubtedly done better in the past generation than it did in the previous ten, but let's still keep matters in perspective—especially about Chinese growth rates. China claimed that its average annual industrial growth between 1951 and 1980 was 12.5 percent. Japan's comparable figure was 11.5 percent. One can reach one's own judgment about whose figures turned out to be more accurate.

Few economists trust modern Chinese economic data; even Chinese Prime Minister Zhu Rongji distrusts it. The Asian Development Bank routinely deducts some two percent from China's official GDP figures, including national current GDP growth rates of eight percent. Some two or three percent of what might be a more accurate GDP growth rate of six percent is useless goods produced to rust in warehouses. About one percent of China's growth in 1998 was due to massive government spending on infrastructure. Some three percent of GDP is accounted for by the one-time gain that occurs when one takes peasants off the land and brings them to cities, where productivity is higher. Taking all these qualifications into account, China's economy is effectively in recession. Even Zhu calls the situation grim.

China's ability to recover is hampered by problems that the current leadership understands well but finds just too scary to tackle seriously—at least so long as East Asia's economy is weak. By conservative estimates, at least a quarter of Chinese loans are nonperforming—a rate that Southeast Asians would have found frightening before the crash. Some 45 percent of state industries are losing money, but bank lending was up 25 percent in 1998—in part, to bail out the living dead. China has a high savings rate (40 percent of GDP), but ordinary Chinese would be alarmed to learn that their money is clearly being wasted.

Some put their hope in economic decentralization, but this has already gone so far that the center cannot reform increasingly wasteful and corrupt practices in the regions and in specific institutions. Central investment—20 percent of total investment in China—is falling. Inter-provincial trade as a percentage of total provincial trade is also down, having dropped a staggering 18 percent between 1985 and 1992. Despite some positive changes during the past 20 years of reform, China's economy has clearly run into huge structural impediments. Even if double-digit growth rates ever really existed, they are hard to imagine in the near future.

In terms of international trade and investment, the story is much the same: Beijing is a seriously overrated power. China made up a mere 3 percent of total world trade in 1997, about the same as South Korea and less than the Netherlands. China now accounts for only 11 percent of total Asian trade. Despite the hype about the importance of the China market, exports to China are tiny. Only 1.8 percent of U.S. exports go to China (this could, generously, be perhaps 2.4 percent if re-exports through Hong Kong were counted)—about the same level as U.S. exports to Australia or Belgium and about a third less than U.S. exports to Taiwan. The same is true of major European traders. China accounts for 0.5 percent of U.K. exports, about the same level as exports to Sri Lanka and less than those to Malaysia. China takes 1.1 percent of French and German exports, which is the highest in Asia apart from Japan but about par with exports to Portugal.

China matters a bit more to other Asian countries. Some 3.2 percent of Singapore's exports go to China, less than to Taiwan but on par with South Korea. China accounts for 4.6 percent of Australian exports, about the same as to Singapore. Japan sends only 5.1 percent of its exports to China, about a quarter less than to Taiwan. Only South Korea sends China an impressive share of its exports—some 9.9 percent, nudging ahead of exports to Japan.

Foreign direct investment (FDI) is even harder to measure than trade but sheds more light on long-term trends. China's massive FDI boom, especially in the past decade, is often trumpeted as evidence of how much China does and will matter for the global economy. But the reality is far less clear. Even in 1997, China's peak year for FDI, some 80 percent of the $45 billion inflow came from ethnic Chinese, mostly in East Asia. This was also a year of record capital flight from China—by some reckonings, an outflow of $35 billion. Much so-called investment from East Asia makes a round-trip from China via some place like Hong Kong and then comes back in as FDI to attract tax concessions.

Even a more trusting view of official FDI figures suggests that China does not much matter. FDI into China is about 10 percent of global FDI, with 60 percent of all FDI transfers taking place among developed countries. Given that less than 20 percent of FDI into China comes from non-ethnic Chinese, it is no surprise that U.S. or European Union investment in China averages out to something less than their investment in a major Latin American country such as Brazil. China has never accounted for more than 10 percent of U.S. FDI outflows—usually much less. In recent years China has taken around 5 percent of major EU countries' FDI outflow—and these are the glory years for FDI in China. The Chinese economy is clearly contracting, and FDI into China is dropping with it. In 1998 the United Nations reported that FDI into China maybe cut in half, and figures for 1998–99 suggest that this was not too gloomy a guess. Japanese FDI into China has been halved from its peak in 1995. Ericsson, a multinational telecommunications firm, says that China accounts for 13 percent of its global sales but will not claim that it is making any profits there. Similar experiences by Japanese technology firms a decade ago led to today's rapid disinvestment from China. Some insist that FDI flows demonstrate just how much China matters and will matter for the global economy, but the true picture is far more modest. China remains a classic case of hope over experience, reminiscent of de Gaulle's famous comment about Brazil: It has great potential, and always will.

It does not take a statistical genius to see the sharp reality: China is at best a minor (as opposed to inconsequential) part of the global economy. It has merely managed to project and sustain an image of far greater importance. This theatrical power was displayed with great brio during Asia's recent economic crisis. China received lavish praise from the West, especially the United States, for not devaluing its currency as it did in 1995. Japan, by contrast, was held responsible for the crisis. Of course, Tokyo's failure to reform since 1990 helped cause the meltdown, but this is testimony to how much Tokyo matters and how little Beijing does. China's total financial aid to the crisis-stricken economies was less than 10 percent of Japan's contribution.

The Asian crisis and the exaggerated fears that it would bring the economies of the Atlantic world to their knees help explain the overblown view of China's importance. In fact, the debacle demonstrated just how little impact Asia, except for Japan, has on the global economy. China—a small part of a much less important part of the global system than is widely believed—was never going to matter terribly much to the developed world. Exaggerating China is part of exaggerating Asia. As a result of the crisis, the West has learned the lesson for the region as a whole, but it has not yet learned it about China.

DOES CHINA MATTER MILITARILY?

CHINA IS a second-rate military power—not first-rate, because it is far from capable of taking on America, but not as third-rate as most of its Asian neighbors. China accounts for only 4.5 percent of global defense spending (the United States makes up 33.9 percent) and 25.8 percent of defense spending in East Asia and Australasia. China poses a formidable threat to the likes of the Philippines and can take islands such as Mischief Reef in the South China Sea at will. But sell the Philippines a couple of cruise missiles and the much-discussed Chinese threat will be easily erased. China is in no military shape to take the disputed Senkaku Islands from Japan, which is decently armed. Beijing clearly is a serious menace to Taiwan, but even Taiwanese defense planners do not believe China can successfully invade. The Chinese missile threat to Taiwan is much exaggerated, especially considering the very limited success of the far more massive and modern NATO missile strikes on Serbia. If the Taiwanese have as much will to resist as did the Serbs, China will not be able to easily cow Taiwan.

Thus China matters militarily to a certain extent simply because it is not a status quo power, but it does not matter so much that it cannot be constrained. Much the same pattern is evident in the challenge China poses to U.S. security. It certainly matters that China is the only country whose nuclear weapons target the United States. It matters, as the recent Cox report on Chinese espionage plainly shows, that China steals U.S. secrets about missile guidance and modern nuclear warheads. It also matters that Chinese military exercises simulate attacks on U.S. troops in South Korea and Japan. But the fact that a country can directly threaten the United States is not normally taken as a reason to be anything except robust in defending U.S. interests. It is certainly not a reason to pretend that China is a strategic partner of the United States.

The extent to which China matters militarily is evident in the discussions about deploying U.S. theater missile defenses (TMD) in the western Pacific and creating a U.S. national missile defense shield (NMD). Theoretically, the adversary is North Korea. In practice, the Pentagon fears that the U.S. ability to defend South Korea, Japan, and even Taiwan depends in the long term on the ability to defend the United States' home territory and U.S. troops abroad from Chinese missiles. Given the $10 billion price tag for NMD and the so-far unknowable costs of TMD, defense planners clearly think that China matters.

But before strategic paranoia sets in, the West should note that the Chinese challenge is nothing like the Soviet one. China is less like the Soviet Union in the 1950s than like Iraq in the 1990s: a regional threat to Western interests, not a global ideological rival. Such regional threats can be constrained. China, like Iraq, does not matter so much that the United States needs to suspend its normal strategies for dealing with unfriendly powers. Threats can be deterred, and unwanted action can be constrained by a country that claims to be the sole superpower and to dominate the revolution in military affairs.

A similarly moderated sense of how much China matters can be applied to the question of Chinese arms transfers. China accounted for 2.2 percent of arms deliveries in 1997, ahead of Germany but behind Israel (the United States had 45 percent of the market, and the United Kingdom had 18 percent). The $1 billion or so worth of arms that Beijing exports annually is not buying vast influence, though in certain markets Beijing does have real heft. Pakistan is easily the most important recipient of Chinese arms, helping precipitate a nuclear arms race with India. Major deals with Sudan, Sri Lanka, and Burma have had far less strategic impact. On the other hand, arms transfers to Iran have been worrying; as with Pakistan, U.S. threats of sanctions give China rather good leverage. China's ability to make mischief therefore matters somewhat—primarily because it reveals that Chinese influence is fundamentally based on its ability to oppose or thwart Western interests. France and Britain each sell far more arms than China, but they are by and large not creating strategic problems for the West.

Hence, it is ludicrous to claim, as Western and especially American officials constantly do, that China matters because the West needs it as a strategic partner. The discourse of "strategic partnership" really means that China is an adversary that could become a serious nuisance. Still, many in the Clinton administration and elsewhere do not want to call a spade a spade and admit that China is a strategic foe. Perhaps they think that stressing the potential for partnership may eventually, in best Disney style, help make dreams come true.

On no single significant strategic issue are China and the West on the same side. In most cases, including Kosovo, China's opposition does not matter. True, the U.N. Security Council could not be used to build a powerful coalition against Serbia, but as in most cases, the real obstacle was Russia, not China. Beijing almost always plays second fiddle to Moscow or even Paris in obstructing Western interests in the Security Council. (The exceptions to this rule always concern cases where countries such as Haiti or Macedonia have developed relations with Taiwan.) After all, the Russian prime minister turned his plane to the United States around when he heard of the imminent NATO attack on Serbia, but the Chinese premier turned up in Washington as scheduled two weeks later.

NATO's accidental May bombing of the Chinese embassy elicited a clear demonstration of China's theatrical power. Beijing threatened to block any peace efforts in the United Nations (not that any were pending), but all it wanted was to shame the West into concessions on World Trade Organization membership, human rights, or arms control. China grandiosely threatened to rewrite the Security Council resolution that eventually gave NATO an indefinite mandate to keep the peace in Kosovo, but in the end it meekly abstained. So much for China taking a global perspective as one of the five permanent members of the Security Council. Beijing's temper tantrum merely highlighted the fact that, unlike the other veto-bearing Security Council members, it was not a power in Europe.

In the field of arms control, the pattern is the same. China does not block major arms control accords, but it makes sure to be among the last to sign on and tries to milk every diplomatic advantage from having to be dragged to the finish line. China's reluctance to sign the Nuclear Nonproliferation Treaty (NPT), for instance, was outdone in its theatricality only by the palaver in getting China to join the Comprehensive Test Ban Treaty. China's participation in the Association of

Southeast Asian Nations Regional Forum—Asia's premier, albeit limited, security structure—is less a commitment to surrender some sovereignty to an international arrangement than a way to ensure that nothing is done to limit China's ability to pursue its own national security objectives. China matters in arms control mainly because it effectively blocks accords until doing so ends up damaging China's international reputation.

Only on the Korean Peninsula do China's capacities seriously affect U.S. policy. One often hears that China matters because it is so helpful in dealing with North Korea. This is flatly wrong. Only once this decade did Beijing join with Washington and pressure Pyongyang—in bringing the rogue into compliance with its NPT obligations in the early phases of the 1994 North Korean crisis. On every other occasion, China has either done nothing to help America or actively helped North Korea resist U.S. pressure—most notoriously later in the 1994 crisis, when the United States was seeking support for sanctions and other coercive action against North Korea. Thus the pattern is the same. China matters in the same way any middle-power adversary matters: it is a problem to be circumvented or moved. But China does not matter because it is a potential strategic partner for the West. In that sense, China is more like Russia than either cares to admit.

DOES CHINA MATTER POLITICALLY?

THE EASIEST category to assess—although the one with the fewest statistics—is how much China matters in international political terms. To be fair to the Chinese, their recent struggle to define who they are and what they stand for is merely the latest stage of at least 150 years of soul-searching. Ever since the coming of Western power demonstrated that China's ancient civilization was not up to the challenges of modernity, China has struggled to understand its place in the wider world. The past century in particular has been riddled with deep Chinese resistance to the essential logic of international interdependence. It has also been marked by failed attempts to produce a China strong enough to resist the Western-dominated international system—consider the Boxer movement, the Kuomintang, or the Chinese Communist Party (CCP). Fifty years after the Chinese communist revolution, the party that gave the Chinese people the Great Leap Forward (and 30 million dead of famine) and the Cultural Revolution (and perhaps another million dead as well as a generation destroyed) is devoid of ideological power and authority. In the absence of any

other political ideals, religions and cults such as the Falun Gong (target of a government crackdown this summer) will continue to flourish.

China's latest attempt to strengthen itself has been the past 20 years of economic reforms, stimulated by other East Asians' success in transforming their place in the world. But the discourse on prosperity that elicited praise for the order-sustaining "Asian values" or Confucian fundamentals was burned in the bonfire of certainties that was the Asian economic crisis. China was left in another phase of shock and self-doubt; hence, economic reforms stalled.

Under these circumstances, China is in no position to matter much as a source of international political power. Bizarre as old-style Maoism was, at least it was a beacon for many in the developing world. China now is a beacon to no one— and, indeed, an ally to no one. No other supposedly great power is as bereft of friends. This is not just because China, once prominent on the map of aid suppliers, has become the largest recipient of international aid. Rather, China is alone because it abhors the very notion of genuine international interdependence. No country relishes having to surrender sovereignty and power to the Western-dominated global system, but China is particularly wedded to the belief that it is big enough to merely learn what it must from the outside world and still retain control of its destiny. So China's neighbors understand the need to get on with China but have no illusions that China feels the same way.

China does not even matter in terms of global culture. Compare the cultural (not economic) role that India plays for ethnic Indians around the world to the pull exerted by China on ethnic Chinese, and one sees just how closed China remains. Of course, India's cultural ties with the Atlantic world have always been greater than China's, and India's wildly heterogeneous society has always been more accessible to the West. But measured in terms of films, literature, or the arts in general, Taiwan, Hong Kong, and even Singapore are more important global influences than a China still under the authoritarian grip of a ruling Leninist party. Chinese cities fighting over who should get the next Asian Disneyland, Chinese cultural commissars squabbling over how many American films can be shown in Chinese cinemas, and CCP bosses setting wildly fluctuating Internet-access policies are all evidence of just how mightily China is struggling to manage the power of Western culture.

In fact, the human-rights question best illustrates the extent to which China is a political pariah. Chinese authorities correctly note that life for the average citizen has become much more free in the past generation. But as Zhu admitted on his recent trip to the United States, China's treatment of dissenters remains inhuman and indecent.

Still, China deserves credit for having stepped back on some issues. That China did not demand the right to intervene to help Indonesia's ethnic Chinese during the 1998–99 unrest was correctly applauded as a sign of maturity. But it was also a sign of how little international leadership China could claim. With a human-rights record that made Indonesia seem a paragon of virtue, China was in no position to seize the moral high ground.

Measuring global political power is difficult, but China's influence and authority are clearly puny—not merely compared to the dominant West, but also compared to Japan before the economic crisis. Among the reasons for China's weakness is its continuing ambiguity about how to manage the consequences of modernity and interdependence. China's great past and the resultant hubris make up much of the problem. A China that believes the world naturally owes it recognition as a great power—even when it so patently is not—is not really ready to achieve greatness.

DOES IT MATTER IF CHINA DOESN'T MATTER?

THE MIDDLE KINGDOM, then, is merely a middle power. It is not that China does not matter at all, but that it matters far less than it and most of the West think. China matters about as much as Brazil for the global economy. It is a medium-rank military power, and it exerts no political pull at all. China matters most for the West because it can make mischief, either by threatening its neighbors or assisting anti-Western forces further afield. Although these are problems, they will be more manageable if the West retains some sense of proportion about China's importance. If you believe that China is a major player in the global economy and a near-peer competitor of America's, you might be reluctant to constrain its undesired activities. You might also indulge in the "pander complex"—the tendency to bend over backward to accommodate every Chinese definition of what insults the Chinese people's feelings. But if you believe that China is not much different from any middle power, you will be more willing to treat it normally.

This notion of approaching China as a normal, medium power is one way to avoid the sterile debates about the virtues of engaging or containing China. Of course, one must engage a middle power, but one should also not be shy about constraining its unwanted actions. Such a strategy of "constrainment" would lead to a new and very different Western approach to China. One would expect robust deterrence of threats to Taiwan, but not pusillanimous efforts to ease Chinese concerns about TMD. One would expect a tough negotiating stand on the terms of China's WTO entry, but not Western concessions merely because China made limited progress toward international transparency standards or made us feel guilty about bombing its embassy in Belgrade. One would expect Western leaders to tell Chinese leaders that their authoritarianism puts them on the wrong side of history, but one would not expect Western countries to stop trying to censure human rights abuses in the United Nations or to fall over themselves to compete for the right to lose money in the China market.

To some extent, we are stuck with a degree of exaggeration of China's influence. It has a permanent U.N. Security Council seat even though it matters about as much as the United Kingdom and France, who hold their seats only because of their pre–World War II power. Unlike London and Paris, however, Beijing contributes little to international society via peacekeeping or funding for international bodies. China still has a hold on the imagination of CEOs, as it has for 150 years—all the more remarkable after the past 20 years, in which Western companies were bamboozled into believing that staying for the long haul meant eventually making money in China. Pentagon planners, a pessimistic breed if ever there was one, might be forgiven for believing that China could eventually become a peer competitor of the United States, even though the military gap, especially in high-technology arms, is, if anything, actually growing wider.

Nevertheless, until China is cut down to size in Western imaginations and treated more like a Brazil or an India, the West stands little chance of sustaining a coherent and long-term policy toward it. Until we stop suspending our disbelief and recognize the theatrical power of China, we will continue to constrain ourselves from pursuing our own interests and fail to constrain China's excesses. And perhaps most important, until we treat China as a normal middle power, we will make it harder for the Chinese people to understand their own failings and limitations and get on with the serious reforms that need to come.

Tokyo's Depression Diplomacy

Yoichi Funabashi

DON'T JAPANIC

DURING THE mid-1980s, when Japan's economic might was reaching its zenith, a French diplomat reportedly declared, "All I wish is that somehow Japan and the Soviet Union would disappear from the earth." On both counts, his dream has almost come true. Japan now confronts the toughest challenges in its foreign relations since World War II. The way it faces up to them will determine whether Japan's meteoric rise to world-power status in the last half-century is transient or sustainable.

Japan is in a deep funk. Its economic debilitation, political gridlock, and rapidly aging population all contribute to a pervasive pessimism and imperil its cherished identity as a nonnuclear, non-weapon-exporting, economically dynamic, democratic, generous, civilian power. And while the Japanese are famed for downplaying future prospects to prepare for a rainy day, this time is different. People genuinely fear the future. Political leaders have consistently failed to lead and the economy has deteriorated for seven years. Increasingly, however, the pessimism is the problem, with far-reaching regional and global implications. Unless the psychological slump reverses, Japan's deflationary cycle will cripple Asian hopes for recovery and destabilize the global economy.

While the world has been collectively keening over the Japanese economy, another death has been in progress—Japan's diplomacy. Economic and financial failure have exacerbated Japanese insecurity at a time when it must confront a complex of foreign policy concerns—Asia's economic meltdown, India and Pakistan's nuclear tests, China's emergence as a major power, and most critically, uncertainty over the U.S.-Japan alliance. Japan, historically disposed to a sense of strategic exposure, is again feeling vulnerable about its place in the world.

ISOLATIONIST JAPAN?

SINCE WORLD WAR II, Japan has based its diplomacy on economic, not ideological, foundations. But the erosion of those foundations has jolted the belief that economic might would translate into diplomatic influence. Japanese hopes for peace through economic development and integration have been compromised.

Worse, Japan is currently amassing a dismal record as the catalyst for world depression. If Japan allows the hemorrhaging banking system to bleed to death and the public refuses to invest in Japan's future, deflation could bring down the world economy and destabilize the entire international system.

Japanese business has already started to withdraw from the world. Foreign direct investment to Asia is slowing down, and even large corporations in the developed world are following suit. Fujitsu has just closed a semiconductor plant within British Prime Minister Tony Blair's Sedgefield constituency. In Asia, Japan's consumers provided the original stimulus for regional economic growth as countries enthusiastically exported goods to Japan. But this "absorber function" is rapidly diminishing because of Japan's consumer

YOICHI FUNABASHI is Chief Diplomatic Correspondent and Columnist at the Tokyo newspaper *Asahi Shimbun.*

Reprinted by permission of *Foreign Affairs,* November/December 1998, pp. 26-36. © 1998 by the Council on Foreign Relations, Inc.

retrenchment. Japan, the locomotive of the regional economy, accounting for about 70 percent of Asia's GDP, has ground to a halt. Depreciation of the yen—now about 40 percent lower against the dollar since April 1995—means that yen loans will shrink in dollar terms. As Japan's economic assistance to its neighbors declines, the couplings between the Japanese engine and the rest of Asia will crack.

Meanwhile, Asia fumbles for an economic formula to solve the problems of globalization. The current model is defunct, and Tokyo has been unable to come up with a revitalized version. Its demoralized bureaucracy, buffeted by scandal and charges of economic mismanagement, is ill equipped to forcefully promote a positive, outward-looking economic or foreign policy. Asian countries are left without new ideas or direction from their erstwhile economic mentor. Japan's strategy of regional integration, particularly with regard to Asia-Pacific Economic Cooperation, has stalled. The recent APEC trade ministers' meeting in Kuching, Malaysia, demonstrated Japan's clumsy attitude toward liberalizing regional trade.

Japan's economic health has deteriorated alarmingly. With public sector debt projected at 106 percent of GDP for 1999, Japan will be one of the most heavily indebted members of the G-7. This dismal performance bodes ill for U.S.-Japan relations. Resumption of "Japan-bashing" in the United States over Japan's perceived economic intransigence has prompted a rise in anti-American sentiments in Japan. Some Japanese even feel that current economic circumstances represent "the second defeat in the Pacific War." Japan will have to fundamentally restructure and streamline its government in the next decade. This move will certainly strain ties with the rest of the world, especially with Washington, which could find its presence in the region undermined as Tokyo cuts defense expenditures and Host Nation Support contributions.

ASIAN CONFLAGRATION

ASIA'S ECONOMIC crisis has rudely exposed the helplessness of the Association of Southeast Asian Nations and APEC. ASEAN simply lacked the stature or intergovernmental institutions to respond to the financial crisis. Its principle of nonintervention in members' domestic affairs precluded a comprehensive collective response, which hastened the downward spiral of Asian currencies. ASEAN's inability to act was mirrored by APEC's, where the creed of "concerted unilateral action" failed to muster a credible response to the Asian conflagration. Now the crisis' unequal impact threatens to rupture the politically fragile framework of regional ties.

This feebleness is especially troubling for Japan. Over the last three decades, ASEAN has been an increasingly important compo-

Japan is burdened by past misdeeds and its ad hoc attempts to resolve them.

nent in Tokyo's foreign policy. Japan sought to develop regional ties to complement its alliance with the United States and its global participation in the G-7 and the United Nations. As Professor Gerald L. Curtis of Columbia University has noted, "The strengthening of Japanese-ASEAN relations is one of the outstanding achievements of postwar Japanese diplomacy." ASEAN's record of friendship with Japan has provided some fulfillment in Japan's search for an international role. This found concrete expression in 1977, when then-Prime Minister Takeo Fukuda proposed a new doctrine for Japan in Southeast Asia that rejected Japanese military power and professed the desire for a "heart to heart" relationship with the region. This tie has underpinned Japanese dealings with ASEAN for 20 years, but it is now in serious jeopardy.

The regional turmoil has also drawn Japanese attention to Asia's seas. With Indonesia occupied by its internal travails, a power vacuum has opened up in waters of critical strategic importance. More than 80 percent of Japan's oil supplies sail through the South China Sea, which also delivers vital oil to China. If instability in Indonesia threatens those supplies, many fear that China will use force to protect them. Chinese seabed resource surveys intruded into Japanese waters near the Senkaku Islands in May and June of 1995, sparking a series of niggling confrontations. China's 1996 missile tests in the Taiwan Strait also strained relations with Japan. As an island country, Japan has always been a major seafaring nation and is thus sensitive to any changes in the maritime status quo. Tokyo's past policy envisaged a strong, stable Indonesia, but this can no longer be assumed.

Japan's primary stumbling block, however, is the burden of past misdeeds and its ad hoc attempts to resolve them. This accounts for Japanese reluctance to lead on the Korean peninsula and, more generally, to address the Asian economic crisis. Japan's relations with South Korea have deteriorated, particularly in 1995 during the fiftieth anniversary commemorations of World War II. Japan's inability to tackle its past has also tainted relations with China. In 1992, Emperor Akihito's visit to China was hailed as a harbinger of future reconciliation. But three years later, Japan and China found themselves pitted against each other over China's nuclear tests, Japan's suspension of grants to China, and territorial disputes. At their joint press conference in 1995, South Korean

President Kim Young Sam and Chinese President Jiang Zemin criticized Japan's handling of the World War II anniversary. In that criticism Japan saw anti-Japanese sentiment in Korea and China amalgamating to portend a troubling geopolitical future, especially with the prospect of Korean reunification.

Historically, Japan has played a unique role as the most socio-economically advanced country in Asia, competing with the West on relatively equal footing. This status as a "member of the club" of modernized nations inspired belief in Japan's role "bridging" the gap between the West and Asia. But now Japan finds disturbing similarities between its own problems and the rest of Asia's. Throughout the region, the lack of transparency and accountability in both financial markets and politics has been cited as a factor in the economic crisis. The acute awareness that these are shared problems has exploded the myth of Japanese uniqueness. At the same time, the concept of "bridging" has proved unnecessary. Western businesses deal with all Asia directly, without needing Japanese intermediaries. Although it thinks of itself as exceptional, Japan has found itself subject to the rules that govern the rest of Asia.

SPECTACULAR SABER-RATTLING

JAPAN'S FAITH in the efficacy of its nonnuclear, pacifist creed has been profoundly shaken by India's and Pakistan's spectacular saber-rattling. Japan, which plays a symbolic role as the sole victim of nuclear weapons, has been ineffective in promoting nonproliferation and relegated to the international sidelines. With the prospect of North Korea going nuclear, these concerns take on increased urgency.

First, the tests demonstrated that Japan's economic aid has not prevented nuclear proliferation in Asia. Second, they revealed the limits of employing official development assistance as a diplomatic tool. No amount of economic assistance persuaded India or Pakistan to forgo their respective nuclear programs. Both countries, India in particular, have questioned the meaningfulness of Japan's nonnuclear stance while it remains under the U.S. nuclear umbrella. The ambiguity of Japan's position has undermined its moral authority in South Asia. India's eloquent criticism of the Nuclear Nonproliferation Treaty regime dividing the globe between nuclear "haves" and "have-nots" struck a note with many Japanese. Japan is still highly unlikely to go nuclear. But Japan is interested in another option—Theater Missile Defense. Nuclear proliferation in South Asia further inflamed the TMD controversy within Japan, a debate given urgency by North Korea's August 31 missile test over Japanese airspace. These new threats will bolster support for a TMD system. Growing threats may also, however, trigger calls for Japan to reaffirm the global community's commitment to nuclear disarmament, challenge the status quo, and perhaps even forgo the nuclear umbrella.

South Asia's nuclear tests also revealed tensions between Japan and the United States and China on the issue. On June 4, the foreign ministers of the five established nuclear powers met in Geneva to fashion a response to the tests. Japan's request to participate was denied, which fueled suspicion that its attempts to endorse nuclear disarmament and nonproliferation lack U.S. support and are being contained by China. Many Japanese resent the exclusion of major nonnuclear powers like Japan and Germany from meetings like those in Geneva, feeling that it rewards the nuclear path to power while punishing the civilian. China claims that only the "club" of declared nuclear powers should discuss nuclear issues because they have a special responsibility. This argument is unacceptable to Japan. A nonproliferation regime can only be truly sustainable through cooperation between the "haves" and the "have-nots," so the "have-nots" should not be excluded.

TRADING PLACES

JAPAN'S PREDICAMENT looks almost surreal when contrasted with its sensational arrival on the world scene—announced by its defeat of imperial Russia—at the beginning of the twentieth century. A hundred years ago, the Greek-born, Japan-residing author Lafcadio Hearn wrote an essay entitled "The Genius of Japanese Civilization" ushering a new Japan into the world. But in 1998, China's rise to world prominence commands the world's attention. The perception that Japan and China are trading places in Asia has started to spread. Although it is hardly accurate, in the recent Asian crisis China has been hailed as a regional stabilizer and Japan condemned as a passive bystander.

Tokyo feels used and abused by Washington.

A rising China will induce critical, painful, and psychologically difficult strategic adjustments in Japanese foreign policy. Japan has not known a wealthy, powerful, confident, and internationalist China since its modernization during the Meiji era. Proximity to China's constant turmoil has sharpened Japan's sensitivity to its neighbor's problems, deepening skepticism about China's prospects for development. Japan has long viewed itself as the leading

Asian country. While most remain unconvinced that China will emerge as a regional leader, other Japanese now wonder if their predominant position in the past century has been an aberration.

China's emergence presents multiple challenges to Japanese foreign policy. Despite Japan's financial largesse and diplomatic engagement, its attempts at rapprochement have been compromised by the perception that China and Japan are natural rivals. China's role on the world stage has recently been getting greater billing, while Japan's star has been on the wane. The old order, with the U.S.-Japan alliance as a bulwark against Soviet belligerence, has given way to trilateral relations coaxing China into the world community. Sometimes the three countries' interests overlap, as when dealing with nuclear weapons and famine in North Korea. More often, however, the intrusion of domestic politics has distorted the triangle, shifting the focus to bilateral concerns at the expense of the third party.

Japan is deeply uneasy about the "constructive strategic partnership" that has evolved between the United States and China. Despite American assurances to the contrary, China is perceived to be trying to outflank Japan while U.S.-Japan relations are particularly shaky. Jiang's 1997 visit to Pearl Harbor came at his request, while this year China put out feelers about a Clinton visit to Nanking, the scene of an infamous massacre by the Japanese imperial army. Tokyo feels used and abused by Washington. Some suspect that the United States enhanced its security ties with Japan in 1996 expressly to strengthen its negotiating position with China. Yet Japan continues to suffer the indignity of being chided by both China and the United States for its economic failures. To Japan, this emphasis on the "Japan problem" is a diversionary tactic, preventing an Asian backlash against U.S. "victory" in the markets and obscuring China's externalization of its "internal contradictions," like currency vulnerability. This is a zero-sum game for Tokyo. China barely conceals its desire to weaken the U.S.-Japan bilateral relationship: witness its pronouncements about the need for a new multipolar world order and the end of Cold War security arrangements.

But at the same time, Japan fears U.S.-China enmity. Should the vociferous anti-China rhetoric emanating from Congress impact policy, warnings of Chinese antagonism may become self-ruling. This would devastate the U.S.-Japan alliance. Unless it significantly compromises its interests, Japan believes that it can live with a powerful China, even one that challenges the U.S.-led liberal internationalist order. Such a belief acknowledges that geography and history matter. Some Americans believe that Japan has no choice but to follow the U.S. lead as China becomes more powerful. In fact, Ja-

pan's actions will depend on how the threat from China takes shape.

JILTED JAPAN

THE MOST problematic factor for Japan's political leaders is that Clinton did not reaffirm, in his talks with Jiang, the stabilizing importance of the U.S.-Japan alliance in Asia. It is as if the alliance was something to be ashamed of, to be hidden from China to avoid friction. The United States and Japan have lost sight of their relationship's overarching purpose. The alliance was reaffirmed with great fanfare in 1996, but tensions over Japanese macroeconomic policy and the U.S. bases in Okinawa have added to widespread doubts about its terms.

During the Cold War, U.S. forces and Japanese support mechanisms formed an elegant security architecture. Few were inclined to tamper with it. The end of the Cold War brought new pressures to bear. There is no rationale for the impressive U.S. presence in Japan without a compelling military threat. Economic tensions between the two countries are rising. American contentions that the three legs of the relationship—security, economics, and a common agenda—can be compartmentalized are disingenuous. It is cruelly ironic that U.S. Treasury Secretary Robert Rubin is busy extolling the virtues of China's state-directed economy without a fully convertible currency while lambasting Japan as an economic miscreant. This downgrading of U.S.-Japan ties is particularly painful because it violates the highest virtue in Japanese society, loyalty. Once an alliance is entered, it is not subject to negotiation, justification, or competition from a third party. The perceived betrayal strengthens Japanese advocates of a "burdenless alliance."

If Korea unifies, domestic pressures will probably hasten the withdrawal of most U.S. military forces. That would certainly prompt some Japanese to call for a drastic reduction in U.S. forces stationed in Japan, declining to be the only nation hosting U.S. troops. The U.S.-China "constructive strategic partnership" has been welcomed in some quarters—in a rather twisted way—for stabilizing Asia. Indeed, advocates of a reduced American presence in Japan argue that China's strategic relationship with America means there is less need for security preparedness between the United States and Japan. With a further reduction in U.S. forces, the two countries could move toward a new alliance based on political relations rather than military strength.

RELUCTANT REALISM

JAPAN MUST define its priorities, policies, and national interests more clearly. Security ties with America must be strengthened; so must dialogue among China, Japan, and the United

States. Although Japan cannot and would not wish to compete militarily with China or the United States, it cannot be left out of regional and global discussions between the two. Tokyo's role may be to ameliorate the hegemonic tendencies of these two great powers. All three countries need to remember that the stabilizer in the recent Asian economic crisis has not been the Chinese renminbi but the U.S. presence and the U.S.-Japan alliance. Rather than feeling victimized by growing U.S.-China warmth, Japan should push for more dynamic trilateral dialogues on a range of issues, including macroeconomic policy, trade, the environment, nuclear reduction measures, and regional policies. This discourse should also be developed within and used to promote multilateral institutions like APEC and the World Trade Organization. Tokyo and Washington should explore the possibility of including Beijing in their alliance—although not until it becomes a democracy and finds a peaceful settlement with Taipei.

Japan and the United States must coordinate macroeconomic policy to forestall the downward spiral of the world economy. These consultations should include China. The United States and Japan, along with South Korea, should also work to involve China in the denuclearization of Northeast Asia through the Korean Energy Development Organization project. Although it has suspended contributions to protest the North Korean missile test, Japan should once again sponsor KEDO. The organization does not merely encourage nonproliferation, it is also a soft-landing for Korean reconciliation and

Japan must send a clearer message about nuclear disarmament.

reunification. If China would get involved, the organization would foster China's cooperative behavior. The quality of security policy coordination between the United States, South Korea, and Japan should be enhanced. A "G-6" dialogue among the two Koreas, the United States, China, Japan, and Russia on peninsular security should be launched.

Finally, Tokyo must develop a rejuvenated nuclear policy. Working with like-minded nations, Japan should prod the established nuclear powers to get serious about nuclear disarmament. The original five should invite representatives of the nuclear "have-nots," such as Japan and Germany, to take part in discussions to coordinate nonproliferation policies. Now is the time for Japan to build momentum for change. An unfortunate consequence may be that the United States misconstrues Japan's rejection of the nuclear status quo as equivocation about the alliance itself. Nevertheless, if Japan is to regain an honorable place in the world, protect Asian stability, and further the cause of nonproliferation, it must send a clearer message about nuclear disarmament.

Japan is evolving from an era of commercial liberalism to one of reluctant real-ism. A weaker economy means that national interests will have to be defined more realistically. Inevitably this will involve scaling back in areas where Japan is overextended. But Japan should remain faithful to its aspirations to be a prototype of a global civilian power. This will continue to strengthen the U.S.-Japan alliance, as Japan's defensive power complements America's offensive might and joint contingency planning is improved. Sooner or later, Japan can and will shed its pessimism. History has taught us that Japan will act quickly and decisively once its people reach a consensus. The new generation of leaders must come to terms with Japan's history, make amends, and move on. Japan's financial system will be revamped, and Japanese business will restructure and launch itself once more onto the global stage. Strong support for development aid, U.N. peacekeeping operations, refugee relief, and a larger (albeit still nonmilitary) role for Japan in the international community reflects the public's strong sense of themselves as stakeholders in a peaceful, orderly international system. In the next decade, the emergence of new political players—especially younger and more internationalist politicians, women, and non-governmental organizations—will create new dynamics in Japanese public life. If Japan's economic and foreign policy edifices are to be restored, new ideas and human resources are urgently needed—these will not come from the bureaucracy but from the burgeoning civil society. Japan's leaders must harness these forces and embrace change.

Toward a Comprehensive Settlement of the Korea Problem

"The ongoing humanitarian emergency and the needs of the North Korean economy provide a major opportunity to transform the security stalemate on the Korean peninsula, to bring North Korea into the world economy, and then watch that system contain and ultimately transform Pyongyang's insurgent and recalcitrant posture."

BRUCE CUMINGS

Millennial fever grips us all as the days count down to 2000. How much more so for the Korean people: for them, the current century has not been a good one. After nearly a half-century of brutal imperial occupation by Japan, the country was divided after World War II, wracked by a vicious civil war, and then returned to its contentious antebellum condition of national division and military confrontation.

Many Koreans thought that this century of troubles would come to an end with the fall of the Berlin Wall in 1989, which appeared to remove the ideological polarities and bloc politics that characterized the cold war, perhaps clearing the way for a long-awaited reunification between the northern Democratic People's Republic of Korea and the southern Republic of Korea. But as 1999 comes to a close, unification remains a distant goal and the cold war maintains its grip on the Korean peninsula as tightly as it did a decade ago. There has, however, been modest improvement on both counts because of several important diplomatic initiatives and the changes that the 1990s have forced on North Korea. Indeed, the humanitarian crisis in the north and the democratic transition in the south could be the prelude to settling this seemingly interminable civil conflict.

THE POLITICS OF FAMINE

Since the death of Kim Il Sung in 1994, North Korea has been visited by two years of flood in 1995 and 1996, a summer of drought in 1997, and a resulting famine that may have claimed the lives of 2 million people. This sequence is a textbook example of the calamities that are supposed to attend the end of the Confucian dynastic cycle, and North Koreans must wonder how much more suffering Mother Nature will mete out before she is done. (Kim's son, Kim Jong Il, waited out the three-year traditional mourning period for the first son of the king before assuming his father's titles; he became secretary of the ruling Korea Workers' Party in 1997, and he inherited the position of maximum leader at the fiftieth anniversary of the regime's founding on September 9, 1998.)

Among the many crises that North Korea has suffered in the past decade, the famine that began in 1997 seems to be the worst. Andrew Natsios, the vice president of World Vision, has argued that North Korea has lost 500,000 to 1 million of its citizens to famine, and if full information were at hand, the total might be closer to 2 million, or nearly 10 percent of the population. An unscientific survey in August 1997 of about 400 Koreans living in China who frequently cross the border into North Korea led to an estimate that 15 percent of the population in towns along the northern border had died. In orphanages, from which have come many of the televised images of this famine, the figure was 22 percent; in poor mining towns in the far north, about 9 percent.

It is not clear that these figures apply to the entire country. Regional differentiation is great in North Korea, with 10 percent of the population living in the highly centralized and much-privileged capital city of Pyongyang. Foreign travelers have not witnessed starvation conditions in Pyongyang, and various visitors to other parts of the country sometimes cannot find them either. For example, an international delegation that visited the upper east coast in August 1997 did not see much

BRUCE CUMINGS, *a* Current History *contributing editor, is the Norman and Edna Freehling Professor of History at the University of Chicago. His latest book is* Parallax Visions: Making Sense of American–East Asian Relations at the End of the Century *(Chapel Hill, N.C.: Duke University Press, April 1999).*

evidence of malnutrition, let alone famine. Regardless of its claims to have eliminated classes, North Korea remains a class society; families who have homes in villages and small cities have small plots of land at their disposal, every inch of which is under cultivation. Foreigners who have visited homes with private gardens have found that they did not need government rations in order to have enough to eat.

On closer inspection, this famine appears to be more a failure of economic infrastructure than a fluke of nature. Although Mother Nature shares much of the blame for North Korea's recent travails, most experts believe that even with the best weather conditions, the north's agricultural problems are irremediable short of major reform. The collapse of the Soviet bloc left North Korea without customers for its exports, exports that had been exchanged at favorable rates for petroleum. A rapid decline in petroleum imports in the 1990s, in turn, hurt the national transportation network and the huge chemical industry, which provided fertilizer to the farms.

Although it is often seen in the United States as an East Asian Albania, North Korea is an industrial society, and the absence of critical fuels and industrial inputs has stymied the economy. For several years now, industry may have been running at less than 50 percent of capacity. Pyongyang's problems therefore seem fairly straightforward: if it can find ways to export goods to the world market to earn the foreign exchange needed to import food, oil, and other essentials, it would not only stabilize but probably prosper. Since the leadership has not carried out the fundamental decisions necessary for this to occur, its reform process has been piecemeal and haphazard.

Administrative politics is also to blame. Bureaucratic lineages and hierarchies often exist as independent kingdoms, creating difficulties in communicating and coordinating with each other. The military has clearly been at odds with the Foreign Ministry in recent years, something that foreign diplomats have witnessed on occasion, but the problem goes beyond that. Generational conflict between an increasingly small but still influential revolutionary old guard and people who range in age from 40 to 60, relative bureaucratic autonomy, the practice of provincial self-reliance, a vast party apparatus organizing upward of one-third of the adult population, the privileged position of the military (receiving 25 percent or more of the annual budget), the death of the only leader the country ever had, and a series of externally generated crises have all resulted in a kind of immobilism in the 1990s.

Decisions are pushed upward through the hierarchy, and at the top no one seems capable of making the hard decision to push the country on a truly new course. North Korea is neither muddling through toward some form of postcommunism, as other socialist states did after 1989, nor is it reforming like

China and Vietnam. The leadership seems deeply frightened by the consequences of opening up the economy, preferring instead to create tiny coastal enclaves (such as the Najin-Sonbong export zone in the northeast). Still, for all the troubles that have come in the 1990s, they have not threatened the stability of the top leadership. It is at the local level that the system is breaking down.

For example, a Korean visitor who recently traveled by car from Pyongyang to the northeastern city of Hamhung told me that he had seen a large barter market operating daily along the riverbank in Hamhung. Hard currency, especially dollars, was in wide if informal use, and highly valued. He believed that the historically centralized, planned delivery of goods and services by the state had almost completely broken down at the local level, with many people telling him that government food rations had not been delivered for months.

Foreign relief experts say that food brought into North Korea is not diverted to the privileged military. Instead, locally produced food stocks go to the elite in Pyongyang and to the vast military, in which one-twentieth of the entire population serves. Otherwise, foreign observers speak of an egalitarian sharing of existing food stocks combined with a triage policy where the young, the elderly, and the infirm are the first to suffer. The government is helping where it can, denying where it will, and keeping the essential pillar of its power—the military—sufficiently fed.

> *The cold war continues on the Korean peninsula, as does the Korean War, in a fragile peace held by an armistice and fortified by the world's largest military confrontation.*

NORTH KOREA'S POTENTIAL

Unfortunately the post–cold war world is almost inured to such humanitarian disasters. Twenty-five nations were scourged by war, human displacement, hunger, and disease from 1993 to 1995, increasing to 65 in the last four years. Raimo Väyrynen has written in *The Age of Humanitarian Emergencies* that "humanitarian emergencies are primarily imbedded in intra-state crises," with stalemates in civil wars playing a large role; unresolved conflicts, like those in Afghanistan and Angola, merely bring death and destruction in their wake.

The Korean War is the most stalemated conflict in the world, unmoving since 1953, and amid all the other problems that have characterized this conflict, we now have a major famine in North Korea. Unlike other humanitarian emergencies around the world, however, this one has provided little evidence of a collapse of state power, except for the breakdowns at the local level. Few significant changes have occurred in the leadership since Kim Il Sung died. There have been defections, many of them hyped in the South Korean press and the world media, but only one—that of Hwang Jang Yop in February 1997—was truly significant. Although the regime was embarrassed and demoralized by Hwang's departure, he had never been a central powerholder and the core leadership still appears unshaken.

Another curiosity in the current crisis is that North Korea suffers as if it were Somalia or Ethiopia, but has a much more developed and modern economy. North Korea historically had a powerful industrial economy and remains relatively urbanized, with less than 30 percent of the population working in agriculture. Until recently, international agencies found that North Korea's life expectancy rates, child welfare, and general public health conditions were all comparatively high. Unlike other countries afflicted by humanitarian disaster, this is not a peripheral dependent state with a weak government and a strong society. North Korea has had effective sovereignty and high state capacity. In short, unlike many other nations coping with humanitarian disaster, serious reform could occur in North Korea once the key decisions are made because this is a country that can mobilize everyone for centrally determined tasks. With its well-educated and disciplined workforce, North Korea could effectively exploit a comparative advantage in labor cost in world markets. Indeed, for years major South Korean firms have hoped to marry their skills with North Korean labor.

In some ways, a comparison of North Korea's problems and other humanitarian emergencies is artificial, or forced, because no other region in the world has the anachronistic and special characteristics that distinguish the Korean peninsula. The cold war continues here, as does the Korean War, in a fragile peace held by an armistice and fortified by the world's largest military confrontation. Nearly 2 million heavily armed troops confront each other on the peninsula, we often hear; what we do not hear enough about, however, is how close they recently came to war.

ON THE BRINK

In mid-1994, the United States nearly plunged into a conflict that the commander of American forces in South Korea, General Gary Luck, estimated would have killed a million people, including as many as 100,000 American soldiers, and would have cost more than $100 billion (about double the total cost of the Persian Gulf War). Yet this near-war, like so much else about Korea, is mostly unknown to the American people. Former Washington Post correspondent Don Oberdorfer's recent book, The Two Koreas, contains a detailed account of the frightening crisis over North Korea's nuclear program, which lasted from mid-May to late June 1994. Based on new inside information garnered from interviews in Washington and around the world, this harrowing account also makes clear that it is time to reevaluate the half-century-long American troop presence in Korea. With the cold war over and the Soviet Union gone, the American people should have a choice about whether they want their sons and daughters involved in another Korean War. At the moment, with 37,000 Americans still manning the ramparts of a little-known "family quarrel," as Oberdorfer aptly calls it, that choice has already been made.

For more than a year the American people have been treated to another media barrage about North Korean perfidy. Indeed, it appeared that war might break out in the spring of 1999—not in Kosovo, but in Korea. The ostensible cause was Pyongyang's intransigence about opening up a mountain redoubt that United States intelligence officials said was a surreptitious site of continuing nuclear weapons activity (a possibility thought to have disappeared with a 1994 agreement that mothballed North Korea's graphite nuclear reactor at Yongbyon). This mini-crisis began with a key intelligence leak, leading to a sensational August 17, 1998, New York Times article revealing alleged nuclear activity inside a mountain northwest of Pyongyang. The article implied that the site had just been discovered, when it had in fact been the object of American surveillance for at least six years. Readers also were not told that fully 8,200 underground installations exist in the north, many connected to the security of a country that has never been able to control the prying eyes of satellites and U-2 aircraft. Readers of the North Korean press at the time, however, learned that North Korea would agree to an American inspection of the facility for a price—$300 million—since the site would be useless to its security after the inspection. Pyongyang finally derailed this particular crisis on March 16, 1999, when it made an unprecedented concession to allow multiple American inspections of the underground facility, and agreed to continue negotiations about its missiles.

Two weeks after The New York Times story, a hailstorm of alarmist press reports claimed that Pyongyang had sent a two-stage missile arcing over Japan, leading to virtual panic in Tokyo—leaving the impression that the missile had barely cleared the treetops. Yet North Korea's press had spoken for weeks of little else but preparations for the celebration of the fiftieth anniversary of the regime. Shortly, Pyongyang announced that its three-stage rocket had put a satellite in orbit—beeping out the "Song of Kim Il Sung." Weeks later—after poring over radar tapes—the United States intelligence community concluded that it was indeed an anniversary fireworks display, and that the satellite had failed to reach orbit. The news was, of course, buried in the media.

This was a major intelligence failure, needlessly inflaming Japanese opinion about a rocket that entered the stratosphere over the northern tip of the country (Tokyo relies on Washington to monitor missile firings). But that did nothing to stop hard-liners in the United States from plying their friends with privileged information. By midautumn rightwing Republicans were once again highly critical of President Bill Clinton's North Korea policies, and moderate insiders in Washington were convinced that they were trying to kill the 1994 agreement. Then the Defense Department leaked a new American war plan that would take advantage of prevalent North Korean infirmities to wipe out the entire regime should the north attack the south: the plan would "abolish North Korea as a state and . . . 'reorganize' it under South Korean control." "We will kill them all," a Pentagon insider told veteran East Asia correspondent Richard Halloran.[1]

---

[1] Richard Halloran, Far Eastern Economic Review, December 3, 1998; Halloran quoted the second statement in his November 14, 1998, story published on the "Global Beat" Internet site: http://www.nyu.edu/globalbeat/asia/Halloran111498.html.

Predictably, Pyongyang retorted with unprecedented propaganda broadsides about taking any new war directly to United States territory—and erasing it instead. That kind of fiery rhetoric, combined with the rocket launch, succeeded only in vastly enhancing the chances that Japan will finally agree to deploy the theater missile defense system that the United States has been pushing on Tokyo for 15 years. It was a perfect illustration of a tit-for-tat minuet between two sets of hard-liners to justify their military and intelligence budgets.

THE SILVER LINING

Despite this volatile confrontation, the limited history of the 1990s suggests grounds for optimism about the seemingly endless Korean conflict. The crisis over the north's nuclear problem that began in 1994 nearly led to war, but the final result was promising: a comprehensive diplomatic agreement in October 1994 to freeze the north's nuclear facilities, build light-water reactors that will help its deficient energy regime, and open relations between Pyongyang and Washington. In 1997 the north finally agreed to "four-power talks" to end the Korean War. The mini-crisis of 1998–1999 also ended with an unprecedented inspection agreement, followed by a major step forward in American policy toward the north under the leadership of former Defense Secretary William Perry. North Korean immobilism—which seems so fearsome whether inside the country or in the interminable negotiations over almost any diplomatic issue—has not stood in the way of significant change in the 1990s. In recent years North Korea has shifted considerably, above all in its basic strategic orientation: long determined to get the United States out of Korea, it now appears to want it to stay involved to deal with changed international circumstances in the 1990s, and help the country through its current, unpredictable transition.[2]

If the 1994 framework agreement froze the north's nuclear program and represented the first time since the Korean War that any serious problem on the peninsula had been solved through diplomacy, the ongoing four-power talks represent the first time since 1953 that any serious attempt has been made to replace the armistice with a lasting peace. In adopting this four-way modality, North Korea erased its long-standing policy of refusing to negotiate with the south about the armistice (Seoul never signed the 1953 document, leaving an opening that the north has exploited ever since); the United States finally became serious about negotiating a peace (which it had not been at the designated peace conference at Geneva in 1954 or at any time since);[3] China offered its own participation and good offices (which it usually was reluctant to do unless Pyongyang first approved); and South Korea showed its own constructive attitude by proposing the talks in the first place when Bill Clinton visited Seoul in 1996.

The four-power talks envision an outcome in which the huge and intense military confrontation in Korea can be replaced by a comprehensive peace mechanism that provides full guarantees for all sides. No one yet knows the shape of a final agreement, and there is little public news of progress in the ongoing talks. But if an agreement is reached, it would allow a significant reduction in forces deployed near the demilitarized zone, various confidence-building measures between the two Koreas, and the eventual withdrawal of American troops.

Despite a phalanx of noisy Beltway opposition and the high-level media din about the North Korean threat (including reports that Pyongyang might unleash the smallpox virus on its enemies), midlevel State Department officials have patiently negotiated one agreement after another with Pyongyang in a long series of bilateral talks on various problems. They also began a six-month-long review of Korea policy in the fall of 1998, which markedly changed the direction of United States policy and culminated in the Perry mission to Pyongyang in May 1998. Perry finally issued a public version of this report (and this policy review) in October 1999, the essence of which is a policy of engagement predicated on the coexistence of two Koreas for a considerable period of time, progressive lifting of the half-century American embargo against the north, a deepening of diplomatic relations, and a substantial aid package for the north. North Korea, for its part, agreed to continue to observe the 1994 agreement, to suspend missile testing, and to continue talks with the United States about ending its missile program, including sales of missiles to countries in the Middle East.

The north has sought to couple these talks with the food problem, linking any further progress to increased external aid. The United States has routinely denied a direct relationship between the two. Of course the two problems are linked, but American diplomats do not want to appear to by playing politics with the lives of famine victims. Still, substantial American food aid has flowed into North Korea in the past several years as various talks continue, creating an informal linkage. (The agreement on inspection of the underground site was in effect a trade-off for $500 million in food aid over the next two years.)

> *Pyongyang is on completely unfamiliar terrain when foreigners bearing gifts knock at the door.*

---

[2]Selig Harrison interviewed a North Korean general who told him that whereas the north may call publicly for the withdrawal of American troops, in reality the troops should stay to help deal with a strong Japan, among other things. See Selig Harrison, "Promoting a Soft Landing in Korea," *Foreign Policy,* Spring 1997.

[3]In 1986 I interviewed one of the American negotiators at Geneva in 1954, the late U. Alexis Johnson, who explained how he had prepared for a peace conference, the result of which, he knew well in advance, would be no diplomatic progress whatsoever, let alone a peace treaty.

A WAY OUT

The way to deal with the issue of talks and food aid is to give food aid and indeed aid of all types to the north—in the near term when it can make a difference—without preconditions related to progress in the four-power talks, the missile-control talks, or other forums. The United States can win friends and influence many people by joining with its allies, South Korea and Japan above all, in a major, multibillion-dollar package of aid for North Korea. There has already been plenty of progress on the critical nuclear issue; Pyongyang can be rewarded for mothballing its billion-dollar investment in the Yongbyon reactor and reining in its dangerous missile program.

Pyongyang does best with its back to the wall; it is a world champion of clever resistance and resurgence in such a situation. It is on completely unfamiliar terrain, however, when foreigners bearing gifts knock at the door. A major aid package will silence the hard-liners in the regime and bolster reformers. The downside risks (diversion to the military, for example) are all tolerable, given the north's current inability to wage anything but a suicidal war. In other words, the ongoing humanitarian emergency and the needs of the North Korean economy provide a major opportunity to transform the existing situation on the Korean peninsula, to bring North Korea into the world economy, and then watch that system contain and ultimately transform Pyongyang's insurgent and recalcitrant posture.

Such a package would also save a considerable amount of money: according to Oberdorfer's *The Two Koreas,* the United States spends between $20 billion and $30 billion a year to maintain its Korea commitment, and it continues to do so long after the purpose of this commitment—to contain Soviet and Chinese communism—evaporated. United Nations agencies have called for food and other assistance to North Korea in the hundreds of millions of dollars, and China, the United States, and other countries have already provided food aid that runs to the billions. But the amount needed is much larger today. The few billion dollars necessary to put the North Korean economy back on its feet and buy out its missile program sounds expensive, but the United States has spent similar amounts in retiring the nuclear weapons of Kazakhstan. And it pales in comparison to the annual American expenditure over the past half-century for all things Korean, let alone the $100 billion that a new war would cost.

If the United States were to spend just $1 billion per year on food and other assistance to the north, it would be making a strategically sound investment in orienting Pyongyang away from confrontation and toward engagement with the United States and the rest of the world. It would prod the regime to open up trade and investment opportunities and move rapidly toward the diplomatic relations called for in the 1994 accord, and this in turn would help bring North Korea out of isolation and support reform elements in the regime. Above all, unlike the endless and seemingly irremediable humanitarian crises and civil wars in Afghanistan, Somalia, Rwanda, Angola, Bosnia, and Kosovo, in North Korea this program might actually defuse the problem.

Large-scale aid to the north, not to mention reconciliation, reunification, and the essential magnanimity needed to bring it about, all seem difficult to imagine because such virtues cut against the grain of Korea's history during the past 50 years. That history teaches us how easy it is to get into a war—indeed it happened overnight in June 1950—and how hard it is to get out: 54 years, and counting. Who would have imagined, when American troops first marched into Seoul in September 1945, that one of the most destructive wars of this century would occur five years later, and that 50 years later, the United States is still not out of it—and that it could happen again?

WHY THE TIME IS RIPE

If this scenario sounds unrealistic, consider that South Korea, facing a far greater threat to its existence than does the United States, has made much more far-reaching changes in its policies toward the north since Kim Dae Jung was elected president in December 1997. With his persistent and patient "sunshine policy," President Kim has done more to change policy toward the north than any South Korean or American president since the Korean War, and he has not allowed provocations by hard-liners in Pyongyang to derail his new initiatives. It was Kim Dae Jung who first urged President Clinton to lift the 50-year economic embargo on North Korea (during a visit to Washington in June 1998), arguing that as long as the embargo continued, one could hardly expect the regime to change its economic policies and open up. At the time his efforts met with indifference from the White House and ill-concealed contempt from national security managers. But now his policy is American policy.

The main reason to push for a large aid package is that the alternatives are all worse. The favored scenario of hard-liners in Washington and Seoul, a North Korean collapse, has not occurred, and will not occur—and it *should* not. North Korea was to have collapsed abruptly in 1989, certainly after the Soviet Union disappeared in 1991, above all after its founding father died in 1994. And how could it possibly survive in the face of the nuclear crisis, new war scares, flood, drought, and famine? But North Korea has not collapsed, and its leaders have warned many times that for the world to hope for its collapse is to hope for the next Korean War.

The political obstacles to a major American effort on behalf of North Korea are many, and we can instantly imagine them: the Republicans will attack Clinton's weak-kneed appeasement, the CIA will leak olds stories about the north's war plans, South Korean hard-liners will accuse the United States of abandoning them and will make life difficult for President Kim and his sunshine policy, and hard-liners in the north will be tempted to take the money and run. With well-constructed safeguards on the uses of this aid, however, and a clear statement of its purpose, a still-popular second-term president like Bill Clinton could make this option happen. Ultimately a peace settlement combined with a large aid package will open the path to reconciliation and reunion, the recompense that the twenty-first century will unquestionably bestow upon the Korean people, sooner or later. Why not make it sooner? This is a golden opportunity for the United States to make a new friend, solve an old problem, and prepare for a twenty-first century that is likely to be much kinder to the Korean people.

Unit Selections

Key Points to Consider

❖ What can the United States and other western countries do to limit the appeal of Islamic fundamentalists such as bin Laden who call for more terrorist acts against the United States?

❖ Explain why you do or do not favor lifting U.S.-backed economic sanctions on Iraq. Be sure to explain whether your position is guided more by humanitarian, pragmatic, national security, or other criteria.

❖ What can be done to promote peace and stability in the Great Lakes region of Africa? By whom?

 **Links**   # www.dushkin.com/online/

These sites are annotated on pages 6 and 7.

The bombing of U.S. embassies in Kenya and Tanzania by Islamic extremists and retaliatory U.S. air raids in Sudan and Afghanistan during the summer of 1998 manifest conflicts between the United States and radical Islamacists. In "License to Kill: Usama bin Ladin's Declaration of Jihad," Bernard Lewis emphasize the importance of Americans understanding what drives Islamic extremists. Lewis describes how the main Islamacists' grievance—the infidel U.S. troops in Arabia—was published in a little-noticed declaration of Jihad by Usama bin Ladin in an Arabic newspaper prior to the bombings. Most Muslims reject this declaration as a gross distortion of America's role in the region and also for advocating the use of terrorism. However, the few who accept the extreme interpretation will continue to use terrorism in the future to rid the region of infidels.

Recurring U.S.–Iraqi confrontations since the Persian Gulf War reached a new level of intensity in mid-December 1998 when the United States and Great Britain launched military strikes against Iraq for 4 days in response to Iraq's lack of cooperation with UN weapons inspectors. After the raids, the United States announced that it would step up efforts to encourage domestic opponents of Salaam Hussein. To date, efforts to reach a new set of terms to permit UN weapons inspectors to re-enter Iraq have failed. While the United States and Great Britain continued to maintain the no-fly zones over southern and northern Iraq, pressures were building throughout the international community during 1999 to lift more of the sanctions on Iraq for humanitarian reasons.

Enis Halliday describes in "Iraq and the UN's Weapon of Mass Destruction" how UN sanctions have placed a moral crisis before the international community. Halliday, the former head of the oil-for-food program in Iraq, asks how anyone can justify the continued killing of children to contain Saddam Hussein. Halliday recently resigned to protest continuation of the sanctions. A fundamental paradox of this conflict is that 8 years of bombing and embargo have strengthened, rather than weakened, Saddam, who uses a permanent state of war to strengthen his power base.

The long-stalled Middle East peace processes were revived after Ehud Barak took office as the prime minister of Israel and implemented a more conciliatory policy toward the Palistinian Liberation Authorities and neighboring Arab states. Israel forced settlers to leave their recently constructed homes on the West Bank while Yassar Arafat moved to implement the final provisions of the Wye agreement brokered by the United States in 1998. Syria's aging President Hafez al-Assad also signaled in 1999 that he was ready to rejoin the Middle East peace effort. UN forces currently separate Israel and Syrian troops who technically have been at war since Israel occupied two-thirds of Syria's Golan Heights in 1967.

Generalizations about political and economic trends in sub-Saharan Africa are difficult to make because conditions vary widely among countries and between sectors in the same country. Marina Ottaway emphasizes in "Africa" that many countries in sub-Saharan Africa are neither on the verge of widespread anarchy nor at the dawn of democratic and economic renewal. Economic growth in Africa is stronger today than in the disastrous 1980s but most countries were adversely affected by the downturn in commodity prices during 1998. Clinton's talk of "a new African renaissance" during his historic visit in March of 1998 seemed premature. Most African economies remain highly fragile economies dependent on world commodity prices and other forces beyond the control of their national policy makers.

Throughout Africa progress in implementing democratic reforms varies. Grassroots demands for democracy continue in most African countries but in several recent elections civilian and military leaders of the ruling elite managed to retain power in manipulated multiparty elections. In contrast, post-apartheid South Africa saw the peaceful transition of power from Nelson Mandela to Tambo Mbeki and democratically-elected civilian rule returned to Nigeria in 1999. Ottaway also notes that the countries of sub-Saharan Africa are now confronting their political problems, but they are doing so in a manner that the international community might not always find acceptable.

Efforts to establish a new balance of power in countries such as the Democratic Republic of the Congo resulted in spreading interstate conflict. Restoration of political stability is likely to require a substantial modification of the territorial and political status quo. Meanwhile, the massive death toll in the Eritrean-Ethiopian war, the long delays involved in the UN effort to send peacekeepers to monitor the ceasefire in Sierra Leone, and Nigeria's scaling back of its military commitment to West Africa's peacekeeping force, ECOMOG, raises serious questions about who will play the role of peacekeeper in Africa in the future.

Middle East and Africa

License To Kill

Usama bin Ladin's Declaration of Jihad

Bernard Lewis

On February 23, 1998, *Al-Quds al-Arabi,* an Arabic newspaper published in London, printed the full text of a "Declaration of the World Islamic Front for Jihad against the Jews and the Crusaders." According to the paper, the statement was faxed to them under the signatures of Usama bin Ladin, the Saudi financier blamed by the United States for masterminding the August bombings of its embassies in East Africa, and the leaders of militant Islamist groups in Egypt, Pakistan, and Bangladesh. The statement—a magnificent piece of eloquent, at times even poetic Arabic prose—reveals a version of history that most Westerners will find unfamiliar. Bin Ladin's grievances are not quite what many would expect.

The declaration begins with an exordium quoting the more militant passages in the Quran and the sayings of the Prophet Muhammad, then continues:

> Since God laid down the Arabian peninsula, created its desert, and surrounded it with its seas, no calamity has ever befallen it like these Crusader hosts that have spread in it like locusts, crowding its soil, eating its fruits, and destroying its verdure; and this at a time when the nations contend against the Muslims like diners jostling around a bowl of food.

The statement goes on to talk of the need to understand the situation and act to rectify it. The facts, it says, are known to everyone and fall under three main headings:

> First—For more than seven years the United States is occupying the lands of Islam in the holiest of its territories, Arabia, plundering its riches, overwhelming its rulers, humiliating its people, threatening its neighbors, and using its bases in the peninsula as a spearhead to fight against the neighboring Islamic peoples. Though some in the past have disputed the true nature of this occupation, the people of Arabia in their entirety have now recognized it.
> There is no better proof of this than the continuing American aggression against the Iraqi people, launched from Arabia despite its rulers, who all oppose the use of their territories for this purpose but are subjugated.
> Second—Despite the immense destruction inflicted on the Iraqi people at the hands of the Crusader-Jewish alliance and in spite of the appalling number of dead, exceeding a million, the Americans nevertheless, in spite of all this, are trying once more to repeat this dreadful slaughter. It seems that the long blockade following after a fierce war, the dismemberment and the destruction are not enough for them. So they come

BERNARD LEWIS is Cleveland E. Dodge Professor Emeritus of Near Eastern Studies at Princeton University. His books include *The Arabs in History, The Emergence of Modern Turkey,* and, most recently, *The Middle East: A Brief History of the Last 2,000 Years.*

Reprinted by permission of *Foreign Affairs,* November/December 1998, pp. 14-19. © 1998 by the Council on Foreign Relations, Inc.

again today to destroy what remains of this people and to humiliate their Muslim neighbors.

Third—While the purposes of the Americans in these wars are religious and economic, they also serve the petty state of the Jews, to divert attention from their occupation of Jerusalem and their killing of Muslims in it.

There is no better proof of all this than their eagerness to destroy Iraq, the strongest of the neighboring Arab states, and their attempt to dismember all the states of the region, such as Iraq and Saudi Arabia and Egypt and Sudan, into petty states, whose division and weakness would ensure the survival of Israel and the continuation of the calamitous Crusader occupation of the lands of Arabia.

These crimes, the statement declares, amount to "a clear declaration of war by the Americans against God, his Prophet, and the Muslims." In such a situation, the declaration says, the *ulema*—authorities on theology and Islamic law, or *sharia*—throughout the centuries unanimously ruled that when enemies attack the Muslim lands, jihad becomes every Muslim's personal duty.

In the technical language of the *ulema*, religious duties may be collective, to be discharged by the community as a whole, or personal, incumbent on every individual Muslim. In an offensive war, the religious duty of jihad is collective and may be discharged by volunteers and professionals. When the Muslim community is defending itself, however, jihad becomes an individual obligation.

After quoting various Muslim authorities, the signatories then proceed to the final and most important part of their declaration, the *fatwa*, or ruling. It holds that

To kill Americans and their allies, both civil and military, is an individual duty of every Muslim who is able, in any country where this is possible, until the Aqsa Mosque [in Jerusalem] and the Haram Mosque [in Mecca] are freed from their grip and until their armies, shattered and broken-winged, depart from all the lands of Islam, incapable of threatening any Muslim.

After citing some further relevant Quranic verses, the document continues:

By God's leave, we call on every Muslim who believes in God and hopes for reward to obey God's command to kill the Americans and plunder their possessions wherever he finds them and whenever he can. Likewise we call on the Muslim *ulema* and leaders and youth and soldiers to launch attacks against the armies of the American devils and against those who are allied with them from among the helpers of Satan.

The declaration and *fatwa* conclude with a series of further quotations from Muslim scripture.

INFIDELS

Bin Ladin's view of the Gulf War as American aggression against Iraq may seem a little odd, but it is widely—though by no means universally—accepted in the Islamic world. For holy warriors of any faith, the faithful are always right and the infidels always wrong, whoever the protagonists and whatever the circumstances of their encounter.

The three areas of grievance listed in the declaration—Arabia, Iraq, and Jerusalem—will be familiar to observers of the Middle Eastern scene. What may be less familiar is the sequence and emphasis. For Muslims, as we in the West sometimes tend to forget but those familiar with Islamic history and literature know, the holy land par excellence is Arabia—Mecca, where the Prophet was born; Medina, where he established the first Muslim state; and the Hijaz, whose people were the first to rally to the new faith and become its standard-bearers. Muhammad lived and died in Arabia, as did the Rashidun caliphs, his immediate successors at the head of the Islamic community. Thereafter, except for a brief interlude in Syria, the center of the Islamic world and the scene of its major achievements was Iraq, the seat of the caliphate for half a millennium. For Muslims, no piece of land once added to the realm of Islam can ever be finally renounced, but none compares in significance with Arabia and Iraq.

Of these two, Arabia is by far the more important. The classical Arabic historians tell us that in the year 20 after the *hijra* (Muhammad's move from Mecca to Medina), corresponding to 641 of the Christian calendar, the Caliph Umar decreed that Jews and Christians should be removed from Arabia to fulfill an injunction the Prophet uttered on his deathbed: "Let there not be two religions in Arabia." The people in question were the Jews of the oasis of Khaybar in the north and the Christians of Najran in the south. Both were ancient and deep-rooted communities, Arab in their speech, culture, and way of life, differing from their neighbors only in their faith.

The saying attributed to the Prophet was impugned by some earlier Islamic authorities. But it was generally accepted as authentic, and Umar put it into effect. The expulsion of religious minorities is extremely rare in Islamic history—unlike medieval Christendom, where evictions of Jews and (after the reconquest of Spain) Muslims were normal and frequent. Compared with European expulsions, Umar's decree was both limited and compassionate. It did not include southern and southeastern Arabia, which were not seen as part of Islam's holy land. And unlike the Jews and Muslims driven out of Spain and other European countries to find what refuge they could elsewhere, the Jews and Christians of Arabia were resettled on lands assigned to them—the Jews in Syria, the Christians in Iraq. The process was also gradual rather than sudden, and there are reports of Jews and Christians remaining in Khaybar and Najran for some time after Umar's edict.

But the decree was final and irreversible, and from then until now the holy land of the Hijaz has been forbidden territory for non-Muslims. According to the Hanbali school of Islamic jurisprudence, accepted by both the Saudis and the declaration's signatories, for a non-Muslim even to set foot on the sacred soil is a major offense. In the rest of the kingdom, non-Muslims, while admitted as temporary visitors, were not permitted to establish residence or practice their religion.

The history of the Crusades provides a vivid example of the relative importance of Arabia and other places in Islamic perceptions. The Crusaders' capture of Jerusalem in 1099 was a triumph for Christendom and a disaster for the city's Jews. But to judge by the Arabic historiography of the period, it aroused scant interest in the region. Appeals for help by local Muslims to Damascus and Baghdad went unanswered, and the newly established Crusader principalities from Antioch to Jerusalem soon fitted into the game of Levantine politics, with cross-religious alliances forming a pattern of rivalries between and among Muslim and Christian princes.

The great counter-Crusade that ultimately drove the Crusaders into the sea did not begin until almost a century later. Its immediate cause was the activities of a freebooting Crusader leader, Reynald of Châtillon, who held the fortress of Kerak, in southern Jordan, between 1176 and 1187 and used it to launch a series of raids against Muslim caravans and commerce in the adjoining regions, including the Hijaz. Historians of the Crusades are probably right in saying that Reynald's motive was primarily economic—the desire for loot. But Muslims saw his campaigns as a provocation, a challenge directed against Islam's holy places. In 1182, violating an agreement between the Crusader king of Jerusalem and the Muslim leader Saladin, Reynald attacked and looted Muslim caravans, including one of pilgrims bound for Mecca. Even more heinous, from a Muslim point of view, was his threat to Arabia and a memorable buccaneering expedition in the Red Sea, featuring attacks on Muslim shipping and the Hijaz ports that served Mecca and Medina. Outraged, Saladin proclaimed a jihad against the Crusaders.

Even in Christian Europe, Saladin was justly celebrated and admired for his chivalrous and generous treatment of his defeated enemies. His magnanimity did not extend to Reynald of Châtillon. The great Arab historian Ibn al-Athir wrote, "Twice, [Saladin said,] I had made a vow to kill him if I had him in my hands; once when he tried to march on Mecca and Medina, and again when he treacherously captured the caravan." After Saladin's triumph, when many of the Crusader princes and chieftains were

taken captive, he separated Reynald of Châtillon from the rest and beheaded him with his own hands.

After the success of the jihad and the recapture of Jerusalem, Saladin and his successors seem to have lost interest in the city. In 1229, one of them even ceded Jerusalem to the Emperor Frederick II as part of a general compromise agreement between the Muslim ruler and the Crusaders. Jerusalem was retaken in 1244 after the Crusaders tried to make it a purely Christian city, then eventually became a minor provincial town. Widespread interest in Jerusalem was reawakened only in the nineteenth century, first by the European powers' quarrels over custody of the Christian holy places and then by new waves of Jewish immigration after 1882.

In Arabia, however, the next perceived infidel threat came in the eighteenth century with the consolidation of European power in South Asia and the reappearance of Christian ships off the shores of Arabia. The resulting sense of outrage was at least one of the elements in the religious revival inspired in Arabia by the puritanical Wahhabi movement and led by the House of Saud, the founders of the modern Saudi state. During the period of Anglo-French domination of the Middle East, the imperial powers ruled Iraq, Syria, Palestine, Egypt, and Sudan. They nibbled at the fringes of Arabia, in Aden and the trucial sheikhdoms of the Gulf, but were wise enough to have no military and minimal political involvement in the affairs of the peninsula.

Oil made that level of involvement totally inadequate, and a growing Western presence, predominantly American, began to transform every aspect of Arabian life. The Red Sea port of Jiddah had long served as a kind of religious quarantine area in which foreign diplomatic, consular, and commercial representatives were allowed to live. The discovery and exploitation of oil—and the consequent growth of the Saudi capital, Riyadh, from small oasis town to major metropolis—brought a considerable influx of foreigners. Their presence, still seen by many as a desecration, planted the seeds for a growing mood of resentment.

As long as this foreign involvement was exclusively economic, and as long as the rewards were more than adequate to soothe every grievance, the alien presence could be borne. But in recent years both have changed. With the fall in oil prices and the rise in population and expenditure, the rewards are no longer adequate and the grievances have become more numerous and more vocal. Nor is the involvement limited to economic activities. The revolution in Iran and the wars of Saddam Hussein have added political and military dimensions to the foreign involvement and have lent some plausibility to the increasingly heard cries of "imperialism." Where their holy land is involved, many Muslims tend to define the struggle—and sometimes also the enemy—in religious terms, seeing the American troops sent to free Kuwait and save Saudi Arabia from Saddam Hussein as infidel invaders and occupiers. This perception is heightened by America's unquestioned primacy among the powers of the infidel world.

TRAVESTIES

To most Americans, the declaration is a travesty, a gross distortion of the nature and purpose of the American presence in Arabia. They should also know that for many—perhaps most—Muslims, the declaration is an equally grotesque travesty of the nature of Islam and even of its doctrine of jihad. The Quran speaks of peace as well as of war. The hundreds of thousands of traditions and sayings attributed with varying reliability to the Prophet, interpreted in various ways by the *ulema*, offer a wide range of guidance. The militant and violent interpretation is one among many. The standard juristic treatises on *sharia* normally contain a chapter on jihad, understood in the military sense as regular warfare against infidels and apostates. But these treatises prescribe correct behavior and respect for the rules of war in such matters as the opening and termination of hostilities and the treatment of noncombatants and prisoners, not to speak of diplomatic envoys. The jurists also discuss—and sometimes differ on—the actual conduct of war. Some permit, some restrict, and some disapprove of the use of mangonels, poisoned arrows, and the poisoning of enemy water supplies—the missile and chemical warfare of the Middle Ages—out of concern for the indiscriminate casualties that these weapons inflict. At no point do the basic texts of Islam enjoin terrorism and murder. At no point do they even consider the random slaughter of uninvolved bystanders.

Nevertheless, some Muslims are ready to approve, and a few of them to apply, the declaration's extreme interpretation of their religion. Terrorism requires only a few. Obviously, the West must defend itself by whatever means will be effective. But in devising strategies to fight the terrorists, it would surely be useful to understand the forces that drive them.

Denis Halliday resigned in October as head of the oil-for-food program in Iraq to protest the suffering inflicted on the Iraqi people by UN sanctions. Here he makes his case.

Iraq and the UN's Weapon
of Mass Destruction

DENIS J. HALLIDAY

Lord David Owen has written that "conflict is cancerous in the way it erodes democracy and trust, brutalizes behavior and destroys civilized values and constraints." His observation is especially apt in regard to the conflict between Iraq and the member states of the UN Security Council. It is time, after years of humanitarian tragedy, to acknowledge that this conflict has turned the resolutions of the Security Council into brutal instruments. The council has sustained economic sanctions, fully aware of their catastrophic impact on the people of Iraq—an action that represents the effective abandonment of civilized values. It is ironic that warfare is governed by conventions, but that unilateral and multilateral economic sanctions are not.

As we have seen conspicuously in Iraq, comprehensive UN sanctions undermine the very spirit and intent of various internationally endorsed instruments, such as the Declaration of Human Rights, the Convention of the Rights of the Child, and even the appropriate provisions of the Hague and Geneva Conventions concerning civilians. Of course, the member states of the United Nations cannot allow a country's leadership to engage in blatant misbehavior. At the same time, member states cannot knowingly resort to devices such as the sanctions on Iraq that have reduced the Security Council to effectively punishing innocent Iraqi citizens, especially the most vulnerable: the children. And having successfully demonized Iraqi President Saddam Hussein, we now face the unfortunate consequences of the political and media demonization of the entire Iraqi people.

DENIS J. HALLIDAY is the former United Nations assistant secretary general and humanitarian coordinator in Baghdad. This article is adapted from a speech given before the London Conference on Sanctions in December 1998.

The UN's Versailles Treaty

Sanctions on Iraq have placed a moral crisis before the international community. Is there really anyone who can justify the continued killing of children and who believes that the death of large numbers is acceptable—is required—to contain Saddam Hussein? Through the deprivation that sustained sanctions have brought about in Iraq, we have the member states of the Security Council themselves undermining the human rights of the innocent and the blameless. Whether the number of Iraqi children who have died because of sanctions is 5 or more than 500,000—the latter in fact the tragic reality—there can be no morally acceptable justification. Thousands are dying each month, and many others suffer from malnourishment, including chronic malnutrition with its long-term effects of physical and mental stunting.

In short, the member states of the Security Council must not continue to punish the people of Iraq because they fear and cannot effectively communicate with the leadership of the country. To blame Saddam Hussein for Iraq's plight is to evade responsibility—a responsibility that member states must share.

I refer to the humanitarian crisis in Iraq today fully aware of the oil-for-food program that I coordinated in Baghdad over a period of 13 months. Yes, the program makes a difference, and the people of Iraq would be worse off without it. But it remains a largely ineffective response to the humanitarian crisis in the country and has not begun to tackle the underlying infrastructural causes of continuing child mortality and malnutrition—an infrastructure destroyed by coalition forces during the 1991 Persian Gulf War, even though it was civilian and thereby protected by international conventions.

Under the oil-for-food program, Iraq is allowed to sell a set amount of oil over periods of six months (initially $2 billion gross, or $1.2 billion net, and now $5 billion gross, or $3 billion net), with the revenues going directly into a UN account. This account is managed solely by the UN controller, who dis-

Iraq's younger generation . . . is maturing in an environment not dissimilar to that found in Germany under the conditions set by the Versailles Treaty.

burses funds to contractors and suppliers of foodstuffs and basic medicines. These have been contracted for by Iraq through its own international bidding process that is under the auspices of the Security Council's Sanctions Committee. Nearly 40 percent of gross revenues is earmarked for the UN's gulf war compensation fund and for UN operating expenses in Iraq.

The program continues to be underfunded even though increased revenues were agreed to by the Security Council; the increases has been effectively halved by lower oil prices in 1998 combined with Iraq's ever-diminishing capacity to produce and pump oil (without new equipment and spare parts, which have been clocked by sanctions since the war and the damage done by coalition forces at that time, and since). The program has sustained imports of supplies, but has failed to diminish malnutrition levels and reduce the monthly death rate of children and adults directly attributable to sanctions.

SECURITY COUNCIL RESOLUTIONS RELATING TO THE OIL-FOR-FOOD PROGRAM

RESOLUTION 661 of August 6, 1990, imposes comprehensive economic sanctions on Iraq, exempting food and medicine, and establishes the 661 Committee to oversee implementation of the sanctions.

RESOLUTION 687 of April 3, 1991, sets terms for a cease-fire and maintains the terms of the embargo.

RESOLUTION 706 of August 15, 1991, establishes the mechanism for the oil-for-food program and authorizes an escrow account.

RESOLUTION 712 of September 19, 1991, confirms the sum of $1.6 billion to be raised by the sale of Iraqi oil in a six-month period to fund the oil-for-food program.

RESOLUTION 778 of October 2, 1992, authorizes transferring back money produced by any Iraqi oil transaction on or after August 6, 1990, and that had been deposited into the escrow account, to the states or accounts concerned for as long as the oil exports take place or until sanctions are lifted.

RESOLUTION 986 of April 14, 1995, enables Iraq to sell up to $1 billion of oil every 90 days and use the proceeds for humanitarian supplies.

RESOLUTION 1051 of March 17, 1996, establishes an export-import monitoring system for Iraq.

RESOLUTION 1111 of June 4, 1997, extends the term of Security Council Resolution 986 another 180 days.

RESOLUTION 1129 of September 12, 1997, decides that the provisions of Resolution 1111 should remain in force, but authorizes special provisions to allow Iraq to sell petroleum in a more favorable time frame.

RESOLUTION 1143 of December 4, 1997, extends the oil-for-food program for another 180 days.

RESOLUTION 1153 of February 20, 1998, allows the export of $5.256 billion of Iraqi oil.

RESOLUTION 1158 of March 25, 1998, permits Iraq to export additional oil in the 90 days from March 5, 1998, to compensate for delayed resumption of oil production and reduced oil prices.

RESOLUTION 1175 of June 19, 1998, authorizes Iraq to buy $300 million worth of oil spare parts in order to reach the ceiling of $5.256 billion.

RESOLUTION 1210 of November 24, 1998, renews the oil-for-food program for a further six-months from November 26, at the higher levels established by Resolution 1153 and including additional oil spare parts.

Source: United Nations, "Basic Facts" of the oil-for-food program, at http://www.un.org/Depts/oip/scrs.html.

The social cost of sanctions has been enormous. Iraqi families and Islamic family values have been damaged. Children have been forced to work, to become street kids, to beg and engage in crime. Young women have been forced into prostitution by the destitution of their families. Fathers have abandoned their families. The many problems single mothers already faced in the aftermath of the Iran-Iraq war have been compounded. Workplace progress that professional and other women had achieved in recent decades has been lost. The education system has collapsed, with thousands of teachers leaving their posts because they are unable to work under existing conditions, and a dropout rate of some 30 percent at the primary and secondary levels. The health services are unable to handle the most basic preventable diseases—such as diarrhea, gastroenteritis, respiratory tract infections, polio—and curtail their spread to epidemic proportions. Hospitals attempt to function with collapsed water and sewage systems, without even the basic supplies for hygiene and minimal care.

Iraq's younger generation of professionals, the political leadership of the future—bitter, angry, isolated, and dangerously alienated from the world—is maturing in an environment not dissimilar to that found in Germany under the conditions set by the Versailles Treaty. A future generation of Baath party leaders may lead Iraq onto the path followed by the Taliban and the fundamentalist right; many of these future political leaders find the present leadership and its continuing dialogue and compromise with the UN to be unacceptable, to be too "moderate." An entire people have been stripped of their pride and dignity; they are humiliated and angry, and may find it difficult to move forward, to collaborate with other nations in the gulf—indeed, with the entire international community. We need to worry about the longer-term social and political impact of sanctions together with today's death and despair.

The Media's Spin

We live in an era when time and distance no longer provide the space for considered thought, careful reactions, and strategic responses. The public has calamities, man-made and natural, broadcast at it on the hour, if not more often. We know that this exposure is selection, often tragically so, failing to provide balance and objectivity. The media responds to what it believes to be the demand of its consumer clients or, in some cases, to the constraints that government decision makers impose. The media "spin" often corresponds to the politically attractive spin of the day; in the end, the general public is grossly misled.

Politicians and decision makers are rushed to judgment and action—or inaction—by the instantaneous television and radio coverage of world events. There needs to be a change whereby the bottom line no longer drives news coverage and the enormous responsibility for evenhanded reporting is understood and mandated. With Iraq we have seen so often the violence inflicted by roaring jets and the deadly reach of missiles. We are only too familiar with the buildup of crisis, the anxiety of tension, and even the excitement of conflict and destruction that, sadly, appeals to many who have not experienced it.

We do not find balance. Have we seen the unending daily tragedy of the malnourished, the slow death from leukemia in the absence of proper drugs, the fatalities caused by waterborne disease, the health effects of children playing in raw sewage? Despite the civilian devastation in Iraq, the television audiences of Europe and North America are largely ignorant of the thousands of deaths every month directly attributable to United Nations sanctions. They also remain unaware that the appalling situation in Iraq is the result of decisions and actions taken by their own elected officials.

"Smarter" Sanctions and Prevention

We need to consider alternative to economic sanctions, including "smarter" sanctions that target the personal bank accounts of and ban travel by a country's leadership. Studies show that sanctions almost always fail to achieve their stated objectives. They tend to miss a country's leadership and hit the innocent. They impact most on democratic societies, but fail to impress the dictatorial regimes whose leaders often remain untouched and whose civilians pay the price. They are in toto notoriously unsuccessful. They are expensive in terms of life and in terms of the economic impact they have on immediate neighbors, and indeed, on the global economy.

This takes me back to the thoughts of Lord Owen. Dismissing conflict as a force destructive of all parties, he has turned to the importance of preventive actions. In so doing he has noted that the skills and discipline to create a preventive health system took 100 years to develop. In today's crisis-prone world we do not have that time. We need to focus on preventive diplomacy and action immediately. We need to anticipate problems within and among countries before they become crises. We need early warning systems and observation mechanisms. We need preventive journalism, humanitarian neutrality, anticipation, and strategic planning for conflict avoidance and resolution.

Preventive skills and political will need to be applied more than ever before. Is there an obligatory and critical role for the United Nations? I believe so. With the advantage of hindsight, how many calamities might have been avoided with proper anticipation, with greater understanding, with viable compromises and political will and resolution? How many sanctions might have been avoided? Could we not have anticipated the Kuwait invasion? The thought was not new, and the intentions were well known, as were the history of Mesopotamia and the root causes that continued into this century.

Another Iraq Policy

We need to find a compromise to address the plight of Iraq. Let us retain all possible control over arms manufacture for and sales of arms to Iraq. Let us retain the capacity to monitor and observe. Remove economic sanctions now and sustain the capacity to prohibit military renewal and the development of weapons of mass destruction. Let's give up the UN weapon of mass destruction: economic sanctions. Let us risk a new approach. In other words, accept the early successes of Unscom (the UN special commission charged with eradicating Iraq's weapons of mass destruction) and reject the continuing and politically motivated search for needles in the military-capacity haystacks of Iraq. Let us restrict ourselves to the wording and intent of the relevant resolutions of the Security Council. Avoid the add-ons of toppling the Iraqi leadership, of assassinating Saddam Hussein; these calls will simply enhance the president not only in Iraq but throughout the Arab and Islamic world. Let us adopt a genuinely evenhanded approach to the pursuit of peace and disarmament throughout the entire Middle East.

Some international lawyers now question the legality of Security Council decisions that yield "criminal" devastation, including large numbers of civilian deaths. Recent history shows that sanctions can be more devastating than a declaration of war. Furthermore, Security Council deliberations, and resulting outcomes that grossly neglect improper behavior of some member states while authorizing retaliatory enforcement on others, are noted with great bitterness in the Arab-Islamic world and beyond. Not only are the reputation and glaringly undemocratic workings of the council severely threatened, but the credibility and the very integrity of the United Nations itself widely questioned. It is time for a distinguishing panel of international jurists to be assembled to review the propriety of Security Council resolutions and actions relating to economic sanctions. Constraints need to be established.

Can we speak of encouraging the development of a community inclusive of all the member states of the Middle East? Can we have vision, and take a longer view? Can we see Iraq not as a problem state, but as an essential part of a larger region that, without Iraq's participation, can never be at peace or exist as a viable community?

Let us acknowledge that the world needs peace in the gulf for its own selfish purposes. Let us reward the private sector (but not the arms manufacturers), respond to human rights concerns and the expectations of people, and end the humanitarian nightmare we have created with legitimate and nonexploitative opportunities. Perhaps then not only the people of the countries immediately concerned, but also the international community, will be rewarded. Finally, let us take the United Nations back to the legal and moral high ground on which it belongs.

War without end

Saddam's Survival in the Ruins

While the world's attention was focused on Kosovo, the U.S. continued to bomb Iraq— to the tune of one attack every three days. After eight years, five bombing campaigns, and a notable lack of success, America is still hoping the pressure will topple Saddam. . . .

The Americans are bombing Iraqi positions? On the outskirts of Baghdad, children are dying of malnutrition? Iraq's hospitals lack medicines? In Latakia, a fine restaurant where the city's upper crust dines, there is no sign of any of this, for the clientele of this place in the fine suburb of Jadiriya are members of the small class of Iraqis who lack nothing—except scruples.

These owners of luxury limousines are war profiteers and courtiers around Iraqi dictator Saddam Hussein. The sanctions introduced to punish Saddam for invading neighboring Kuwait in August, 1990, do not trouble the people in Latakia. Nor do the bombs still being dropped by the American planes that Washington hopes will shake the dictator's hold on power. So the regime's favorites celebrate as if Saddam Hussein had not driven his nation into poverty. They eat as people used to, when Iraq, with its enormous oil reserves, was the economic miracle of the Arab world.

Until recently, enjoying such wealth was frowned upon in Baghdad. Those who had profited from the war preferred to indulge in luxury out of the public eye. But now they flaunt the money they make by cigarette smuggling, illegal oil trading, and black-market dealing in food and medicine. These people seem to fear that every party could be their last— that they are dancing atop a volcano— because tomorrow the anger of the wretched people of Iraq could sweep Saddam and his supporters away.

Except for jokes about Saddam, the new rich can dare anything. They have made their money in rampant real-estate speculation or in dubious businesses dealing televisions, computers, and cameras. The days when the police would arrest profiteers to keep them in line—or even shoot some on the spot—are long past. The government has accepted that the social gap has widened. "Two decades of war, deprivation, and the indifference of the rest of the world have destroyed the social fabric," says a government official. "Now everyone thinks of himself."

The collapse of the currency has worsened the disaster. The average monthly salary of a mid-level government employee—three quarters of all those working work for the government—is 4,000 dinar, or $3.30. Even a short cab ride costs 300 dinar, and a grilled chicken costs 5,000 dinar, or what a teacher makes in a month.

The education system is at the edge of ruin. There are not enough books or supplies. Child labor, formerly not allowed in Iraq, is now the order of the day. Kids sell snacks, shine shoes, scrub sidewalks, wash cars, or simply beg.

For a tiny sum, every Iraqi receives supplies of sugar, tea, flour, meat, oil, soap, and detergent, but the monthly amounts barely cover two weeks. And how long Baghdad will be able to provide even this, given its apparently empty treasury, is not clear.

Iraq can now harvest just 30 percent to 40 percent of what it needs from its farms, partly because of the worst drought in memory. In spite of the United Nations' "Oil for Food" program, humanitarian aid provides just $175 per capita per year. According to official Iraqi statistics, since the embargo began in 1990, more than 1 million Iraqis have died of malnutrition.

Heads of families that own a car often try to make it as taxi drivers. Gasoline is comparatively cheap: One dollar buys about 13 gallons, but this is what a civil servant would work 10 days to earn. The cars are rickety, for

Reprinted from *World Press Review,* August 1999, pp. 16-17. Originally appeared in *Der Spiegel,* May 24, 1999 and reprinted by permission of The New York Times Syndication, Paris, France.

spare parts are not available. Even basic engine components are classified as having military use, so their import is banned by the UN. The embargo also limits the numbers of replacement parts for turbines that can be bought, so electricity generation is rationed. The current is cut off twice a day—for three hours each—in Baghdad and other cities.

The national health service, once splendid, now exists only on paper. The doctors at the hospitals, often the products of the world's finest medical schools, continue to provide good diagnoses, but patients have to bring their own drugs, and medicine is usually available only on the black market, for dollars. As a result, child mortality is especially high.

In order to survive, people are leaving Baghdad. It is easier to find food and housing in the countryside. While threshers and tractors stand idle because spare parts are difficult to find, farmers using sickles and scythes are still able to harvest enough wheat, barley, and potatoes to earn a small profit.

Iraqis have long believed that the West has condemned them to their fate. Saddam Hussein's propaganda machine has told them that the American-led embargo is the source of all

their misery. More recently, Iraqis are becoming disappointed in their Arab brother nations. Aid from neighboring countries has diminished, complains the head of the Red Crescent in Kerbela, a city in the south. "Neither our fellow Shiites in Iran nor our fellow Arabs in Saudi Arabia or the Emirates show any sympathy," the official says.

Kerbela is the center of Shiite opposition to the Sunni Saddam, so the south has suffered more under his repression than other parts of the country. In February, opposition Ayatollah Mohamad Sadiq al-Sadr was assassinated, a killing apparently allowed by those around Saddam. That set off the worst unrest in years, and the region threatened to get out of Baghdad's control.

But even in Kerbela no one dares speak publicly against the president. The dictator, with his army of spies and agents, has the country well in hand. On April 28, the man who has thwarted two American presidents celebrated his 62nd birthday. Saddam was feted by parades and ceremonies throughout Iraq. For the biggest party, held in his native village of Audsha near Takrit, the president brought in 5,000 foreign guests, among them

Arab and Eastern European politicians and intellectuals, but also 150 Russian athletes and two Armenian football teams. A huge portrait depicted the leader as a modern-day Nebuchadnezzar, mounted on a chariot and shooting down American jets with his bows and arrows.

Both the bombing and the embargo, contrary to Western expectations, have strengthened, rather than weakened, the despot. The permanent state of war is his basis of power, and he has turned the suffering of his people into patriotic pride. "Saddam is showing everybody what an Iraqi can do," enthuses a customs officer, Amr Amir, at the Kuwaiti border.

Diplomats in Baghdad see the crass behavior of the war profiteers as the "social explosive" that could destroy the regime. The poor are bitter. "I could no longer watch while these new-rich used the millions they earned with the help of Satan to humiliate us," complains carpenter Ghassan Juman, who is leaving Baghdad. But Juman still harbors the naive hope that Saddam Hussein will "clean out that bunch."

—*Dieter Bednarz and Volkhard Windfuhr, "Der Spiegel" (liberal newsmagazine), Hamburg, May 24, 1999.*

AFRICA

Much of the world sees Africa as one of two extremes. Either it is a continent beset by genocidal warfare, corrupt leaders, and rampant poverty or it is a region that is about to enter a renaissance. But Africa is neither on the verge of widespread anarchy nor at the dawn of democratic and economic renewal. These misperceptions are shaped by a mixture of old red herrings, new myths, and hasty conclusions.

by Marina Ottaway

African Instability Is the Legacy of Artificial Colonial Borders

No. It is true that colonial powers established African boundaries. Some of these borders cut across old African states or separate people anthropologists classify as members of the same tribe—regardless of whether or not these individuals ever considered themselves as such in precolonial days. [See box "What Is a Tribe?"] But what else is new? All borders, except perhaps those of small island states, are artificial. Many borders separate members of distinct ethnic groups, and in countries with long histories, the modern state is superimposed on a veritable graveyard of obsolete political entities.

What makes Africa unstable is not the artificiality of its borders but the artificiality of its states. African states attained independence through agreements with the former colonial powers, not through the emergence of strong leaders and governments that could establish effective control over territory and extract the resources necessary to sustain an independent state. During the Cold War, the rival power blocs imposed an artificial, tenuous stability on the continent by propping up the corrupt leaders of client states. Had these African nations been forced to defend themselves against powerful neighbors and establish their political and economic viability—as states have had to do historically—few would have survived.

In recent years, economic decline and the decay of administrative structures have further weakened the capacity of most African states to govern effectively. The authoritarianism of many African governments, coupled with their incapacity to project power throughout their countries, has provided a fertile breeding ground for armed opposition movements. This situation has given way to a paradox wherein governments can easily arrest political opposition leaders in their capital cities but have little capacity to curb even minor armed insurgencies in rural areas. Civil wars further undermine economic conditions and weaken the governments' already tenuous hold on power. War becomes a means of livelihood for young men without prospects. [See map on next page.]

A New Generation of African Leaders Is Committed to Economic Reform and Democracy

Sadly, no. A new generation of leaders is beginning to emerge, but its members are not committed to democracy. They are intent on building government apparatuses that can discharge the basic task of maintaining security and stability over their entire territories. They are determined to promote economic development and to reconstruct the state administrative capacity. But they remain extremely

MARINA OTTAWAY *is a senior associate at the Carnegie Endowment for International Peace. Her latest book,* Africa's New Leaders: Democracy or State Reconstruction?, *has just been published by the Endowment.*

Turbulent Africa

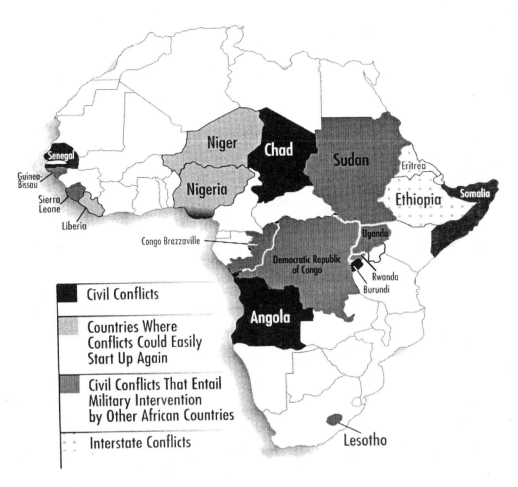

Civil Conflicts

Countries Where
Conflicts Could Easily
Start Up Again

Civil Conflicts That Entail
Military Intervention
by Other African Countries

Interstate Conflicts

Primary Sources: *African Research Bulletin, New York Times, Washington Post.*

suspicious of popular participation and even more so of party politics. Among the so-called new leaders are Ugandan president Yoweri Museveni, Eritrean president Isaias Afwerki, Ethiopian prime minister Meles Zenawi, and Rwandan vice president Paul Kagame.

These men represent a new generation in terms of their ideas, not their ages. All have come to power by winning a civil war and, consequently, they believe in the importance of force, strong organization, and good strategy. Contrary to most African leaders of the "old generation"—Julius Nyerere of Tanzania, Kwame Nkrumah of Ghana, or, even today, Robert Mugabe of Zimbabwe—who were largely economic illiterates, they have a good grasp of the imperatives of the market. In so far as they have a model of economic and political development, it is neither the "African socialism" of the early days of African independence nor the Marxism-Leninism that

guided them when they started their own wars. It is not even the democracy-and-free-market model that multilateral and bilateral donors preach. This new generation believes in a mixture of strong political control, limited popular participation, and economic liberalization that allows for a strong state role in regulating the market—South Korea, Taiwan, and even Singapore are viewed as models to be emulated.

The African Renaissance Has Come and Gone

Think again. The idea of an African renaissance—a term given currency by South African deputy president Thabo Mbeki—caught hold for a while as an apt metaphor for a series of positive events occurring on the continent, a corrective to the horrors of Rwanda, Sierra Leone, and Somalia. Apartheid ended in South Africa, economic growth showed signs of renewal even in countries long-considered basket cases such as Mozambique, and stability returned to Eritrea, Ethiopia, and Uganda after decades of civil unrest. This perception of a renaissance prompted President Bill Clinton to visit Africa and, amidst much fanfare, call for a partnership with the "new leaders" who seemed to personify this change.

Then, three months after President Clinton left Africa, Ethiopia and Eritrea almost went to war over a seemingly trivial border issue. President Laurent Kabila revealed his mediocre abilities as a leader when he failed to consolidate power in the Democratic Republic of Congo. The country slipped into crisis with Uganda and Rwanda backing antigovernment rebels, and Angola, Chad, Namibia, and Zimbabwe coming to Kabila's rescue. It was, as one American official observed, Africa's first world war. Suddenly, the renaissance was out, anarchy was back in.

But not so fast. Renaissance and war are not necessarily antithetical—the European renaissance was hardly a period of peace and stability. The most important precondition for a sustained revival in Africa entails restructuring its many failed states. While the idea of reviving failed states by embracing democracy and the free market is appealing, it is unrealistic. Elections and economic reform do not cause domestic armed movements to disappear, nor do they prevent conflicts in decaying neighboring states from spilling over borders.

The Age of Empire has truly ended in the 1990s. The political order imposed by the colonial powers and maintained until recently by U.S.–Soviet rivalry and French interventionism can no longer be taken for granted. States will survive only if they can establish domestic control and defend themselves against outside infringement. African nations must make up for lost time and establish a balance of power on the continent that they can maintain on their own. Diplomacy undoubtedly has a role to play here, and Afri-

What Is a Tribe?

Africans who readily admit that it is impossible to understand African politics without reference to ethnicity bristle at the use of the word "tribe." Europe has national minorities, other parts of the world have ethnic groups, but "primitive" Africa has tribes.

Anthropological definitions do not shed any light on the political use of the term. Like all people in preindustrial societies, people in precolonial Africa identified with small local groups or clans. But the tribes with which we are familiar are an invention of the colonial powers, the product of the same intellectual outlook that was busy classifying European nations in the nineteenth century.

Consider, for instance, the history of the Zulus. At the beginning of the nineteenth century, the Zulus were one of many small clans speaking a N'guni dialect. They numbered a few hundred at most. Along came Shaka, a local chief who revolutionized military technique, built an empire, and made everybody he conquered a Zulu. Then came the British, who suffered a humiliating defeat at the hand of the Zulus at Isandhlwana in 1879 and gained tremendous respect for them as a great warrior tribe. With the British came missionaries and their Bibles. The Bibles needed translating, which prompted the development of linguistic studies. Language built another empire: Anyone who spoke one of the N'guni dialects became part of what linguists called the "Zulu" family, or simply, the Zulus. Finally, along came apartheid with its official classification of people into races and tribes. Today, there are about 9 million Zulus, inhabiting a territory many times larger than what Shaka conquered.

But invented identities—whether called tribal, ethnic, or national—can become real. Postindependence politics in most African countries has been based largely on ethnic appeals. Civil wars tend to be fought along ethnic lines and democratic political parties form on the same basis. Pointing out that Hutus and Tutsis are historically the same people will not stop conflict in Rwanda any more than pointing out that Bosniacs, Croats, and Serbs have a common origin will bring peace to the Balkans.

—M.O.

cans are attempting to negotiate solutions in many conflicts, from Burundi to Sudan. But it is unlikely that a new balance of power, sustainable without outside intervention, can be established without conflicts. History suggests otherwise. Conflict is probably an intrinsic part of an African renaissance and not necessarily a sign of the so-called coming anarchy.

Africans Must Take More Responsibility for Solving Their Own Problems

Yes, and they are beginning to do so. But have African leaders been shouldered with the burden of implementing non-African solutions to their own problems? And is the rest of the world willing to live with African solutions that they do not necessarily favor?

Consider, for example, the U.S.-sponsored African Crisis Response Initiative, which mandates the training and equipping in some countries of military units that can be mobilized and deployed in peacemaking and peacekeeping operations. These units would enforce policies blessed by the international community, obviating the need for non-African troops in trouble spots such as Sierra Leone or Rwanda. Many African countries, including South Africa, have been leery of the initiative, suspecting that it is simply a means to get Africans to implement policies not of their own making.

When it comes to issues such as conflict resolution and economic development, genuine African solutions vary considerably. The international community has approved some of these initiatives, such as the attempts of the Inter-governmental Authority on Development—an East African agency that changed its focus from the threat of drought and locust infestation to that of conflict—to negotiate an agreement in Sudan. Others are more controversial, such as the interventions led by the Economic Community of West African States Ceasefire Monitoring Observer Group (ECOMOG) in Liberia and Sierra Leone. The world placed its stamp of approval on ECOMOG as a laudable African peacemaking effort—but in doing so glossed over an unsettling development. Successive Nigerian military governments provided the bulk of ECOMOG peacekeeping forces, raising the specter of a growing Nigerian hegemony over West Africa.

Other African solutions have been condemned outright by the international community as crude and unethical, even when the rest of the world has been unwilling to support the principled alternatives. The elimination of the Hutu refugee camps in eastern Zaire by Rwandan troops and the forces of Kabila in 1996 is a prime example. The refugee camps were dominated by Hutu forces guilty of genocide. These forces were reorganizing and rearming even as they were being fed and housed by humanitarian agencies that did not have the means to separate bona fide refugees from members of murderous military groups. The international community was unwilling to send in a UN force capable

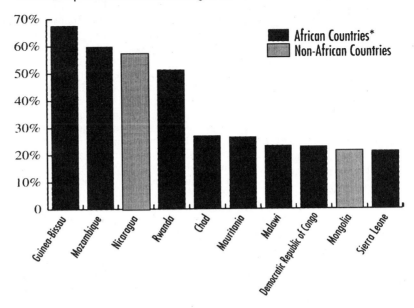

African Countries Are Among the Most Aid-Dependent in the World . . .

Ten Most Aid-Dependent Countries: Aid as Percentage of GNP

of separating refugees from members of militias because of both the danger and expense involved. Rwanda could not afford to let the *genocidaires* rearm on its borders and broke up the camps by force. The international community condemned the action.

This story illustrates a perennial dilemma: Africans do not have the means to develop textbook solutions to difficult problems. Theoretically, the international community has the means to implement these solutions but is unwilling to do so. Africans intervene and provide solutions in line with their means and inclinations. The international community has the luxury to denounce the outcome.

Africa Is a Major Financial Burden on the International Community

Not at all. Africa is disproportionately aid dependent, but it does not receive a disproportionate amount of aid. This misperception confuses the actual amount of money African countries receive, which is relatively small, with the importance of that assistance relative to the countries' gross national products (GNPs).

Collectively, sub-Saharan Africa receives a little more than one-fourth of all official multilateral and bilateral assistance in the world. It receives approximately 7 percent of U.S. foreign aid. About one-tenth of official development assistance to sub-Saharan Africa consists of emergency funds to victims of natural and

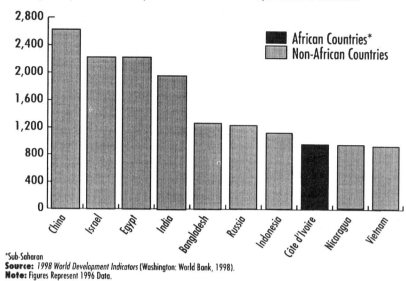

... Yet Only One is Among the Largest Recipients of Foreign Aid.

Ten Largest Recipients of Net Development Assistance and Official Aid, in Millions of U.S. Dollars.

African Countries*
Non-African Countries

China, Israel, Egypt, India, Bangladesh, Russia, Indonesia, Côte d'Ivoire, Nicaragua, Vietnam

*Sub-Saharan
Source: *1998 World Development Indicators* (Washington: World Bank, 1998).
Note: Figures Represent 1996 Data.

veloped and globally integrated country, falls well below world averages on most indicators of global integration.

While current conditions are dismal, some trends look promising. Foreign direct investment more than doubled in the 1990s. Even more significantly, at least some of the new investment is going to countries such as Uganda that are not big oil or mineral producers, indicating that investors are beginning to look at new opportunities. And although investors, particularly American ones, remain shy of a continent where they have no experience and which they perceive as politically unstable, the number of corporations, particularly small ones, interested in exploring opportunities in Africa is growing steadily.

There is also a growing web of informal contacts linking Africa to Europe and the United States. As African immigrant communities grow in both regions, so does a flow of remittances and information that does not appear yet in official statistics. African diasporas support families at home and provide funds for investment. And they provide an unprecedented conduit for information: Few Africans have e-mail yet, but there are enough of them to link informal communications networks—the African *radio trottoir* (radio sidewalk), or "bush telegraph"—into a global network, with information about yesterday's events in an African city discussed in Washington today and vice versa.

human-made catastrophes. On a per capita basis, the region receives slightly more on average than other low-income countries but only about one-fifteenth as much as Israel.

African countries, however, continue to depend so heavily on international aid because their economies are so small and so depressed that even modest amounts of funding represent a huge percentage of their GNPs and government budgets. Twenty-two of the thirty most aid-dependent countries in the world are in Africa. [See charts above.]

Globalization Is Bypassing Africa

True. By any standard, African countries remain marginal to all global trends. The basic facts are discouraging. With just over 10 percent of the world population, sub-Saharan Africa accounts for only about 1.5 percent of world trade. It receives less than .6 percent of foreign direct investment, while portfolio investment is essentially nonexistent, except for South Africa. Sub-Saharan Africa has only 15 telephone mainlines per every 1,000 people, compared with a worldwide average of 133 per every 1,000 people. A reliable estimate of how many personal computers, fax machines, and mobile telephones Africans own is not even available. Information is poorly distributed—access to newspapers, radio, and television is the lowest in the world. The continent is economically, socially, and culturally marginalized. [See charts "A Continent Left Behind."] Even South Africa, its most de-

France Is Africa's Worst Enemy

Get over it. It is time to stop obsessing about the French in Africa. Their influence is rapidly waning. With the passing from the political scene of the old generation of Gaullist Africanists, Paris is becoming more concerned about the cost-benefit ratio of its Africa policy. Military intervention is no longer an automatic response to African crises.

More fundamentally, no evidence exists to suggest that the political and economic problems of Francophone countries are different from those of the rest of the continent. None of the countries facing the most critical problems at present—Angola, Democratic Republic of Congo, Nigeria, Rwanda, Sierra Leone, or Sudan—were French colonies.

South Africa Is the Engine That Will Modernize the Continent

Possibly, but not right away. South Africa must first restructure its own economy. With a GNP representing about 45 percent of the total for sub-Saharan Africa, a per capita GNP of $3,520 compared with a continental average of $490, good roads and railroads, numerous ports, an extended electricity grid, and adequate telecommunications networks, South Africa appears to be a "First World country in Africa," as white South Africans used to argue.

But look again. South Africa's economy is heavily dependent on the export of minerals, particularly gold, and gold prices have been low for years and will probably remain so. Its industry has been highly protected, its agriculture highly subsidized. Unless major reforms are undertaken, South Africa will be unable to compete easily in the world markets. The list of necessary changes is daunting: greater flexibility in the labor market, lower wages for unskilled entry-level workers, land reform, privatization, reform of the tariff structure, and massive investment in education and training—in other words, a complete overhaul.

Politically, these reforms are extremely difficult to implement. Apartheid has left a dismal social legacy of immense urban squatter camps and rural areas too crowded for agriculture, a population insufficiently educated for the needs of a modern economy, and a lasting desire to redress old grievances. The powerful labor unions, closely allied with the ruling African National Congress, are making economic restructuring more difficult. South Africa's estimated unemployment rate is over 30 percent, and its crime rate is among the highest in the world, not only for violent crime but also for white-collar crimes such as corruption, embezzlement, and, reflecting the country's greater technological sophistication, computer crime. Economic statistics reflect the situation. In 1998, the stock market fell by more than 30 percent (in U.S. dollar terms), and the rand was devalued by 20 percent. The country lost 100,000 formal-sector jobs because of international competition and domestic restructuring. After years of sluggish growth, GNP has started contracting, fueling fears of a prolonged recession. It will be a while before this engine can pull a continent.

WANT TO KNOW MORE?

Many of the issues discussed in this article are analyzed in greater depth in Marina Ottaway's *Africa's New Leaders: Democracy or State Reconstruction?* (Washington: Carnegie Endowment for International Peace, 1999). Every serious scholar who has studied ethnic problems in Africa has concluded that the tribes we know are a colonial construct, but the myth of primordial tribalism does not die. Two particularly good treatments of the issue are Crawford Young's *The Politics of Cultural Pluralism* (Madison: University of Wisconsin, 1976) and Leroy Vail, ed., *The Creation of Tribalism in Southern Africa* (Berkeley: University of California Press, 1989). Yahya Sadowski sheds light on the origins of the Rwandan genocide in **"Think Again: Ethnic Conflict"** (FOREIGN POLICY, Summer 1998). On the problem of artificial states, in Africa and elsewhere, Robert Jackson's *Quasi-states, Sovereignty, International Relations and the Third World* (Cambridge: Cambridge University Press, 1990) still offers the best insights. On the specific problem of African states, I. William Zartman, ed., *Collapsed States* (Boulder: Lynne Rienner, 1995) remains an important source. An in-depth analysis of France's relations with its former colonies, written by a disillusioned insider, is found in Serge Michailof's *La France et l'Afrique* (Paris: Éditions Karthala, 1993). Robert Kaplan sets forth the ultimate counterrenaissance scenario of African disintegration in his often cited but extremely misleading **"The Coming Anarchy"** (*Atlantic Monthly*, February 1994). Opposite views on the new generation of African leaders can be found in Dan Connell and Frank Smyth's **"Africa's New Bloc"** (*Foreign Affairs*, March/April 1998) and Joel Barkan and David Gordon's **"Democracy in Africa"** (*Foreign Affairs*, July/August 1998). Reliable statistical information on current economic trends in Africa is always scant, with the best sources remaining **World Bank publications** and the country profiles published by the **Economist Intelligence Unit.**

For links to relevant Web sites, as well as a comprehensive index of related FOREIGN POLICY articles, access **www.foreignpolicy.com.**

Post-Imperial Africa at War

The "African renaissance" heralded less than a year ago has been left a stillborn hope. Marina Ottaway explains why Africa remains gripped by conflict—and why that remains the continent's future.

MARINA OTTAWAY

The last 12 months have seen increasing conflict in parts of Africa, dashing hopes that the continent might finally achieve political stability and economic growth. While some countries are undertaking state reconstruction, political liberalization, and economic development, others are sinking into chaos. The major cluster of conflicts has arisen in Central Africa, where shock waves originating from the 1994 genocide in Rwanda have spread to Congo, which has now become the center of the fighting, as well as to Angola, Uganda, and the Congo Republic. Even countries that do not share borders with Congo, notably Zimbabwe, are affected. Other, smaller groups of conflicts have developed to the west, centering around Sierra Leone, and to the east, centering around Sudan.

These recent conflicts are fundamentally different from the past wars that have afflicted Africa, and they have troubling implications. They are more complex, drawing in larger numbers of countries from a broader geographic area; United States Assistant Secretary of State for Africa Susan Rice has aptly referred to the fighting centered around Congo as Africa's "first world war" because of the intricacy of the alliances among the many countries involved. Moreover, their resolution will also require a substantial modification of the territorial and political status quo, since many of the states involved have decayed to the point at which they are no longer capable of discharging even minimal responsibilities and are unlikely ever to develop such capability. Congo, Sudan, and Angola are among these decaying states.

MARINA OTTAWAY *is a senior associate at the Carnegie Endowment for International Peace. She is the author, most recently, of* Africa's New Leaders: Democracy or State Reconstruction? *(Washington, D.C.: Carnegie Endowment for International Peace, 1990).*

Each cluster of conflicts has its own causes and its own dynamics. Underlying all of them are common factors that explain why conflict has erupted simultaneously in different parts of the continent and why most are unlikely to subside soon. Two developments in particular deserve attention. One is a worldwide phenomenon that could be defined as the end of imperial order—that is, of an order imposed on a region by more powerful countries outside it. Imperial orders have ended not only in Africa but also in the Balkans, Central Asia, and the Caucasus, leading to much turmoil. The second is the aforementioned disintegration of many African states, which is not a new phenomenon but is becoming more evident now that it is no longer concealed by the stability imposed from the outside.

Some of the countries engaged in conflict at present, most notably Ethiopia and Eritrea, cannot be defined as decaying states. On the contrary, they are states that have been rebuilding, and rather successfully. Their continuing border war, which started in May 1998, is an unfortunate part of this process of state reconstruction. It points to the fact that even if some of the decaying states succeed in stabilizing and undertaking a process of reconstruction, conflict may continue because strong states defend their perceived interests vigorously, and often aggressively.

THE END OF IMPERIAL ORDER

From the 1960s to the early 1990s, the African state system was remarkably stable. While many countries were troubled domestically, experiencing civil strife and repeated military coups, the overall structure of independent Africa did not change.

It is well known that African governments opted for stability when they founded the Organization of African Unity (OAU) in 1963 and adopted two principles to guide their foreign policies: noninterference in each other's affairs and respect for colonial borders. Proud of their newly acquired independence but uncertain of their real strength, African governments unanimously disliked the borders bequeathed by the colonial powers but also feared that challenging them would lead to chaos. Their pledge to respect colonial borders was hailed, deservedly, as a demonstration of statesmanship.

But stability was not maintained by African goodwill alone. The former colonial powers, especially France, had economic and political interests they wanted to protect. The United States and the Soviet Union, as newcomers to the continent, sought to enlarge their spheres of influence. While their cold war policies could have had a destabilizing effect, in reality neither power cared enough about Africa to make a major investment to increase its influence. Instead, both played a cautious game of counterbalancing each other's efforts, a game that in the end helped preserve the status quo.

African state borders thus remained basically stable. Despite the numerous grievances and occasional skirmishes over the demarcation of boundaries, attempts to bring about major modifications were rare and invariably failed. Somalia tried twice, in 1963 and 1977, to annex the Ogaden region of Ethiopia, but in both cases it lost diplomatically as well as militarily, with no African country accepting the legitimacy of its quest. The secession of the Katanga (now Shaba) region from the former Belgian Congo in 1960 was reversed less than three years later. The secession of Biafra from Nigeria in 1967 was quickly brought under control and received minimal support from African states. And in Ethiopia, Eritrean nationalists fought the central government for over 30 years without receiving support or recognition from African countries, despite their claim that Eritrean statehood was in accordance with OAU principles; as a former Italian colony, Eritrea said it was entitled to independence within colonial boundaries.

The stability of the African state system was part of a global trend. After the end of World War II, the cold war froze the borders of much of the world. While the number of independent countries multiplied as a result of decolonization, existing states were guaranteed survival, no matter how inept their governments or how limited their economic resources, because the United States and the Soviet Union did not want destabilizing changes. In Central Asia and the Caucasus, order was maintained through incorporation in the Soviet Union. In the Balkans, order depended on the survival of Yugoslavia, a state improbably cobbled from pieces of old Balkan puzzles and kept together by President Josip Broz Tito's political skills and even more by the interest of the superpowers in maintaining the equilibrium of a fragile region. The imperial order came to an end abruptly after 1990 in these Eurasian regions. In 1991 Yugoslavia broke apart, sliding into war. That same year the Soviet Union ceased to exist, and many of the successor states were themselves threatened by secessionism and infighting. Instability, uncertainty, and war replaced imperial order.

In Africa, the first sign of the change came in Eritrea, which finally became independent in 1991 after winning, in alliance with other Ethiopian movements, a military victory against the regime of Mengistu Haile Mariam. OAU members and the rest of the international community accepted the change they had long opposed. In part, this was because Eritrean nationalists and the new Ethiopian government had reached an agreement, making opposition by outsiders moot. It was also because the emergence of this new state was little more than a footnote to the massive reconfiguration of entire regions and states occurring elsewhere.

Soon there were other signs that outsiders were no longer interested in safeguarding the stability of the African state system. When Somalia sank into chaos in 1992, the United Nations and the United States intervened diplomatically and militarily, not only to alleviate a humanitarian crisis but also to reestablish the Somali state. By 1994 they had decided to leave Somalia to its own devices, a position that continues to the present. In 1994 not even the crisis in Rwanda that led to the brutal murder of at least 800,000 people could prompt an international response to stop the killing, except for a brief intervention by the French. In 1996, when Rwanda sent troops into Zaire to support the rebel movement of Laurent Kabila and above all to stop the incursions into Rwanda by armed groups sheltering in the refugee camps, nobody reacted. It was abundantly clear that the international community was no longer inclined to maintain an imperial order in Africa.

THE CRISIS OF THE AFRICAN STATE

The second factor fomenting conflict in Africa is the weakness of many states. Artificial creations of the colonial powers, many African states were weak at independence, with poorly developed human and physical resources, rudimentary administrative systems, and, inevitably, inexperienced leadership. But the imperial order guaranteed their survival, no matter how powerless some of these states were. In the last 30 years, African countries have become a much more diverse group. Some have managed to consolidate governments capable of fulfilling at least the minimum requirements of statehood: control over their territory, maintenance of an administrative system, provision of basic public service, and establishment of domestic security sufficient to allow normal life and economic activity to continue. Such states are not necessarily democratic, or even well governed, but they are states; Kenya, Ghana, Ivory Coast, and Zimbabwe are examples, and many more could be added to the list. But other countries no longer have even minimal attributes of "stateness." Among them are not only small marginal countries such as Somalia or Sierra Leone but major ones such as Congo.

But the imperial order maintained a superficial stability, allowing the severity of the decay of many states to be ignored. It was well known, for example, that Zaire under President Mobutu Sese Seko did not function as a state: the government had no reach outside the capital, civil servants and even the military were not paid, revenue went to Mobutu rather than to the state treasury, and the country's infrastructure had deteriorated to the point that linkages among the regions were tenuous. Yet Zaire continued to receive United States assistance,

French and Belgian troops helped put down insurgencies, and the international community in general continued to pretend that there was still a Zairian state.

As the foreign powers that had guaranteed the overall stability of the African state system disengaged, the fiction of stateness could no longer be maintained. Failed states were revealed for what they were, and conflicts multiplied, both domestically, as factions fought over control and resources, and internationally, as neighboring countries sought to protect themselves and further their interests.

AFRICAN GEOPOLITICS

There are three ways in which countries have historically established a new order in the aftermath of empire. The first is to attempt to reach a balance of power through a politics of alliances and mutual defense pacts; the second is by building a bureaucratic order based on an agreement to abide by common rules and on the existence of multilateral organizations to enforce them. Historically, attempts at creating a balance of power are the classic response to the dissolution of the overarching order created by imperial control. Bureaucratic order has emerged as the solution of choice only in this century, first with the creation of the League of Nations and then with the formation of the United Nations and other multilateral organizations. Europe represents the most far-reaching example of a conscious transition from a centuries-long and ultimately vain attempt to create a stable balance of power to an order maintained by a web of agreements and bureaucratic organizations.

The third way a new order can be reestablished is from the outside, through the imposition of a new imperial order. In such a case, the countries of the region again become secondary players.

Looking at Africa, it is possible to see all three approaches to creating a new order playing out simultaneously. The dominant approach, underlying the major conflicts, is the politics of the balance of power. Unfortunately, attempts to create a balance are contributing to clusters of interrelated conflicts rather than establishing a durable peace. Parallel to these efforts to create a balance of power are the attempts by African regional and subregional organizations to encourage negotiated solutions. These efforts have not been effective and will remain so because of the weakness of the organizations involved and the paucity of the means at their disposal. Finally, a demand is also developing in Africa for the reimposition of order from outside through international intervention. It is unlikely that this demand will be heeded, however. Although African governments want greater international involvement, Europe and the United States are hesitant to make a commitment. For the foreseeable future, African countries will continue to pursue the politics of the balance of power, perpetuating conflict in the process.

CONGO AND THE BALANCE OF POWER

The cluster of conflicts that best exemplifies the politics of the balance of power is centered around Congo. In this cluster Congo, Rwanda, Uganda, Angola, and the Congo Republic are the first-tier actors, with Zimbabwe, Zambia, Namibia, and the Central African Republic in the second tier. It is open to discussion when this conflict started—the partition of Africa by the colonial powers and their policies in the decades of imperial control would be a legitimate starting point. More recently, and somewhat arbitrarily, the conflict can be traced to 1994, when a series of relatively unconnected political threads started to become entangled into one major snarl.

The first thread was ethnic conflict in Rwanda. With ethnicity highly politicized since colonial times, the demographic composition of Rwanda—14 percent Tutsi and 86 percent Hutu—was a dangerous mix. Belgium had favored the minority, as colonial powers tended to do everywhere. But with numbers on their side, Hutus dominated the politics of the independent country, after a showdown in 1959 sent several hundred thousand Tutsis fleeing across the border into Uganda. Tutsi exiles supported Yoweri Museveni (now president of Uganda) in his fight for power in the early 1980s, gaining both political and military support for their own cause. The result was the formation of the Rwandan Patriotic Front (RPF), which launched its first attacks into Rwanda in 1990. With the help of other countries in the region, the conflict was halted, and a promising agreement to form a government of national reconciliation and an integrated national army was reached in Arusha in 1993. However, the implementation of the agreement was opposed by Hutu extremists in the military and by the Hutu militia known as the Interahamwe. When President Juvénal Habyarimana, a Hutu, was killed in a still unexplained plane crash in 1994, Hutu extremists launched a mass slaughter of Tutsis and moderate Hutus. In turn, the RPF launched an all-out attack on Rwanda. When the country settled after several months of horror, an estimated 800,000 people were dead, the RPF was in power in Kigali, and 2 million people, including both refugees from the massacre and its perpetrators, were living in camps in eastern Zaire.

There the thread of ethnic conflict in Rwanda became entangled with that of the domestic politics of Zaire in the waning days of the Mobutu regime. Zaire was in reality a country without a government. In Kinshasa, an ailing Mobutu still manipulated allies and foes to prevent the formation of another government, but he had little or no control over the rest of the country and little hope of reestablishing it.

> *As the foreign powers that had guaranteed the overall stability of the African state system disengaged, the fiction of stateness could no longer be maintained.*

For Rwanda and also for Uganda, the weakness of the Zairian state posed a problem. Opponents of the Ugandan government operated from eastern Zaire with the support of Sudan. In the refugee camps, members of the Rwandan army and the Interahamwe militia were reorganizing and rearming. In an attempt to protect itself from raids by Hutu extremists rearming in the camps, the new Rwandan government, with the help of Uganda, chose a radical solution: it destroyed the camps from which the attacks were being mounted, and it sought to replace the Mobutu regime with one it hoped would be friendlier and more capable of controlling Zairian territory. So advanced was the disintegration of the Zairian state that a weak guerrilla force, supported by Rwanda and Uganda and headed by a virtually unknown local warlord, Laurent Kabila, marched across the country and seized power in a few months.

But President Kabila proved to be an incompetent leader. He quickly alienated most domestic groups and never gained the confidence of the international donor community, whose help the country badly needed. He also soon lost the support of the Ugandan and Rwandan governments, disillusioned by his lack of political acumen and even more by his inability to control the eastern part of the renamed Democratic Republic of the Congo. With their enemies once again rearming in that region, Rwanda and Uganda abandoned Kabila in 1998 and threw their support behind a new movement dominated by Congolese Tutsis, the Congolese Union for Democracy (RCD). The new round of fighting gathered more threads into the growing tangle.

One of these threads was the struggle between the Angolan government, dominated by the Popular Movement for the Liberation of Angola (MPLA) and rebels of the National Union for the Total Independence of Angola (UNITA). The second-oldest conflict in Africa after the Sudanese civil war, the rivalry between UNITA and the government dated to the 1960s, when both were fighting the Portuguese government for the independence of Angola. The first round was won by the MPLA, which assumed power when Angola became independent in 1975. But UNITA did not accept this victory, and with the support of South Africa and the United States went to war against the MPLA, which in turn received the backing of the Soviet Union and Cuba. The conflict in Angola thus turned into a proxy war between the superpowers.

This phase came to an end in late 1988, when an agreement provided for the withdrawal of the Cubans and South Africans. With this settlement, the United States and the Soviet Union became mediators of the continuing rivalry between the MPLA and UNITA. A peace agreement was signed by the two groups in 1991, but it did not hold. After losing elections in 1992, UNITA returned to war. A new agreement negotiated in 1994 was never implemented completely. As a result, in 1998 Angola headed again for war at the same time as the new conflict in Congo flared.

To wage war anew, UNITA needed channels through which to import weapons and fuel into the country; the financing was provided by the smuggling of diamonds. Under Mobutu, Zaire had been a source of support for UNITA, and as a result UNITA had supported Mobutu against Kabila, while the MPLA government had backed the insurgency; both, however, had been minor players in that fight. In 1998, Angola continued to back Kabila, hoping that he would stay in control and repay Angola by blocking supplies going to UNITA. Inevitably, UNITA supported the rebel RCD.

The Congolese conflict picked up many other, though lesser, threads as well. One was domestic. Mobutu's generals in charge of his elite corps had not put up much resistance against Kabila, choosing exile in South Africa instead. When the RCD started its war against Kabila in 1998, some of the generals decided to open their own front in the northwest of the country, the region from which Mobutu and his closest supporters hailed. This intervention is likely to be significant, because the generals not only have some support in the region but are also involved in the international arms trade.

Other foreign components were added to the growing imbroglio. Zimbabwe, whose president, Robert Mugabe, has mining interests in Congo, sent planes and troops to Kabila's defense, probably with the financial support of Libya. The Congo Republic, whose government is supported by Angola and had ties to Kabila, nevertheless allowed—or was incapable of preventing—Mobutu's former generals from using its territory to launch attacks. Zambia, which initially tried to stay out of the conflict and play the role of the peacemaker, lost much of its neutrality when Angola, angered by the Zambian refusal to allow it to use Zambian territory to fight UNITA, allegedly carried out a series of bombings in Lusaka as a warning to the government. To avoid strife with Angola, Zambia in turn discontinued supplying fuel to southern Congo, hoping that this would convince Kabila to curb UNITA activities based in his country.

There are more pieces to this puzzle, but it should be clear that in the attempt to further their interests and protect themselves against enemies, governments and opposition movements have not attained a new balance of power. Instead, they have created a web of alliances that pulls more and more players into the conflict, making peace and stability increasingly elusive goals.

UNITED WE STAND?

As conflict has spread, so have attempts by regional organizations like the OAU and subregional organizations such as the Economic Community of West African States (ECOWAS) or the Southern Africa Development Community (SADC) to establish a bureaucratic order based on adherence to common rules and principles enforced by multilateral organizations. These efforts have been unsuccessful because of problems with the principles to which these organizations adhere, because of inadequate resources, and because of the role played by the very governments that fuel the conflicts. None of these conditions is likely to change soon.

The principles guiding the OAU and the subregional groupings have not changed. The OAU expects African countries to respect colonial borders and refrain from interfering in each other's affairs. This is unrealistic. Interference is the rule rather the exception in entire regions of the continent. Respect for borders means little when the state no longer exists: the borders of Somalia are intact, but they enclose a vacuum. Thus African organizations adhere to principles that fail to address the situations from which the worst conflicts stem.

Additionally, African regional organizations, funded and staffed by African countries with serious economic problems, are inevitably poor in resources. Yet the problems to be addressed are increasingly complex. Consider the tangle of issues involving Congo. Restoring stability would require, first, reaching an agreement among the major domestic and foreign parties. Second, it would require, minimally, bringing under control the armed factions that roam the Congo: Kabila's ragtag army, the RCD and the obscure local movements and warlords with which it has formed alliances, Mobutu's generals, the remnants of the old Rwandan army and the Interahamwe militia, and, increasingly, assorted mercenaries. It would require rebuilding the state in Congo—a country that has not had an effective government for decades, where administrative institutions and the physical infrastructure have deteriorated, and where there is no longer even a common currency. It would require the removal of other countries and political forces from the conflict, which is unlikely to happen unless the problems that encouraged intervention in the first place are settled: the conflict between UNITA and the government in Angola; the conflict between Hutus and Tutsis; and the Congo Republic's infighting. The disparity between the magnitude of the task and the capacity of African organizations is enormous.

Finally, there is the issue of the regional and subregional organizations' lack of independence. The same governments that control these organizations are involved in the fighting, presiding over decaying states, and violating the major principles to which the organizations are devoted. The problem becomes more acute as some of the largest and most important countries sink deeper into conflict. Congo, Sudan, and Ethiopia are all at war. Nigeria, which through ECOMOG (the ECOWAS Monitoring Group) became the peacekeeper in Liberia and Sierra Leone, did so while under the worst military governments in its history. The pool of influential African countries that are not part of any conflict is shrinking, weakening all African organizations. Thus, establishing an effective African bureaucratic order—the most desirable solution to the present conflicts—remains a distant goal.

A NEW IMPERIALISM?

The escalation of conflict, coupled with the evident incapacity of regional organizations to cope with the magnitude of the problem, has led to renewed demands among African governments for greater external intervention. Such interest is not expressed without ambivalence, but it is becoming more pronounced, leading to a curious reversal of roles. African governments that in the past condemned foreign intervention in Africa as motivated by neocolonialism and neo-imperialism

are now pleading for greater United States and UN involvement in controlling conflict. Outsiders, however, are reluctant to be cast in the role of imposing order.

The ambivalence of African governments about external intervention remains great, however. It is revealed, for example, by the hesitant reaction of many countries to the United States African Crisis Response Initiative, a program to train African troops to participate in peacekeeping operations in Africa. While training has taken place in a number of African countries, others whose participation would be central to the success of the initiative, such as South Africa, refuse to participate. And there is not agreement on when, by whose decision, and under whose command the troops that have received training would be deployed.

For its part, the international community is unlikely to make a major commitment to reestablishing order in Africa. The United States and Europe have no vital interests in Africa. African conflicts compete for attention with those elsewhere, particularly in the Balkans. And intervention always creates resentment: the experience of the United States in Somalia shows that it is easy for the intervenor to be hailed as a savior one day and denounced as an enemy the next. The failure of earlier intervention is also a deterrent: after a decade of efforts in Angola, the desire of the international community to remain involved has dissipated and the UN has withdrawn its peacekeeping force. Finally, as more countries disintegrate—perhaps beyond restoration—the role of the international community becomes problematic: should it labor to prop up failed states, or should it contribute to a new partition of Africa?

POST-IMPERIAL FLUX

Attempting to establish a balance of power fuels rather than diminishes conflict; an African bureaucratic order is not likely any time soon; and the international community is reluctant to impose a new order on Africa and may not have the capacity to do so in any case. Conflict will not end soon in Africa.

Increasingly, the settlement of conflicts cannot be separated from the task of consolidating African states, new or old. Conflict festers in the vacuum of power that exists where governments are only nominally in control. Unfortunately, state consolidation can itself lead to conflict, as is happening in Ethiopia and Eritrea. Such are the dilemmas Africa faces in this post-imperial phase.

Dismal as the situation is in the countries most affected by disintegration and conflict, it is important to remember that there are also countries in Africa where the state is holding its own and economic and political conditions are improving. Conflict is not bound to spread through Africa like a virulent infectious disease; some countries will continue to move ahead politically and economically. But others will become more deeply mired in conflict, and may not survive.

Unit Selections

Key Points to Consider

❖ Do you support current efforts to increase the role of UN peacekeeping forces, or should UN activities be limited to preventive diplomacy and more modest peace maintenance operations such as monitoring elections and referendums?

❖ What proposals do you support to solve the UN's current fiscal crisis? Be specific.

❖ Should NATO countries be withdrawn from communal conflicts in the Balkans and leave peacekeeping duties in such varied places as Kosovo, East Timor, Haiti, and Sierra Leone to the UN and regional organizations? Who should pay and supply the troops for these peacekeeping operations?

❖ Can the international community do more to regulate the activities of modern mercenaries?

❖ What is the most effective way to prevent the use of child soldiers? Should the international community do more to help integrate former child soldiers into societies after peace settlements are negotiated?

 **Links**

www.dushkin.com/online/

These sites are annotated on pages 6 and 7.

The most visible international institution since World War II has been the United Nations. Membership grew from the original 50 in 1945 to 185 in 1995. The UN, across a variety of fronts, achieved noteworthy results—eradication of disease, immunization, provision of food and shelter to refugees and victims of natural disasters, and help to dozens of countries that have moved from colonial status to self-rule.

After the Persian Gulf War, the UN guided enforcement of economic sanctions against Iraq, sent peacekeeping forces to former Yugoslavia and to Somalia, monitored an unprecedented number of elections and cease-fire agreements, and played an active peacekeeping role in almost every region of the world. However, the withdrawal of the UN mission in Somalia, the near-collapse of the UN peacekeeping mission in Bosnia prior to the intervention of NATO-sponsored troops, and the delayed response of the UN in sending troops to monitor cease-fire agreements in East Timor and Sierra Leone in 1999 raises doubts about the ability of the organization to continue to be involved in peacekeeping worldwide. Some observers now call for the United Nations to scale back its current level of peacekeeping in order to focus more effectively on global problems that nobody else can or will tackle.

Pressures to reduce UN peacekeeping efforts are also being fueled by the realities of scarce resources created largely by the refusal of many member states, including the United States, to pay back dues. The United States has withheld payments of back dues for several years as part of a campaign led by conservative members of the U.S. Congress. For several years these congressmen have demanded that the UN undertake extensive internal reforms and reduce the amount of the United States' contribution before the United States pays its back dues. The United States narrowly averted losing the right to vote in the General Assembly by agreeing at the end of 1999 to pay a portion it's $1.02 billion debt over a 3-year period.

The delays and continuing refusal of the U.S. Congress to pay the United States' entire debt is costing the United States prestige and influence in the UN. Although resentment toward America was muted within the organization in the past, this resentment is now expressed openly, especially since the U.S. government announced an unexpected budget surplus in 1999. Critics within the United States respond by charging that current UN Secretary-General Kofi Annan failed to implement required organizational reforms and exceeded his mandate from the Security Council in negotiating an agreement with Iraq's Saddam Hussein. An internal UN study published at the end of 1999 added fuel for UN critics with it's finding that the Office of the Secretary-General failed to heed warnings from other UN offices that momentum was building toward a genocidal campaign by Hutu extremists in Rwanda months before it started in 1994.

The willingness of major nation-states to take action without first gaining the approval of the UN's most influential decision-making body, the Security Council, also undermines the ability of the United Nations to play a central role in international conflicts. In "Bewitched, Bothered, and Bewildered," Richard Butler describes how NATO's decision to bypass the United Nations and begin military action against Yugoslavia without the Security Council's approval raises new questions about the Security Council's ability to function as the guardian of international peace and security. According to Butler, "fixing" the Security Council will require changes to the permanent members' veto and to the current approach to arms control.

In the absence of involvement by the United Nations or major world powers, a variety of nonstate actors play influential roles in communal conflicts. One of the more important actors in many recent conflicts are modern mercenaries. David Shearer in "Outsourcing War," describes the role of modern mercenaries in a number of conflicts. In several areas of instability, private security businesses are booming, as governments, corporations, nongovernmental organizations (NGOs), and the media increasingly contract for their services. While mercenaries have been involved in international conflicts for hundreds of years, the average soldier of fortune today wears a suit and works out of a corporate office in Great Britain or South Africa. David Shearer examines this new type of international actor to determine whether mercenaries are murderous profiteers or the future of international peacekeeping.

Many of the most intractable communal conflicts around the world continue because combatants enlist children to serve as their foot soldiers. In "Children under Arms: Kalashnikov Kids," writers for *The Economist* describe how children are being used to fight wars, at great cost to themselves and their societies. Today, an estimated 300,000 children in over 60 countries are soldiers. The use of child soldiers in armed conflicts also aggravates peace settlement efforts as the resources necessary for demobilization and reintegration of child soldiers are usually lacking in developing countries, where children constitute nearly half the population.

The UN Convention on the Rights of the Child (CRC), signed in 1989 and ratified by more than 160 nations, was one effort designed to address this abuse by establishing 15 years as the minimum recruitment age for child soldiers. However, several influential nation-states, including the United States, have not yet ratified this treaty. Until the use of child soldiers is ended, post-conflict reconstruction efforts will have to continue to find ways to demobilize and reintegrate former child soldiers into societies with high rates of unemployment and limited education facilities, where children constitute nearly half the population.

A number of thorny issues related to the question of "who should fight for whom" are likely to remain controversial in future decades. These issues promise to raise problems for politicians in developed countries where older people will increasingly comprise an ever larger portion of the population. The trend toward graying populations in developed countries will co-occur with demographic changes in many developing nation-states where the average age of the population is 18 or younger. Many societies must also deal with extreme social dislocations due to continued poverty and an unprecedented death rate caused by the AIDS epidemic among adults. These trends may do more to reshape our collective future than more familiar security problems and threats.

International Organizations and Global Issues

Bewitched, Bothered, and Bewildered

Repairing the Security Council

Richard Butler

For the first half of the decade since the Cold War's end, the atmosphere in the U.N. Security Council was decidedly improved. With less East-West divisiveness, the council met more frequently and did more business. Only seven vetoes were cast in the post-Cold War period, versus 240 in the first 45 years of U.N. life. Twenty peacekeeping operations were mandated, more than the total for all the preceding years.

But then the initial optimism about the Security Council's ability to get its job done in a vetoless world turned sour. Particularly dismaying were the last 12 months, during which the council was bypassed, defied, and abused.

It was bypassed when NATO began military action against Slobodan Milošević's Yugoslavia without first seeking the Security Council approval that NATO countries knew would be vetoed by Russia and China. The fundamental significance of NATO's slight was not diminished by the post-conflict agreement of NATO and Russia to seek Security Council endorsement and

RICHARD BUTLER is Diplomat in Residence at the Council on Foreign Relations. For the past two years, he was Executive Chairman of the United Nations Special Commission, the body charged with disarming Iraq. Prior to that, he served for five years as Australia's Permanent Representative to the United Nations in New York.

U.N. participation in the policing and administration of Kosovo.

The Security Council was defied by Saddam Hussein, who correctly assessed that he could get away with disobeying the council's disarmament resolutions thanks to a combination of influential friends on the council, a general loss of will within the body, and a sympathetic secretary-general. During the past eight years, many but not all of Iraq's weapons of mass destruction have been eliminated. Disarmament tasks remain to be completed, however, and monitoring and verification systems need to be secured to ensure that Saddam does not reconstitute his illegal weapons. Yet the Security Council has been unable to reach a decision that would restore, even in a modified way, the implementation of its own law. Indeed, some members—including, incredibly, Canada, a nonpermanent member of the council—have sought to lower the standard of Iraqi compliance.

Council procedures have also been abused. China prevented minor peacekeeping operations from proceeding in Guatemala and Macedonia and threatened to do the same in Haiti, merely because those countries had dealt with Taiwan. Although vetoes driven more by national interest than any sense of collective responsibility were common during the Cold War, they have been less so since, with nothing comparable to these Chinese vetoes, delivered and threatened. Such use of the veto is dramatically distant from that

Reprinted by permission of *Foreign Affairs,* September/October 1999, pp. 9-12. © 1999 by the Council on Foreign Relations, Inc.

envisioned at the 1945 U.N. founding conference or by reasonable people today.

The five major powers were given permanent seats on the council to ensure their commitment to the new body. They were given the veto for a very limited and specific reason: to allow them to prevent a council decision authorizing the use of force against them. Beyond that, they were expected to exercise collective responsibility for "the maintenance of international peace and security."

Yet the Security Council's ability to function as the guardian of international peace and security has been thrown into question by the incidents depicted above. In all these cases, permanent members have weighted their narrow national interests over collective responsibility.

FIXING IT

Clearly, the Security Council is not working adequately. To fix it, two key areas must be addressed urgently. First is the veto, which has been abused by permanent members in defense of interests, client states, and ideological concerns that very often had nothing to do with maintaining international peace and security. Even if it is accepted for argument's sake that the profligate use of the veto during the bitter contest of the Cold War might have forestalled its worst consequence—nuclear holocaust—it is no longer appropriate, much less necessary, to view the veto power in such a context. Today's world is more interdependent and, if threatened, it is by weapons proliferation, not superpower rivalry.

The veto issue is a vexed one. Clearly, the major powers will not give up their veto power voluntarily, and the charter allows them to block any proposal that it be removed. The question thus becomes whether they can voluntarily agree to a more constructive interpretation of the veto's nature and the uses to which it may legitimately be put. Only if they succeed in doing so can the Security Council be rescued from its present breakdown.

It would be best if the proposed rules were informal. They should reinforce the distinction between substantive and procedural issues—and permit vetoes of the former only. Some may point out that this distinction already exists in the U.N. Charter; however, permanent members still have, on innumerable occasions, successfully threatened the veto on procedural issues. Any agreed rules would need to prevent this and take into account threatened vetoes in addition to those that are actually delivered. New rules would also necessarily include other understandings on substantive issues.

Such rules would diminish use of the veto, a move that would cause some heartburn in capitals and par-

liaments. But if the Untied States, the undisputed lone superpower, indicated a willingness to discipline the use of its veto, it could then ask other permanent members to do the same. Certainly, in the absence of an American concession, nothing will change. But if others will not agree, then nor should the United States.

Such an American initiative would have another advantage: it would temper the growing anxiety within the international community about the unipolar world and the policies of its one superpower. A move by the United States to effectively share authority would speak volumes. Naturally, restraining the use of the veto would complicate the lives of permanent members. Less free to throw their weight around, they would have to argue their cases more cogently. They would have to consider issues in more detail than would perhaps immediately meet their interests, taste, or judgment. But the benefits would be many, including a long overdue revitalization of the Security Council's rigid and tired political environment.

A FAREWELL TO ARMS

Arms control is the second area requiring urgent attention, and forging changes there may prove even harder than achieving a new understanding on the use of the veto. The effect on global security and the Security Council's authority, however, is potentially more far-reaching.

Thirty years ago, the international community began a process of drawing up treaties on the nonproliferation of weapons of mass destruction, starting with nuclear, and then working through biological, chemical, and missile technologies. One of the key questions that inevitably arose under such treaties is who would enforce them, especially in the event of a detected breach. Typically, the answer given—sometimes in writing within a particular treaty, but certainly in political terms—was the Security Council. The Security Council is the custodian of nonproliferation. It has the task of providing confidence to the international community that the tapestry of treaties designed to ensure that weapons of mass destruction do not spread is enforced and kept whole. There is simply no other body that can do this job, and this is widely understood.

But how does the Security Council's decision-making methodology, including the veto, square with its expected obligation to enforce the nonproliferation treaties? For example, will a decision by the council on noncompliance with such a treaty be held hostage by national interests and thus vetoes by permanent members?

A case in point: North Korea clandestinely continues nuclear weapons development in contravention of its obligations under the nuclear Nonproliferation

Treaty (NPT). Because of Chinese, and to some extent Russian, interests, the Security Council has responded inadequately, failing a crucial test. Instead, the attempted solution to the problem was agreed on largely outside the council, and is not proving viable.

Iraq represents an even more profound failure. Saddam Hussein has broken all of Iraq's nonproliferation undertakings. He has lied to the United Nations' weapons inspectors. Data indicate that he continues to conceal illegal weapons of mass destruction. Unquestionably, he retains the capacity to make them. These facts are known in the Security Council, including by those permanent members who have given Saddam strong support. Russia, Iraq's strongest backer in the council, is fully aware of Iraq's weapon status, not least because the Soviet Union was Saddam's major supplier of arms and the means to manufacture them.

The authority of the council is deeply challenged when objective cases of treaty violation like these end up being judged on a narrow, subjective political basis by veto-wielding permanent members. Were this to become the council's standard way of dealing with weapons proliferation, it would amount to a profound and, I suspect, mortal failure.

No reflection on arms control and the responsibilities of permanent members would be complete without noting the need for them to keep their own promises concerning nuclear disarmament. Among other things, the survival of the NPT is at stake.

Permanent membership in the Security Council and its associated veto power is a privilege, not a right. The continuing legitimate enjoyment of that privilege, as history has shown with respect to similar privileges, rests on its responsible exercise. This requires a thorough revisiting of the nature and uses of the veto, and the Security Council must prove itself able to fulfill the responsibility it has been given to enforce the weapons of mass destruction nonproliferation treaties. Both of these reforms require action, above all, by the permanent members. They would help the Security Council get over its *annus horribilis*, and serve the interests of the international community in the 21st century.

Outsourcing War

by David Shearer

For nearly three centuries, the accepted international norm has been that only nation-states should be permitted to fight wars. Not surprisingly, the rise of private military companies in the 1990s—and the possibility that they may view conflict as a legitimate business activity—has provoked outrage and prompted calls for them to be outlawed. The popular press has labeled these companies "mercenaries" and "dogs of war," conjuring up images of freebooting and rampaging Rambos overthrowing weak—usually African—governments. At a press conference convened in June 1997 to discuss the ongoing civil war in Sierra Leone, Secretary General Kofi Annan bristled at the suggestion that the United Nations would ever consider working with "respectable" mercenary organizations, arguing that there is no "distinction between respectable mercenaries and non-respectable mercenaries."

But is this depiction fair? Certainly these soldiers might meet the three most widely accepted criteria defining a mercenary: They are foreign to a conflict; they are motivated chiefly by financial gain; and, in some cases, they have participated directly in combat. They differ significantly, however, from infamous characters such as Irishman "Mad" Mike Hoare and Frenchman Bob Denard, who fought in the Congo and elsewhere in the 1960s. What most sets today's military companies apart is their approach. They have a distinct corporate character, have openly defended their usefulness and professionalism, have used internationally accepted legal and financial instruments to secure their deals, and so far have supported only recognized governments and avoided regimes unpalatable to the international community. As Enrique Bernales Ballesteros, the UN's special rapporteur on the use of mercenaries, has noted, personnel working for these companies, "even when they have a military background and are highly paid" cannot be considered as "coming within the legal scope of mercenary status."

Dismissing private-sector military personnel as little more than modern-day soldiers of fortune would not only be simplistic but would obscure the broader issues that these military companies raise. Why have they emerged in the 1990s? What role might they play in the future? Can they be regulated? Practitioners and academics who specialize in conflict resolution typically argue that private military companies hinder efforts to end wars and broker peace. Yet, the evidence suggests that coercion is often essential to breaking deadlocks and bringing opposing parties to the negotiating table. In this context, military companies can be seen not as part of the problem but as part of the solution—especially for struggling but legitimate governments that lack the resources to field effective fighting forces. As the political and economic costs of peacekeeping continue to escalate, it may increasingly make sense for multilateral organizations and Western governments to consider outsourcing some aspects of these interventions to the private sector.

THESE GUNS FOR HIRE

Private military forces are as old as warfare itself. The ancient Chinese, Greek, and Roman armies employed large numbers of mercenaries, and mercenaries comprised about half of William the Conqueror's army in the eleventh century. During the fourteenth century, Italian city-states contracted private military forces, known as *condottieri,* to protect themselves—an early acknowledgement that hiring mercenaries can often prove more cost-effective than maintaining standing armies. Private forces have also served states' immediate strategic interests. The United Kingdom, for example, hired 30,000 Hessian soldiers to fight in the American War of Independence to avoid conscripting its own citizens. In the late eighteenth century, foreigners comprised half of the armed forces of Prussia and a third of the armies of France and the United Kingdom. Mercantile companies were licensed by the state to wage war to serve their countries' economic interests. In 1815, the East India Company, which colonized India on behalf of the British government, boasted an army of 150,000 soldiers.

But with the rise of nationalism in the nineteenth century, the idea of fighting for one's country rather than for commercial interests gained currency. Governments came to command a monopoly over violence and became increasingly keen on limiting the risks to their neutrality that arose when their

DAVID SHEARER *is a research associate at the International Institute for Strategic Studies in London. He was a senior adviser to the UN Department of Humanitarian Affairs in Liberia and Rwanda in 1995 and 1996.*

Reprinted with permission from *Foreign Policy,* Fall 1998, pp. 68-81. © 1998 by the Carnegie Endowment for International Peace.

citizens fought other peoples' wars. Conscripted armies under the control of the state became the norm—apart from the activities of a few individuals that capitalized on the upheavals caused by African independence throughout the 1960s and 1970s.

In the past decade, however, the increasing inability of weak governments to counter internal violence has created a ready market for private military forces. This demand has also been fueled by a shift in Western priorities. The strategic interests of major powers in countries such as Mozambique, Rwanda, and Sierra Leone have declined with the end of the Cold War. As a result, Western countries are more reluctant to intervene militarily in weak states, and their politicians are disinclined to explain casualties to their electorates. Furthermore, Western armies, designed primarily to fight the sophisticated international conflicts envisaged by Cold War strategists, are ill equipped to tackle low-intensity civil wars, with their complicated ethnic agendas, blurred boundaries between combatants and civilians, and loose military hierarchies. The failed U.S.–led involvement in Somalia in 1993 reinforced American resolve never to enter a conflict unless vital domestic interests were at stake.

The increasing inability of weak governments to counter internal violence has created a ready market for private military forces.

Meanwhile, UN peacekeeping efforts have fallen victim to Western governments' fears of sustaining casualties, becoming entangled in expanding conflicts, and incurring escalating costs. The number of personnel in UN operations has fallen from a peak of 76,000 in 1994 to around 15,000 today. Multilateral interventions appear increasingly likely to be limited to situations where the UN gains the consent of the warring parties rather than—as allowed under Chapter VII of the UN Charter—to be designed to enforce a peace on reluctant belligerents. Bilateral, as well as multilateral, commitments have also been trimmed. France's long-standing deployment of troops in its former African colonies, for example, has declined: French troops will be cut by 40 percent to about 5,000 by 2000. Paris has stated that it will no longer engage in unilateral military interventions in Africa, effectively creating a strategic vacuum.

Into this gap have stepped today's private military companies. Most such enterprises hail from South Africa, the United Kingdom, the United States, and occasionally France and Israel. They all share essentially the same goals: to improve their client's military capability, there by allowing that client to function better in war or deter conflict more effectively. This process might involve military assessments, training, or occasionally weapons procurement. Direct involvement in combat is less common, although two companies, Executive Outcomes (EO) of South Africa and Sandline International of Great Britain, advertise their skills in this area. EO has provided training and strategic advice to the armed forces of Angola and Sierra Leone; its apartheid-era soldiers have fought in both countries.

Portrait of a Private Army

In its promotional literature, Executive Outcomes (EO) describes itself as a company with a "solid history of success," thanks to the efforts of its "highly effective work force." This work force is essentially a demobilized army for hire. Based in South Africa, the company was established in 1989 by Eeben Barlow and is staffed almost exclusively by veterans from the former South African Defence Force. EO claims to be able to draw on over 2,000 personnel and forces, all of whom are assembled on a contract-by-contract basis and recruited chiefly by word-of-mouth. This policy has not only ensured quality control but a preexisting military hierarchy of highly experienced troops. EO personnel have distinguished themselves from other companies by entering into combat, claiming that accompanying the client's troops increases their effectiveness and confidence.

EO's first major contract was in Angola in May 1993 to rescue the Soyo oil fields in the north from the rebel National Union for the Total Independence of Angola (UNITA). The Angolan government then hired over 500 personnel from September 1993 to January 1996 for an estimated $40 million a year (including weaponry) to train nearly 5,000 soldiers. EO's arrival, coinciding with the lifting of the arms embargo on Angola, helped reverse the course of the war, and UNITA suffered significant defeats. EO's second contract, this time with the Sierra Leonean government in May 1995, lasted 22 months and cost $35 million—about one-third of the country's defense budget. EO, working with local civilian militias, battered the Revolutionary United Front into submission. In February 1997, EO was subcontracted to the British military company, Sandline International, to train and plan military operations against the Bougain-ville Resistance Army in Papua New Guinea.

EO's military effectiveness testifies to its expertise in low-intensity conflict. It has planned its operations closely with government officials and uses government equipment, although it has arranged the purchase of weaponry. Its hallmark has been its highly mobile operations using MI-17 helicopter troop carriers, on occasion supported by MI-24 helicopter gunships and Soviet-made ground attack aircraft. But EO's biggest strength has been its use of intelligence capabilities, particularly through the cultivation of local populations, augmented with night-sighting and radio intercept devices. Casualties have remained relatively light: EO acknowledges that 11 of its personnel died in Angola, with seven still missing, and four killed in Sierra Leone. Two others died from accident and sickness.

—D.S.

Other companies, such as Military Professional Resources Incorporated (MPRI), a Virginia-based firm headed by retired U.S. army generals, has limited its services to training and has hired former U.S. military personnel to develop the military forces of Bosnia-Herzegovina and Croatia. Some organizations engage in more passive activities, such as protecting premises and people. The British company Defence Systems Limited, for example, guards embassies and protects the interests of corporations working in unstable areas. Other outfits provide businesses with risk analyses, and several have developed specialist expertise in resolving the kidnapping incidents that plague firms operating in Latin America.

Military companies are unfettered by political constraints. They view conflict as a business opportunity and have taken advantage of the pervasive influence of economic liberalism in the late twentieth century. They have also been quick to adapt to the complex agendas of civil wars. Their ability to operate has been enhanced by an expanded pool of military expertise made available by reductions in Western forces. Many recruits come from highly disciplined military units, such ass the British Special Air Service and the South African and American special forces. Likewise, cheap and accessible Soviet-made weaponry has helped strengthen the companies' capabilities.

When help from other quarters was unavailable, Sir Julius Chan, prime minister of Papua New Guinea, claimed in 1997 that he was forced to "go to the private sector" to counter Bougainville Revolutionary Army (BRA) insurgents. After negotiations with the BRA collapsed, Chan signed a $36 million contract with Sandline International to train his national forces and plan an offensive against the separatists. The government was particularly anxious to reopen Bougainville's Panguna Copper Mine, once the source of 30 percent of the country's export earnings.

Western mining corporations also stand to benefit when a private military company restores order, thereby raising questions as to whether these business entities share any formal ties. In April 1997, the London *Independent* reported that Anthony Buckingham, a director of Heritage Oil and Gas and Branch Energy, introduced EO to the governments of Angola and Sierra Leone. But Buck-

Outright victories, rather than negotiated peace settlements, have ended the greater part of the twentieth century's internal conflicts.

ingham has emphatically stated that "there is no corporate link between Executive Outcomes and the Branch Heritage group." EO officials likewise strongly deny any financial or operational/business links with mining companies. While critics decry even this nebulous relationship as neocolonialist behavior in the worst tradition of Cecil Rhodes, Buckingham observes that "If there is no stability there is no investment and no one benefits."

The lure of rich resources and the risks of exploiting them in unstable areas are powerful incentives for companies to maintain stability in weak states. This motivation can also chime with a government's own wishes. A mining company depends on security to protect its investments; a beleaguered government buys increased security to shore up its rule, while the prospect of mining revenues can supplement its coffers. Furthermore, a military company, while strengthening its client government's military performance, protects a mining company's operations because revenues from these sources guarantee its payment. In the developing world, minerals and hardwoods may soon emerge as the currency of stability. The source of payment is a crucial difference between the intervention of a military company and that of the UN, which is funded by donors, not by the state in question. Coupling multinational companies with an external security force potentially gives foreigners powerful leverage over a government and its affairs—a risk that some governments appear willing to take.

Another trend, reminiscent of the privateers of earlier centuries, is the will-

ingness of private military companies to act as proxies for Western governments. MPRI has specialized exclusively in military services, originally for the privatization-minded U.S. Department of Defense. MPRI's first two major international contracts were with the Croation government in 1994 to update its Warsaw Pact–oriented military. When the sophisticated Croatian offensive, Operation Storm, took the Serb-held Krajina enclave in August 1995, there was inevitable suspicion that MPRI was involved. The operation played an important role in reversing the tide of war against the Serbs and—consistent with American policy—in bringing both sides to the negotiating table. MPRI, although denying that it had played a role, has benefited from these rumors. In 1995, the company was contracted, in the aftermath of the Dayton accord, to strengthen the Muslim-Croat Federation's army in order to deter Bosnian Serb aggression. Since it is funded by the contracting government, MPRI has delivered a cheaper service and done so at less political risk than would have been possible had U.S. troops been used. The scenario serves as an example of how the private military sector can allow policymakers to achieve their foreign-policy goals free from the need to secure public approval and safe in the knowledge that should the situation deteriorate, official participation can be fudged.

Other American companies have also worked to further administration policy. Corporate giants such as Science Applications International Corporation and Braddock, Dunn & McDonald, Inc. and its subsidiary Vinnell Corporation are primarily high-technology suppliers to the military-industrial market but have also diversified into military training. They are contracted by the Saudi government to upgrade and train its armed forces in the use of mainly U.S. weaponry. Some British companies have also supported government interests: The London-based Saladin Security, for example, trains Omani government forces working alongside British Army officers who are seconded there. But on the whole, British companies are smaller and less diversified than their U.S. counterparts and have tended to focus on protecting commercial interests. Nonetheless, they maintain close contacts with Britain's Ministry of Defence and are an important source of intelligence.

THE FUTURE OF PEACEKEEPING?

Some private military companies, such as EO, possess sufficient coercive capability to break a stalemate in a conflict. Unlike multinational forces, they do not act impartially but are hired to win a conflict (or deter it) on the client's terms. EO and Sandline International have argued that military force has an underutilized potential to bring conflicts to a close. However, bludgeoning the other side into accepting a peace agreement runs in diametric opposition to most academic studies of conflict resolution. These studies center on consent: bringing warring sides together with the implicit assumption that each wants to negotiate an end to the war. To a large degree, the international community has responded to civil wars in this manner, especially those of limited strategic interest. Ceasefires act as holding positions; mediation seeks to bring combatants to an agreement. Peacekeepers, acting under mandates to be evenhanded and to use minimal force, are deployed to support this process.

The flaw in this approach is that according to recent empirical studies, outright victories, rather than negotiated peace settlements, have ended the greater part of the twentieth century's internal conflicts. Combatants in Angola, Bosnia, and Sierra Leone consistently resisted a negotiated, consent-based settlement. There appeared to be little chance of a breakthrough until more coercive measures were applied. So why has the international community continued to persist with negotiated settlements and even-handedness in cases where one side was clearly at fault? The reason, for the most part, is self-interest. Such an approach avoids direct intervention and the subsequent political risks.

Yet when it suits them, Western states have also been proponents of "battlefield diplomacy" to resolve conflicts. This approach was favored throughout the Cold War when the object was to limit Soviet expansionism. More recently, the United States tacitly supported the aims of Laurent Kabila's military campaign to oust President Mobutu Sese Seku in the former Zaire. France allegedly backed former military ruler Denis Sassou Nguesso's overthrow of Congolese president Pascal Lissouba in September 1997. And by condoning the Croatian capture of Serb-held Krajina, Washington was implicitly recognizing the value of resolution through force.

> *There is little to stop military companies from working for rebel movements in the future.*

However, the likelihood that a military solution can bring durable peace to a country depends on the nature of the peace agreement, as well as on how effectively follow-up measures such as demobilization, cantonment of fighters, and rehabilitation are implemented. Despite EO's involvement in Angola, for example, peace is still not finally secure. Nevertheless, its military involvement was instrumental in turning the tables of war in favor of the government's side, a development that coerced the National Union for the Total Independence of Angola (UNITA) to negotiate and eventually sign the 1994 Lusaka Accords. Similarly, in Sierra Leone, EO battered the Revolutionary United Front (RUF) faction into submission, creating sufficient stability to hold the first elections in 27 years. Later military offensives compelled the RUF to return to the negotiating table and sign a peace accord in November 1997. But just three months after EO left, the government was overthrown by disgruntled members of the armed forces, highlighting the importance of implementing postconflict measures.

These shortcomings are often seized upon as proof that the efforts of military companies have failed. But EO has always acknowledged its limitations. The UN did not engage members of EO in Sierra Leone, possibly because it chose to label them as mercenaries and therefore as untouchable. The entire episode illustrates that it is better to acknowledge the existence of military companies and engage them politically than to ignore them and hope that somehow a peace agreement will stay intact.

REGULATING THE MARKET

Since the demand for military force is unlikely to end anytime soon, military companies, in their various guises, appear here to stay. Should there be some attempt to regulate them, or is it the right of sovereign states—as with the purchase of weaponry—to employ who they wish as long as they ensure that their employees behave within acceptable bounds? There is widespread discomfort with a laissez-faire approach, most of it caused by military companies' lack of accountability. Although most military companies have only worked for legitimate governments, there is little to stop them from working for rebel movements in the future.

To make matters even more complicated, deciding which is the "legitimate" side in a civil conflict is not always straightforward. Many modern governments were once classified as "insurgents" or "terrorists" while in opposition, among them South Africa's African National Congress and Ugandan president Yoweri Museveni's National Resistance Army. The governments that grew out of these movements are now internationally recognized.

Military companies are motivated first and foremost by profit and are responsible primarily to their shareholders. Consequently, financial losses, in spite of any strategic or political considerations, may prompt a company to pull out. There are also few checks on their adherence to human-rights conventions. The problem is not a lack of human-rights law. During times of war, the employees of military companies fall under the auspices of Common Article 3 of the Geneva Conventions, which is binding on all combatants. They are also bound by a state's obligations to UN human-rights conventions as "agents" of the government that employs them. What is absent is adequate independent observation of their activities—a feature common to all parties in a conflict but especially characteristic of military companies that have no permanent attachments to national governments.

Efforts at controlling mercenaries through international law in the 1960s and 1970s were led by African states that faced a skeptical reception from the United States and major European powers. The most accepted definition of a mercenary, found in Article 47 of the 1977 Additional Protocols to the Geneva Conventions, is so riddled with loopholes that few international-law scholars believe it could withstand the rigors of the courtroom. International apathy is palpable. France and the United States have not signed the Additional Protocols, and the UN's 1989 International Convention against the Recruitment, Uses, Financing, and Training of Mercenaries has attracted only 12 signatories. Three of these signatories, Angola, the former Yugoslavia, and the former Zaire, have gone on to employ mercenaries. Most states have domestic laws that ban mercenaries but few, if any, have acted on them. Britain's Foreign Enlistment Act, for example, was introduced in 1870, and there has yet to be a prosecution.

The drive to regulate military companies has been most passionate when home governments—not those who contract them—are affected. The British government is currently investigating regulation after Sandline International, claiming it had clearance from the Foreign and Commonwealth Office, appeared to violate UN sanctions by supplying arms and military expertise to the ousted Sierra Leonean government. Sandline executives, portrayed in the media as "mercenaries," embarrassed Britain's new Labour Party government, which had entered office touting its platform of an "ethical" foreign policy.

South Africa too has come under both domestic and international pressure to control the increasing number of companies based there. Its parliament passed the Regulation of Foreign Military Assistance Bill in May 1998. Privately, however, most commentators in South Africa believe that while the legislation provides a framework for government policy and satisfies its critics, its real impact will be limited. Military companies are mostly registered offshore and can easily relocate to other countries, making it difficult to pin them down under specific jurisdictions. A growing trend is for international companies to form joint ventures with local companies, avoiding the effects of the legislation in any one country. Angola, for example, has over 80 security firms, many of them in joint ownership. Companies can also easily disguise their activities by purporting to be security companies performing protection services while actually engaging in more coercive military operations.

The principal obstacle to regulating private military companies has been the tendency to brand them as "mercenaries" of the kind witnessed in Africa 30 years ago, rather than to recognize them as multinational entrepreneurs eager to solidify their legitimacy. Consequently, regulation can be best achieved through constructive engagement. This process would likely expose governments and international institutions to accusations of sanctioning the use of "soldiers of fortune" to shore up the international system. Yet, this tack offers the international community greater leverage to influence the activities of companies that believe legitimacy is the key to their future growth and prosperity. In an effort to broaden their appeal, for instance, military companies have offered greater transparency. Sandline International maintains that it is prepared to place itself under the scrutiny of international monitors and accept an international regulatory framework. This pledge is a necessary step; a careful audit would establish corporate links that might affect the company's operations.

Engagement could well begin with dialogue between key multilateral institutions and the private military sector. Liaison at senior levels of the UN, for example, is needed, and the Department of Peacekeeping is an obvious starting point. UN field personnel should be permitted to contact military companies and plan strategies for conflict resolution where appropriate. Had there been a structured transition between EO's departure and the planned deployment of UN observers, the military coup in Sierra Leone might have been averted. EO could have maintained a threat of enforcement that would have bought time for the UN to fully implement postconflict programs, allowing RUF combatants to become confident enough about their future that they might demobilize. Direct engagement could also provide an opportunity to lay out a code of conduct that might incorporate more specific operational issues rising from the work of military companies. Observation of companies such as EO to ensure that they adhere to basic principles of warfare is needed, something in which the International Committee of the Red Cross could take a lead.

The prospect that private military companies might gain some degree of legitimacy within the international community begs the question as to whether these firms could take on UN peacekeeping functions and improve on UN efforts. Military companies see this as an area of potential growth and are quick to point out the advantages they offer. There is no denying that they are cheaper than UN operations. EO cost Sierra Leone's government $35 million for the 22 months it was there, versus a planned UN operation budgeted at $47 million for eight months. Likewise, its annual cost in Angola was a fraction of that of the UN's operation—for example, in 1996–97, UNAVEM III cost $135 million. Admittedly, EO and other such firms provide military support, not peacekeeping, but there is no doubt that they can mobilize more quickly and appear less sensitive to casualties. However, accepting a UN mandate or conditions may also undermine a company's effectiveness. As any soldier who has served in a UN operation will attest, a peacekeeping mission is only as effective as the operation's mandate.

GIVE WAR A CHANCE

Policymakers and multilateral organizations have paid little attention to private-sector involvement in wars. Yet low-intensity conflicts—the type that military companies have specialized in up to now—will be the wars that prevail in the first part of the twenty-first century. Their virulence and random nature could undermine the viability of many nation-states. These wars defy orthodox means of resolution, thus creating the circumstances that have contributed to the expansion of military companies into this area.

Conflict resolution theory needs to look more closely at the impact of coercion, not dismiss it. Military companies may in fact offer new possibilities for building peace that, while not universal in applicability, can hasten the end to a war and limit loss of life. Moreover, there is no evidence that private-sector intervention will erode the state. Despite the commercial motives of military companies, their interventions, if anything, have strengthened the ability of governments to control their territory. Yet, military companies are unlikely to resolve conflicts in the long term. Political intervention and postconflict peacebuilding efforts are still necessary.

Although the UN's special rapporteur on the use of mercenaries has acknowledged the difficulties in equating military companies with mercenaries, the debate has not moved beyond that point. Admittedly, the UN is in a sticky position. Although some member states have condemned the use of military companies, others have employed their services or condoned their operations. Meanwhile, the future of private military interests looks bright. "Now entering its eleventh year, MPRI has over 400 employees," declares the company's Web site, noting that in 1997 the volume of business exceeded $48 million. Even with a mercenary label and its associated moral stain, EO and Sandline continue to tout their services to beleaguered governments. Other companies are likely to emerge that offer EO's services, particularly in terms of low-key military training and advising for governments. The most rapid expansion is likely to be linked to the protection of commercial interests, although these can act as a springboard for more aggressive, military actions alongside local companies and power brokers. Mainstream companies, from the United States in particular, are also likely to encroach into low-intensity conflict areas. With backing from a cautious administration not wanting to forgo strategic influence, the temptation to use military companies might prove irresistible.

Regulation of military companies will be problematic, given the diversity of their services and the breadth of their market niche. Yet, in many respects, the private military industry is no different from any other sector in the global economy that is required to conform to codes of practice—except that in the former's case, the risk of political instability and social mayhem is amplified if more unscrupulous actors become involved.

There is good reason to glance back in history to a time when private military forces operated more or less freely. Historian Anthony Mockler notes that one hundred years after the first *condottieri* entered Italy: "The lines had become crossed and tangled: mercenaries had become rulers and rulers had become mercenaries."

WANT TO KNOW MORE?

Mercenaries have been around for as long as warfare itself. For detailed accounts of their history, see Anthony Mockler's *Mercenaries* (London: MacDonald, 1969) and Janice Thomson's *Mercenaries, Pirates & Sovereigns: State-Building and Extraterritorial Violence in Early Modern Europe* (New Jersey: Princeton University Press, 1996).

Several recent articles and studies scrutinize private military companies and their activities worldwide: David Shearer's *Private Armies and Military Intervention, Adelphi Paper 316* (New York: International Institute for Strategic Studies, February 1998); William Shawcross' *"In Praise of Sandline"* (*The Spectator*, August 1, 1998); Al J. Venter's *"Market Forces: How Hired Guns Succeeded Where the United Nations Failed"* (*Jane's International Defense Review*, March 1, 1998); Ken Silverstein's *"Privatizing War"* (*The Nation*, July 28, 1997); and David Isenberg's *Soldiers of Fortune Ltd.: A Profile of Today's Private Sector Corporate Mercenary Firms*

(Washington: Center for Defense Information, November 1997).

The legal status of mercenaries is addressed in Francoise Hampson's *"Mercenaries: Diagnosis Before Prescription"* (*Netherlands' Yearbook of International Law*, No. 3, 1991) and Edward Kwakwa's *"The Current Status of Mercenaries in the Law of Armed Conflict"* (*Hastings International and Comparative Law Review*, vol. 14, 1990).

Martin van Crevald examines the changing dynamics of conflict in *The Transformation of War* (New York: The Free Press, 1991). Two studies provide empirical evidence that outright victory, rather than negotiated peace, has ended the greater part of the twentieth century's internal conflicts: Stephen John Stedman's *Peacemaking in Civil Wars: International Mediation in Zimbabwe 1974–1980* (Boulder: Lynne Rienner, 1991) and Roy Licklider's *"The Consequences of Negotiated Settlements in Civil Wars 1954–1993"* (*American Political Science Review*, September 1995).

On human rights, see a series of reports by the UN's special repporteur on mercenaries that are available online: *Report on the Question of the Use of Mercenaries as a Means of Violating Human Rights and Impeding the Exercise of the Right of Peoples to Self-Determination.*

For links to this and other relevant Web sites, as well as a comprehensive index of related articles, access **www.foreignpolicy.com.**

CHILDREN UNDER ARMS:
Kalashnikov Kids

**Increasingly, children are being used to fight wars,
at great cost to themselves and their societies.
Discouraging the trend is tricky but not impossible**

We were trapped between acts of heaven and acts of hell," says a young woman in Sierra Leone who spent two unwilling years under arms in her country's civil war. "When the rebels laughed, we laughed." When they were angry, she was punished savagely. Dragged by rebel fighters with 27 other members of her family from their village into the jungle, she found herself a slave to unpredictable violence.

The youngest were forced into Small Boy and Small Girl Units, where they carried stolen goods, ammunition, water and food. They were taught to punish and even kill other children who disobeyed or sought to escape. Each day she and her comrades sang an anthem glorifying their struggle:

Go and tell the president that Sierra
  Leone is my home.
Go and tell my parents they see me
  no more.
When fighting in the battlefield I am
  fighting for ever.
Every Sierra Leonean is fighting for
  his land.

After two years, 19 of her family were dead, but she escaped.

Such a story is common in Sierra Leone, where, although the civil war may at last be ending, 6,000 children were recently combatants, according to Radda Barnen, a Swedish charity. It is also common elsewhere.

The United Nations reckons that children, defined as those under 18 years old, are active participants in conflicts stretching from west and central Africa to the Balkans, Latin America, Sri Lanka and Afghanistan. In Uganda, for example, the UN Children's Fund, Unicef, estimates that as many as 8,000 have been abducted by rebels since 1995. Another 15,000 are said by Amnesty International to be in the ranks of Colombia's security forces and many more are in paramilitary groups there. According to the Coalition to Stop the Use of Child Soldiers, a group of religious and peace groups headquartered in Switzerland, 300,000 children in over 60 countries are soldiers.

Are these figures accurate? Do they represent a worrying increase on past practice? It is impossible to say. The phenomenon of child soldiers is far from new. For generations, young men

in Africa have taken up weapons alongside their fathers to defend their villages, just as they worked in the fields in peacetime. Drummer boys led armies into battle in America's revolutionary war. In Europe, too, child recruits were common. Admiral Horatio Nelson, like other great seafarers, began his naval career as a ship's boy and saw action in the Indian Ocean. By the end of the second world war, Berlin was defended by 15-year-olds against the might of the Allies. Children have played an active part in wars since at least spartan times.

Then there are problems of definition. What is a child? Is it the same in all cultures? A Tamil might well be married at 14 and expect to fulfil other manly duties, but it is against the law in Britain to take a wife at that age. A 12-year-old gun-toter seems clearly unacceptable; a 17-year-old, less so. And what is a soldier? Not all of them fight, or even risk their lives. Many ordinary children suffer horribly during the kind of vicious civil war that throws up lots of child soldiers. At least the soldiers are likely to get a handful of food for their pains.

Despite these ambiguities, two trends are worth thinking about. Children tend to be used heavily as soldiers during prolonged civil wars; and such civil wars abound at present. And although children were once recruited only when the supply of adult fighters ran short, the youngest are now often recruited first.

There are logical reasons for this. First there are more children around. Thanks to demography, poverty and persistent fighting, in much of Africa south of the Sahara, for example, half the people are now under 18 years old. Then too children are often easier to attract than adults. Entertainment is in short supply in most villages and what organised recreation there is (watching "Rambo" on mobile video players in rural Liberia and Sierra Leone) may well spur young people to sign up on the spot. Children in most parts of the world can be lured by a gun and a bit of drill into militias or street gangs.

When they cannot be tempted into the ranks, children can be forced more easily than adults. Once secured, they are more readily moulded into unquestioning fighters. Give them only a little alcohol, marijuana or gunpowder to sniff; tell them, as in parts of west Africa, that a magic incantation or membership of a secret society will protect them; give them mirrors and a woollen toy to steer enemy bullets away: then many, more credulous than grown-ups, will run fearless into battle. The youngest will often develop the sort of loyalty that stems from knowing no other way of life.

Despite—sometimes because of—their size, children can do valuable work as scouts, spies, messengers and decoys. Even ten year-olds can learn to carry and use lightweight but lethal weapons, such as M16 semi-automatic rifles or the omnipresent aluminium Kalashnikov AK-47s. They may be more willing than older companions to do the most dangerous jobs, such as laying and clearing mines, serving as suicide bombers or infiltrating villages that are due to be attacked. With no sons or daughters, wives or husbands to think of, they are frequently less terrified of death than most older people.

Finally, children are an economical addition to the force. They need less food than adult soldiers, take up less space and can do without a wage. One Congolese rebel officer explained why *kadogos* (boy fighters) "make very good soldiers": it was because "they obey orders; they are not concerned about get-

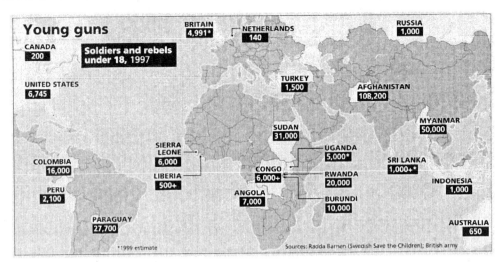

Young guns

Soldiers and rebels under 18, 1997

CANADA	200
UNITED STATES	6,745
BRITAIN	4,991*
NETHERLANDS	140
RUSSIA	1,000
TURKEY	1,500
AFGHANISTAN	108,200
MYANMAR	50,000
SUDAN	31,000
UGANDA	5,000*
SRI LANKA	1,000+*
COLOMBIA	16,000
SIERRA LEONE	6,000
LIBERIA	500+
CONGO	6,000+
RWANDA	20,000
INDONESIA	1,000
PERU	2,100
ANGOLA	7,000
BURUNDI	10,000
PARAGUAY	27,700
AUSTRALIA	650

*1999 estimate   Sources: Radda Barnen (Swedish Save the Children); British army

ting back to their wife or family; and they don't know fear."

Girls and boys come out to kill

War takes an enormous toll on the young in general. Olara Otunnu, the UN Special Representative for Children and Armed Conflict (and a man with particular knowledge of the subject from his earlier days as spokesman for President Obote of Uganda), says that 2m children have been killed in situations of armed conflict since 1987, and three times that number have been seriously injured or permanently disabled. As civilians' share of casualties in war has rocketed this century (up from 5% in the first world war to 48% in the second and around 90% today), the involvement of children has also grown. They are victims of crossfire and of deliberate attacks, as the evidence of mass graves in Kosovo shows. They are particularly prone to treading on landmines, catching diseases, being poisoned by pollutants. Others are taken hostage or used as human shields. Many simply starve.

But for child soldiers in particular there are more risks. On top of the obvious dangers of injury or death during combat, they tend to live harsh lives. Some are punished, or killed, for making mistakes. Children who have fought for the Lord's Resistance Army in Uganda, for example, report being beaten for dropping a tub of water while under enemy attack. In the same army, if a child fails to raise the alarm when a friend escapes, he is executed by his comrades.

Day-to-day injuries from carrying heavy loads, as well as damage to ears and eyes from gunfire, are well documented. Drug addiction, malnutrition

and sexually transmitted diseases are common among bands of child soldiers in different continents.

Then are the emotional effects. Large numbers of children have seen atrocities. In Kosovo, says the UN High Commissioner for Refugees, half of those who fled were under 18 years old. In 1996 Unicef estimated that half of all Rwanda's children had witnessed a massacre. But child soldiers are also made to commit atrocities. Rachel Brett, the author of a book on child soldiers*, argues that "the general brutalisation of child recruits is often a deliberate policy; even in exceptional cases involving ritual cannibalism." Sometimes, in order to humiliate a village under attack and destroy its social order, the youngest boy in the ranks of the attackers is ordered to execute the village chief. Another trick of rebels in Sierra Leone is to use abducted children to attack their own villages and families. Why? So that, feeling cast out from their communities, they will cling to the rebel group.

The impact of all this not only on the child but on society as a whole is dreadful. Children who have had no training or education beyond the use of a gun or a rocket–propelled grenade are harder to demobilise and bring back into routine life than grown-up fighters. Mr. Otunnu argues that groups that recruit child soldiers tend to find themselves with a big problem when peace comes, or even when it does not. "They find a generation of children carrying guns, who know only the gun culture, who hang around on streets everywhere with guns," he says. In Congo, for example, even rebel leaders are keen to see children de-

*"Children: The Invisible Soldiers". Radda Barnen, 2nd edition, 1998.

mobolised, as some child fighters are, it seems, impossible to control.

Where conflicts have dragged on—in Sri Lanka, Afghanistan, Sierra Leone—many rebel leaders, officers and co-ordinators turn out to have taken part in war first as children. The Taliban leaders in Afghanistan learned to fight as teenagers in the refugee camps of Pakistan. Some of those who abduct children today in Sierra Leone were abducted themselves when the war began in 1991; others started fighting as children in the civil war in neighbouring Liberia. Conflicts involving child soldiers, in other words, may be particularly hard to end.

Under age and under arms

This week about 100 government representatives, UN staff and aid workers gathered in Montevideo, the capital of Uruguay, for the second of four international conferences on child soldiers. They discussed how to stop recruitment of children by armies, paramilitary groups and civil-defence bodies.

That is a difficult (and some would say impossible) task. The differences among the three categories are immense. Some child soldiers are recruited, openly and legally, into national armies where care is taken over their training and welfare. A second lot, such as those with self-defense committees in Mozambique or the "village guards" in Algeria, fight to protect their families and villages. A third type those who are taken away from their communities, often forcibly, by groups that may have started life with a political agenda but frequently end up as common criminals.

The first sort are the easiest to do something about but the least in need of rescue. It is not illegal under international law to recruit a 15-year old as a soldier. The UN Convention on the Rights of the Child, signed in 1989 and ratified by all members except America and Somalia, establishes the age of 18 as the end of childhood. It forbids, for example, the death penalty for children and sets other standards for their protection. An exception has been made for soldiering, allowing recruitment at 15.

The British navy, for example, recruits 16-year-old school-leavers. The British army starts hiring them at 17 and now has 4,991 under-18-year-olds (1,000 more than two years ago) in its employ. Seventeen of them are serving in the Balkans; one of the 381 17-year-old soldiers serving in the Gulf war was killed. The American army, too, re-

cruits and deploys 17-year-olds. Jo Becker of Human Rights Watch, a non-governmental organisation based in America, says that in 1997 the American army had 2,880 17-year-olds on active duty.

The minority of countries that recruit at this age argue that, if they left it any later, the young people would turn to other employment. Some make a different point, that society benefits if lads without job prospects are taken off taken the streets and into useful training before unappealing habits form.

Their opponents say that only the most careful system—for example, that in Australia, where young recruits are monitored by a host of psychologists, chaplains and other folk as well as given training suitable to their age—can protect children from what they see as the unhealthy rigours of military life. It is consistent, they say, for governments that do not allow young people to vote, buy alcohol, drive, marry without their parents' consent or accept certain kinds of civilian employment to send them into mortal danger instead.

Their campaign to realise the minimum age for soldiering from 15 to 18 is gradually gaining momentum, though perhaps not for the reasons put forward. Many western countries want to reduce their armed forces anyway and raising the minimum age is a painless way to cut. Last year Denmark and South Africa increased their recruitment ages to 18. Sierra Leone's government has also said that it will no longer hire soldiers younger than 18. Burundi, Canada and the Netherlands are thinking of raising their recruitment age, and the Netherlands already keeps its youngest soldiers out of combat. So, to some extent, does Britain: soldiers younger than 18 are not sent to patrol the streets in Northern Ireland, though they do go to other trouble spots. The UN, for its part, refuses to employ soldiers younger than 18 in its peacekeeping forces and prefers 21-year-olds for the tougher assignments.

Another step has been taken. On June 17, members of the International Labour Organisation voted unanimously to ban the employment of those younger than 18 in hazardous work, including prostitution, drug-smuggling and soldiering. (Only young conscripts are prohibited; young volunteers will still be allowed—though definitions of "voluntary" among the very poor could prove a touch theoretical.)

Is 18 a reasonable cut-off? It smacks of an attempt by developed countries to force their values on the rest of the world, where children get down to

things earlier. But at least, points out Miss Brett, if 18 becomes the legal minimum, then—even allowing for the difficulty of telling a child's age in places where malnutrition may make him look younger than he is or hard labour make him older—13- and 14-year-olds are less likely to end up clutching Kalashnikovs.

If the minimum recruiting age is raised by amending international agreements, (and America and Britain are notable stand-outs against it), it will affect only national armies. A far bigger worry is unofficial armed groups, the civil-defence or rebel-cum-criminal gangs that draws boys and girls during prolonged civil wars. They are not confined to poor countries: a few children fight for the KLA (Kosovo Liberation Army) in Yugoslavia and rather more for the PKK (Kurdistan Worker's Party) in Turkey.

Harder to handle

Civil-defence groups recruit children to fight for their communities along with their friends and fathers. Children with the Kamajors, a secret hunting society turned militia in Sierra Leone, man road blocks, search vehicles, fight and perform rituals in battle. Some children are made to dance naked into battle in order to intimidate the enemy. Algeria's village guards and defence committees in Latin America fall into the same category. They often recruit children at a much earlier age than the government (as young as 12 or 13 in Sierra Leone).

Stopping such groups from using children as soldiers is much harder than stopping governments, as they are unlikely to be much affected by the opinions of either international do-gooders or voters (who might anyway—who knows?—consider enlisting child soldiers preferable to communal destruction). But because these groups usually defend villages, and thus move around less than rebel bands, their activities can be monitored more easily. Some outside carrots and stocks—money to demobilise, the threat of harsh penalties if recruiting child soldiers comes to be classified as a war crime—could have some effect. It is, frankly, a long shot.

Even longer are the odds against winning hearts and minds among the third group. Yet the sort of child soldiers soldier for whom life is worst, and from whom the greatest threat to stability and peace is later likely to come, is an abducted child who becomes a fighter. Wrenched from his community, like the 3,000 or so children in the Lord's Resistance Army in Uganda, such a child risks losing all identity except that which his gun gives him. "Orders have gone out recently from the LRA officers to abduct younger and younger kids. Eleven to 13 is now the preferred age, though they will take up to 17-year-olds," says Keith Wright, Unicef's programme chief in Kampala. "They are slave soldiers, enduring an endless cycle of brutality." In other countries, children as young as three are grabbed, sometimes to secure the loyalty of older siblings, and trained to fight almost as soon as they can walk.

In many civil wars, banditry and competition for resources are as important for the rebels as any political objective. Soldiers do not necessarily fight to win territory but to keep control of wealth. In Uganda a new rebel group, the Allied Democratic Forces, also uses about 500 child soldiers to preserve its sources of revenue. In Colombia factions fight in part for control of the drug trade. In west Africa, Angola and Congo, much of the fighting is for mineral wealth, especially diamonds. Children in such "guerrilla" groups often learn as much about crime as warfare—and perpetuate it.

Authorities that have so far proved unable to halt these groups' obviously criminal activities are unlikely to succeed in stopping their merely immoral ones. But some things could still be done to make it harder to employ children as soldiers. Mr Otunnu is probably optimistic in reckoning that the trade and production of small arms can be limited. But foreign countries and institutions, he argues, should make it clear to any rebel group aspiring to govern that recognition and aid will be harder to win if the group has used child soldiers. This may sound like pie in the sky, but such arguments are making a little progress. The Sudan People's Liberation Army has pledged not to use child soldiers. So have both the Tamil Tigers and the Sri Lankan government.

Until 1998, the UN Security Council had not even discussed the issue of child soldiers. Since then, however, the subject has been raised several times, and expert witnesses have been questioned. The fate of children under arms is now recognised as an important part of peace negotiations in many parts of the world, with implications not only for successful demobilisation but also for policies on health, education and nurturing democracy. As with the campaign to ban landmines, it is the gradual realisation of the problem, rather than any multilateral posturing, that has the best chance of solving it in time.

Index

AE Article Review Form

We encourage you to photocopy and use this page as a tool to assess how the articles in **Annual Editions** expand on the information in your textbook. By reflecting on the articles you will gain enhanced text information. You can also access this useful form on a product's book support Web site at ***http://www.dushkin.com/ online/.***

NAME: _____ DATE: _____

_____

TITLE AND NUMBER OF ARTICLE:

_____

BRIEFLY STATE THE MAIN IDEA OF THIS ARTICLE:

_____

LIST THREE IMPORTANT FACTS THAT THE AUTHOR USES TO SUPPORT THE MAIN IDEA:

_____

WHAT INFORMATION OR IDEAS DISCUSSED IN THIS ARTICLE ARE ALSO DISCUSSED IN YOUR TEXTBOOK OR OTHER READINGS THAT YOU HAVE DONE? LIST THE TEXTBOOK CHAPTERS AND PAGE NUMBERS:

_____

LIST ANY EXAMPLES OF BIAS OR FAULTY REASONING THAT YOU FOUND IN THE ARTICLE:

_____

LIST ANY NEW TERMS/CONCEPTS THAT WERE DISCUSSED IN THE ARTICLE, AND WRITE A SHORT DEFINITION:

_____

ANNUAL EDITIONS revisions depend on two major opinion sources: one is our Advisory Board, listed in the front of this volume, which works with us in scanning the thousands of articles published in the public press each year; the other is you—the person actually using the book. Please help us and the users of the next edition by completing the prepaid article rating form on this page and returning it to us. Thank you for your help!

ANNUAL EDITIONS: World Politics 00/01

ARTICLE RATING FORM

Here is an opportunity for you to have direct input into the next revision of this volume. We would like you to rate each of the 43 articles listed below, using the following scale:

1. Excellent: should definitely be retained
2. Above average: should probably be retained
3. Below average: should probably be deleted
4. Poor: should definitely be deleted

Your ratings will play a vital part in the next revision.
So please mail this prepaid form to us just as soon as you complete it.
Thanks for your help!

RATING

ARTICLE

1. Dueling Globalizations: A Debate between Thomas L. Friedman and Ignacio Ramonet
2. The Future of Civil Conflict
3. The New Interventionism and the Third World
4. International Political Economy: Beyond Hegemonic Stability
5. Toward a New International Economic Order
6. Capitalism's Last Chance?
7. Trade and the Developing World: A New Agenda
8. Helping the World's Poorest
9. Against Nuclear Apartheid
10. Russia: The Nuclear Menace Within
11. Troubled Treaties: Is the NPT Tottering?
12. Bombs, Gas and Microbes: The Desperate Efforts to Block the Road to Doomsday
13. Life after Pax Americana
14. Ham-Fisted Hegemon: The Clinton Administration and Russia
15. Rethinking United States Policy toward the Muslim World
16. Americans and the World: A Survey at Century's End
17. How Many Deaths Are Acceptable? A Surprising Answer
18. No-First-Use for NATO?
19. Canada's Water: Hands Off
20. The International Relations of Latin America and the Caribbean: Defining the New Era

RATING

ARTICLE

21. Colombia at War
22. Economic Crisis in Latin America: Global Contagion
23. The Search for a Common Foreign Policy
24. Enemies and Colleagues
25. The Revolutions of 1989 Reconsidered
26. Unlearning the Lessons of Kosovo
27. Life with Boris: Rousing, Infuriating, Always Surprising—Yeltsin the Singular
28. Still Soul Searching
29. The Baltics: Between Russia and the West
30. Chaos in the Caucasus
31. Is the Asian Financial Crisis Over?
32. Tigers Ready to Roar?
33. Does China Matter?
34. Tokyo's Depression Diplomacy
35. Toward a Comprehensive Settlement of the Korea Problem
36. License to Kill: Usama bin Ladin's Declaration of Jihad
37. Iraq and the UN's Weapon of Mass Destruction
38. Saddam's Survival in the Ruins
39. Africa
40. Post-Imperial Africa at War
41. Bewitched, Bothered, and Bewildered: Repairing the Security Council
42. Outsourcing War
43. Children under Arms: Kalashnikov Kids

(Continued on next page)

245

We Want Your Advice

ANNUAL EDITIONS: WORLD POLITICS 00/01

BUSINESS REPLY MAIL
FIRST-CLASS MAIL PERMIT NO. 84 GUILFORD CT

POSTAGE WILL BE PAID BY ADDRESSEE

Dushkin/McGraw-Hill
Sluice Dock
Guilford, CT 06437-9989

NO POSTAGE
NECESSARY
IF MAILED
IN THE
UNITED STATES

ABOUT YOU

Name _____   Date _____

Are you a teacher? ☐   A student? ☐

Your school's name _____

Department _____

Address _____   City _____   State ___ Zip ___

School telephone # _____

YOUR COMMENTS ARE IMPORTANT TO US !

Please fill in the following information:

For which course did you use this book?

_____

Did you use a text with this *ANNUAL EDITION*? ☐ yes ☐ no
What was the title of the text?

_____

What are your general reactions to the *Annual Editions* concept?

_____

Have you read any particular articles recently that you think should be included in the next edition?

_____

Are there any articles you feel should be replaced in the next edition? Why?

_____

Are there any World Wide Web sites you feel should be included in the next edition? Please annotate.

_____

May we contact you for editorial input? ☐ yes ☐ no
May we quote your comments? ☐ yes ☐ no

300 A4 FM 344
06/07/00 33700 SELE

DATE DUE

GAYLORD			PRINTED IN U.S.A.